## Star Crossed

OTHER BOOKS BY HEATHER DUNE MACADAM

*999: The Extraordinary Young Women
of the First Official Jewish Transport to Auschwitz*

*Rena's Promise: A Story of Sisters in Auschwitz*

*The Weeping Buddha*

OTHER BOOKS BY SIMON WORRALL

*The Poet and the Murderer*

*The Very White of Love*

# STAR CROSSED

*A True Romeo and Juliet Story in Hitler's Paris*

**HEATHER DUNE MACADAM**
and
**SIMON WORRALL**

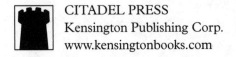

CITADEL PRESS
Kensington Publishing Corp.
www.kensingtonbooks.com

*For Michele*

*In memory of Annette*

## LES ENFANTS QUI S'AIMENT

*Les enfants qui s'aiment s'embrassent debout*
*Contre les portes de la nuit*
*Et les passants qui passent les désignent du doigt*
*Mais les enfants qui s'aiment*
*Ne sont là pour personne*
*Et c'est seulement leur ombre*
*Qui tremble dans la nuit*
*Excitant la rage des passants*
*Leur rage leur mépris leurs rires et leur envie*
*Les enfants qui s'aiment ne sont là pour personne*
*Ils sont ailleurs bien plus loin que la nuit*
*Bien plus haut que le jour*
*Dans l'éblouissante clarté de leur premier amour.*

—JACQUES PRÉVERT

## CHILDREN WHO LOVE ONE ANOTHER

*The young lovers embrace standing up*
*Against the doorways of the night*
*And passersby who go by point a finger at them*
*But the young lovers*
*Aren't there for anyone*
*And it is only their shadow*
*That trembles in the night*
*Arousing the rage of the passersby*
*Their rage their scorn their laughter and their jealousy*
*Young lovers are not there for anyone*
*They are elsewhere much further away than the night*
*Much higher than the day*
*In the wonderment of their first love.*

# Contents

## ACT THREE: 1941–42

# Introduction

The mercury tops 90 degrees Fahrenheit (36 degrees Celsius) when I arrive in Paris. On the train from Charles de Gaulle Airport, children are crying; old people sit hunched over, sweating and exhausted. My shirt clings to my back, wet with sweat. In the metro from Gare du Nord the heat is even more infernal. Seeing my discomfort, an African woman passes me her spray bottle of Vichy spa water. Everyone in Paris is carrying them, and the fine mist of cool water feels good on my face.

I have flown from London to meet Michele Kersz, the mother of one of my wife's dearest and oldest friends, Laurence, and her partner, Ron, with whom we spend almost every August in the Hamptons of New York. Over the years we have watched Michele's grandchildren grow from toddlers wading in the shallows to teenagers and young men diving into waves. The Kersz families have enjoyed seaside vacations since Michele was a child.

Arriving at Michele's spacious apartment in Montmartre, we sit at a large dining table covered in letters, newspaper articles, and photos of Annette. A vibrant ninety-one-year-old who still travels to play bridge tournaments, Michele is the younger sister of Annette Zelman, the heroine of our book. Dressed in a white skirt and a blouse decorated with red tulips, with her thinning red hair brushed back off her face, she hands me a photo of Annette, aged nineteen, taken in 1941 outside the Academy of Beaux-Arts in Saint-Germain-des-Prés, where her sister was a student. A radiant Annette stands in front of a marble column, wrapped in a billowing, brown-and-white check pattern outfit, cinched at the waist. "I helped her sew that dress," Michele says with a smile. "She made all her own clothes."

Over the next five hours, the memories pour out, while I film and record her. Worried that she must be exhausted by the heat, I suggest we take a break at midday, but she insists that we continue. She has wanted to tell Annette's story for many years. She is not going to let a heat wave stop her now.

It is five in the afternoon when I finally kiss Michele goodbye, on both cheeks in the French fashion. I tell her that Heather Dune and I think there is enough material in her archive for a book and we would like to write it. She smiles and nods. "It is so important that the world knows Annette's story." She touches my arm. "But don't wait too long. I am ninety-one years old."

She is now ninety-four.

—*Simon Worrall*

*Annette twirls in front of the École des Beaux-Arts in a Zazou-style dress she sewed with the help of her younger sister, Michele.*

# ACT ONE

## 1941 Paris

À l'homme de mes vies
à ses risques et périls
à son amabilité
à ses cheveux blonds....
mon admiration sincère et...

Annette Zelman

# *Annette*

Café de Flore

*Flore was a place halfway between a workers' cafeteria
and a cenacle where "fantastic," "madly interesting"
people met.*

—SIMONE SIGNORET

**PARIS, JANUARY 1941**

HERE IS ANNETTE ZELMAN, just nineteen, celebrating her ac-
ceptance into the Beaux-Arts, the most famous art school in

all of France. She has only been in Paris for a month and already she has found her niche. Her mane of thick, dark blond hair gleams in the sunlight, pinned in a fashion all her own. Curls akimbo. A headband hauls them back off her face, almost. She is still a teenager; the baby fat has not yet fallen from the cheeks of her face. Her eyes squint in the winter light and crinkle in a full-on smile. It is cold out, but today is a day for photos. A day to celebrate. Annette is starting her first semester at the Beaux-Arts. The announcements have been made. She is going to be an artist!

*They* are artists! Another of the newly accepted students, Salvatore Baccarice, has a camera and has coaxed Annette to pose with the sculpture she drew for the entrance exam. He has a roll of film he wants to develop, with a few frames left to spare, and is eager to preserve the memory. He already has a crush on the vivacious Annette.

The courtyard of the Beaux-Arts is a forest of classical Greek and Roman sculptures. Annette quickly discards her woolen coat and climbs onto the pedestal of the *Discobolus* statue. She swings her arm around the thick marble neck, presses her head against the figure's, and arches away as if she is a bow being pulled into his embrace. She had never drawn anything so complicated before. Her parents are tailors, so she is more versed in patterns than physique, but she smudged and shaded his rippled washboard abs, his swollen biceps, dimpled butt. His penis. She had never drawn a penis before. She looks as if she might be in love with him. Perhaps she is. He is the reason she is here. Now. The reason for her success. She is laughing. Always laughing. Linked in this pas de deux, her partner frozen in time, the camera clicks. Salvatore winds the film.

*Your turn!* we can almost hear Annette say to her new friend Yannick Bellon.

Sixteen-year-old dark-haired beauty Yannick hugs the discus thrower and smiles down at the newly named artist, as

Annette looks up at her friend, beaming. There is another metallic click, then a plastic whoosh as Salvatore winds the film forward to the next frame.

When he looks up again Annette has her coat back on, buttoned up to defend against the bitter air. Some say this is one of the coldest winters in living memory, but for the moment Paris is free of snow. Hands half in and half out of her pockets, Annette stands as if at attention. With her feet placed firmly together, wearing pale tights and heavy socks with her sensible shoes, nothing can move her from this moment in time. Tilting her head, as quizzical as a puppy, she asks with her eyes, *What's next? Where to now?* Her smile radiates secret amusement.

Hold it!

Salvatore focuses his lens and her gaze changes in that instant to one of adoration. She looks into the camera and is captured as a fleeting thought about this day and all its possibilities crosses her face. Everything that is happening in her life is meant to be, even the friend who is memorializing it all on black-and-white Agfa film, even the curl that falls across her cheek as the shutter clicks.

Perfect.

They are all laughing now. What is not to laugh about? They are the crème de la crème. They belong here. And even though Annette is a new arrival to the capital—a refugee, in fact—Paris has opened her arms to embrace her. *You are mine, now*, Paris whispers. *You're an artist.* It is all Annette has ever wanted.

SOMEONE HAS THE idea to go to a café and celebrate. Perhaps it is Yannick who suggests the idea. Her famous mother, Surrealist photographer Denise Bellon, frequents the Café de Flore, and they are just a few blocks away.

Tucking her portfolio under her arm and swinging a hefty black purse over one shoulder, Annette sets off down Rue Bonaparte with a growing group of fellow art students. Yannick and she link arms, hurrying ahead until they are only the click of heels syncopated by staccato laughter. Curls bee-bop off their scarved necks, swing with the sway of shoulders, the sashay of hips. *Ooh la la.*

Passing an eleventh-century church and its wartime worse-for-wear garden, the girls pause on Boulevard Saint-Germain. This is the heart of the Latin Quarter, the hippest part of Paris, where smoky music clubs are still allowed to play American jazz, and lust, if not love, is always in the air. Annette can hardly believe that she has arrived here, a student in the City of Light.

Standing outside of the café Les Deux Magots is a clump of "Green Beans," as the Wehrmacht soldiers are known because of the color of their uniforms. With them are some "Gray Mice," their female counterparts. You can always tell Germans because they look like they own even the sunshine on the street. Annette is not interested in sharing the watery winter sun with the enemy. Reminded how the war has deprived her of her adolescence, Yannick scrubs the ground with her eyes. After fleeing the capital ahead of the invasion, she has only recently returned to Paris with her mother and younger sister, Loleh. Annette's ebullience and confidence are infectious, though. She big-sisters her younger friend, loops her arm on Yannick's waist, and slows to allow the boys to catch up with them. "*Sale Bosch,*" one of them murmurs as they catch up to the girls. *Dirty Germans.* The rest laugh, daringly.

Since the Germans marched into Paris over eight months ago, there has been an incessant show of military strength along the Champs-Élysées, tanks and goose-stepping as if they own the streets. But today the Beaux-Arts students are the parade. In a city whose pride has been battered by the invasion, the hope and innocence of youth help the capital's spirit flicker.

Half a block away the scalloped white-and-green awnings of the Café de Flore beckon. Named after a statue of the antique goddess of flowers and gardens, the mother of spring, the Flore is where the artists and writers hang out. The communists and anti-fascists. The painters and dancers. The in-crowd. There are no Germans here. The brass doors open and the students usher one another inside. No one looks up.

It is the hour of the aperitif, and the Flore is packed. Everyone who is anyone is here or on their way. On any given afternoon, Annette might find the smoldering intensity of Picasso, furiously smoking Gitanes with Brancusi and Dora Maar. A particularly elegant dark-haired woman with her hair turbaned and coifed in a bun, Simone de Beauvoir, sits with a small group of confidantes. Absent is her owlish, bespectacled paramour, Jean-Paul Sartre, who is being held in a German Stalag. In another corner, gypsy guitarist Django Reinhardt is back in Paris, after trying to escape across the Swiss border. The young sparks flitting into the café are his idea of innocents whose hearts will soon be broken by his love songs.

Overhead, six magnificent Lalique chandeliers bathe the brows of the Floristes in dim yellow light. The boys grab a center table and pull out chairs for the girls, then tussle for the best spot. The waiter takes their order. Ersatz coffee. There is a "celluloid bell" of macaroons in the center of the table. Annette pops one into her mouth, only to find that it is nothing like the prewar macaroons of her hometown. This is a mystery recipe, lacking coconut, almond, and real sugar. A secret formula of sawdust and something?

Students gravitate to the Café de Flore for good reason: It is the only café in the Latin Quarter with decent heat. A large coal stove occasionally belches smoke and flames, but it is still the centerpiece of the room. On cold winter mornings, Simone de Beauvoir has been known to arrive before the doors are unlocked to get a seat close to the fire while she writes. Being cold is as common and uncomfortable as being hungry, but the cold is easier to remedy. Students and artists in threadbare corduroy coats lean against it for warmth and nurse their imitation coffees, forcing the dregs to last for hours in order to postpone the inevitable exodus to the cold streets and icy winds whipping up off the Seine. A survey of faces shows some creased with worry, while others look smooth and confident. Everyone over thirty looks tired. Being occupied is exhausting.

Around the room, debates rage between the Surrealists and Dadaists, anarchists and Trotskyists. Join the resistance, commit to pacifism, flee? What is the best way to fight fascism? Art or guns? Should art be political or stay above the fray? Annette picks up on the conversations that interest her: art, jazz, ration cards. Eavesdropping is an art form of its own. The voices are as varied as their ages. Some speak with hushed urgency, others with bored superiority. Polish-, Czech-, Russian-, and Spanish-accented French are as common as the nasal tones of true Parisians. Annette herself has a provincial accent. She should lose it, she thinks. Lose that old Annette who came from far-away Nancy in eastern France. She should become a new, shinier Annette—à la Parisienne.

Not the kind of girl to be easily overwhelmed, Annette may be a refugee from the provinces, but aren't they all refugees now? Being occupied makes you a stranger in your own country. You no longer own the laws or the spirit of your homeland. Someone else does.

Here amid the poor students from the Beaux-Arts, Annette feels drawn to move closer to the stove, where the hubbub of conversation is the thickest. She wants to be in the middle of things and the heat of conversation. The Café de Flore is like a drug—try it once and you want more.

Her initiation complete, Annette watches the animated conversations encircling her. In the mirror there is a *mise en abyme* effect: multiples of herself watch herself, watch herself, each Annette in a separate frame of the same reflection, as if she were stepping back in time or moving sequentially forward into the world around her. She watches her selves amid the others reflected in the mirrored walls.

Lost in thought, she thinks of ways to paint this reality, but not in realism. She wants to abstract it, push the boundaries of her mirrored selves. If she can begin to emulate these people, modulate her accent, and grasp the meaning of those more worldly by soaking this place up in all its smoke-filled atmosphere, she can become a new Annette. A different Annette. She wants to be more than simply tolerated or, worse, ignored.

Annette wants to belong. The great feat of walking into a Paris café is to have somebody recognize you, somebody to acknowledge your presence when you walk through the door. It only takes a nod to exist.

# Petit Matin du Flore—
## *In the Small Hours at the Flore*

*In fairy tales, the pumpkin carriages take you to Maxim's but there are others that take you to the Flore, to princes who are handsome, intelligent, gifted, generous, funny, and poor.*

—SIMONE SIGNORET

ONE OF THE NEW REALITIES of the Occupation was that France was forced to pretend it was in the same time zone as Berlin, which is normally one hour earlier. That meant winter nights fell earlier than ever, a metaphor for the dark mood infecting the city.

In the gloaming of late afternoon Annette and the other students leave the Flore, warmed by ersatz coffee, sweetened by saccharine and a sense of belonging. They huddle close together to fend off a bitter wind sweeping up from the Seine and dash for the stairs of the Saint-Germain-des-Prés metro. Kiss, kiss. "*Au revoir!*" "*À demain!* [See you tomorrow!]" Annette boards the Number 4 line. Seven stops later she disembarks at Strasbourg–Saint-Denis, a heavily Jewish neighborhood, and hurries up the stairs for home.

A CURRICULUM OF art history. Life drawing. Color theory. Beginning painting. Annette was in a delirium of charcoal-dirty fingers and turpentined perfume. Heaven was the shuffle and scrape of charcoal willow sticks on paper, and the solemn voices of those working in studios down the hall.

The Flore was part of her curriculum too now. With the self-assurance of youth, Annette, Salvatore, and a few other newly accepted artists from the Beaux-Arts descended upon the Café de Flore after classes, in a kind of foreign invasion of their own. Perhaps one or two waved to someone they knew, but the students formed their own clique. Once inside the brass doors, they claimed a table as near as possible to the coal stove, near another group consisting of well-educated, eclectic, and wealthy young Frenchmen. Both groups had one thing in common: they were all trying to establish themselves amid a world gone mad.

Within a few weeks of discovering the Café de Flore, Annette met a stylishly dressed Jewish girl who was studying at the Sorbonne. Bella Lempert was tall, smart and a Trotskyist. Girls bond in situations where they are the minority. Bella Lempert, Yannick Bellon, and Annette found themselves not only to be kindred spirits but among kindred spirits. Bella was studying philosophy and was friends with the well-educated young men at the table next to the Beaux-Arts students. Among them was Bella's neighbor, an up-and-coming film-maker and ethnographer named Jean Rouch. Annette began table-hopping. Yannick joined her.

Jean Rouch had a seductively exotic life story. His father worked as a marine biologist on an Antarctic exploration ship called the *Pourquoi-Pas?* (Why not?), captained by the legen-dary French explorer Jean-Baptiste Charcot. After the voyage, a shipmate introduced his sister to the young scientist, and they were married.

Born in Paris in 1917, Rouch spent much of his childhood accompanying his parents to places like Casablanca and Greece. During his studies at the Sorbonne, he and his friends became familiar faces in the hip circles of Montparnasse, cruis-ing the latest Surrealist art shows or hanging out at the Hot Club de France in Saint-Germain, listening to "gypsy jazz" by Django Reinhardt or the latest American swing bands. Rouch also painted, wrote sentimental poetry, and loved the cinema. He watched every film on offer at the Cinémathèque Française and was keen on photography. At one point, he bought a cam-era in a Paris flea market and began to make nocturnal trips to the Luxembourg Gardens, hoping to emulate Brassaï's night photos of Paris. Like many of the Surrealists, Rouch was fasci-nated by *l'art negre* (African art). It was in the jazz he heard at Hot Club de France, in the African masks that inspired Picasso, and in the dancing on Rue Blomet, where the mixed-race crowd danced freely together.

YANNICK BELLON WAS only sixteen, but liked to espouse free love. Coming from a sophisticated, artistic family, she was more worldly than the older girls. Annette found her amusing and charming. Six years older than Yannick, raven-haired Bella Lempert was an activist and a fashionista, who wore trendy round shades over her eyes and a man's zoot suit jacket. Bella was the epitome of cool—a Zazou.

Being a Zazou was about being free. Young Parisians adopted this new fashion aesthetic as a form of rebellion and resistance. Zazous got their name from the swing song by American jazz artist Cab Calloway, called "Zah Zuh Zaz." Anything American was anti-German. Zazou men wore their hair past their ears and slathered brilliantine to shine and shape it, in what was known as *la mode*. Their trousers were drainpipe-style, wide at the top, tapering in at the ankles, and cinched tightly at the waist. Their shirts had high collars kept in place by a pin and, when they could afford them, the Zazous wore suede shoes with brightly colored socks.

Sporting different fashions was part of the fun. Zazou women wore their hair shoulder-length or teased high over their foreheads. Blond was their go-to color. Sunglasses were round and dark. Lips were bright and red. In defiance of the fabric rationing imposed by the Nazis, they wore their skirts full and dresses full-skirted—the more pleats the better!—and, for some reason, brown-and-white check was the pattern for these rebels.

This was not just a fashion craze, though. As Jean Rouch recalled:

> Our only weapon was the scandal of our outfit. For quite naturally, we had found a path of protest, by taking the opposite view of the appearance of German soldiers of our age: we contrasted our long hair with their shaven necks, our long jackets (Zootsuits) with their "shaved" jackets, our high-collared English shirts with their low necklines, our narrow trousers with their too wide breeches, our thick-soled English shoes (already the latest stocks from J.-M. Weston) with their iron boots. Some of us had

fought against them in the first round of the war
[1940–41] and we knew that, for the time being, we
could only fight their *blitz-krieg* with swing, and
against their goose step and *Sieg heil!* with our double step danced at the Boissière club to the chanted
silences of "In the Mood."

Bella had her Zazou look down. The only missing element
was the bleached hair; hers was ink black. Romanian by birth,
Bella and her family had emigrated when she was a child. While
she had grown up outside of Paris, in the middle-class suburb
of Asnières, she was a chic city girl. When she began her studies,
she moved to an apartment on Rue Saint-Jacques, near the Sorbonne. Bella was a regular fixture at the Flore and became one
of Annette's closest friends.

Two years older than Annette, Bella had a bit more experience with men, but in the photo Rouch snapped of his friend
she looks more like a bookworm than a temptress. Bella and
Annette were so lively and animated that Simone de Beauvoir
noticed the "blond Czech" (which was how she always identified Annette) and Bella, the "little brunette, [with] creamy
skin...also Israelite, and ravishing," whose boisterous laughter
lit the room.

The young women at the Flore were the planets that men
circled like satellites. Not only were they beautiful and interesting, young and innocent; they were not your run-of-the-mill
"decadent artists" whom Simone de Beauvoir described as "the
Shock Brigade, pale haired creatures, all to a greater or lesser
extent ravaged by drugs (or alcohol, or just life) with sad
mouths and shifty, restless eyes." Young Jewish women were
seen as a little more exotic, independently minded, intelligent,
and, their admirers hoped, sexually liberated.

Attracting the attention of so many young intellectuals was
an endorphin rush for Annette, Yannick, and Bella. Twenty-

three and world-wise, with a sportsman's physique and curly brown hair, Rouch was the epitome of the Montparnasse scene. Annette liked him at once. Besides working in the art studios at the Beaux-Arts, all she wanted was to hang out in some handsome guy's apartment, spin jazz discs, and discuss the Surrealist revolution.

Rouch had two especially close friends he called his *copains comme cochons,* or pig buddies, a French colloquialism for "close friends." Pierre Ponty and Jean Sauvy studied together at the École Nationale des Ponts et Chaussées (the School of Bridges and Roads) and had fought together in the defense of France. Twenty-year-old Claude Croutelle, who was studying philosophy at the Sorbonne, was also part of Rouch's clique at the Flore, as was Claude's close friend, Jean Jausion, a poet with elfin features and the lithe figure of a dancer. These attractive, well-educated young men immediately latched onto Bella and her new friends, Annette and Yannick. But who would go out with whom?

The table was set. The future stretched before them.

# Les Réverbères

*A print from Les Réverbères zine*

*To Jean Jausion, whose work will please young people
as it should but will always please the forever young.*
—MICHEL TAPIÉ

A WELL-KNOWN FIGURE IN PARIS'S Surrealist and Dadaist circles, Jean Jausion had made his name as one of the leading

lights of a group known as Les Réverbères, or The Streetlamps. Les Réverbères was made up of about thirty artists and writers and produced both Surrealist and Dada theater—events a bit like the Happenings of the 1960s—as well as beautifully designed graphic magazines.

Jausion's friend, the artist Michel Tapié, was a great-great-nephew of Toulouse-Lautrec and had studied art with Marcel Duchamp. As well as being the graphic-artist-in-chief for the Réverbères' magazine, Tapié was also a jazz musician playing the clarinet in Les Réverbères' own band. L'Orchestre Hot played American jazz at Camille-Desmoulins, a cellar bar near the Palais Royal. Everything from Duke Ellington and Sidney Bechet to their beloved Louis Armstrong, whose performances had electrified Parisian audiences in the 1930s. It was their signature ragtime Tin Pan Alley opener, "Le Pas des Pélicans," that really drew crowds, though.

No sooner had the piano player struck up *les pélicans'* stride baseline than hundreds of young people flung themselves onto the dance floor to engage in an eccentric pigeon-toed dance of flapping arms, bobbing heads, and gaping mouths, imitating the gobbling of fish. Dada Jazz was fun, weird, and highly energetic and "took on the appearance of sarcasm," Dadaist Georges Ribemont-Dessaignes wrote in a rare description of the dance.

A bit circus-like, the minor chords of the music lent an ominous edge as the dancers, women with women, men with women, and, depending on the club, men with men, sashayed around the room in a fast 2/2 time of syncopated chaos. Think a foxtrot on cocaine.

The "foxtrot is kind of a blank slate of dances," Dr. Colin Roust says as he plays the chords on the piano, while explaining the notes. "It's linear movement, but then you throw in additional movements to it as your skill and inspiration strikes."

Here is Michel Tapié's beak-like nose and thin face, looking like a Cubist painting, craned over his clarinet, tapping his feet furiously. Ladies' man Django Reinhardt faces the crowd, an ascot knotted at his neck, his suavely mustachioed lips smiling as he sings:

> *"Toward the shore, while staggering strongly,*
> *A pelican was driving seriously,*
> *Belly in front, the children following him.*
> Clopin-clopant!*"*

Waddling like pelicans, the dancers push their bellies out like overstuffed birds, wagging their bottoms and shouting, "*Clopin-clopant!* [Hobbling along!]" They laugh and croak like pelicans as well.

What happier song than one where everyone gets to eat! The Pelican Dance was exactly what Tristan Tzara meant by Dada and Dadaism's performance art. If it made sense, it wasn't art. Everyone has to dance to their "own boom." That was Dada.

Packed into the tiny cellar venue, its air blue with smoke, patrons danced while smoking their pipes and cigarettes and applauded the band before settling back for the cabaret part of the evening: comedy sketches mocking the French police, Surrealist and Dada poetry, essays on art, perhaps an avant-garde theatrical performance, and, of course, more dancing.

On Les Réverbères' opening night, Jean Jausion stepped out onstage and treated the audience to a recitation of a poem by the father of Dadaism, Tristan Tzara:

> *"Tombo Matapo the vice king of nights*
> *They lost the arms Moucangama*
> *They lost the arms Manangara*
> *They lost the arms, irregular polygon,"*

he intoned, in French. The audience was rapt. Tzara had not been performed onstage in almost twenty years. A whole new generation eager to experience the avant-garde gathered the nonsense into their hearts and revered Jean Jausion of the Réverbères all the more.

For all their musical and theatrical experimentation, the Réverbères were actually best known for a cutting-edge zine that was launched, with typical irony, on April Fool's Day in 1938. Dedicated to André Breton, the high priest of Surrealism, it contained a potpourri of contributions: an essay on psychoanalysis and art; a translation of a poem by Edgar Allan Poe; three prints by Michel Tapié, on the theme of Narcissus, in Dadaist style; and an essay on composer Erik Satie (one of the heroes of the group). It also featured announcements inviting people to dances at the cellar bar in the Latin Quarter every Wednesday night with L'Orchestre Hot and an advertisement for a record shop on Boulevard Raspail where "Les Réverbères buy their records."

Renaissance man Georges Hugnet, who personally knew Joan Miró, Marcel Duchamp, Pablo Picasso, and Man Ray, was one of Jean Jausion's closest friends. With financial backing from his father, Hugnet established the publishing company Les Editions de la Montagne with the intention of releasing his own work and that of his friends Jean Jausion and Gertrude Stein.

Hugnet also printed the Réverbères' exquisite limited-edition graphic magazines. One vertical chapbook, *Polypheme—ou l'Escadron Bleu,* is no wider than a bookmark, with quixotically colorful illustrations by Michel Tapié and experimental Dadaist poems by Jean Jausion.

> *The Virgin with a white smile of fear…*
> *Vigorous as an April morning…*
> *Like goats from Portugal.*

Hugnet took on the new medium of photography with the joie de vivre of a prankster and sexual frivolity. In one photo, for L'Orchestre Hot, he placed the nude torso of a woman beside a flaming euphonium trumpet. It didn't take long for Hugnet to be excommunicated from the Surrealists; André Breton would not stand for offshoots to the movement or his manifesto, and his authoritarian stance was anathema to the young Surrealists coming of age in a prewar Europe. Hugnet and Jausion and others like them wanted to change the status-quo boring old world of the bourgeoisie and embrace artistic and sexual freedom, while also being deeply committed to political and philosophical values that would help free society.

But the onset of war brought the Réverbères to a halt. "Suddenly, all had disappeared, it hit us right in the face and after that it was never the same," Jean Rouch recalled. The last and final edition of the Réverbères' zine closed with the words: "There is only a small margin between a normal man, an imbecile and a madman." And then France fell to a madman.

Jean-Paul Sartre, Jean Rouch, and other regulars from the Flore Surrealists joined together to fight for France. Jean Jausion was exempt due to arrhythmia, a condition he jokingly ascribed to "the syncopated rhythms of Hot Jazz."

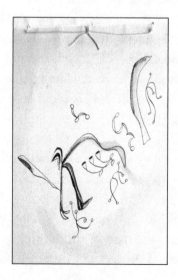

DESPITE THE OCCUPATION, in the spring of 1941, the Réverbères decided to continue their mission of disrupting societal norms and mount a show to re-create their prewar heyday. Jausion and other members of the group met at the studio of Jean Marembert, a Surrealist known for painting the invisible. This was Parisian bohemia, writ large. Amid liters of ether and empty morphine ampoules discarded by Marembert's junkie wife, a Great Dane wandered around the studio, placing his giant head on laps, knocking over glasses with a sweep of his tail. Occasionally, he defecated majestically in front of the debating artists and left the room.

Genevieve La Haye, Jean Marembert's wife, spent more time in a drug-induced dream world than in Surrealist reality and believed that the studio was actually a mansion, filled with servants. In truth, her home was a dirty *chambre de bonne,* an unoccupied maid's room, where she would shoot up heroin.

Chaos was the preeminent theme of the meetings at Marembert's studio. What should they do? How should they do it? They had been separated for two years, and most of them had been to war. These were not the same young men they had once been. Preparations were riven with personality clashes and infighting. Michel Tapié accused the others of being disorganized. Ten days before the opening Jean Marembert had not even produced a catalogue. There were no posters or records; no theatrical masks, no programs. Not even a venue!

Finally, somebody secured the Galerie Matières et Formes off Rue Bonaparte, not far from the École des Beaux-Arts and Café de Flore. Here they found a building with a large courtyard, various different rooms, and a cellar where they could mount the paintings, drawings, records, and posters created by Marembert, Tapié, and the other remaining members.

The Réverbères launched their first show in occupied Paris on Sunday, July 20, 1941. Many of the guests remembered the earlier shows from 1938–39, but there were also newbies in the

audience, like Annette and Bella, who had heard of the Réverbères but never seen the type of mania that was about to be
unleashed on the audience.

At 3:00 P.M. a large crowd of artists and spectators gathered
outside the gallery. A performer dressed in the orange, red, and
blue striped uniform of a Swiss guard, complete with the white
ruffled collar, black beret, and sharpened halberd, herded the
spectators into the gallery space. The venue was full to standing,
and extra chairs had to be brought in from a nearby school.
Three representatives from the German Propagandastaffel, the
body responsible for overseeing Paris's cultural life, were also
in the crowd. Dressed in full German regalia, they were not in
costume.

By four o'clock the show still hadn't gotten underway. The
crowd was restless. There were no hors d'oeuvres, no alcohol,
nothing to take the edge off ration-hungry Parisian appetites.
A cornucopia of decorative fruit and vegetables was being used
as part of the art installation. Finally, two hours late, the Swiss
guard gave a flourish and introduced soprano Olga Luchaire,
who performed several of the renowned Dadaist composer
Erik Satie's melodies. Jean Jausion followed with a few poems;
La Haye and a few others performed a Dadaist's work. When
three paintings were unveiled by an unknown artist, revealing
a formless scrawl applied with a cigarette butt, the Parisians
guffawed.

"*Merde!* You call that art?"

Catcalls rang out. Someone threw one of the decorative ap-
ples at the stage. The apple was followed by an orange and a
zucchini. The Swiss Guard grabbed one of the fruits and
hurled it back at the audience. The evening ended with audience and performers pelting each other with fruit. Thinking
it was all part of the show and a satirical statement on the avant-
garde, the German propaganda team applauded.

# Hitler and Annette

*It was easier for Hitler to start World War II than it was for him to face a blank square of canvas.*
—STEVEN PRESSFIELD

## FRANCE, JUNE 22, 1940

ON JUNE 22, 1940, the French delegation signed the armistice agreement imposed by Germany at the very location of the 1918 armistice signing. This entailed France's surrender in the Second World War.

At 1:35 in the morning of June 22, 1940, Hitler was in Belgium awaiting the news. He ordered the lights turned out and windows opened, so that his dining companions could hear the bugler announce the armistice. "A thunderstorm must have been brewing in the distance," the German architect Albert Speer recalls, and "as in a bad novel, occasional flashes of heat lightning shimmered in the dark room." The next day, Speer was "astonished" to find himself personally invited to tour the French capital with two other artists: the architect Hermann Giesler and Hitler's favorite sculptor, Arno Breker. It seemed

23

Hitler was truly dedicated to preserving the city "he himself had called the most beautiful in Europe, with all its priceless artistic treasures."

Like Annette, Adolf Hitler had dreamed of being an artist. Unlike Annette, his drawings and paintings were so bad that, at the age of eighteen, he failed the entrance exam to the prestigious Akademie der bildenden Künste, Vienna's equivalent of the French École des Beaux-Arts. The future Führer was reduced to earning a lowly living by drawing billboards for an antiperspirant powder called Teddy and working as a painter-decorator, an occupation that earned him the derisive nickname the House-Painter from Bertolt Brecht. Hitler's bitterness at being a failed artist and his resentment of those more talented and successful found focus in the concept of *Entartete Kunst,* or "decadent art," which he associated with Jews, Bolsheviks, and Freemasons.

Paris was not safe from his resentments. On the first stop of his tour—the Palais Garnier, the Opera House—Hitler divulged, "In the past I often considered whether we would not have to destroy Paris. But when we are finished in Berlin, Paris will only be a shadow. So why should we destroy it?" Considering how he had annihilated Warsaw, it was not an idle threat. "Although I was accustomed to hearing Hitler make impulsive remarks," Speer wrote, "I was nevertheless shocked by this cool display of vandalism."

The Opera House was Hitler's favorite building in the city. Speer watched as the Führer "went into ecstasies" before the grand rotunda, sweeping stairways, and gilded parterre. Scrutinizing the neo-Baroque landmark of world architecture, Hitler's eyes "glittered with excitement," Speer recalled. "Berlin must be made far more beautiful," Hitler instructed the architects.

The dictator had informed his staff that he was "not in the mood for a victory parade." But he did take an early morning photo-op tour of the Arc de Triomphe, Napoleon's tomb at the

Invalides, and the Eiffel Tower. Somber-faced, striding down the Champs-Élysées, Hitler led his retinue of generals, dressed in regimental overcoats, regulation visor caps, and polished black boots. Behind the cortege, the skeleton of the Eiffel Tower rose and clouds encroached from the west. Drizzle dampened the sidewalks. It was as if Paris herself was crying.

Their last stop was Sacré-Cœur, where Hitler and his entourage surveyed the spectacular panorama of the city he had conquered. "It was the dream of my life to be permitted to see Paris," he told the men around him. "I cannot say how happy I am to have that dream fulfilled today." Just three hours after arriving, having neither eaten nor gone to the toilet, Hitler and his three artists departed. It was nine in the morning.

The clouds broke up. Temperatures soared to almost 80 degrees and rays of sunshine dried the tearstained streets. Paris herself seemed to sigh with relief.

ONE OF HITLER'S obsessions, and a trigger for the war, was seizing back all the territories that Germany had been forced to surrender by the Treaty of Versailles in 1919, after its defeat in World War I. Among them was Alsace-Lorraine, a wealthy region that straddles the border with Germany, in northeast France. And it was here, in Nancy, the capital of Lorraine, that Annette Zelman was born on October 6, 1921.

Set in a deep, circular valley, like an amphitheater, Nancy is a place of baroque beauty, lush gardens, and golden gates that must have shaped Annette's artistic sensibilities and appreciation for art and beauty. It was the birthplace of Art Nouveau, and young Annette grew up surrounded by works of the École de Nancy, a group of renowned artisans and designers like Louis Majorelle, who revolutionized furniture design, and Émile Gallé, who created exquisite works in glass. Perhaps even more important for Annette and the rest of the Zelman children was that Nancy is also the birthplace of the culinary delight "Macarons de Nancy," those lush, pastel-colored cookies that will make a dent in your pocketbook but not in your stomach.

That one of Nancy's most famous benefactors was the deposed King of Poland, Stanislaw, who became Duke of Lorraine in 1736, may have added to its appeal for Moishe Zelman, a Polish émigré who was looking to create a new life with his new wife. Nancy offered the promise of work in its textile factories. So, like many Polish and Russian Jews, Moishe immigrated west to escape the pogroms devastating Eastern Europe. Nancy had a large Jewish population. Moishe Zelman secured work and found a role in the local synagogue as their cantor; his bell of a voice pure enough to make you weep when you heard him sing. With a job secured and an apartment rented, Moishe sent to Lodz for his young wife, Kaila, and their nine-month-old baby boy, Guy. It was 1920.

Moishe was a tailor by trade, but he was also a showman with a Chaplinesque flamboyance and sense of theater, leaping at everything in life with full-on energy and enthusiasm. As a young man he had moved to St. Petersburg, Russia, to study ballet, then he briefly served as a Cossack soldier. Looking at a photo of him from that time, standing at attention with his curved saber and enormous fur hat, one wonders if he decided to enlist simply so he could dress up in the elaborate uniform. Russia was one of his passions. But he was also a passionate Francophile who embraced the language and culture of France so completely that he was soon going by the French name Maurice.

Like her husband, Kaila Wilf grew up in a Polish upper-middle-class Orthodox family. She was dark haired with an oval face, and well-built. She had a manner of looking directly at one with a mixture of mirth and strength in her eyes. Kaila was the ground wire for the high-voltage cable Maurice. "Opposites attract" was certainly true for the couple. Where Maurice thrived on drama, Kaila was a no-nonsense, practical woman, who dealt with whatever life threw at her with a shrug and a smile. No sooner had they settled in Nancy than the industrious young couple began to hone their skills as tailors while building their family. Annette was born in Nancy, two years after Guy, and Charles came soon after. Annette was the middle of the Zelman sandwich. The cream cheese. Their father's adored daughter.

Maurice and his sister, Hélène, got a stall at the market where they sold fabrics, took orders, measured customers for suits and dresses, and spent the rest of the week sewing the designs and creating Zelman couture. Annette was five years old when Vétements M. Zelman De tail, Confections des Hommes, Zelman's Tailor's, Clothing for Men opened on Macaron Street. To celebrate the occasion the family lined up outside the entrance and splurged a few francs on a professional photographer who memorialized the event in celluloid. Dressed in his own tailored suit and tie, Maurice looks earnestly at the camera, a gold watch chain looped into his breast pocket. Hélène is on the other side, and the only one smiling at the camera. Kaila still has her apron on and looks like she is about to smile but hasn't quite caught her breath yet. The couple stands beside their growing brood, stacked on a stepladder, in order of age. Guy at the bottom looks slightly bored. Above him Annette has a large bow adorning her mop of blond hair. On the top is toddler Charles, with a knit cap on his head.

Initially, the family lived upstairs from the shop, where the children raced in and out with little care for customers or clothes. The *clackity clack* of the sewing machines syncopated the family's rhythm. They were well dressed, well fed, well off.

Like most women, Kaila had her hands full with work, at the shop as well as shopping, cooking, and changing and washing diapers and clothes for the brood of children that arrived in rapid succession. After a brief hiatus, a third son, Cami (Camille), was born in 1927. And a year later, the baby of the family, Rachel, emerged into what was by now a big, raucous, and loving family.

Five in eight years! Maurice and Kaila moved their brood down
the street to a larger apartment where there was a courtyard that
the youngest could play in under the watchful eye of their elder
sister. It was a happy childhood. Nancy was the sort of idyllic
city where children could be raised without too much parental
oversight. With both parents working in the shop, the children's
days were spent playing either amid the fabric cuttings on the
floor or in the Pepinière gardens, on the other side of Place Sta-
nislaus, the baroque heart of the city.

Constructed in the mid-seventeen-hundreds by Duke Sta-
nislaus, in honor of his son-in-law, Louis XV of France, the
Place is set between the old medieval part of town and the
newer, enlightened one that the duke envisioned. This vast outdoor space combined three squares surrounded by Baroque
buildings, an Arc de Triumph, sculptures, and ornately crafted
gates with gold railings. A colonnade flanked by an allée of trees
(four deep) allowed for the morning cavalry parade, as well as
for horse-drawn carriages to enter the square.

In the heat of the summer, the Zelman children cooled themselves in the fountains that sprayed water across the flagstones
in a fine mist. At the far end of the square, elaborate rococo
statues of Neptune and his wife, Amphitrite, and their scantily
clad attendants riding on dolphins stood beside the giant
wrought-iron and gilded gates of the Pepinière gardens, a 21-
hectare park, where the Zelman children spent many happy
hours. This was the city's "green lung," where families came to
stroll or picnic, or listen to music performed at the Kiosk Mozart, an ornately decorated bandstand set in an English-style
garden that also hosted community dances in the summertime.

Other pleasures included summer camping trips with
other Jewish children and holidays to the mountains or the
seaside. As the family grew, the children were lined up in
order of age, dressed in their Sabbath best, for memorial photos, often with cousins sprinkled in and always ordered eldest

to youngest. They were contented, industrious, and the children were decidedly French.

That was why it was such a shock when Rachel came home from school one day in tears. Other children had taunted and bullied her at recess.

"They called me a 'dirty Polack' and 'dirty Jew,'" she told her sister. "I thought we were French."

Furious, Annette marched up to their parents and insisted that they change Rachel's name to something French sounding. If Moishe could become Maurice, why couldn't Rachel become Michele? She was Michele from then on.

ANNETTE MANIFESTED AN independent streak early on, refusing to attend temple regularly. In most families this might have created strife, but Maurice and Kaila accepted her decision. As cantor at the nearby synagogue, Maurice worked the High Holy Days as well as the Sabbath. Despite that, Annette decided that she would attend only Yom Kippur and Rosh Hashanah services. Religious orthodoxy had little appeal, and she influenced the rest of the children with her opinion.

During the traditional fasting holiday of Yom Kippur, which is supposed to be a day spent in the synagogue in prayerful reflection on the past year and atonement for one's sins, Annette babysat her three younger siblings, while their parents were at temple. Later in the afternoon, she was supposed to bring the children down for the blowing of the shofar, the ram's horn. Tired of the grumbling in her stomach, Annette looked at her brothers and sisters and said, "Come on, let's go to a restaurant and eat."

So, they ate before joining their parents at synagogue.

Another year, "Annette dragged home a pine tree that she had found and decorated it in the family living room, so that we could celebrate Christmas," little sister Michele recalls. "Annette never acted like other people."

Nor did Maurice.

On a whim, in 1936, he packed everyone into the family car and drove from Nancy to Paris, where he had rented a spacious apartment. Rue de Belleville was a busy, commercial street in the east of Paris, made famous by Maurice Chevalier's song "Ma Pomme" and by Edith Piaf, who, according to legend, was born in the doorway of No. 72.

Transporting the sewing machine with them, Maurice and Kaila set up shop in the apartment and began making clothes. Guy and Charles sold their "vétements" in street markets all over Paris. Meanwhile, Annette did what was natural to her: pushed boundaries and experimented. Theater was her new passion. She was just fifteen, but that didn't stop her signing up for acting classes with two up-and-coming young actors, Serge Grave and Marcel Mouloudji. It is possible she even met Yannick Bellon in class, as Yannick would eventually become good friends with Mouloudji. And Annette would meet him again amid the regulars at the Café de Flore.

As the August heat suffocated Paris, the ever-mercurial Maurice announced that the family was decamping to the seaside resort of Paramé, near Saint-Malo in Brittany. Situated on France's Atlantic coast, Paramé had a grand seafront esplanade lined with villas and cafés, miles of sandy beaches for the children, and a casino for Maurice. Every afternoon, attired in a dinner jacket and bow tie, he left the family behind and went dancing at the casino. Kaila never went with him. Perhaps she knew to give her flamboyant husband a long leash; he certainly always returned home at night. Well, almost always.

Always the leader, Annette entered the children in volleyball, gymnastics, and sundry other entertaining competitions available to visiting tourists. One contest involved making costumes out of copies of newspapers. Annette spent days creating whimsical outfits and hats for Cami and Michele to wear for the fashion show. Zelman Couture won, of course.

At the end of the season, the children climbed onto a life-guard stand for their annual photograph, eldest on top. Annette's face is sun-kissed and sea sprayed. Her tousled hair is pulled back off her face with a headband. Beaming and tan, she is back-to-back with her elder brother, Guy, the only one in the group not dressed in a swimsuit. With his hair slicked back, wearing a button-up T-shirt, Guy looks like he is ready for work or flirtation, carrying his teenage self with a suave sophistication that in a few years will have the girls lining up to date him. Below Guy and Annette, Charles grins from ear to ear in a sleeveless striped T-shirt. In the sand, a gap-toothed Michele, with sun-kissed cheeks and sea-frizzed hair, hugs her beloved brother Cami. Heads touching, their arms are flung around each other's necks.

Maurice decided the family should stay in Paramé for the winter and enrolled the children in school. Then Brittany weather did what Brittany weather does best—it changed. Storms came in off the Atlantic and ravaged the beaches. Umbrellas blew inside out in cold, drenching rains. Worst of all, "they closed the casino!" Michele says. So "Maurice packed everyone back up in the car and they returned to Nancy. That's how Maurice was."

GUY AND CHARLES had cut their teeth on the family retail business, helping potential customers peruse fabrics, buttons, and design patterns. Now that they were teenagers, they got jobs working at Boucherard, the city's leading department store. During the day Annette kept an eye on the children, but on Saturday evenings she and Guy would attend dances at the gazebo, Kiosk Mozart, in the Pepinière gardens or at a Jewish youth club in the center of town. Like her father, Annette loved to dance, and she was a popular dance partner. One man was so smitten with her that he snapped a photo of the two siblings. Guy, looking astonishingly handsome, admires his little sister, who is beaming and full of life, as always.

To improve the family's fortunes, Maurice began driving through the surrounding countryside to sell parcels of clothes from the trunk. Farmers needed to be clothed, as much as city people. Sometimes they traded food and eggs for Zelman-tailored attire. "We were always well-dressed," Michele remembers.

The family business continued to thrive right up to the outbreak of war with Germany, after its invasion of Poland and the Czecho Slovak state, in September 1939. Only 120 kilometers from Saarbrücken, Germany, Nancy's industries became an immediate target for the Allies. RAF bombers pounded the city from the air and the mayor issued a mandatory evacuation. The Zelmans had just fourteen days to pack up and leave. One of the first things they did was divine a secret whistle to help them find one another in the crowds Maurice knew they would face. The children practiced the Zelman whistle until they could all trill perfectly to one another.

With true sorrow Maurice and Kaila pulled down the shutters on the family business and fled, along with thousands of others. Most evacuees left with no more than they could carry on their backs. As usual, the Zelmans were different. Kaila insisted that they bring the *lessiveuse*, a cylindrical laundry tub on legs, made of galvanized metal.

Who would carry a metal tub and mangle hundreds of miles on a train? A family of seven would. They might be refugees, but they were going to have clean clothes. Kaila also made sure that the tub was packed with crockery, kitchen utensils, the family china, valuables, and silverware. She wrapped everything up with her linens, so the family had napkins and tablecloths, too. "Without these we will become animals eating with our hands," she told Maurice. He didn't argue.

Guy and Charles lugged the tub down the street to the railway station. Annette, Cami, and Michele carried the suitcases. Kaila hoisted a bulging ball of sheets and pillowcases over her shoulder. Maurice schlepped his precious sewing machine and trusty balalaika. As long as they had the sewing machine, they could make a living. They had to leave the piano behind.

The designated reception area for what would become a mass evacuation—six hundred thousand citizens from the Alsace-Lorraine region—was the southwest of France. An arduous journey in the best of times, it lasted three days and covered 500 miles. There were numerous stops, long hours on station platforms waiting for the next connection or the next one, if the train was full. Livestock wagons had replaced passenger cars. Stamped on the outside was the phrase *8 horses 48 men*. "If you were lucky, the wagons had wooden benches to sit on," Michele recalls, and they had multiple sections, designated for ten people in each area. As the Zelmans were only seven, Maurice persuaded a couple and their child to travel with them. Some wagons offered no privacy or seating and were filled with families, their belongings, and a few pets.

Overhead, the skies rumbled from enemy aircraft scouring the landscape for ground targets. Evacuees lived under the constant fear of bombardment.

BEING A REFUGEE is an act of desperation, a last-resort effort to survive. Flight is safety. Vulnerability is a permanent state of mind. As a victim of circumstance, you are aware that larger forces are at work in your life. You have no control. Violence and danger are the only certainties, so you risk everything for the unknown, hoping that it will lead to something safer or more manageable. To get there, you must give up everything you have ever known. Everything you have created. Worked for. Loved. Life is reduced to sustenance. Food. Staying together. A whistle.

The piano may have been left behind, but every wagon the Zelmans entered was filled with their songs and stories. Maurice entertained everyone as darkness descended across France.

Evacuees were treated with varying degrees of welcome. Rural people were considered uneducated, uncouth, and unclean. And not only were many people city dwellers, they were Jews. Small rural communities felt inundated by outsiders, with their different accents, regional traditions, and religions. Refugees received a daily maintenance allowance from the government—ten francs per adult, six for children—but locals were struggling as well. Why were these incomers receiving handouts while simultaneously looking down on the very people whose communities they had fled to for refuge? Locals blamed the evacuees for making life harder on them. Food and housing were already hard to come by, and inflation was on the rise.

The first stop on the Zelmans' flight from Nancy was the village of La Lande-de-Fronsac, in the winemaking region to the east of Bordeaux. Fully aware of the issues facing the locals, Maurice encouraged the family to integrate themselves into the community. With typical Zelman ingenuity and vitality, Maurice and Kaila began to build their clothing business back from scratch. The teenagers rallied around their parents to help make money.

The Vendanges, the annual grape harvest, is a French tradition that begins in October and is a chance to make money, no matter who you are. Hell, high water, or German invasion, nothing was going to stop the Vendanges. The French might let the German panzer division roll over their fields and homes, but not even the Germans touched vineyards. The Germans wanted wine, too.

Guy and Charles got work as field hands and spent the first two weeks picking bunches of ripe purple grapes. The work was hard, but the rewards were good—food, wine, and buxom country girls. The boys' participation in the harvest helped endear the Zelmans to the community. Within weeks, Annette befriended the local priest, at the Church of Saint Pierre. An open-minded, educated man, he became a kind of mentor to the teenage girl. "He's the most intelligent man in the village," Annette told her brother Charles. Her intellectual curiosity and freedom from religious prejudices drew her to spend hours at the vicarage, talking about books, religion, and life. When she wasn't babysitting, that is.

As autumn waned and winter turned the leaves from red and orange to crisp browns, Maurice decided to continue Annette's tradition of celebrating Christmas. It was so unseasonably warm he announced they would have Christmas dinner outside and invited their neighbors and the priest to join them.

With seven in their family and neighbors with their own broods, you can imagine how many tables and chairs were needed. Furniture was hauled up the road by hand and by wagon. The linen tablecloths Kaila had schlepped from Nancy in the *lessiveuse* were steam-pressed, and out came the family china, the silverware, the glasses. The local vintner supplied the wine.

Sitting at the head of the table, Maurice raised his glass and clinked it with his knife. The chatter of children quieted and everyone looked up as Maurice stood to make his toast. "Remember, *mes enfants,* that in the winter of 1939 you had Christmas dinner outside, among the vines. *Salut!*"

"*Salut!*"

The Zelmans and their neighbors, adults and children, clinked their glasses, looked one another in the eye and sealed the toast. There is nothing so special as drinking wine while standing on the soil where that wine was born, and a few of the more sentimental poured a little wine on the earth, giving back to her what she had given so freely to them. Then they drank. For Michele it was her first taste of wine. She made a face at Cami, who squinched up his nose back at her.

MICHELE DOESN'T REMEMBER why they left La Lande in the spring of 1940, but the reason probably had to do with making a living. Rural life was less lucrative than urban, especially for a tailor. Few needed a new suit in the midst of a war. Rents were skyrocketing, and now that the harvest was over, food was in even shorter supply. Inevitably the Jews among the refugees received the bulk of the opprobrium. A survey conducted by French authorities in 1942 showed that 85 percent of the people living in Limousin were "declared anti-Semites." Negative rhetoric spread by the collaborationist press blamed Jews for driving food prices higher by engaging in black-market activities. It was probably a variety of these factors that caused the Zelman family to move to the city of Bordeaux.

Settling in the suburbs, Maurice and Kaila picked up their tailoring business. Guy and Charles returned to retail and worked at the Bordeaux location of Boucherard, the same department store they had worked at in Nancy. Annette stayed home to look after the smaller children and tried not to tear her hair out. The situation was deteriorating fast, though. Maurice held a family meeting to discuss plans for escaping to England. He had worked in London in the past, and they had cousins there. If they could find a smuggler and get across the Channel, they could set up the family business in England. Smugglers were expensive, but he and Kaila had saved a fair amount of money. The plan was hatched.

Then, on June 18, 1940, the Wehrmacht marched into Bordeaux. The German occupation of Bordeaux was particularly brutal, especially toward Jews. Almost immediately, all French Jewish citizens had to register at their local *mairie,* or mayor's offices. The Zelmans joined the queues and watched with unease as their blue French Republic passports were stamped with the word *Israelite*.

When Annette registered, she was required to list a profession, despite the fact that she was a teenager. Her ID now listed her as an "apprentice seamstress." She was infuriated at the label.

"I don't like this," Maurice complained at dinner that night. They were too vulnerable, living on the outskirts of the city.

A vote was brought to the table—everyone wanted to relocate. This time they decided on the center of the city, where they could merge with the population at large.

A stone's throw from the mighty Gironde River, they found a sizeable residence on Rue des Pontets. It was a good thing the house was large because family members from all over France started showing up on their doorstep. Kaila's first cousin, Leon Wilf, arrived with his wife and four boys. Their eldest, Joseph, was Guy's age. Maurice (namesake of his uncle) was close to Charles's age. Abraham was fourteen and palled around with Cami. Jean and Michele were eleven. Their home was full to bursting. You didn't have to be a Wilf or a Zelman—anyone desperate for a place to sleep was welcome, though beds were in short supply. Michele recalls twenty people living there, at one point, and every available surface became a makeshift bed.

The war soon caught up with them. The British pounded Bordeaux from the air.

An airport north of Bordeaux, in Mérignac, and an Italian submarine base just a few miles upstream were prime targets. Bombers came in the dead of night, accompanied by the shrieking and wailing of air-raid sirens that woke even the most dedicated sleepers. Even Charles. Zelmans and Wilfs and whoever else was in the flat rushed for the air-raid shelter, but Charles always took his time getting dressed. "He would even put a tie on!" Michele recalls with a laugh.

There was probably a girl in the same shelter, whom he had a crush on.

"*Allez! Vite!* Hurry up, Charles!" Annette would shout as Michele leaned against her, sleepy eyed. But he was always last. And always well-dressed.

Autumn leaves fell with the bombs. In addition to the threats from the air, in October 1940 France's puppet Vichy government, headed by Marshal Pétain, passed its first *statut des Juifs,* statute on Jews. Tightening the definition of Jewishness, it excluded Jewish citizens from a wide array of professions, including the army, the civil service, education, the press, and many industrial activities. Maurice's sister, Hélène Goldman, had sent news that there was an empty apartment in the same building as hers in Paris's 10th arrondissement.

"Come to Paris," she entreated.

On the night of December 8, 1940, a massive squadron of forty-four RAF aircrafts attacked the submarine base. Bombs rained on the city, killing sixteen and wounding sixty-seven civilians. Even the bomb shelters shivered and quaked.

The next morning, Maurice called a family meeting. They had a chance to move to Paris, he announced. "This is a great opportunity!" Maurice told the children.

Kaila was against the idea. "Paris is too dangerous!"

"And Bordeaux is safe?"

"There are Nazis there! Listen to reason, Maurice."

"They aren't bombing Paris. We have to get out of here. People need clothes in Paris. The business will do better there."

With a strange fascination Michele watched their parents bat arguments back and forth. Their mother rarely raised her voice or disagreed with their father.

"We are refugees! We are Jews!" Kaila almost shouted at her bullheaded husband.

"We are Zelmans! We will survive!" Maurice thundered back at her.

The children froze. Their mother and father never argued. The disagreement revealed a seriousness to their circumstances that Michele could not imagine.

"We will vote." Maurice asked for a show of hands.

No one was surprised when Annette agreed with their father. As usual, the rest of the children voted with Annette. She was their leader, after all.

Outvoted, Kaila sighed. But she was not leaving her trusty *lessiveuse* behind. They piled their china, silverware, linens, and valuables inside the washtub and boarded a train to Paris. A new stage in the family's story was about to open.

*"Zah Zuh Zaz!" Jean Huguet, dressed in Zazou style and dancing.*

# ACT TWO

## 1940–41

At the International Surrealist Exhibition held in Paris in 1938, model Sonia Mosse was the only plastics artist to exhibit, and one of a few women (the mannequin is her likeness).

# The Circus Comes to Town

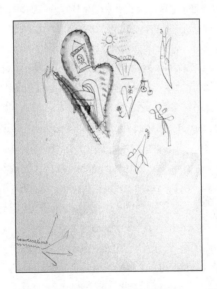

*The Zelman circus, as we continue to be called in the*
*Latin Quarter. We are famous, old man.*

—A<small>NNETTE</small> Z<small>ELMAN</small>

C<small>OULD</small> A<small>NNETTE AND HER FAMILY</small> have chosen a worse moment
to arrive in Paris? Temperatures were well below freezing. The

skies were leaden. Frequent bouts of rain and snow chilled the air. There would be no dining outside amid the vines this year.

Mornings were dark. Afternoons were darker. In between it was gray. Food was scarce and strictly rationed. Oil and coal were in short supply, so people used anything they could burn, even old ashes. Churches were forced to turn off their furnaces; Nazis did not approve of Catholic prayers any more than Jewish. Writing in her diary in the dank chill of her apartment on Rue de Beaujolais, the writer Colette praised the heat-giving properties of gold jewelry.

Despite the cold, the Nazi soldiers parading up and down the Champs-Élysées, the military vehicles rumbling over cobblestones, and the giant swastikas hanging from government buildings, Paris was a welcome respite from the smoke and terror of Bordeaux. She opened her feeble arms to our small group of fugitives and swept them up in an invisible embrace, hiding them from the prying eyes of pro-German informants and goose-stepping invaders.

Collaborationist papers like *Paris-soir* proclaimed, "The Purification Begins: Jews at last expelled from all public jobs in the country" as private enterprises were targeted. All Jewish shops now had to display a sign saying *Judisches Gesellschaft* and *Enterprise Juive*. This was not the carefree Paris where they had frolicked as children four years earlier.

The raft of anti-Semitic legislation passed by the Vichy government had clamped down on educators as well. "At the Lycée Camille Sée—as in all the *lycées* [schools]—I was made to sign a paper where I swore under oath that I was not Jewish nor affiliated to Freemasonry," Simone de Beauvoir wrote. "I thought it repugnant to sign, but no one refused: for most of my colleagues, as for myself, there was no way of doing otherwise." Sartre wrote that he disapproved of her decision, but she reminded him that as he was in a POW camp, he didn't need to pay for food or a roof over his head.

Sporadic acts of resistance occurred. Before the Zelmans arrived, on November 11, the anniversary of the armistice of World War I, a massive demonstration had taken place at the Arc de Triomphe. Parisians gathered together and sang the Marseillaise; students and schoolchildren carried signs displaying the Cross of Lorraine—the symbol of resistance adopted by the Free French army under de Gaulle.

Paris police were in charge of handling civil disorder, but how could they arrest French patriots for singing the national anthem? Their hesitation was fatal. German troops charged the crowds with fixed bayonets. In the scuffle one patriot raised his fist at a German soldier, then disappeared into the crowd. An innocent bystander was arrested. When Jacques Bonsergent was asked to divulge the name of the man who threatened the soldier, he accepted responsibility for the incident. Found guilty of *"Beleidigung der Wehrmacht,"* insulting the Wehrmacht, Bonsergent was executed two days before Christmas and a curfew was imposed across the city from midnight to 6:00 A.M.

"For the first time these 'correct' Occupation authorities were telling us, officially, that they had executed a Frenchman for failing to bow before them in the approved manner," Simone de Beauvoir wrote. The streets were plastered with posters threatening punishment to vandals defacing the announcement of Bonsergent's fate. Despite the threat, posters were immediately defiled. Police turned a blind eye. Then, in typical French fashion, Parisians turned tragedy into artistic outpourings of grief. Overnight, flowers, WW I paper poppies, and tiny tricolor flags appeared under the posters. It was much harder to quash these memorials.

Still, Maurice expressed nothing but enthusiasm as they schlepped their ever-trusty washtub, sewing machine, and belongings past these shrines to the new apartment at 56 Boulevard de Strasbourg. Like a fata morgana, Paris was an oasis of art, music, culture, and books, all the things they held dearest. The pastries weren't half-bad either.

WALKING DOWN THE long entrance hallway that ended in a tiny kitchen, Kaila took stock of their new surroundings. Two doorways like a backward F led to a bedroom and a dining room. She pushed back the drapes, unlatched the window to look down into the courtyard, and spotted the latrine. First things first, they needed fuel to light the stove in the kitchen. She sent Guy and Charles to forage for wood or garbage and shut the window before a cold blast of wind could stir dust up from the floor. She had cleaning to do, unpacking and sleeping arrangements to organize. After the stove was lit she had supper to get on the table, but she could make this place a home. It even had a piano.

The dining room was the center of the family's universe. Everything of importance happened at this table. It was a stage for the Zelmans' own Comédie-Française, a podium for debate, a pillow for a tired head, a place to do homework, a dormitory for Annette and Michele, even Annette's art studio. Dinner was eaten there too.

The long wooden table seated eight comfortably. On Maurice's left sat the eldest. Dark and swarthy, Guy had movie star good looks but was "a bit of a narcissist," Michele admits. Where Annette was intellectually stimulated by reading, writing, and art, the "only thing that really interested Guy was appealing to girls." He spent hours in front of the family mirror doing his hair and adjusting his outfits. But he was also a protective big brother who escorted his kid sister to dances and was ready to punch the lights out of anyone who didn't treat her with respect.

Guy was her mother's favorite. Annette was her father's. The leader of the children, she and her father were the family's decision makers. At times, she could seem a bit peremptory, but the children always agreed with her. Annette sat at Maurice's right hand.

Sitting beside Annette was Charles, "the odd philosopher." Thin and narrow-waisted, he had a melancholy face under an unkempt mop of hair. What Charles lacked in looks he made up for in charm and character. He was the family eccentric, intellectual and blessed with a quirky sense of humor. Annette adored him. Their kindred spirits formed a nucleus that underpinned the family.

On the other side of the table was another nucleus of sibling devotion: Camille and twelve-year-old Michele. They played, fought, and kicked each other under the table while waiting for dinner. They were inseparable. Dinner was not a ceremonious affair. Kaila generally deposited a pot in the middle of the table with a terse, "Help yourselves," then walked away.

Guy was always the quickest to dive in, but Charles and Cami were the hungriest. No matter, none of the brothers were so rude as to forget to leave enough for their parents and sisters. Rationing meant meals didn't last long.

Providing the family's anchor in the turbulent seas of the world's multiple crises was Kaila, the perfect foil to her flamboyant husband. She practiced a laissez-faire parenting style. "My mother was always very laid-back," Michele remembers. "'Go and ask your father,' she would always say. Nothing bothered her. Even with all the chaos in the apartment, she remained unflustered."

As a lay rabbi, Maurice was soon officiating at neighborhood weddings, while Kaila made food for the receptions. Weddings were a good way to market proper attire as well. Once word got around that a tailor of Maurice Zelman's reputation was in town, everyone wanted a pair of his fine-fitting trousers. The building was already home to Zelman relatives, and soon, Michele recalls, "There were people coming and going from the other apartments. My mother would make cake and tea for them. And we would sit around the table. We talked. We read. We remade the world."

Maurice thrived on the bedlam. This elfin, impeccably dressed man was a born entertainer who did everything with panache. Even if Jews were rich enough to have radios, it was illegal to own one. Entertainment came from Maurice's imagination or memory. He loved to sing the Russian songs that he'd learned as a young man in St. Petersburg, the Polish songs of his homeland, French songs, and Jewish songs. From his place at the head of the table, Maurice could simply turn his chair around and pound the ivories to regale the family with after-dinner entertainment. They shared their dancing, singing, game playing, boisterous jokes, storytelling, and laughter with the entire apartment block. Their father's performances and flights of fancy were regularly greeted by an ironic Kaila saying, "Thank you, Sarah Bernhardt!"

Maurice would often conclude the evening's entertainment with his favorite Russian ballad, the tear-jerking "*Ochi Cherny* [Black eyes]":

*Dark eyes, flaming eyes*
*They implore me into faraway lands*
*Where love reigns, where peace reigns*
*Where there is no suffering, where war is forbidden*

As the last notes of his passionate voice faded, Maurice would dab his eyes, and the children would fall into a reflective silence. The only other time the Zelman household was quiet was when everyone was asleep.

ACROSS THE ROAD was a cinema where Annette and her brothers took the children to watch the latest movies. A few blocks away, Cami and Michele registered for school. Around the corner from the school was the communal bath where the family took their weekly ablutions. "We shopped in the morning with Annette, and then she took us to school. She always made sure I was well turned out with a good outfit and plaited my hair." Ben Guigui, an Algerian who adored bon vivant Maurice, ran the neighboring vegetable stand. "Maurice used to come into the kitchen at five P.M. and make soup. I can see it today," Michele says. "He used to say to my mother: 'There we are; I've made the soup.' A bouillon with chicken or *ravioli a la Juive*."

Not everyone in Paris was happy to see new faces seeking refuge and anonymity. Getting work outside of the Jewish quarter was impossible. Annette secured a part-time mending and embroidery job with Eva Singer, a seamstress who lived upstairs, while Guy and Charles worked the streets selling Zelman couture. On Sunday mornings, young Jewish men would gather at Place de la République, a fifteen-minute walk from the apartment, and skirmish with gangs of fascist French youths. With bloodied noses and boosted egos, Charles and Guy would return home in time for supper, boasting they'd given those bastards as good as they got.

Urban living was more familiar to the Zelmans than the rural lifestyle they had led in La Lande. The metro shuffled them from one region of Paris to another, but it was the Latin Quarter that held a special fascination for Annette. An autodidact, she was always reading or going to the theater. The creative energies around her were a banquet for her spirit to dine on, and she soaked them up. She simply couldn't get enough of all Paris had to offer. That was how she learned that the École des Beaux-Arts was taking students for the winter session.

Since she did not have a baccalaureate, Annette had to take an entrance exam, which consisted of a drawing test. Up until that point, no one in the family even knew that Annette wanted to be an artist. So they were more than a bit surprised when she arrived breathless in her aunt Hélène's apartment, having hurried back from the Beaux-Arts and Café de Flore. Her mother and Aunt Hélène were sitting with Annette's cousin Simone. Michele and the other children looked up from their playing.

"I passed the test! I've got in!" Annette shouted proudly, unrolling the newsprint with a charcoal sketch of the famous Greek sculpture of a naked discus thrower, penis and all.

"It's *Discobolus!*"

Aunt Hélène screamed and covered Simone's eyes. "Don't look!"

Kaila burst out laughing.

ARTISTIC SKILL MAY be bequeathed at birth, but it takes time to develop the physical skill sets. Artists need to develop their eye, that steadiness of hand, and most important a vision for what they want to say through art. Annette doodled constantly. She loved caricatures and cartoons, delighted in humor and irony, but it took raw skill to look at the complicated dimensions of a sculpture like *Discobolus* and render it in charcoal well enough to be accepted into the Beaux-Arts without any formal training or even a sketch class. Annette had an eye. Like her father and mother, she could reproduce whatever she saw. Whether it was a pattern for an outfit or a muscle-bound, anatomically correct man.

She entered the world of the Café de Flore with the same confidence. For young artists and writers, hungry for a sense of direction and place, the Flore was the perfect oasis in a country whose sense of identity had been shattered by occupying forces. Every morning now, on her way to the Beaux-Arts, Annette would drop Michele and Cami at school, then walk to the Strasbourg–Saint-Denis metro and descend beneath the green copper patina of the Art Deco metro sign that still bedecks the station today. Seven stops later she would mount the stairs to find herself in a new world of Saint-Germain-des-Prés in the Latin Quarter on the Left Bank. A world that she was about to make her own.

# A Surprise Visit

*The reason why this war is so "undiscoverable" is because it's everywhere.*

—JEAN-PAUL SARTRE

NEW YEAR 1941 ARRIVED WITH a snowstorm. Much of the country, including Paris, was paralyzed. Parts of the Seine froze over and a hill in a park in Saint-Cloud was turned into a ski run. An army of Parisians, unemployed and not, were sent out to clear the streets, but blankets of white still covered the ground on the day a black German staff car, flying swastikas from its hood, drew up outside the École des Beaux-Arts.

Clambering out of the car, a short, plump Wehrmacht officer with a head like a potato waddled across the snow-covered courtyard under the watchful eyes of Annette's *Discobolus* and the other classical statues lining the courtyard's entrance.

The choice of fifty-five-year-old Captain Heinrich Ehmsen as the Nazi liaison to engage with the director of the Beaux-Arts, Paul Landowski, was a clever one. Originally from Düsseldorf, where he had trained at the School of Decorative

51

Arts, Ehmsen was a veteran of the First World War and a painter himself. Like Hitler, he held France's artistic heritage in high regard. Unlike Hitler, Ehmsen had made several art pilgrimages to Paris and the South of France as a young man.

He also knew, from firsthand experience, all about the political control of art. In 1933, Ehmsen was arrested by the Gestapo. Four years later, his work was branded as *Entartete Kunst,* or "decadent art." He must have made a full recantation, because he was now installed at the Propagandastaffel, the Nazi propaganda department, at No. 52 Champs-Élysées, which was in charge of overseeing cultural life in Paris. A German in charge of French culture? That was an oxymoron Landowski was careful to keep to himself.

Squeezed into an ill-fitting uniform, Ehmsen entered the great hall of the Palais des Études and crossed the geometric-patterned marble floor. Supported by ornamental columns and arches decorated with the classical Greek and Roman statues, its famous leaded-glass ceiling extended into a bisque-colored overcast sky. Designed by the architect Jacques Félix Duban in 1830, the Great Hall was modeled after the magnificent courtyard of a Florentine palace, where Duban had studied. It is still the centerpiece of the school and one of the finest architectural examples of the Beaux Arts style.

For Ehmsen, arriving under this edifice was inspirational. He stood in the cradle of French painting, where so many of the great artists he admired, from Degas to Renoir, had been trained. But as part of the *Kultur* group in Paris, Ehmsen's job was to see that the Beaux-Arts was falling in line with Goebbels's policies on Aryan culture.

Climbing the marble stairway and heading along the second-floor hall, Ehmsen could look down upon the galleried arches and their sculptured nudes. Ornamentally painted wall panels with stenciled waves and fruits hanging along two-story periwinkle and deep russet-red panels of circling vines lined the passageway. This was the grandeur that Ehmsen passed on his way to the office of Director Landowski. The hallways echoed with the first clicks of Nazi jackboots, each step like a ticking bomb. The question was, how much time would Landowski have to protect the school and his students?

A tall, bearlike man with a domed forehead and goatee, Landowski was a celebrated sculptor, not just a pencil pusher.

Ehmsen held his palms forward in an open gesture of greeting, clicked his heels, and said, "*Es ist mir eine Ehre, Sie kennenzulernen, Herr Direktor.*"

At least he hadn't *Heil Hitler*ed, Landowski noted in his diary later that night.

A taller and more elegantly dressed German in civilian clothes interjected, "Herr Ehmsen does not speak fluent French. I am his interpreter."

Landowski took offense that the head of French culture spoke no French. Surely, the Germans could have found someone who spoke the language. But he kept his thoughts to himself as he offered Ehmsen a seat. Pleasantries were exchanged, cigarettes lit. There was an awkward pause.

"*Keine Sorge; wir sind nicht hier um Ihnen etwas wegzunehmen.*"

"Don't worry; we're not here to take anything away," the interpreter translated.

Landowski sighed with relief. Under the direction of Reichsmarschall Hermann Goering, the Nazis had plundered thousands of artworks since the Occupation began. Paintings by Goya, Rembrandt, da Vinci, and other Old Masters had disappeared into Germany.

"We are here to help," Ehmsen continued.

Help? Landowski considered the offer a veiled threat, but the Germans were in charge now. He and Ehmsen discussed the heating problems in the ateliers and the dwindling supply of art materials for the students. "I would also like to visit the workshops," Ehmsen explained. "And get to know the students."

Landowski raised a bushy eyebrow. The last thing he wanted was the Nazis snooping around. But he had his own agenda: the fate of several hundred of his former students, who had enlisted in the French army and were being held in German internment camps. "There are rumors that give hope for massive releases. Is it true?" he asked.

"That's not my department, I'm afraid," Ehmsen replied. "But I will make inquiries for you."

Landowski wondered what he would have to give up for the information. As the meeting drew to a close, Ehmsen repeated his desire to visit the workshops and again assured Landowski that he was available to help with any difficulties that might arise. Landowski was not fooled. He knew the real goal of the visit was to investigate the Beaux-Arts and ensure the Aryanization of the academy.

"Let's keep in touch by phone." Ehmsen clicked his heels together again and this time gave a peremptory Nazi salute.

Landowski felt sick as he described the meeting in the diary he kept throughout the war. Painstakingly recording his daily life at the École, Landowski chronicled every conversation and worry he had. And he had cause to worry.

For his Jewish students, like Annette Zelman, the sudden appearance of a Nazi officer was alarming. Up until now, the École des Beaux-Arts had, like the Café de Flore and the rest of the Latin Quarter, felt like a safe space, free of German interference. But the Nazis and their French collaborators were tightening their control of the capital's cultural life and intensifying their campaign against the Jews. The writer François Fosca ran a column in the collaborationist journal *Je Suis Partout*, where he railed against "the hordes of Jews" who had corrupted French art, expressly calling for the Fine Arts to be Aryanized and Jews banned from all cultural events.

The mission of the Nazi Propaganda Department that Ehmsen served was to force the defeated French to accept

Nazi ideology through censorship and the control of information. The importance the Nazis attached to this work can be seen by the size of the department: a staff of more than twelve hundred serving seven sections dealing with radio, literature, cinema, theater, music, art, and culture. Under the leadership of the German ambassador, Otto Abetz, a new German Institute was established in the elegant Hotel de Monaco on the Left Bank, where he hosted cocktail parties, lectures, German-language classes, and exhibitions.

These organs of Nazi propaganda tried not to be overtly heavy-handed but rather practiced a process of "seduction." It was hoped that French artists and writers would accept German culture more easily if they were given enough freedoms that they wouldn't wince at the pain of Occupation. The Jewish question required a more head-on approach, however. The name of the Théâtre Sarah-Bernhardt was changed to Théâtre de la Cité, to expunge Bernhardt's Jewish identity. The publishing house Calmann-Lévy, which had issued the work of such pillars of French literature as Flaubert and George Sand, was renamed Éditions Balzac.

Ehmsen was determined to bring the Beaux-Arts to heel, as well. Two weeks after his first visit, he summoned the head of the Grande Masse, or student union, Philippe Mondieux. This time it was a meeting of intimidation. Arriving at the Propagandastaffel's headquarters on the Champs-Élysées, the young Mondieux was escorted through the confiscated building to Ehmsen's office, where he was peppered with questions about his fellow students and teachers.

"Are your fellow students patriotic? Are they seeking revenge?" Ehmsen asked. "Is it true Jewish women are posing as models? When I visited it seemed there was one. Why are Jewish women there? Is it to illustrate racial characteristic differences?" Ehmsen then launched into a diatribe about racial purity, national identity, and how Jews were an alien race and subhuman.

Mondieux was so upset by the meeting that he went at once to see Director Landowski. Distraught, Mondieux confessed that he was afraid his responses might harm his fellow students. Later that night, in his diary, Landowski railed at the threats Mondieux had experienced. "It was more like gossip, even espionage. Can you imagine more gross silliness? Men seriously engaged in this hunt. And to think that in France there is a commissariat of Jewish affairs! What fools if they really do this!"

The vise squeezed even tighter in February, when Landowski himself was summoned to the Propagandastaffel. Though junior in rank, Lieutenant Herbert Lucht was a career Nazi and, as Ehmsen's superior, a far more dangerous man. Everything about Lucht was pale, his hair, his skin, even his cold blue, expressionless eyes. His green jacket was badly cut, too short. Leave it to a Parisian to note a Nazi's lack of style.

As they sat in comfortable armchairs, Lucht launched into "a profession of faith" and his deepest concerns. "I am a good German," he told Landowski. "You are a good Frenchman. But there is a Jewish question. What do you think about it?"

"I have met Israelites in my life," Landowski replied cautiously, "who have rendered me such great services that I am not an anti-Semite on principle." He refused to use the word "Jews." He then added, pointedly: "As director of this school, I will bow to the instructions of the *French* government. The number of Israelites here is so small, anyway, that the question does not arise." With that, Landowski stood up and took his leave. But he felt Lucht's ice-blue eyes following him out the door.

Landowski was concerned not only for his students but also for himself. The previous fall, he had been investigated and questioned about being Jewish. Suspected of being a Freemason, he was accused of embezzling 100,000 francs from the school coffers. The investigations went nowhere, but he was a target. At the same time that he was under suspicion, he was secretly helping one of his female students, an "unfortunate Hungarian Israelite," escape Europe. He cared deeply about the young artists in his charge.

Because so many students were struggling to make ends meet and would spend money on paint more quickly than food, the École supplied free lunches. Landowski raised funds for competitions with cash prizes that could then be shared among all artists. When two sisters delivered 30,000 francs to the school from an anonymous donor, Landowski distributed the money to his most needy students.

Throughout the spring of 1941, Landowski recorded increasing anxiety and frustration: "At this moment this agitation of being the director, the decisions which must be taken, the measures which must be applied by [German] orders, so contrary to what one thinks, do not simplify life. . . . If I resigned, immediately people would spread the rumor that it was because I am Jewish. I am not an anti-Semite, quite the contrary. But I do not like...that people say I am Jewish."

His reluctance to resign as director had an even deeper reason than the trouble it would cause his wife and children. He was secretly giving student cards to compatriots who otherwise could not move freely about Paris without getting arrested. The director was working his own private arm of the resistance.

Jewish students like Annette were registered as foreign students. This may have been a way to "cook the books" against the Germans and hide Jewish students. Annette's name is not recorded in the academy's regular student register, but as an *auditrice libre,* or visiting student. That meant she did not have to go through normal bureaucratic checks and would not be suspected of being Jewish. She also benefited from the influx of female students during wartime. Many male students had been conscripted and ended up as POWs, which meant that some 64 percent of students at the academy were female. "It's like the start of a girls' high school!" Landowski wrote.

The precise number of Jewish students attending the Beaux-Arts in 1941 is unknown, but the German statute on Jews in September 1940 set the limit at no more than 3 percent of the student body in any institution of higher education. The absence of attendance figures in the school's archives suggests that the lack of documentation may have been intentional.

UNDER PRESSURE FROM the authorities, some of Landowski's colleagues curried favor with the Nazis. Every May, the Beaux-Arts judged submissions from the state schools, in order to find young artists outside of Paris. On the day of the competition, Captain Ehmsen and his superior, Lieutenant Lucht, arrived at Rue Napoleon with a group of plainclothes officers to watch the session. Landowski was "shocked by the flat and disgusting way" some of the professors were being chummy with Ehmsen and Lucht and happily denigrating Jews with the heads of the propaganda department. "Why anyone would enter into a relationship with the Germans, when they are not forced to do so by their position!" Landowski fumed.

His pro-German colleagues were mounting a campaign of disinformation against Landowski, trying to force him out. A few weeks after his meeting with Lucht, a sympathetic colleague warned him that Ehmsen and Lucht wanted to "chase out all Jews" from the academy, including Paul Landowski. "They say you are not Aryan!"

"That is stupid!" The director laughed. The gargantuan, open-armed *Christ the Redeemer* statue he had created overlooking Rio de Janeiro should have been proof enough for anyone that he was Catholic.

"It's very serious, Paul."

Landowski had a signed statement from the investigation back in the fall that proved he was not Jewish. His friend encouraged him to deliver the documents to Ehmsen at once. Back at their apartment, Landowski and his wife assembled the documentation and arranged to have it delivered to 52 Champs-Élysées. Two days later, he attended a meeting with the head of the French education authority to discuss "this question of Aryanism."

"What stupidity!" he wrote later that evening. "What cowardice to accept to defend oneself." But his situation was a precarious one. He had to "risk everything, imprisonment, deportation, even being shot at random, as a hostage" to remain in his position and continue helping his students.

# Becoming a Floriste

*I entered the luminous cave, noisy, full of feminine
boys and wanton goddesses. The ashtrays I remember
well, filled with Lucky Strike cigarette butts stained
with red kisses.*

—CHARLES MATTON

THE PARIS CAFÉ HAS A special culture all its own. In the 1940s,
no one at the Café de Flore made much money. Many of its
regulars were communists, and everyone read *Le Populaire* or
*l'Humanité,* two left-leaning newspapers. Today, the café has a
slightly different culture, but one thing remains the same: patrons rarely look up to see who has entered. Who arrives is of
no importance, if you belong.

Simone de Beauvoir often spent mornings and afternoons
at the Flore, despite the absence of her lover and fellow professor, Jean-Paul Sartre. Then toward the end of March, Sartre
surprised de Beauvoir by arriving back in Paris after escaping
from his German stalag. Reentry was not seamless; de Beauvoir writes that he'd made a commitment with his fellow

60

inmates "never to compromise, to reject all concessions" with the occupying forces. This was a difficult proposition, she notes, "in Paris, where simply to be alive implied some sort of dim compromise."

Even cigarettes were now currency, rationed just like food and dealt on the black market—the higher the quality of the cigarette, the more valuable. In a valiant effort to avoid compromise, Sartre grubbed his way through the Paris gutters and ashtrays to find "dog-ends and dottle to fill his pipe," de Beauvoir recalled. Other pipe smokers created concoctions from dried grass, weed, flowers, or whatever they could find, which "made the Café Flore smell like an herbalist's shop." Smoking did more than warm cold hands and calm nerves; it stemmed hunger.

ABOUT THE SAME time that Annette was finding her seat at the Flore, another young Jewish woman walked through the frosted-glass doors. No one looked up at her either. The same age as Annette, Simone Signoret would have been hard to miss because on her first afternoon she decorously knocked over the jar of macaroons on the table. The waiter was not happy.

Despite the faux pas, when Signoret stood up to leave, the famous Surrealist and artist's model Sonia Mossé "smiled at the new girl.... She was terribly nice and I never saw her without a smile during the months that followed." Of course, Signoret didn't realize that Sonia was making a pass at her. Sonia Mossé, whose body had inspired artists like Giacometti and Man Ray and who was close friends with Picasso and Dora Maar, held court with her acolytes in the lesbian corner of the café.

On any given day, you might find Dora Maar, "her big dog with her on the lead," with Picasso, Giacometti, and Solange Bertrand sitting in one corner, across from the Beaux-Arts and Sorbonne students. Signoret's place was at a table full of actors, directors, and the poet/screenwriter Jacques Prévert. Wannabes and stars mingled together at the Flore.

Like Annette, Simone Signoret quickly became one of the young female regulars. "All of the men seem to wear tweed," Simone de Beauvoir described. "And black turtlenecks. The women have no uniform, there are only a small handful of women to be counted, and they are unique in that. Not fashionable with any sense of style. They were their own fashion."

WHAT WAS THIS social vortex called Café de Flore? Was its attraction the red moleskin banquettes? The coconut-less macaroons? The fake coffee? The weak beer? Were the men more handsome there than in the rest of Paris? Were they more intelligent? Perhaps. But really they were a family of black sheep. Floristes were well-read, well-informed Parisians, but best of all, Germans avoided them.

In an occupied city, where individualism could be fatal and the terror of the Gestapo was beginning to hang over everyone, the Flore had an inescapable allure. Here women were not hushed or taken for granted. Coffee might grow cold, but feet stayed warm. One elderly gentleman might whisper the BBC news in the ear of Sartre or someone else and soon everyone knew what was happening outside the censored world of France.

Before the year was out, Paul Boubal, the owner of Café de Flore, would be hiding the painter Francis Grüber from the Gestapo. When a young Jewish man named Mimile Cercan fled into the café off the street, Boubal ushered him through a side exit and helped him escape. The Flore's clientele were "resolutely hostile to fascism and collaboration and unafraid to conceal it," Simone de Beauvoir noted.

For a young, impressionable artist striving to find her place in the world, the Flore provided an education not offered anywhere else in occupied Paris. Annette may have been learning the classical techniques she would need to become a real artist, but her mind hungered to be stretched as much as her canvasses. No different from any other teenager, she was eager to experience life in fistfuls, and circled the flame of Paris's intellectuals and artists, like a fluttering blond moth. In a world that was strangling thought, the religions of Surrealism, existentialism, and humanism worshipped at the Flore were even more important than school.

Though she didn't know it yet, becoming a Floriste was what Annette had been waiting for all her life.

# The Zazous

*Zazou, what you're gonna do? There's a lot of people
gunning for you. Zazou, comment allez-vous? Knock
on the door in the night*
          —PET SHOP BOYS, "IN THE NIGHT"

THE ZELMANS HAD SEVEN PEOPLE living in the two-room apartment on Boulevard de Strasbourg. They washed and dressed in the kitchen, and slept everywhere! Michele claimed the long bench by the piano. Annette had a mattress pad under the dining table, which allowed her to work at night, while the rest of the family snored. The boys slept on thin mattresses or mats in their parents' bedroom. Guy had the corner by the window; Charles slept along the wall, Cami in the other corner. Their parents had the only bed. On a table beside the bed sat their most precious possession, the sewing machine. "That was the soundtrack of our lives," Michele says. "That wheel spinning. It was the sound of earning money."

Maurice and Kaila could work all day long thanks to their live-in domestic—Annette. When she wasn't studying at the

Beaux-Arts or sitting in the Café de Flore, she had the unglamorous task of babysitting. "Whenever we were bored, we could count on Annette or Charles to add some creative activity. Charles was the master of inventing games and comic stories to entertain us. If you needed to know something about your homework or were curious about something else, you asked Annette," Michele recalls. "She always knew what to do. Full of ideas. Always busy. Always convinced of her views and always spoke her mind forcefully."

Annette longed to spread her sketchbooks across the dining table and draw. Art students have exercises to perform: Sketch one hundred hand gestures in a week, feet, eyes, lips, noses. Draw in the metro, in cafés, on the street. Draw your family and friends. Draw everything you see. Quick sketches. Capture the line. The gesture. The last thing she wanted was distracting children around, but they depended on her.

"We're bored" was the refrain of their childhood. And like their father, Annette or Charles would create a new game to play or give them a project. "Okay. Let's do this!" They would make Michele a doll or a dress; when Cami was younger they made soldiers. In the spring of 1941, Bella and Annette decided to make original dresses with convenient pockets on their sleeves, so they didn't need to carry purses while dancing. Excited about the challenge to design something unique, Annette solicited Michele to help. She wanted to make something with loads of pleats. Something with brown-and-white checks. Something Zazou.

Annette sketched her idea on a scrap of paper: a dress with a pleated skirt and a button-up belt; "she even made a matching hat and umbrella" with the leftover fabric, Michele remembers. Nothing Annette did was halfway. Michele helped take her sister's measurements: waist, bust, hips, shoulders, arms, et cetera, and they began the mathematical equations necessary to determine how much fabric to buy. This was not simple math. Michele and Cami were learning complicated equations that were part of the family business. Calling out the measurements, Cami wrote down:

A=Waist
B=Skirt length
C=Seam allowance

Plus a waistband. The same formula was used for the bodice and sleeves. The pleating in the skirt was going to be the hardest part to construct. Annette wanted lots of pleats! So the skirt would swirl when she spun. This wasn't just fashion; it was a political statement against Germany's textile rationing! And real math. She taught them how to triple her waist size and double the seam allowance (3A + 2C) to get the length of fabric required. Then they added the desired skirt length to the seam allowance (B + C) to get the width.

Michele does not recall how Annette got enough ration cards to make her outfit. But she recalls scouring the bolts of fabric, until Annette found the perfect checked print for her outfit. Back at home they gathered some cellulose tape and old newspapers. Now the children had to practice some geometry! The circumference of Annette's waist was entered in the middle of large sheets of taped-together newsprint. She used a tape measure to draw a circle that was the precise circumference of her waist. Then she showed them how to measure the diameter and radius of the circle. Cami now multiplied $2\pi \times r$ and divided his answer from Annette's waist measurement to arrive at the radius.

The wooden pattern master that Maurice and Kaila used for their own creations was now needed. This curved ruler helped Annette draw the lines she needed from the radial circle of her waist. Using Cami's measurements and the pattern master, she folded the newsprint into quarters and traced a quarter circle in the folded corner, so when Michele cut it out they would have a perfect circle for her waist. Opening up the pattern, they had to cut a circular hem too, so the skirt would flare when she spun on the dance floor. It was all in the planning and the pattern. The slightest miscalculation could make the outfit too small.

She and her sister carefully pinned the pattern to the fabric and outlined it with blue fabric chalk. While Annette cut out the skirt, Michele and Cami cut the sleeves and waistband and a few other small pieces. Once the skirt was cut, Annette took a piece of old cardboard the width of her pleats and assigned Michele the task of measuring and marking the width of the pleats onto the skirt section with blue tailor's chalk, three marks per pleat: "Think of A, B, and C and you are matching A to C; B is the fold." The skirt looked like a huge fan hanging off the edges in the middle of the dining-room table.

Ironing the pleats and basting them flat was Annette's job. The heavy iron had to be heated on the stove, and she had to set a towel on the table for pressing. Sprinkling water on the fabric with her fingers, she took the waistband strip of fabric and double-folded it over the interfacing to stiffen the band, so it would hug her waist. Then she sandwiched the pleats with the band and pressed until steam hissed. Pin and press, pin and press, all with the help of her handy little sister. The scent of damp wool filled the room.

The sewing machine they lugged across France was probably a hardy, black Bernina, manufactured in Switzerland. Bernina was the first company to manufacture a household sewing machine in 1932 and by 1938 had a zigzag machine on the market that was of workhorse capacity. Each shiny metal part had a specific dial, one for the bobbin winder, one for wheel balance, another for thread tension. Large spools of thread unrolled from the top of the machine, above the stitch regulator.

Maurice and Kaila were proud of the work the girls were doing and supportive of the effort, but night was the best time to get access to the sewing machine. After supper, Annette sewed while Maurice sang.

The outfit may have premiered at the Flore, but it was Salvatore Baccarice, Annette's fellow student and friend, who captured her, swinging her skirt seams in the air, outside the Beaux-Arts. Smiling coquettishly for the camera, her feet crossed in a mock curtsy, she was the perfect Zazou. Later that evening she and Bella went to the Hot Club, where Annette took to the dance floor. She *was* the hot spot that night, lighting the floor with her effusive spirit and radiant smile. Zazou boys in their baggy pants sashayed and swung her, so her skirt flew horizontal to the floor and whipped her thighs. The ultimate "Zah Zuh Zaz" Zazou babe. All she needed was red lipstick!

———————

*If [Parisians], in spite of the disgraceful defeat of their country, wish to dance, it is in the German interest not to prevent them from doing so.*
—SCHOOLS AND CULTURE DEPARTMENT,
MILITARY GERMAN COMMAND (MBF)

IT WAS A double-negative revocation of the Vichy government's ban on dance clubs. Of course, dancing was still considered highly immoral. Not that most Parisians cared as long as they could dance. There was a catch, though—dancing was only legal if it was part of a dance lesson. Only a certain number of couples could be on the dance floor at any time. And there could be no jazz and no live music. Dance schools immediately sprung up around Paris.

For Zazous, circumventing the imposed regulations on dance venues was part of the fun. Like the punks of the 1980s, Zazous used their distinctive, rebellious way of dressing to protest against rationing, conservatism, curfews, and the law. But their favorite pastime was dancing. They even had their own provocative choreography. In front of swastika-draped public buildings, they would yell, "Swing!" hop on the spot, and yell, "Zazou hey hey! Hey za Zazou!" slap their hips three times, shrug their shoulders twice, and turn their faces to the side. It was a dangerous game.

The Vichy government condemned the Zazous as degenerates, a poke in the eye for the ideals of masculinity, obedience, and conformity that Vichy and the Nazis espoused. The collaborationist press attacked them as lazy, selfish, and part of a "Judeo-Gaullist" conspiracy to undermine the morals of French youths. The pro-Nazi paper *La Gerbe* railed against "the decline of critical faculties, the follies of 'nigger' jazz and swing, the contagion of our youth by American cocktail parties." Zazous were rounded up in bars and beaten up on the streets. "Scalp the Zazous!" became the favorite slogan of the fascist youth organization Jeunesse Populaire Française, and squads of young JPF activists armed with hair clippers shaved their freedom-loving contemporaries. Many Zazous were arrested and condemned to forced farm labor.

After months of lockdown, confined to cafés and bars devoid of live jazz, Zazous and young Parisians leapt to "study" at dance schools as the city went into full swing mode. Paris had a vibrant nightlife once again.

Swarthy, mustached Eddie Ruault, who changed his name to Eddie Barclay and would become a famous postwar music producer, was among the most rebellious of the dance club owners. He simply ignored the ban on live music and opened his dance hall under the guise of a "school" at 37 Rue Boissière, where Annette and her contemporaries congregated. So began a game of cat and mouse.

The police shut down Barclay's club almost weekly because he refused to register his "school." A week later, he would open back up, often somewhere else. Finding the next "surprise party" before the police located it was part of the entertainment. Because Eddie was good friends with Django Reinhardt, whose band was willing to risk playing live, his club attracted well-heeled young Parisians as well as Zazous. Annette and her brothers flocked to Eddie's clubs.

Zazous could also be found hanging out in the Latin Quarter or the Hot Club de France, where they listened to jazz and traded the latest American novels and records. The Hot Club was infamous. On any given evening (when he wasn't at Barclay's) Django Reinhardt could be found dressed in his signature white suit, cradling his battered Selmer guitar. Inspired by American swing bands, Django and his Nouveau Quintette were the hottest sound in town. It only took a nod for the band to launch into his rendition of "Mabel" and Annette and the rest of the crowd to jump up and swing.

The whole Latin Quarter came to the Hot Club, where regulars included students from the Sorbonne, like Jean Jausion and Claude Croutelle. Rebel girls donned zany-looking hats made of crepe paper or painted cardboard, a slap in the face for the rationing system that allowed only one hat per person. There were Zazous with their dark sunglasses, bleached hair, and brown-and-white-checked outfits. At the bar, watered-down drinks flowed like water. The rich had coupes of champagne. The poor had jugs of beer.

Django was their idol. Young men grew mustaches in homage to him. Dancers in the aisles made Indian banshee war cries, like the ones they'd heard in American movies about the Old West. They danced until the sweat poured from their armpits and perfumes gave out. They danced past sore feet and side stitches. They danced until curfew. Then, like Cinderella racing for her pumpkin carriage, Paris's youth made a mad dash for the last metro.

Leaping down four steps at a time to catch the train, they threw themselves between closing doors. Propping doors open for friends and strangers, they packed into carriages full of entertainers and musicians, theatergoers and students. Often musicians continued playing, an accordion here, a guitar there, a hat passed for spare change. Because it was Paris, there had to be lovers kissing as the train swayed and rumbled through the dark tunnels. Conversations were of concerts, art shows, theater. The revelers shared laughter and stories of losing friends at one club only to find them again on the train home. "What happened to you? Where did you end up?" Some couples hauled their half-full champagne bottles with them and finished off the last of the bubbly in pilfered glasses on the way home.

*Paris will never be crushed!* That is the silent toast. The feeling, the hope, in the metro cars before midnight.

# The Moon Prepares Her Nightly Toilette

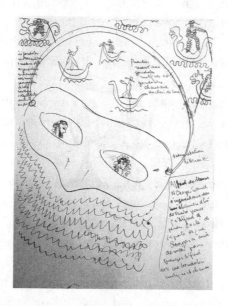

*Glory to he who brings dispute.*

—JEAN ROUCH

THROUGHOUT THE SPRING OF 1941, Annette and Jean Jausion circled each other, like stars, but for the moment Annette's attentions were taken by the other Jean, Jean Rouch, the alpha male of the Flore's young students and artists.

Rouch and Jausion had a great deal in common intellectually, but they were physical opposites. Where Rouch was a tall, muscular Adonis, who liked wearing casual outdoor clothes, Jausion was a slighter man who always dressed in a well-tailored suit. Both had a wicked sense of humor.

Annette and Rouch were clearly attracted to each other. Four years older, the well-traveled Rouch was not only to-die-for handsome, intelligent, and world-wise; he had the kind of tireless intellect Annette cleaved to. On top of his engineering course, he had begun studying ethnology at the Sorbonne and Musée de l'Homme, where Marcel Mauss, the father of French anthropology, mentored him. It is a testament to Annette's magnetism and intelligence that this daughter of a Jewish tailor, living in a third-floor walk-up with her family on Boulevard de Strasbourg, was mixing with some of Paris's brightest up-and-coming intellectuals.

Rouch liked vivacious and independent young women, like Annette, the kind of girls "with whom he played and to whom one could entrust his dreams and imaginations," Annette told her brother Charles. Annette put great stock in dreams, and Rouch loved to explore the dreamscape of the psyche that Surrealism espoused. She was just the "sort of girl he was attracted to," Jocelyn Rouch, his widow, confirms. "Rouch liked strong, intelligent women."

He was also a ladies' man. Annette was not the only attractive girl in the room, nor was he the only handsome young man. The two were perfect foils for each other. And they were about to drive each other crazy.

THE CAFÉ DE FLORE's cliques were mostly drawn up along artistic lines. But the tables were close and table-hopping was as normal as bed-hopping. The young women there, many Jewish or half-Jewish, were close in age and temperament. All had the same aspiration—to escape the conventional. "The person I am today was born one evening in March 1941 on a banquette in the Café de Flore," Signoret writes. The same could be said of Annette.

The conversations swirling around Annette were freighted with political and artistic revolution. Living under the thumb of an occupying force was an art in itself. Robbed of innocence and naïveté, French youths struggled with the hard realities that tainted their lives. Surrealism was a safe haven, a way to express one's inner life. André Breton had written about the rights of imagination in *Surrealism in Service of the Revolution,* sixteen years earlier. His message was just as relevant for young artists living under occupied rule. They needed a purpose for art. A direction. Surrealism suggested that art could be "free, spontaneous, playful, and imaginative." Everything that Annette would soon embrace, demolishing what she called the "barriers of reason" forced upon her by "the oppressive rules of modern society."

The war of independence in the Surrealist movement was not just against the Germans but against logic and reason. A metaphor for Paris herself, under the yoke of oppression. If they couldn't be physically free, they would become spiritually, intellectually free.

Annette had arrived at the École des Beaux-Arts a blank slate, ready to be tutored and mentored by classical artists. Classical education *was* theory and rules, though. As she honed her skills, her hand learned to accomplish what her mind ordained. She devoted herself to learning the tricks: How the human body is divided into heads, seven and a half. How to create that linear illusion of perspective.

Here is gouache. Here is charcoal. Here is color theory. Pen and ink. Shading. Perspective. Negative space. Here is oil and turpentine and linseed. Here is homework: Sketch. Thirty or more per day. Quick sketches with no detail. Just the line. The gesture. Now larger with more detail. Sketch hands and feet, eyes, and mouths. What about ears? Develop the muscles of your hands until your fingers and palms ache.

It was grueling work. Not "playful" at all.

But Annette hungered to learn the rules. How else could she break them?

# Flea in a Glass Cage

*DADA is a state of mind....DADA applies itself to everything, and yet it is nothing, it is the point where the yes and the no and all the opposites meet, not solemnly in the castles of human philosophies, but very simply at street corners, like dogs and grasshoppers.*

—TRISTAN TZARA

HERE IS ANNETTE WITH A toehold in adulthood, on the brink of leaving childhood, balancing between the two. Ready to step off one moment and retracting the next. She wants to play more. She wants to make believe. She wants to create. "Do you still think it's possible that we can find friends like those crazy people we played with on the train or from the loony bin or at the post office?" she asks her brother Guy. "I doubt it and it pains me." But those were exactly the kind of people she had found in the Surrealists. Even though "psyche" was a term still being defined, the Surrealists knew its mysteries existed. The new Annette was undeciphered, undefined, open to exploration. Searching for herself.

Her infatuation with Rouch was a bit of a lark. She had never wielded so much power over a man, nor had a man become so tied up in knots over her. And she liked it. Testing how far she could push the boundaries of their relationship, she sashayed around him, in a Pelican Dance of courtship. She was exhausting.

Like most young men, Rouch was impatient for consummation. He had fought the invaders, seen death and mayhem, been decorated with the War Cross and Combatant's Cross for his service. He wanted love, by God. He wanted sex! Annette wasn't ready. She was on again, off again—hot, then cold.

As their relationship progressed, Rouch became adamant about leaving Paris for the Free or Unoccupied Zone. Established in June 1940, after the defeat of France, the Vichy government under Marshal Pétain was allowed to govern the southeastern portion of France, stretching from the Swiss frontier to the Spanish border.

As a Jew, Annette could not legally travel to the Free Zone even if she had wanted to. And she didn't. She had only just arrived in Paris. Why would she swap her City of Light for the provinces she had just left? Neither girl thought the boys would be gone for long. Paris was in their blood. Meanwhile, the dashing Claude Croutelle had caught Bella's eye; Bella had caught Guy's eye, and Jean Jausion was trying to catch Annette's.

It had been too cold when the Zelmans arrived in Paris; now it was too hot. On the anniversary of Hitler's visit to Paris in June 1940, a heat wave descended and temperatures climbed. Streets became kilns, baking good natures into short-tempered outbursts. Even the Seine lost its breeze. The only places to escape this kind of heat were the municipal swimming pools. With her brothers and sister, Annette was soon watching the boys from the Flore lift weights and play Ping-Pong instead of debating the merits of Dadaism versus Surrealism. They were getting tan too.

Annette's love life and the heat were not the only reason to go to the pools.

"The mouth has ears," Michele says. "There was a kind of network or bush telegraph for Jews. We told each other this is safe or you can't go there, but you can go here. Everyone in our building was Jewish. We were always telling each other the latest news and tips for what was safe and what wasn't." Jews were now being collected randomly off the streets and never seen again. Instability and insecurity were constant threats to peace of mind. But, as Michele recalls, "the Germans never came to the swimming pool because they couldn't come into the changing rooms to ask for people's identity cards." The pools were among the safest places in Paris for Jews. And many Jewish youths, as well as Floristes, congregated at the floating pools on the Seine on Saturday afternoons. The most famous of the pools was the Olympic-sized Les Bains Deligny, which was constructed in the 1800s and designed to look like Roman baths. It boasted Corinthian pillars and a balcony overhead for bystanders to enjoy food or refreshment, though in 1941 few people could afford such luxuries. On the promenade below as many as a hundred people might be milling around in the water and on the decks.

To get in, bathers lined up under the shade of the mature chestnuts. Women in dresses and sensible shoes carried their bathing costumes in their pocketbooks and folded a small towel over their arms. Men in suits and ties carried even less. Swinging on the guide ropes, Michele and other impatient children wished the line would evaporate into the humid air. On a hot day, the line could extend past the houseboats moored along the quay.

A billboard above the entrance assured customers that they would find filtered running water and varnished decks. Since there were no lounge chairs, bathers lay on the decking with or without towels. Bathing suits were baggy, less than formfitting, and were often just cotton bloomers or undergarments. A crowd of young men and women hung out in groups or pairs, talking in the sun or lying prone to soak up the rays. Two Ping-Pong tables offered an opportunity for exercise; there were even some weights to lift. Outside the communal changing rooms, lockers lined the pool's edge so that customers could secure their clothing and purses.

When the pool was constructed, there was no filtration system for the water and according to historians the water in the pool took after its source, the Seine—part sewage and part garbage dump. "Dirty, cloudy, often foul smelling and unhealthy," was how one Parisian journalist described it in 1844. Even as late as 1954, newspaper captions stated the municipal pool did not always have a "heavenly scent." Michele remembers the water as being clean, though. The Zelman children counted on Annette taking them at least once a week. "It was a time of freedom for us. It was like we were on holiday. We sat on the benches or on the side of the pool with our feet in the water and watched people."

There were no lifeguards, so at the beginning of the summer Annette made sure that Michele knew how to swim. "Annette was a good swimmer and very sporty, and looked good in a bathing suit," Michele recalls. Annette taught her kid sister a few basic strokes, then left her and Cami in the shallow end to play.

Annette's preferred position was sitting at the edge of the deep end, hanging her feet in the water and laughing with Bella and Yannick. In case boredom struck, she always had a pad to sketch on and book to read. As bookish as his sister, Charles was reading Nietzsche's *The Birth of Tragedy* while they hung out at the pool. Guy didn't read. He was too busy being a chick magnet. Twenty years old and an inveterate flirt, Guy strutted around the decks, hoping to catch Bella's eye.

With wry humor, Annette watched her brother trying to seduce the "deeply mystical" Bella Lempert. Guy "will ruin himself with flippant champagne dinners and gifts for her," Annette confided to Charles, and dismissed Guy's delusions of philosophical conversations with Bella as "a bunch of indiscreet confidences about other people's lives and loves." Where the money for these meals came from was a mystery. Were Charles and Guy working a covert income stream through the dance clubs on Rue Boissière?

As THE SUMMER fun progressed, a new clique formed around the girls. It wasn't just Jean Rouch and his pig buddies in their orbit; Claude Croutelle and his close friend Jean Jausion were just a bath towel away. Jean Jausion and Guy enjoyed playing Ping-Pong and talking jazz, while Claude and Charles punned together. As Annette sketched and read, Bella let her pale skin turn copper in the sun. Cami and Michele splashed in the shallows. And poor Salvatore Baccarice, Annette's adoring photographer friend from the Beaux-Arts, felt his heart break.

A communal phonograph was available for entertainment. Guy and a few others enjoyed bringing their discs in to play. Of course, it didn't take long for catastrophe to strike. Punching a ball back and forth in the air in a kind of slow-motion volleyball game without a net, a pretty young woman by the name of Paula accidentally hit the ball into the phonograph, broke Guy's favorite record, and damaged the player. The Zelmans' flamboyant Don Juan was not happy. But Paula was pretty and apologized profusely.

In high summer, amid the high jinks and aquatic fun, Guy announced he was suffering from pulmonary issues due to urban living. This seemed especially odd as the weather was hot and humid and he wasn't even coughing. Even Maurice thought Guy should get away, though. Almost immediately Guy was packed up and moving back to Bordeaux, where he planned to stay with their Aunt Alte. It never occurred to Michele that anything other than Guy's health was at stake.

ANNETTE'S FIRST LETTER to "Frater Bella" Guy is one of her funniest and most virtuoso pieces of correspondence. Using satiric humor and language that would become her trademark, she is tart tongued and sharp-witted. "Sorry to tell you that Bella hardly ever talks about you. She is much more interested in me and intends to make me her 'best friend.' Jean Rouch is currently very complex doing everything he can *not* to be in love with me. He tries to forget with other girls—impossible."

Stylizing her writing after the Charlie Chan detective books and movies of the 1930s, she imitates the detective's affectations, confessing she is "unable to speak differently from my revered model" (Charlie Chan). She is having so much fun with her riff that she explains the growing complications of her love life as the crime scene detective would:

> Consider (Bella, Claude and I) Jean Rouch as a guinea pig reacting differently according to experience.
>
> Compare Jean Rouch to a flea locked in a glass cage and making desperate and useless leaps to get out. Glass cage = his nickname for me.
>
> Competent authorities = Bella, Claude and me. Life in Paris is exciting. Three scientists waiting with fever, for the purposes of curious experiments. Results are assured in advance.
>
> A story full of interest.

She remarks that her handsome brother has "already found an amiable concubine" with whom Annette is assured he "gently indulged in playful and pastoral love....I hope older brother enjoys the spiritual flavor of postcards. Discoveries in a foul tobacco shop paid six cents. Huge deal. A way to have fun and make people laugh inexpensively." Having found old-fashioned pornographic postcards of scantily dressed women covered in feathers to send wayward, Guy, Annette puns, "full of glass and very French spirit," referring to the glass-half-full idiom and poking fun at French pessimism.

EVERY AUGUST, PARISIANS flee for the coastlines or mountains in a time-honored holiday tradition, as Paris needs to close her eyes for a siesta. War notwithstanding, residents were eager to depart for cooler climes, but those without property or family in the Free Zone could not cross the Demarcation Line without permission. They had to slip across in secret. Such was the case for Simone de Beauvoir and Jean-Paul Sartre.

Since Sartre had escaped from a German prison camp, he was not legally a free man and could not travel safely on the metro or anywhere else, unless he was formally decommissioned—something that could only be done in the Free Zone. If he tried to get decommissioned in the Occupied Zone, he would be arrested and thrown back into a prison camp, or worse. That summer, "it was not so very difficult to cross the border between zones if you sauntered through without luggage, hands in pockets," Simone de Beauvoir writes.

In order to walk luggage-free, they sent bicycles and a package of clothes, which was "permissible," to a friend on the other side. Traveling by rail to Montceau-les-Mines, a coal-mining town about 350 kilometers from Paris, would have taken a full day. From the station, de Beauvoir and Sartre made their way to a café, where they contacted a *passeur*, to help them cross the border safely. One of the locals had recently been caught smuggling people into the Free Zone, though. Everyone was on edge and cautious.

"Toward evening a woman in black, about forty years old, sat down at our table and offered, for a very reasonable fee, to take us across country that same night." They understood the risks that their *passeur* was taking and held their breath whenever she motioned to be still, but the night was dark and warm and the woods free of search patrols. The couple followed their guide until she announced, "*Nous sommes ici. Arrivé.*" Having "defied one German prohibition, I felt as though I had regained my freedom," de Beauvoir concludes.

They headed for a nearby inn, which was full of people who had also just arrived in the Free Zone. Sleeping arrangements were floor-strewn mattresses, six people per room.

There were ways to cross the frontier legally in 1941 as "measures were taken to bring together families of refugees who wanted to stay in the non-occupied zone." Yannick's mother, Denise Bellon, probably took advantage of that window of opportunity to relocate with her daughters, Yannick and Loleh, to the family summerhouse on the Côte d'Azur, where the girls' stepfather, the journalist Armand Labin, was living and working in the resistance.

Close on their heels, Rouch and his pig buddies prepared to follow, hoping to get civil service jobs in the Free Zone. Before they left, Annette and Bella sewed bright, colorful ties for them to wear and included their ingenious pocket sewn on the sleeves of their shirts. The boys were delighted with the gifts and promised to write. Then they either crossed legally, using the Ponty family's château in the Alpes de Haute Provence as their address, or illegally with a *passeur*.

The departure of their male friends was not a terribly happy event for Bella or Annette. The swimming pool and the Flore felt empty. Surprisingly, Rouch's sudden absence made Annette feel sad and lonely. She regretted not holding on to him tighter. She didn't know that his "holiday" in the Free Zone would be permanent.

Rouch had leapt free of his "glass cage."

AUGUST AT THE Flore was as dull as the Paris streets. The dance clubs only offered unattractive, poor, and rather sleazy stragglers in search of easy women. Stuck in their hot, muggy apartment and babysitting her siblings at the municipal pools with other impoverished Parisians and Jews was about to drive Annette crazy. But she refused to allow abandonment to defeat her. She had art to make.

It was probably Salvatore who snapped the photo of Annette at the Saint-Dizier pool, one of the other swimming pools she frequented. The scene at the pool probably went something like this: Annette asks him to take a few quick snaps, while she poses. Standing on tiptoe, she plays with her hair. Looks at the camera with a coquettish tilt of the head. As the eye of the lens captures her, does she know that her gaze is so powerful as to unstring Salva's heart? She is only interested in her idea, not the effect she might be having on the young man who has been taking photos of her for months.

Salvatore wasn't handsome or worldly, but with Rouch out of town he thought he finally had a chance. If he just did whatever she asked, she would see his devotion and return his love. So, he brought her to his dark room. Showed her how to develop the negative and manipulate it. Altering the negative, she scraped the image down to the silver gelatin, and the background down to the paper.

Annette as Venus has silver skin and only the barest facial features. With blue ink from a fountain pen she draws herself—nude. Blue hair is piled high and tumbles softly over her bare shoulders. Ringlets of blue curls cascade to her knees. Standing on tiptoe, she looks as if she is about to dive into the water. One arm is raised to her head. At her feet, the swimming pool deck and railings are just visible. The spirit of the wind holds a mirror on her left. Beneath her is a face behind a veil. On her right, under an apple tree a cobra rises from a pot to whisper in Annette's ear. In the background a man walks a tightrope. Strewn at her feet are childish flowers.

She played with the image until she had created a cross between Chagall's *Adam and Eve* and Botticelli's *Birth of Venus*—a marriage of classicism and Surrealism, the École des Beaux-Arts meets the Café de Flore.

On the back of the finished work, scribbling in her florid script, she writes: "Behind the page, the moon prepares her nightly toilette and casts a coquettish eye at the sleeping earth, in the hope of waking it. Adam, the eternal dreamer, walks elegantly on the wire of existence leaving his wife, the one and only Eve, to entertain herself with temptation's snake. Limit, on a magician's chair, corrects his concrete beauty in a mirror, reducing the man who is forgetful of his duties as a husband."

"I've just painted a 'cure of youth' in the buff (very good)! I am literally in awe of myself and my talent," she writes to Guy.

As August descended, Bella left to visit her parents in the suburbs and Charles made plans to visit Guy in Bordeaux. Annette and the children had to be more careful about what time they left the pool now. Sometimes there were Germans at the exit asking for papers. The grapevine sent warnings into the changing rooms, so Jews either waited inside until the guards gave up or they departed among large groups surrounded by gentiles. Being blond probably helped. "They never checked our papers," Michele says.

Others were not so lucky. German authorities were ramping up Jewish persecutions in Paris. Leading this onslaught was the fanatic Jew hater Theodor Dannecker.

# Eichmann's Man in Paris

*Down with books of Gide, Malraux, Aragon, Freud, the Surrealist books—the pacifist books, the anti-Nazis—which have troubled the relations between Europe and France.*

—AU PILORI, OCTOBER 18, 1940

TALL, BLOND, ATHLETICALLY BUILT THEODOR DANNECKER fit Hitler's requirements for the perfect Aryan and SS candidate: a German national, single, tall, at least five feet, nine inches. The only caveat standing in the young Theodor Dannecker's way was his criminal record, an oxymoron, as he had attacked a Jew.

Dannecker hadn't always been anti-Semitic. As a young man he had fallen in love with the girl next door, Lisbeth Stern, a Jew. Lisbeth's and Theo's parents were shopkeepers on the same street, but the youngsters were also bonded by the loss of their fathers due to World War I. In the midst of the economic crisis of 1929, Theodor's elder brother abandoned the family, leaving a raft of debts behind. Theodor was left running the family clothing store and caring for his seriously ill mother. It was a lot of responsibility for a sixteen-year-old.

When Lisbeth and Theodor fell in love, her mother sold their shop to Gustav Lion, a Jew, and moved Lisbeth away. Furious at the Sterns, Dannecker organized a group of friends to vandalize Lion's shop and urged neighbors to boycott Lion's business. The situation got so bad that Lion closed up shop and immigrated to France, to escape the teenage Dannecker and his hoodlum friends.

The Nazi Party was the perfect place for disgruntled, unemployed young men of the "lost generation," who had grown up feeling shame, anger, and resentment over the humiliation Germany suffered at the Treaty of Versailles. It promised work and provided an outlet for burgeoning anti-Semitism, claiming that Germany was only defeated because of the Jews. The Nazis overlooked the number of Jewish soldiers who had fought and given their own lives in the Great War.

Hitler's tirades stoked Dannecker's hatred of Jews and feelings of victimization. He learned the Führer's speeches by heart and internalized their message, adopting Hitler's invective of race hatred. Jews were "parasites" and "scum," not human beings. Dannecker's official writings never refer to the Jews as people. They were "material" to be taken care of and had no right to be treated humanely.

Two of Dannecker's friends who vandalized Lion's shop joined the SA, or Sturmabteilung, a paramilitary organization also known as the Storm Troopers. Attracted by the notion of a German elite and the master race, Dannecker plumped for the SS, where many *Judenberater* (Jewish advisors), like Adolf Eichmann and Alois Brunner, worked. Anti-Semitism was a route to career advancement.

Dannecker began his career as a prison guard. Within a few years, he was working at a prison in Berlin run by the Gestapo.

In its violent, brutal environment, communists and political opponents to the Third Reich were beaten and tortured.

Dannecker began drinking so heavily that he was suspended and demoted for being intoxicated while on duty. Fortunately for him, Nazis had short memories when it came to bad behavior. Within the year he joined the Security Service of the Sicherheitsdienst des Reichsführers-SS (SD). Run by Heinrich Himmler, this new department oversaw internal security and intelligence and was given sweeping powers to arrest anyone deemed a threat to the Nazi state. Dannecker's direct superior was SS-Obergruppenführer Reinhard Heydrich, who was recruiting highly motivated young functionaries dedicated to the idea of freeing Germany of Jews. Dannecker was appointed to oversee the suppression of Jewish businesses and enforce Jewish emigration. It was a job Dannecker had spent his youth preparing for.

Dannecker was sent to Vienna to assist Heydrich's underling Adolf Eichmann. Together they developed a plan to force Jews out of their homes and expropriate their wealth. It was the same formula that Dannecker would put to use in Paris.

From Vienna, the two men turned their attention to Poland, where they developed the "Nisko Plan" and forced Jews living in German-occupied areas onto a "reservation" near Lublin, much as the European settlers in America had done to its indigenous people. In Poland, Dannecker gained valuable experience in the logistics of transporting and resettling large numbers of human beings by focusing on how cattle and hogs were transported over long distances for slaughter.

Shortly after the Nazis marched into Paris, Heydrich promoted Dannecker to the plum job of *Judenbrater* (Jewish Advisor) for Paris. The experience he had gained in Vienna and Poland was now to be focused on an even bigger project: the forced expulsion of all Jews from France.

---

SICHERHEITSPOLIZEI (SIPO) HEADQUARTERS were located on Avenue Foch, Paris's most expensive street, in the palatial home of the Jewish banking family the de Rothschilds, who had fled to safety in Switzerland. Dannecker's suite of offices for the Jewish Section (Judenreferat) were on the first floor of the de Rothschilds' luxurious mansion. Here his team set to work executing his plan to isolate and eventually imprison the French capital's Jews. Gestapo headquarters were next door at No. 72 Avenue Foch.

Captain Heinrich Ehmsen's visit to the Beaux-Arts was part of this overarching plan to control and monitor France's cultural institutions. By March 1941, Dannecker had established the *Institut d'Etude des Questions Juvies* (Institute for the Study of Jewish Questions), which disseminated propaganda against the Jews and fed the collaborationist press with anti-Semitic articles.

Paris is for lovers, and even Nazis were not immune. Shortly after Dannecker arrived in the capital, he met an attractive brunette from Berlin named Ilse Warnecker, who was working in a typing pool for his boss, Helmut Knochen. As a well-educated woman, fluent in English and French, as well as having worked as a journalist, Ilse had a lot going for her. And her Nazi credentials, as a member of the BDM, Bund Deutscher Mädel (German Girls Association), and the Nazi Women's Organization, were impeccable. They were soon stepping out together, exploring Paris and seeing the sights. Ilse would remember her time in Paris as the best time in her life.

After dating for a year, Dannecker applied for permission to get married. In typical German fashion, it was a bureaucratic nightmare. Ilse had to fill out pages of questions, proving that she was Germanic and Aryan and a good German woman. Her boss, Helmut Knochen, provided a reference. She was also required to prove that she was fertile. Since she was already carrying Dannecker's child, there was no need for a formal gynecological examination.

A photo of their wedding shows the happy couple outside a church in Berlin. Dannecker, in full SS uniform and sunglasses, looks sternly into the camera. Next to him, Ilse beams in a simple ivory dress that clings to her slight figure, a huge bouquet of roses in her hand and an elaborate white hat on her head. They returned to Paris for their honeymoon, but Ilse soon went back to Berlin in order to attend obligatory courses for German officers' wives at the Reichsbräuteschule (Reich's Bride School). Reich brides were taught skills that every Nazi wife should know: cooking, childcare, ironing, pet care, and how to polish their husband's boots and daggers. She also had to swear an oath of loyalty to Adolf Hitler and pledge to raise her and Theodor's children as Nazis. It was the Third Reich's version of *The Stepford Wives,* only scarier.

Sadly, Ilse had few opportunities to polish her husband's dagger. Though Dannecker repeatedly insisted on his desire to visit her, his crusade against Paris's Jews and obsession with French whores left him little time for conjugal visits. Even after the birth of their first son, Theodor-Karl, he stayed in Paris. He was soon gaining a reputation for heavy drinking, violent outbursts of temper, and frequenting Paris's nightclubs and brothels, some of which it is suspected he had a financial stake in. A malfunctioning upper esophageal sphincter caused him to constantly clear his throat, a nervous tic that made the guttural sounds of his Swabian German even more unpleasant to the French ear.

The new Commissariat Général aux Questions Juives (Commissariat-General for Jewish Questions), was headed by a staunch anti-Semite, Xavier Vallat, who wore a Fritz Lang–style monocle over one bad eye and walked with a stick. He practiced what he called "state anti-Semitism," which viewed Jews as "foreign in thought and language" and unassimilable to French culture. Only baptism, he maintained, could be accepted as proof of non-Jewishness, and he personally hunted down Jews with forged baptismal certificates and arrested them. He also advocated for identity cards bearing the word "Juif," something even the Germans had not thought to do, yet. As if that were not enough, Vallat established the Police aux Questions Juives (PQJ), or Police for Jewish Affairs, to monitor infractions against the *statut des Juifs*, which was praised as an "elite troop" by Dannecker.

The ultimate goal of Dannecker's policies was the internment of Paris's Jews. In May 1941, over six thousand foreign Jews were ordered to report to the authorities for a so-called review of their situation. Only about half obeyed the order. They were immediately arrested by French police and imprisoned in camps at Beaune-la-Rolande and Pithiviers.

While Annette and her friends were swimming at the pool playing at adulthood, other anti-Jewish measures had been put in place. In June 1941, the Vichy government introduced a second *statut des Juifs*, which greatly broadened the scope of the original statute of 1940. Jews were now barred from working in a long list of professions, from lawyers to cinematographers, theater managers, publishers, realtors, and even forestry operators. The only way any Jew could be involved in banking, mercantile, or real estate business was through menial labor. On July 22, 1941, Jewish property was placed under government administration. All foreign Jews were to be interned, and Jewish businesses were to be "Aryanized."

When a German soldier was wounded in an attack in August, the Nazi authorities organized a violent crackdown on opposition groups. Two communists were executed and on August 20, Dannecker gave the green light for the largest roundup of Jews to date. Entire city districts were sealed and searched. A total of 4,323 Jewish men were arrested, among them, for the first time, French Jews. They were sent to a newly opened detention camp called Drancy.

# *Family Crisis*

*I gave my subconscious a camera, and promised not to interfere.*

—BARBARA ROSENTHAL, AVANT-GARDE ARTIST

CHARLES HAD DISAPPEARED. HE HAD gone to visit Guy in Bordeaux about the same time Rouch and everyone else in Paris skived off for August holidays, but Charles never arrived at his destination.

The family was distraught. Guy had no news. Annette and the children floundered with doubt. Maurice even stopped singing.

Late at night, Annette fretted about her brother. Where was he? What had happened? She had to channel her anxiety somewhere. She was interested in the Surrealist practice of automatism and automatic writing. Opening her mind and closing her eyes, Annette released her conscious mind and allowed the subconscious to emerge through her pen. In the pale flicker of candlelight, she let her hand roam automatically across the page. A face behind bars appeared under her pen.

CONSIDERED THE INTELLECTUAL of the family, Charles was as autodidactic as Annette. Like many middle-class provincial children, he had left school to work and help the family. The onset of war hadn't changed that work ethic; it was just harder to find work. Both Guy and Charles had to have been concerned about the welfare of the family and their inability to support the family. In the midst of their summer fun at the pool, something else must have been going on in the Zelman universe. The black market may have been illegal, but it was also common, a matter of survival. Just about everyone had their hand in it. Desperate circumstances meant people took risks, and young people tend to take more risks than most. The question is, did Maurice and Kaila know? The answer is, probably.

"There was always a chicken in the pot, or something on the stove," Michele says. Maurice had always worked every angle he could to keep the family fed and afloat. The dance clubs on Rue Boissière were also a popular place to make black market connections, and Guy and Charles had been frequenting the clubs since the spring.

As luxury goods were scarce in the provinces, Charles used visiting his brother as a reason to travel and boarded the train for Bordeaux. He had hidden silk lingerie and stockings under his clothes to sell on the black market. But his contact in Bordeaux turned out to be an undercover gendarme. Charles was promptly arrested and sentenced to three months in prison. Annette's artistic premonition was accurate—her brother was behind bars. The Zelmans were *not* invincible.

News of his arrest turned the lives of the family upside down. Kaila packed up food, blankets, and clothing and caught the night train to Bordeaux. Though no one in the family has ever suggested that Guy and Charles were working together, Guy quickly slipped over the border into the Free Zone and began living in the town of Bergerac.

With Kaila gone and Maurice peddling his wares on the street, Annette was now the only adult in charge of the house, "a kind of hell!…populated by children of all kinds, who scream, play basic matches…bang on the poor piano, open all the drawers, play the flute with equal inexperience, make pancakes in the kitchen, send love letters and learn to walk on roller skates… All Day Long," Annette complained to Charles.

Michele recalls with a chuckle, "We roller-skated down the hallway or out on the sidewalk. We ran up and down the stairs playing hide-and-seek; we played cards, or guessing games, like 'What Am I Thinking?' Our cousin Camille was always asking questions. He drove Annette crazy."

Annette's letter is a play-by-play account of her life under the occupation—not of Germans, but of unruly children. A comical version of *Lord of the Flies*. Without parental authority, the house was entirely under Annette's Surrealist version of supervision. An oxymoron:

We have become very intimate with our neighbors,
and their children are in our house all the time.

They are no less boisterous than any children their age. And I'm sick of it, literally. This means that Camille Goldman [their cousin] receives his harem, made up of all the girls of the apartment house, here. And they are accompanied by a large number of little brothers and sisters.

"Camille! Come back. Where are you going? Camille…," the girls whined and whimpered after the handsome boy.

"Annette! Annette! What should we do now?" Camille banged and stomped into the dining room on his metal roller skates.

"Shut up!" Annette roared.

Her lovely singing voice, the "delight of our family evenings" that she used to charm the family with, "is reduced to a pitiful state of whispering from having shouted, howled, and begged these children of the devil to be silent for a little.

"A few vulgar 'Camille shut ups' to restore order and I'm yours again."

Their upstairs neighbor, who paid Annette pin money for doing mending and embroidering, had two small children. "Marcel was so small, he would rap on the door with his foot, so we could hear him," Michele remembers. His big sister, Surèle, who was five, had a crush on Charles and loved to visit the apartment, even though her heartthrob was gone.

"We have the assiduous visits of your friend Surèle," Annette assured her brother, "and her brother Marcel proves to be a talented and very gifted musician, which is expressed by vigorous punches on the family piano, accompanied by howls that do honor to the strength of this child's lungs. I am obliged to note that he has an iron and hell constitution this child, as well as the devil in his body."

"Shut up!" she screamed once more.

Disappearing down the stairs, the crew of children finally left Annette in peace and she was able to eloquently tell Charles just how much she missed him. Pausing, she became aware of "an acrid and heavy smoke spread throughout the house which doubtless came from some kitchen in the courtyard. Living in an apartment block is so annoying, especially with thoughtless neighbors who leave the cooker on, thereby disturbing my thoughts and musings."

Annette opened the dining-room window. "Where is all that smoke coming from?" she screamed into the courtyard. "Who are the stupid, clumsy cooks who let their food burn on their fires?"

Smug in her criticism, she turned around and found "to my indignant astonishment" smoke billowing into the dining room from "our own kitchen."

Camille roller-skated through the doorway, sweeping his hands through the air and laughing. "So, Annette is cooking today?" In the foyer Michele and the other children were in fits and giggles.

"Shut up!" No wonder her throat hurt. She raced into the kitchen to rescue what was left of supper.

She should have been in the art studio or at the Café de Flore, not babysitting ungrateful children, she wailed to her confidant. "To leave me in this house alone after this culinary adventure! All this, I tell you, is unfair."

In the depths of teenage despair, Annette took her last school photo, stuck a pin in the nose, and, with a measured string, began to draw a circle around it. When the line was dark enough, she trimmed the edge to make the photo round. She used the photo to draw circles. "Sometimes, that is all she would do," Michele recalls. "Stick a pin in the nose and draw circles around the outside of the photo. She was very inventive." Either that, or the children really were driving her mad.

Chafing at her nanny predicament, Annette felt trapped in the apartment. The pools were closed. Paris was inundated with rain. Slick, gray streets were gutter gushers. Autumn rushed forward with the intensity of a German panzer division. She bemoaned that Guy and Charles were gone. Her mother was away every weekend, to visit Charles. Her father was out selling clothes. And none of her friends at the Flore had returned from their holidays. Some never would.

To add to the dismal onslaught of fall, on the fifth of September 1941, L'Institut d'Étude des Questions Juives opened a huge, multimedia exhibition, Le Juif et la France, at the Palais Berlitz. Underneath a four-story-high billboard of a bearded Jew clawing the globe, well-dressed men and women milled about outside the entrance. Inside, a massive sculpture of a naked woman, symbol of the New France, lifted a child up on her shoulder. A well-formed Aryan, in the Arnot Breker tradition, she has her knee on the neck of a bearded Jew greedily groping the globe. Many Parisians cringed at the sacrilege against their French Marianne, the symbol of *liberté, égalité, fraternité*. This German rendition had nothing to do with the ideals of the French Revolution. Ideals had little place in the New France, though. Dannecker and his co-organizer, Commissioner of Jewish Affairs Carltheo Zeitschel, celebrated the crowds arriving through the doors of the Palais Berlitz. Notables from both governments attended, as did the chief of police, Admiral François Bard. In the lobby of the exhibit, displays compared the diameters and profiles of stereotypical hook-nosed Jewish men alongside finer-featured Aryans, supposedly proving racial superiority. Other displays revealed the negative influences of Jews on everything from literature to commerce, radio to film, the press, industry, fashion, banking, and of course politics. A promotional film reel revealed how many Jews were in the cabinet and ministries in 1936 and then, horror of horrors, the war followed. All the fault of whom? The Jews.

People flocked to see the propaganda, and while some were there to protest, one photo by Roger Berson recorded Captain Vézille presenting a gift to the one-hundred thousandth and first visitor.

"The Jewish art dealers have fled, and their shops are occupied or closed," crowed the conservative writer Camille Mauclair in *Le Matin*. "There are no longer any Jewish officials and ministers in the Fine Arts Department or in the National Education Department who were there for twenty-five years. The Jewish advertising brokers, disguised as art critics, have been expelled from the press. The shame is over. It's a great cleansing, long overdue."

KAILA RETURNED FROM visiting Charles in prison, deeply worried. She did not burden the children with her concerns, but their odd little philosopher had haunted eyes and bruises on his face and body. Her most sensitive child should have been wading through stacks of books in the library, not incarcerated in one of the worst prisons in France.

Bordeaux's Fort du Hâ was infamous. Inmates were locked in communal cells twenty-four hours a day. They slept on mattresses infested with parasites. Basic hygiene was impossible. Typhus and tuberculosis were rampant. Their diet consisted of watery broth with a few crusts of bread. Guards carried whips and administered frequent beatings or locked uncooperative prisoners in a special punishment cell. Interrogations of prisoners included being immersed fully clothed in a water trough in the courtyard. Kaila could do little but show up on visiting day with extra food and encourage Annette's letter-writing campaign to keep Charles's spirits up.

# Dangerous Liaisons

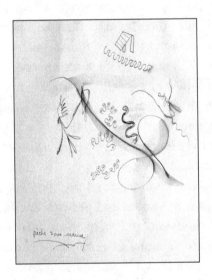

*Don't waste your love on somebody, who doesn't value it.*
　　　　—William Shakespeare, *Romeo and Juliet*

Finally, people were returning from their summer holidays, Annette announced to her brother. "And the season is in full swing between Café Capoulade and the Flore." Any day now Rouch would return and everything would get back to normal, she hoped. Neither she nor Bella had received a single postcard from the pig buddies, though.

The girls sat alone at the Flore, sipped their ersatz coffee, and waited to see who would sit down at their table. Salvatore hovered, but they weren't interested in a fellow student. Enter handsome Claude Croutelle and Jean Jausion, both looking fit and tanned from their August holiday in the Free Zone. Jausion nodded to de Beauvoir and Sartre. A few days earlier, they had snuck over the border together. There was nothing like crawling under barbed wire to bond a group of friends.

Bella and Annette were delighted to see the young men and begged for news of their holiday. They had been on the Mediterranean coast, in the towns of Sanary-sur-Mer and Bandol. There Jausion had made contact with Frédéric Dumas, who was active in a new sport called *plongée*, or scuba diving. A champion free diver, Dumas had met the young Jacques Cousteau and another diver, Philippe Tailliez, in 1937. The three men were master engineers and had created equipment to breathe underwater.

Jausion had even donned mask and fins to explore this underwater world with Dumas and perhaps even Cousteau. Jean, Claude, Bella, and Annette's conversation meandered. While Jean talked about his scuba adventures, Bella made doe eyes at Claude. Taller than Jean, Croutelle had swept-back fair hair, a slim build, and high cheekbones; he also wore a suit and tie. Like Rouch and Jausion, he spoke the impeccable French of the upper classes and dabbled in poetry. But of the three men, only Jausion was a seriously published and recognized poet.

As Bella watched Claude, Claude watched Annette. Chatting with his best friend, Annette gave all her attention to Jausion, and Claude found himself attracted to the girl with the Ashkenazi eyes. The problem was that not only did Claude find both girls alluring, but both girls were attracted to Claude. Over the next few days, a love triangle formed with Claude at its apex. Depending on the time of day, Claude could be found having a private tête-à-tête with either Annette or Bella. Regulars at the Flore took note.

"I can talk to you in a way I cannot open my heart to Bella," Claude confided to Annette. "We are more like-minded." Annette agreed. The problem was he was just as infatuated with Bella as Guy had been over the summer. Bella was serious about Claude in a way she had not been with Guy, though. And she and Claude consummated their relationship in his tiny romantic hideaway, a *chambre de bonne* that had once served as a maid's room. They were each other's firsts.

Having no idea that their affair had become that serious, Annette continued to maneuver for Claude's affections.

"I swear to you that I am easy about my fate," she assured Charles. "I know that if I let everything go it will unravel between Claude and Bella."

The wait would not be pleasant. To escape the emotional pressure of her own desire, Annette plunged herself into art class, working "with the courage of Michelangelo," she claimed.

JEAN JAUSION BEGAN to become Annette's confidant now, but it was Claude Croutelle who had the upper hand in her affections. A week into this isosceles triangle of love, Annette found a miserable Claude sitting alone in his banquette at the Flore. Secretly pleased that she was there to assuage his grief over Bella, she listened as he poured his heart out.

"Needless to say, my role in the discussion is mostly ironic and strongly biased," Annette explained to her brother. She offered a sympathetic ear and allowed Claude "to suffer Bella-Tyza, the sadist," but worried that Bella was bad for someone as sensitive as Claude. Sadly for Claude, "Bella-Tyza is better than no Bella at all...."

"You are in the deep end," she told him. He was, in fact, drowning. She rubbed her "pencil-black hands against each other in a somewhat vulgar gesture of contentment" and made her move. The life raft she threw Claude was an escape. "I've been thinking of going to work the Vendanges," she told him. She wanted to get out of town, escape these love entanglements, be one with nature, and make some money. She had even written to her friend the priest in La Lande, who had written back a letter full of secrets about his life and the vintner's address. All they had to do was write and ask for jobs. "The weather is good there," she coaxed Claude. They could work among the field hands and get the last rays of the sun on their skin.

That night, she was pleased to tell Charles that she and Claude were coming to pick grapes. "On the way back, we will visit you in prison. Claude will be very happy to see you. He loves you, that boy!"

She mailed the letter in the morning and headed off to school. That afternoon, she found Claude sitting and staring into a cold cup of coffee.

"Why the long face?" she asked.

"Bella begged me to meet her. She's late. She doesn't care about me. What should I do?"

Once again, Claude was "the husband, the cuckold, and beaten. He seems happiest when he is miserable." Annette assured him that he would feel better once he got away. He just needed space and perspective. They would have fun picking grapes and singing under the stars.

Forty minutes into her plan, the brass doors swung open.

Enter Bella, in high dudgeon.

Thick black hair bouncing off her shoulders, rouged lips pulled back in a wicked smile, she glared at Claude and Annette.

"I have no need of you now!" Bella shouted. Heads turned. "And you will reimburse me for my inconvenience of coming all this way for nothing." She turned on her heel and flounced out the way she had come in.

Claude ran after her.

Left alone, Annette fumed. "I blame myself for wasting my time with this mop and I blame him for making me believe in a good guy when he is only a rag. When I think that I would have succeeded in restoring him a little dignity and self-confidence. All of that is ruined. It's like he never knew me. Bella has seduced him back into her clutches." Annette had been bested by her best friend. Her former best friend.

"It reminds me of a Boccaccio tale. Several of them." The Flore was its own *Decameron*.

"I am going to leave Paris with real pleasure to slave away in the countryside," she wrote Charles. "Where I no longer have to deal with these dirty and stupid stupidities. I really need to wash all this off me. I'm tired of their sentimental stories. I need to detox and everything! I will surely come to see you, my Chailo! We'll cry together to pretend Dad is here. I will bring you classic oranges! Or buckwheat pies! I'm sure this story comes back as an obsession in my letters. You must be fed up with it too. You are right."

Burned out by the Flore's *liaisons dangereuses,* Annette packed for La Lande. Alone. She ended her letter to her beloved brother with a poem:

> *Ah! Finally comes the time*
> *So anticipated*
> *To bring you my soul*
> *in my hands*
> *Wrapped hollow and*
> *let my secret tears*
> *Sadly lit*
> *dry up in the well*
> *Of my joy recovered*

*I'll see you again,*
*In your sad prison*
*Your white and flowery beard*
*Will run softer and silkier*
*Your dancer's feet*
*will still sigh*
*As in the beautiful, early days*
*From my chapped and salivating lips*
*The kiss of restrained and costly passion with a*
    *Machiavellian gaze.*
*Mine love song*

# Topography of Terror

*I would never have believed the time would come when, in my own country, fanaticism would manifest itself in such a way!*
— RAYMOND-RAOUL LAMBERT

JUST BEFORE ANNETTE LEFT FOR La Lande, some of Paris's synagogues were bombed. The attacks began in the early hours of October 3, starting with a prayer house on Avenue Montespan. Over the next few hours, the historian Finley-Crosswhite writes, explosions "lit up the night sky and shattered windows, damaged support pillars, blew out doors and windows, destroyed walls and furniture, and spewed debris in all directions." By the end of the attack, five of Paris's synagogues and prayer houses, including the Grand Synagogue, had been bombed.

The bombings were ostensibly carried out by a far-right group called the Mouvement Social Révolutionnaire (MSR), whose mouthpiece was *Au Pilori* (To the Scaffold), the most rabidly anti-Semitic newspaper published in France. Led by Eugène Deloncle, a former naval engineer who prided himself on his resemblance to the Italian dictator Mussolini, the conspirators planned the strikes to coincide with Yom Kippur, the Jewish Day of Atonement. Fortunately, Deloncle and his cronies did not understand the Jewish calendar or Jewish customs. They not only got the date wrong; they thought that the fasting tradition from sundown to sundown meant that people would be in the temple in the middle of the night. Their ignorance saved lives. Only six people were injured; two were German soldiers.

Almost half of Paris's synagogues were destroyed or seriously damaged. These were not just places of worship but beautiful buildings, designed by leading architects in the nineteenth or early twentieth century, including Alexandre-Gustave Eiffel. A stained-glass skylight etched with the Star of David inside the sanctuary at the Copernic Street Synagogue, which would be the target of another terrorist attack in 1980, was shattered and rows of pews ruined. The psychological damage was even more devastating.

Though the bombs were planted by Deloncle's MSR, the organization pulling the strings was actually the German SD, under the direction of Dannecker's boss at the Sicherheitsdienst, Helmut Knochen, who arranged for the explosives to be transported from Berlin to Paris. To save face with Parisians who disapproved of such violence, Dannecker laid the blame at the door of the Jews themselves, claiming they had done it to generate sympathy and provoke agitation. Then Heydrich said the attacks were "punishment" against French "Jewry, previously so powerful in Paris." The Nazis couldn't even get their stories straight. But clearly the Nazi high command was moving from arrest and internment to a new way of solving the "Jewish question."

A few weeks earlier, Otto Abetz, the German ambassador to Vichy France, had met with Hitler and Heinrich Himmler and presented Dannecker and Carltheo Zeitschel's plan for deporting thousands of French Jews. That evening, Himmler scribbled on a notepad: "Jewish Question. Resettlement East."

# *Detox*

*I like Frenchmen very much, because even when they insult you they do it so nicely.*

—JOSEPHINE BAKER

LA LANDE-DE-FRONSAC HAD NOT CHANGED a bit in the year since Annette had lived there with her family. But Annette had. Everything seemed smaller, more provincial, less important, than she remembered. Still, she had arrived for her break and was going to make the most of it. Here she would be the center of fun. She would enjoy conversations under the stars, she would receive accolades for her entertaining wit and joie de vivre; she would sing folk songs. She would dance amid the vines in true Bacchanalian tradition; well, perhaps she'd keep her clothes on. She might even fall in love with some swarthy son of the soil and toss aside those faux Parisian artistes, Rouch and Claude.

But Annette's fantasy of a pastoral idyll was heading for a reality check. Our city girl arrived during an unusually hot harvest season. Called to the fields before the sun broke, she had no time for the leisurely breakfast she had imagined—a baguette with creamy butter and homemade damson jam, washed down with a big bowl of milky coffee. Slinging a pannier on her back before six in the morning, she picked up a pair of secateurs and followed the others down the dusty path to the vines to clip bunches of grapes.

Picking grapes that are at waist or shoulder height is not so bad, but bending over to gather the low-hanging fruit, with the sun beating down on your back, is brutal and tiring work. At midday, the pickers returned to the farm for lunch and a brief siesta in the heat of the day, before returning to the fields until the sun sank to the horizon. After eight hours of hard labor, every muscle in Annette's body screamed. Her back ached; her fingers were stained purple; her hair was full of dust and sticky with sweat.

The accommodations offered her had no hot shower or bathtub to soak in, just cold water in a basin and a bar of soap. At least she could fall into one of those high "very soft and very hospitable beds" common in the French countryside "with very white sheets," she wrote to Charles "under a weak and sad lamp. Everything is so dismal," she scrawled. "If I moan, oh my sweet brother, it is not, believe it, because I am writing to you. If I grieve it's because my kidneys, knees, thighs, shoulders, and back of my neck hurt."

Why wasn't she in Paris seeking a new crowd? At the very least, she should be singing jaunty French melodies. Instead, "the music that accompanies this tirade closely resembles the funeral march." Her fellow workers were not intellectually stimulating or even pleasant company:

> Here is a sample of the table conversations in which I am absolutely unable to play a role.
>
> "I was going to buy needles, but my husband says to me that 'you still have some.' Then I say: 'No, I do not have enough.'"

"The cow will calve in two months."

"You picked the merlot today."

"The grapes are beautiful this year."

"The cellar is filled with barrels."

If it had been Dadaist theater, she would have enjoyed it. Instead, the conversational pabulum made Annette feel as if she were about to go mad. "Everyone considers me a 'non-talkative' girl. Bored to silence is more like it!" To keep herself from telling them what she really thought, she stuffed her face with all the delicacies of the table. "I will come back with a flourishing face and plump hips."

Her romantic dreams of canoodling under the stars were also reduced to the attentions of a seventeen-year-old "boy in boots" who threw her "long, languid glances" as he passed the bread. He spoke at length about his friends in Bordeaux, including the son of a coffeehouse owner. "You see the kind," she quipped. Not even a year in Paris and Annette was a full-blown snob!

Her conversations with the village priest were also disappointing, although she had enjoyed them a year earlier. He was "the nicest type of La Lande," but she had outgrown him. A year ago, she was a refugee looking for her place in the world; now she had found it. Annette was no longer at home with provincial life. She was at home in Paris.

Then it began to rain. But the Vendanges stop for no one. Not even Annette Zelman. On Saturday, after barely eight days, she became "irresistibly fed up." If she didn't leave at once, she was going to say something she would regret. And then she did.

"I'm leaving," she announced at the breakfast table. "I cannot stand your drivel any longer and these stingy, filthy rich owners....And I loathe your dirty Bordeaux accents!"

With that, Annette "left the peasants, the harvest, the rain, the grapes, the priest, and two pairs of men's trousers and took my bag, my zimmel [coat], my toothbrush, my legs around my neck, and the bus to Bordeaux. The bosses were well annoyed."

"We are burnt for La Lande," she confessed to Charles, unapologetically. "We can never go back there again. I left too bad an impression."

ANNETTE NOW FACED the reality of transportation under the Occupation. Nothing was on time. "I arrived in Bordeaux with the bridges in my mouth imprinted with my teeth from the despair of having missed the hour of visitation because of these imbecilic coaches, trams and trains which are not concerned about getting travelers to their destinations quickly." Unable to see Charles, she passed the time by making a visit to Aunt Loupa (their mother's sister) "and then, with unparalleled pleasure, went to the nearest train station hotel because I needed to wash myself. I mean, *wash* myself!" That is to say: "collapsed into a bathtub filled with deliciously warm and scented water," where she sank up to her neck and let the soreness fade as the hot water seeped into her skin. She scrubbed the purple from her fingers and from under her fingernails and watched her skin

turn pink again and the cuts and callouses from the vines and clippers soften.

She didn't feel guilty or ashamed. She was delighted by her indulgence and there in the bath determined a new vision for her future. She would step beyond the doldrums of a hum-drum life. She would climb the heights of artistic endeavor. As the steam dissipated and the bathwater went tepid, her thoughts spiraled upward. She would create a new Annette and take on the world. Love was nothing compared to art!

Renewed and scrubbed clean, she stepped from the bath, toweled herself dry, and caught the next train to Paris.

# I'm Feeling Extremely Kittenish

*Art was for her like a battlefield where she would give the best of her strength.*

—CHRISTIAN ZERVOS, ABOUT JEANNE BUCHER

## SUNDAY, OCTOBER 12, 1941

NO ONE WAS HOME WHEN ANNETTE returned to Boulevard de Strasbourg. Why should they be? She wasn't expected for another week. Standing in the kitchen by the Mirage cooker, "the sight of which alone gave the illusion of fire," she waited for two hours for someone—anyone—to return. The apartment's silence got on her nerves. She gave up waiting and decided to go to the one place where she could get warm, the Flore.

Getting a table near the stove was not always easy on chilly days, but Annette got lucky and found a warm seat. Settling down to write to Charles about her escape from La Lande, she explained the catalogue of errors that had thwarted her visit and made the mistake of mentioning her hot bath, adding: "I'm so happy with myself and the 'big city' that I think I've just built it."

The letter is a bit manic, as if she is packing everything into it, in hopes of gaining Charles's forgiveness. She pokes fun at his last letter, which questioned some of her literary references, as proof of his "clearly insufficient culture. We'll take care of you," she boasts. "We are pretty good guys at le Flore. We are the intellectuals of the Saint-Germain-des-Prés district."

The next day, a Monday, she returned to the "suave and spiritual school" of the Beaux-Arts for the fall semester of classes. She worked furiously, her hair a mess, her brow sweaty. Before the summer break, she had been working on a drawing of a nude man, the only man waiting for her in Paris "with outstretched arms."

After school she stopped by the Flore to have tea with friends. Sitting in their old corner, Claude and Bella completely ignored her when she walked in. She didn't stay long and headed home to read, have dinner, and paint a little. Since the Vendanges, she had been eating like a peasant and complained that her appetite was the result of a curse from Bella, "because I eat like eight and I gain weight like a well-fed newborn."

Over the next twenty-four hours Annette imbibed a cultural cocktail of theater, music, and art. She and her cousin Dora went to see a play and ran into an old friend from home, who had appeared as Marianne in Alfred de Musset's classic play *Les Caprices de Marianne*. Evidently, Josette was "dazzling" in the role.

None of Annette's exuberant epistle went over well with Charles, who had expected her to visit and was crushed when she failed to arrive. Her excuses, however elaborate and humorous, did not amuse him. She had not only failed to keep her word; she had forsaken him for a hot bath. He wrote a blistering retort. She was no longer a teenager. Maybe she should start acting like an adult. She was bored? Try being in prison, where he was not allowed to bathe at all! How self-centered could she be? Their mother came every week. Annette couldn't show up once?

It was the kind of response that only a sibling could get away with, and Charles called her out. She was selfish and flaky. Unreliable. Egocentric. She cared more for her friends at the Flore than she did about her own brother, languishing and miserable in hell.

Their epistolary tiff resolved in a few days. Almost as soon as he sent his angry letter, Charles wrote an apology. Annette responded in kind:

> My dear Charles, elder brother, and whose presence now regretted within this worthy united family was for me the remedy for my misfortunes...I thank you again and again for the kindness which toward me is accumulated in a vast, immense and flattering heap in the letter that you sent me.
>
> I see with indescribable pleasure that you are always the maker of complex words and that, as usual, the letter is full of sentences and spiritual expressions and especially so personal. How to describe the admiration that I felt for you by reading puns as funny and as new as: how are you—emptied of poetry or another play on words of the same (good) taste....
>
> Don't worry, my *Chailo*. You are a good guy. And don't worry so much about what I thought of your attitude. I am not an indifferent critic. I'm your old sis and I don't give a damn about the attitude you have. I pray for you.

He would always be her younger brother, whom she deeply loved, even when she failed him.

To make amends, she promised to write a letter every day. "It will be even better than having me visit for an hour," she assured him. And so, Annette began a daily diet of letter writing—sometimes two per day, sometimes one spread out over several days—to entertain Charles with the hilarities of her life at the Flore spiced with gossip about Guy's girlfriends and sexual escapades. And soon, she secretly hoped, her own.

WHEN DECIPHERING ANNETTE'S letters, it is important to remember that she was young and often wrote in a quick hand. Sometimes the ink has faded beyond repair. The originals have never been found and only photocopies remain. In places it is hard to be certain what she wrote. She also used a wide variety of papers—graph paper, lined paper, blank paper, blue paper, or Flore letterhead. Some letters are dated; some only have the day of the week at the top. Many are not dated at all.

Her handwriting also shows a wide variety of styles and idiosyncrasies. Generally, it is forward sloping, but individual letters vary greatly. Her capital *A* does not have a horizontal bar, it's just one vertical stroke, looped at the top; her lowercase *q* is written like a *p*. Sometimes she scribbles notes down the side of the page and draws an arrow to show their placement. Often her thoughts seem to be moving faster than her pen; her missives include crossing outs, blots, and a profusion of sideways doodles. She used a couple of different fountain pen nibs, so her script vacillates from fine and feathery to broad and bold.

Andrea Paganini, Jean Rouch's biographer, notes:

> Annette wrote very good French (for a 19-year-old, no less!), and she uses a rich and colorful and facetious language. She makes almost no mistakes, spelling, syntax, or otherwise—she does, however, handle abbreviations, contractions, innuendos, wordplay, etc....Annette belongs fully to this beautiful, rich, virtuoso and very cosmopolitan French culture, and particularly to the Parisian culture of

the Roaring Twenties. What a beautiful mastery of writing! Nimble and facetious, humorous and ironic, light and severe, casual but also serious...

She invents words....Handles languages: French, of course—in various registers, with a fine collection of popular expressions and varied literary quotations; sometimes playing with accents and regional sayings. And she reads a lot (really reads): classics (Chateaubriand, Balzac, or Stendhal, to whom she seems close; and even Boccaccio!) and "moderns" (from Verlaine to Gide and Cocteau, from Giono to Delteil and Dos Passos...); also touching upon philosophy (Sartre).

However, sometimes her wordplay and puns, specific to her brother, fall on our deaf ears or are lost in translation. It would take another volume to fully decipher all her hidden meanings.

ANNETTE'S BIRTHDAY HAD fallen in the midst of the Vendanges, where no one had cared that she was twenty and no longer a teenager. Now that she was home, gifts were arriving. Ginette Kobrinec, Annette's favorite cousin, had arrived in Paris with her husband, Henri, and daughter, Eliant. They were staying upstairs with Aunt Hélène. Ginette was a beautiful girl with jet-black hair "and magnificent blue eyes like her mother, the color of the sea," Michele recalls. "She and Annette got on like a house on fire. It was a marvel! They told stories and laughed. It was always a joy when Ginette came to the apartment." She gave Annette a beautiful leather-bound book with *Place Stanislas,* the main square in Nancy, embossed on the cover.

Maurice, their "generous Father," had also given her a rabbit-fur coat, dyed to look like ocelot, "which cost 2,500 francs" but had the "effect of at least 25,000," she bragged to Charles. She delighted in proudly prancing around Paris in her new "walk-with-success" *très* chic three-quarter-length coat. In fact, she had just written that sentence when Jean Jausion came through the frosted-glass doors of Café Flore. He looked very pleased to find Annette alone for once.

"Continue this letter at home," she scribbled across the page.

JEAN JAUSION IMMEDIATELY scooped Annette up and invited her to come and see a few underground art exhibitions. They spent the afternoon perusing the latest in Surrealist art. She loved having real conversations about art and found Jausion's insights into artistic technique both sensitive and discerning. Their last stop was Galerie Jeanne-Bucher Myrbor, on Boulevard du Montparnasse, a center of artistic resistance. Bucher never announced the shows in advance, but Jean Jausion had an inside scoop. His dear friend from the Réverbères, Georges Hugnet, lived upstairs.

At fifty-one years old, Bucher had been promoting the work of Cubists, Surrealists, and abstract artists since the 1920s. That art, now dubbed *Entartete Kunst* by the Nazis, gave her a new cause. She vigorously promoted the works of painters like Lipschitz, Kandinsky, and Miró and was responsible for placing many of her artists' works in museums outside of occupied France, where they would be safe. In a brilliant sleight of hand, Bucher hosted German officers with all the finesse of a native German. She smiled politely as they mocked the art hanging on her gallery walls, all the while hiding resisters above *les Boches'* heads and secretly showing "degenerate art."

With her graying hair pulled back in a loose bun, Bucher looked a bit like a schoolmarm. A photograph of her by Man Ray shows a discerning woman with piercing eyes and a serious mouth. Annette described Bucher as having "a beautiful Alsatian accent but infallible taste." Perusing the paintings hanging on the gallery's white walls, Annette and Jean spoke with Bucher and listened to her wisdom. This was destiny.

Clandestine. Important. Real. Meeting the gallerist with Jean was an artistic leg up the ladder, and Annette knew it.

Georges Hugnet still had the printing press Jausion and he had used to create Les Réverbères' zines, but the press was now used to forge papers. Bucher was running a dangerous operation. The attic above Hugnet's flat served as a safe house both for art and for human beings. Resisters hid in the loft, while Hugnet printed new identity papers. One medical student woke up in the morning to discover paintings by Picasso and Braques under his bed.

Bucher began working for the resistance immediately after the invasion and published a poetic manifesto against the Occupation, titled *Non Vouloir* (Non-willing). It featured four poems by Jean's close friend Georges Hugnet, accompanied by four engravings by Picasso. A special-edition frontpiece was created by Joan Miró. Only four hundred copies were printed.

Head *by Pablo Picasso from the illustrated book* Non Vouloir, *1942*

*You are looking for the diamond*
*from the darkness of day to day*

*there are magical alleys*
*in this strawberry hearted hope*

*noble sleep to sleep*
*the eye like a murderess*

*sleep under your portrait that is old*
*wait in the wind that sparks*
                              —*Georges Hugnet*

Spending the day with Jean Jausion was how Annette dreamt life should be, awash with art and conversation about art. It gave her pause. Maybe Claude Croutelle wasn't the right man for her after all. Maybe Jean Jausion was.

Finally, this Surrealist poet with his dancer's physique, elegant clothes, and keen artistic sensibility had attracted her attention. But, as they left Bucher's gallery and headed back to the Flore, Jean Jausion began to plead Claude's case. Claude had missed her when she disappeared to work the Vendanges and was worried that his behavior had irreparably damaged their friendship. "You know, Claude loves you very much. You should be nice to him."

"I am nice to him!" Annette laughed. "Thanks for the unnecessary information and advice." Now she was really confused. Claude wouldn't even look at her, but Jausion was saying Claude was in love with her? Had Jausion only taken her to see Bucher and the galleries for Claude—not to be in her company or for the love of art but to plead his friend's case? As Jean held open the doors to the Flore, Claude held out a chair for Annette and welcomed them. It was a stitch-up.

Claude tried to be "very kind and very affectionate," smoothing her ruffled feathers and assuring her that he hadn't been ignoring her; he had been protecting her from Bella's jealous temper. Jean Jausion sat beside Claude, nodding.

Feeling manipulated and disappointed, Annette stood up and wrapped her fur coat around herself. It was time to get home. The men groveled all the way to the Saint-Germain-des-Prés metro stop, vying to outdo each other. At the top of the stairs, under the deco-illuminated sign, they stammered their goodbyes. Jean tried to thank her for accompanying him to the exhibitions but became tongue-tied. Claude got tangled in his words of apology.

"We are going away for a few days to the country," Claude stammered.

"I don't care," Annette snapped, and flounced down the stairs, leaving them to "unravel in the slime I threw under their feet." She caught the metro feeling "very happy" with her day. It didn't get much better than leaving two men speechless. The Vendanges had been far more of a success than she had imagined. "I'm feeling extremely kittenish," she told Charles.

She purred all the way home.

# I Am Afraid of
# Becoming a Woman

*One is not born, but rather becomes a woman.*
—SIMONE DE BEAUVOIR

**WEDNESDAY, OCTOBER 15**

THE FLORE WAS NOT HOME TO sharks, but plenty of other places in Paris were. Annette began to frequent those darker dives without any escort—fraternal or romantic—after her father refused to give her 30 francs for spending money. Maurice's refusal was an affront to Annette's sense of justice. She was expected to babysit the children in exchange for room and board. He sent money to Guy but refused her 30 francs to go dancing? What was Guy doing to support the family? Why should girls have a different set of rules than boys?

Maurice had his own economic reasons for refusing her request. He had given her an expensive coat. She had just worked the Vendanges. Why didn't she use her own money? Because she had spent it all on a hotel, a hot bath, and coffee at the Flore.

Like any teenager, Annette wanted to be treated like a grown-up, but she wasn't ready to support herself. And while

Maurice may have wanted his daughter to develop adult values, he wasn't ready for his little girl to be an independent adult. They were too much alike and too strong willed for either to give in to the other. Annette was not about to relinquish her independence by staying at home. No wallflower, she headed for one of Eddie Barclay's "surprise parties," as she referred to his pop-up clubs on Rue Boissière.

It wasn't free to enter the dance "schools," but there was a burgeoning economy in favor of young women. Annette wasn't frivolous, stupid, or loose, but she wanted to dance and was learning how to game the system. She found someone to pay her entrance fee.

Enter Mr. Suzanne. This name crops up repeatedly in Annette's letters. It is not clear who he is, but it seems likely he is one of Charles's contacts from the black market. It is clear that Charles knew Mr. Suzanne, and perhaps worked with him, before he was arrested and jailed in Bordeaux. When he introduced himself by his alias, Annette "laughed like crazy," she told her brother.

Not far from the Champs-Élysées, in the chic 16th arrondissement, Rue Boissière was part of Paris's red-light district, the haunt of collaborators, black-marketeers, and *poules de luxe,* high-class prostitutes who plied their trade with the wealthy businessmen who frequented the area. It was a walk on the wild side. Sleazy. Sexy. Dangerous and intoxicating. It was all a lark to Annette. "There were a lot of people. Funny people!" she bubbled to Charles.

Like her father, Annette was a popular dance partner and "danced all evening with a friend of Mr. Suzanne's," she told her brother. "A refueling inspector. Very clever! Very cynical! Very ladies' man. Very enterprising."

She also ran into the family's dentist, Jacques Maillet. "He's the perfect guy to ridicule the fun." Without Guy or Charles there to protect her from the wolves, Maillet took on the responsibility of keeping an eye on the wild child flitting around this rough-and-ready scene. Though married, Maillet was often out on the town without his wife and was critical of Annette's dance partners. As she stepped out on the dance floor with Mr. Suzanne's friend the refueling inspector, Maillet watched with a wary eye. When she paused for refreshment, he admonished, "Your mother is not at all wrong to say that you know too many men."

The night ended with Mr. Suzanne escorting her to the metro and offering Annette her choice of books from his library. He knew how to sway her attentions. She accepted a copy of the newly released French translation of *Gone with the Wind* and intended to borrow more books but then got angry with him. "I don't want to owe him anything," she wrote late that night. The flirtations of the evening left a sour aftertaste in her mouth.

"Mr. Suzanne is too much of a man. I don't like it. Without being defensive, he is not trusting like with Jean Rouch and Claude or Jausion." She was realizing that many men had ulterior motives and were not interested in her intellect. "It doesn't amuse me," she told Charles. She didn't want to be an object of lust. Love, yes. But not outright greed. "Mr. Suzanne is like that and Guy too, for that matter.... Maillet is not like that. You neither," she assures Charles. "I can't wait to go out with you and Guy again. At least, when I am with my brothers, I don't have to defend myself or play the coquette or the cabotine [poseur]."

Annette's personality was constantly inconstant. Up one day, down the next. In love, out of love. Happy, then miserable. Having hoped to find a new start with a different crowd, she was quickly disillusioned by the dance club scene and waxed nostalgic for the Café de Flore. "Mr. Suzanne and his friends are *men*. That is, they are all at least 30 years old," she complained.

"Apart from their relative elegance, extensive knowledge, and a rather ridiculous smugness, all these guys are morons. I miss the milieu of Jean Rouch, Ponty and Sauvy, even Claude. Those guys are real kids, and you can always count on their sincerity and enthusiasm. I think I am stupid to hang out with this dance crowd. First of all, because I only represent a pretty woman whom they desire....A woman who attracts male desires does not amuse me because he 'finds *that* it is enough.' I don't like men. They are really too strong for me and I don't want to deal with them. You must be surprised at this categorical statement. But you know, I don't like women either."

Sexual desire was not enough for Annette, but then she had not yet awoken sexually. And she was "afraid of becoming a woman too quickly."

**THURSDAY, OCTOBER 16, 1941**

"I was kicked out of the 10th arrondissement town hall library!" What kind of intellectual gets kicked out of the library? An Annette kind of intellectual.

Annette had forgotten to return Charles's books, including Nietzsche's *The Birth of Tragedy*. Bent over by the weight of the books, which were already four months overdue, Annette felt like a poor old granny and "suffered a lot," she assured her brother, on the ten-minute walk to the town hall.

At the counter, she bowed her head, feigning remorse. The crotchety old librarian was not amused. She demanded a hefty fine.

Annette protested. Her brother was in prison. She was returning them for him.

Four months late? The librarian pointed her finger. "Out!" Annette fumed:

> I am dispossessed of a healthy literary interest and economic distraction. Oh, and "you will be removed

from the list of readers. Never mind. You will have
my books. By the way, can we send you some?"
   *(laughter)*

Back at the apartment, Annette found Cami seated at the dining-
room table, studying with Theo Hecht and their cousin Camille
Goldman. Both Cami and Camille were named after their pater-
nal grandfather, a twinkly blue-eyed man who looked a bit like
a Jewish Father Christmas.

   Dashing copper-haired Camille was finishing his studies in
Paris before joining his father in the Free Zone, where a grand
residence was being prepared for Aunt Hélène and their children. "They were quite rich," Michele remembers.

   "I like reading *Le Crapouillot*," Camille told the others. Annette shook her head. *Le Crapouillot* was a satiric paper with
leanings to the right.

   "I prefer John Dos Passos or Dostoyevsky," Cami Zelman
responded, parroting the authors Annette read.

   "You are so pretentious," Theo taunted.

   "Quiet!" Annette blurted, quickly recording the blow-by-
blow account for Charles. "I am obliged from time to time to
interrupt this letter to impose silence on the happy student trio:
Theo and the two Camilles, who tell their daily activity with delicious details."

   "Seeing the movie *The Lights of Paris* was a beautiful hu-
manitarian experience," Theo was saying about the French
comedy.

   Annette rolled her eyes but kept transcribing. "This boy
walks with dignity in the direct footsteps of all the stupid and
bourgeois," she joked.

   When Camille Goldman pulled a harmonica out of his
pocket and breathed into its reeds, Cami grabbed it away sur-
reptitiously and filled the room with deafening blasts. Michele
and the rest of the children at the table burst out laughing.

Annette buried her head in her hands. How had such bedlam become her life?

This was why she needed to go dancing at night. No one seemed to understand the importance of hanging out with people her own age. Instead, she was judged and warned. Even Jacques Maillet and Jean Jausion were voicing their concerns that Mr. Suzanne "was not an honest type." She was fed up! They have "no recognition for his kindness toward me. Especially, since I am not *with* him at all." All she asked for was a bit of fun and some free books to read. Camille and Cami wrestled each other for the harmonica. Camille ran down the hallway blowing victory with a thunderous herd of children hard on his heels, screaming with laughter, and Cami shouting "Give it back!"

"Believe me, I am in very bad temper.... *Toinette.*"

# I'm Only Good When I Have a Boy in Mind

*America is my country but Paris is my hometown.*
—GERTRUDE STEIN

**SUNDAY, OCTOBER 19**

KAILA SLOWLY MADE HER WAY up the stairs to the apartment, having slept on the night train from Bordeaux. The family gathered around to hear their exhausted mother's report on Charles. She suggested they start collecting things for a care package to boost his spirits and his diet. Annette was in charge of books. Determined to send Charles so many books he'd have a private library in his cell, she began selecting volumes. Her package had to be limited to weight restrictions, though. "It would have weighed 30kg, if it would have been allowed!" That Sunday was the opening of the Beaux-Arts Fall Salon. Prizes had been awarded on October 11 and announced in *Paris-soir*. A young painter, Mademoiselle Rolland, had won third prize. How long would it be before Annette was winning prizes, if she continued "working with the courage of Michelangelo"?

Nodding to her fellow artists and friends and seeing the notable faces in the crowds, Annette walked through the galleries with her cousin Dora Goldfarb. There was Paul Landowski, director of the Beaux-Arts, and Philippe Mondieux, head of the student union. Even Captain Ehmsen's cronies from the Propagandastaffel were in attendance.

"There were 'good' paintings, but I would have liked to be there with someone who loved painting as much as I did," Annette confessed to Charles. Dora Goldfarb knew nothing about art, and her indifference or perhaps incomprehension made Annette feel nervous and a little embarrassed. She should have come to the salon with someone more sophisticated, who would appreciate the techniques on exhibit. Someone like Jean Jausion. Annette strove to instruct Dora about art but found she lacked intellectual curiosity. At least she was pretty.

Dora's lush red hair turned more than a few heads and the two of them together "undoubtedly had a successful effect" on men. "If Claude read this," Annette joked, "he would utter howls of indignation. Our superiority complex revolts him and God knows (I am obsessed with him) he envies this sense of always being in a good mood and happy with oneself.

"Dora has a haughty nonchalance that I do not have but want to have," but she "has even more enthusiasm for me, if that is possible, than I have for her. She finds me physically amazing." They were a mutual admiration society. "[It is] a real aesthetic pleasure to watch Dora walk, sit or just be." While Annette was struggling to find her identity amid the dance hall girl, the artist, the newborn intellectual, and her role in the Zelman circus, Dora already knew who she was and how she fit into the world.

After the salon and the Flore, the girls went to see Molière's *Le Misanthrope*, starring Alice Licea and Robert Le Vigan at the Théâtre des Ambassadeurs. In the lobby of the theater, they met Pauline Matusiewicz, with whom Annette had gone to school in Nancy. She "goes with her pack of little geese," Annette joked about Pauline's mother, who thought Annette was too debauched for her daughter. Pauline was not allowed to go dancing on Rue Boissière, let alone meet Annette at the Flore. "'The accommodating people are the most skillful.' *La Fontaine*," she writes with a sharp tongue.

The fable "The Heron and the Fish" is not that dissimilar to the lyrics of "Le Pélican," except the lesson in "The Heron" is: don't be too picky or you may go hungry. Like most fables, it has made the rounds over the centuries and been retold with mice, birds, hunters, and virgins. La Fontaine's other version, "The Maid," is about a woman who is too persnickety about the rich young men courting her and ends up with a poor "cripple"—a warning against being an independently minded young woman.

"If [Pauline's mother] knew what to expect from her daughter's virtue, she wouldn't be so eager to keep her," Annette scoffed.

Despite a day packed with art, theater, and coffee at the Flore, Annette arrived at home for dinner feeling "bored despite all the distractions that are within my reach. I don't see anyone except Dora. I am missing something [or someone] to enjoy all the things that I used to enjoy and still enjoy but I neglect. I am missing a sentimental concern." This from a girl who felt like she owned Paris just seven days earlier. "I am only good and living well when I have a boy in mind."

EDUCATING DORA BECAME Annette's new pet project. "I intend to do everything I can to impose her on" the Flore. "This ambition must seem quite mind-boggling to you, and above all very arbitrary…but you have to laugh a little."

As Annette finished writing her letter, Maurice leaned across the table and scrawled upside down across the top of the page: "I'm going to write you a big letter from me, your father kisses you."

"Life is not always a rose. Ronsard does not kiss you well," she concluded, with another literary reference to entertain her brother.

The poet Pierre de Ronsard wrote "Ode à Cassandre" in 1555, for Cassandra Salviati, when she was the same age as Annette. Accompanied by the lute, his poem was courtly love at its most romantic, not Rue Bossière lasciviousness. That Sunday evening, Annette felt the emptiness of being single and alone, despite her boisterous family around her. She closed her letter with an uncharacteristic, "Je ne t'embrasse [I don't embrace you]." For all her sardonic humor and poking fun at Pauline's mother, her cousin Dora, and her own shortcomings, Annette longed for a soul mate to share her life with.

She didn't realize she had already met him.

# Re-Enthusiasm for a Boy

*Paris intimate like a room.*

—ANAÏS NIN

CHARLES CHIDED ANNETTE ABOUT FREQUENTING the Café de Flore too much. "But old man," she wrote back, "it's the nicest café in Paris and forces me to go to school since it's so close." Her entire life was now structured around her classes and work snacks at the Flore. When she walked in, the owner, Paul Boubal, and his wife nodded to her. Pascal, the headwaiter, who was known to discuss literature and philosophy with the customers, personally served her coffee. Even the cat purred in her favor. She was a true Floriste now and, like Sartre and a handful of others, got her messages delivered there. She was even getting commissions for art.

Since Claude and Jean Jausion had left town for a few days, Annette was left to sit alone at their table. Dolf, one of Charles's friends, began meeting Annette at the Flore in their stead. On a Monday afternoon in late October, he invited her to a house-warming party, so she could meet his new love interest, who was unfortunately "provincial" and middle-class.

"A lot of curious people were there. There was also a girl who called herself a journalist but looked mowed down. You can see from there, who is fake Montparnasse. A music teacher for a wealthy family, with girls like a devout waitress in a convent [or] a male nun for a poor people's hospital. Finally, something unheard of!" Annette joked. Feeling superior both intellectually and artistically, she walked around, listening to "people discussing art and music in a thoroughly conventional and horrifying way. I felt like a fish in a cage with birds." Now there was a subject for a Surrealist painting!

The only people with whom she felt the slightest connection were Dolf and the pianist. "Why has Dolf fallen in love with a girl from this stupid environment? 'Bizarre, bizarre,' as Jouvet would say."

The phrase she refers to was from a hit film she and Charles had seen before the war, *Drôle de Drame*. In the scene, the actors Michel Simon and Louis Jouvet have an absurdist conversation over dinner, repeating the word "bizarre."

Famous in French comedy, "Bizarre, bizarre" is the equivalent of Abbott and Costello's "Who's on first?" or Monty Python's "Nobody expects the Spanish Inquisition!" It became a catchphrase that is still recognized today.

SADLY, EDDIE BARCLAY's Sunday surprise parties were getting "uglier and uglier and there's never anything to drink," Annette reported. "Uglier" may refer to the Germans slumming it on Rue Boissière. The Green Beans were everywhere. And that meant Annette had to avoid them. What else was there to do, if she couldn't go dancing? Occasionally Annette stopped at Café Capoulade on Boulevard Saint-Michel. Capoulade had a different crowd. It was a popular Zazou hangout, but it wasn't the Flore, where love trysts and triangles were starting to resemble one of Shakespeare's comedies. Between the decadent Surrealists and so-called freed intellectuals, Annette joked that she was

losing what "little moral and intellectual health" she had left.
And then she discovered she had even lost her flea, Jean Rouch.

ROUCH HAD SENT an Interzone card, but it was so impersonal that
"he could have sent this card to Claude, as well as to Bella or to
the Pope," she complained. But Interzone cards were meant to
be impersonal. These forms provided just enough space for contact information and a two-line message that could be read by
censors. The only legal way to correspond between the Free Zone
and the Occupied Zone, they were often written in code.

Longer letters—like those from Guy—were carried by cou-
riers going back and forth across the Demarcation Line, where
they could be mailed safely. "But enough about these dirty,
horny ants!" she blurts on the page. "I have re-enthusiasm for
another boy" and have "started to love Fernandel. He makes
me laugh." As he should have. Fernandel was a horse-toothed
French comedian of stage and screen. Annette was nothing if
not funny herself. She added a poem to the end of her missive:

> I
>
> *ah tell me so*
> *ah tell me so*
> *what*
>
> *what my says about me:*
> *they say about me:*
>
> II
>
> *We call*
> *you we call you*
> *the duke*
> *the duke*
>
> *etc., etc.*

Annette had started creating an illustrated encyclopedia depicting her social circle—a series of humorous portraits based on etchings of women posing in a real encyclopedia, *Cent Ans de Mode Francaises 1800–1900 (One Hundred Years of French Fashion)*. In typical Surrealist manner, she picked pages out of the book and renamed the models with witty, often-barbed captions. Mr. Suzanne is a coquette leaning on one arm, touching her chest with her free hand in a most inviting way—to trade or barter? A double entendre for his black-market activities and indiscriminate hunt for sex.

The model for Surrealist André Breton wears a Roman tunic with a turban on her head and an ostrich feather dangling in the air—*The Digression*. The collaborationist playwright and poet Jean Cocteau is in a white taffeta dress, framed by a short essay, full of political allusion that fingers Cocteau as an ally of Marshal Pétain. *Mr. Indecision*, Claude Croutelle, is yet another coquette, with a low bodice, holding a flower. Jean Jausion's friend Michel Tapié is *Good Faith*.

And what about Jean Jausion? She took her time turning the thick pages of the encyclopedia, looking for just the right image to illustrate her growing feelings for him. A young woman with an off-the-shoulder bodice covered in lace, a balloon of a hat, and ringlets of curls. Laughing, Annette scrawled his name and the word "Humility."

She was sitting at the Flore sketching patrons when Claude and Jean Jausion walked through the door, having just returned from their trip to the countryside. They walked directly over to her, but before sitting down, Claude took her hand in his and kissed it. Her heart flip-flopped. She couldn't help noticing the attention they were receiving from all corners of the room. Perhaps he was Mr. Indecision no more?

"Now when we sit together, Boubal, the patron, looks over to us with affection and the manager comes to shake our hands. We have become the celebrities of the place," she gushed to Charles. "I appreciate more and more the friendship tinged with love and desire that Claude Croutelle has for me, with whom I am at my best. You will be very surprised when you return to see our intimacy. A very good boy, moreover, with an admirable understanding. He sends friendship."

Within a few days that story changed.

# I Rejoice Like a Thief

*He who contemplates the depths of Paris is seized
with vertigo. Nothing is more fantastic. Nothing is
more tragic. Nothing is more sublime.*

— VICTOR HUGO

**WEDNESDAY, OCTOBER 22**

"FINALLY, I HAVE SOMETHING TO tell you."

A light drizzle dappled gray Paris streets. Prepared for real
rain, Annette arrived at the Flore with her matching brown-
and-white-checked umbrella, hat, and Zazou dress. She didn't
have classes on Wednesday and had gone to a musical matinee
with Dolf and Dora, before adjourning to what she now enjoyed calling "the Flora." Enter Claude Croutelle. Sitting down
at their table, Claude announced that Jean Rouch had found a
courier to send a letter to Bella. A far more personal note than
anything Annette had received. Everyone's interest was piqued,
as Claude divulged the real reason why Rouch had not written
to Annette.

Rouch had gone to see Yannick Bellon in Saint-Raphaël and invited her and her sister, Loleh, to Pierre Ponty's château in Brunet. This remote hilltop village in the Alpes-de-Haute-Provence was about two and a half hours outside of Cannes, though "château" should be used loosely. It was a semi-ruin, but it offered a holiday free of the worries and war and parents. The young people cooked meals over the fireplace, slept under the stars, and frolicked about the estate in perfect bliss. And fell madly in love.

"Yannick for Rouch and Loleh for Sauvy," Annette told Charles. "Yannick gave herself to Rouch in the family park with the adorable confidence of a virgin girl. The mother was very understanding. Surrealist mothers are usually great for this sort of thing. The high life, the sun, enough money, and pretty daughters."

It must have smarted, especially as this was just the sort of madcap adventure Annette would have loved. The sisters had found a trunk full of old clothes in the attic and played dress-up, acting out silly scenes before the camera. Yannick wore a lacy Victorian white dress and gingham pantaloons; Rouch, in a polka-dotted ascot, has a pencil-thin mustache on his top lip. The photo of the young lovers is full of frivolity and innocence, rare joie de vivre captured amid war. Beaming from ear to ear,

the rugged Rouch carries Yannick in his arms as she kicks her feet and laughs. Her diaphanous white dress sweeps across bare legs; her feet are pointed with pleasure; one arm is wrapped around his neck, as if he is carrying her over their honeymoon threshold.

Though younger than Annette, the Bellon girls were more sexually liberated. Along with her famous mother and stepfather, Armand Labin, a well-known journalist who had founded the newspaper *Midi Libre*, Yannick had the kind of professional connections that appealed to the ambitious Rouch.

Though Annette was determined not to be bound by her Jewish background, she wasn't interested in bed-hopping or giving her virginity to a man she did not love. Rouch may have been handsome, but she hadn't been smitten. Yannick, who was also Jewish, had grown up with a far more bohemian attitude to sex. She was also truly in love with Jean Rouch and he with her. Yannick's parents had even begun to think of Rouch as Yannick's fiancé. Annette wrote:

> I think I am beaten in this box by the young Yannick, who was much more in love (with him) than me, since she went so far as to make that famous, well-known sacrifice of her beautiful virginity, which I felt unable to do. First, because she thinks she loves him and because she spouts her pro–free love opinion aloud. Funny concept for a 17-year-old girl.

Not only did Annette feel betrayed by her old boyfriend Rouch, but by her current love interest, Claude, and her former best friend. The recipient of Rouch's confessional was Bella, who knew that if she told Claude the news of Rouch's affair, it would get back to the one person it would hurt most—Annette.

While Dolf and Claude laughed at the sex antics of Rouch and his friends, they missed the cues of the women sitting with them. Only Dora knew how the knife plunged and twisted deep into Annette's heart.

It was at that moment that Jean Jausion appeared at the Flore, "a fiery steed in a nimbus image, wearing a shining white shirt."

"Annette, we missed you!" He kissed her on both cheeks and looked into her eyes. "We talked about you so much, while we were away."

Annette perked up as Jean sat down next to her. Sandwiched between Claude and Jean, she felt Rouch's betrayal fade.

And then Bella arrived.

Outside, there was sudden bedlam. A tiny Citroën, missing a wheel, clanked, panted, and groaned up to the front of the Flore. It was still rolling to a stop when Bella opened the door and stuck one long leg out, unwinding her body like a contortionist through its narrow door. Brushing herself off, Bella stormed into the café.

"*Bonjour! Bonjour! Bonjour!*" Her smoldering eyes flicked back and forth between Jausion and Claude. "What the shit is going on here? *Bélier de merde!* Shit-rams!"

The entire café fell silent.

"Why are you sitting here? What are you doing here?" Bella berated Claude. "Didn't I tell you to stay away from her?"

"Yes, ma'am," the lamentable Claude, "the dishcloth," answered.

Even Jausion looked chagrined. They answered "the hairy fury of Bella" in soft and fearful voices.

"A little war waged before our eyes," Annette told Charles.

Watching the furious Bella's dramatic tirade, Annette realized all was not lost. Rouch might be gone. But Claude and Jean Jausion were not. All she needed was a boy—or two—in mind.

"I have rarely had such a good time," she confessed in an epic letter describing the whole fiasco. "I am judged so important and so dangerous that Claude and his friend Jausion are formally told not to sit at my table!" As for Rouch? His "exploits are no longer of interest to me. It actually makes me happy. I no longer remember what attracted me to that charming boy in the first place. I am no longer in love with him at all, quite the opposite. I rejoice like a thief."

ANNETTE HAD GOTTEN a watercolor portfolio and some brushes, in order to try her hand at Surrealism. She created a kind of visual diary for herself, a way to divert people, events, and places into subconscious form. She called it *Solutions Tardives—Late Solutions*.

That night, as the rest of the family was slumbering, Annette opened a fresh page in her watercolor book, diluted some of her father's indigo fountain pen ink, so it worked like gouache, and painted a hairy one-legged satyr-like creature, targeting an airborne wineglass. The limb is a sledgehammer and spiky cacti are snapping off a purplish-blue spanking paddle. Bella-Tyza. A small curving figure—Claude—is being digested and her foot is stomping on a frail flower: Annette. She titled it *Femme Fidele,* or *Faithful Woman.*

# Solutions Tardives—*Late Solutions*

*Very strong never missed.*
—JEAN ROUCH

## THURSDAY, OCTOBER 23

ALL IS FAIR IN LOVE and war—but between Bella and Annette it was now all war. Despite Claude's previous professions of love, he and Bella were back together the next day. Claude now showed Annette "contempt and indifference." Bella ignored her.

"That little prank she pulled makes her think she is very strong," Annette wrote scornfully. "Bella's done well, she's got him back in her sights. She doesn't have any feelings for him but has the satisfaction of winning over me. At least she thinks so. In fact, she hasn't gained anything at all since I'm not doing anything to try to change this sudden reversal of the situation. Claude, like a fool that he is, has fallen back into the vamp, whose great means of seduction are caresses, rancid perfumes under her armpits, and the look of a punished little girl.

"When I leave school, I go to Flore. And when I leave the Flore, I come home and when I go to bed, I don't cry. I don't have time to complain." That was Annette's life. She didn't care about men anymore. She'd had enough. All she wanted was to paint and sit at the Flore and discuss painting. And that was how Jean Jausion came to find her, sitting with Dolf at the Flore. Finally, Jean Jausion made his move. He asked Annette to go out with him.

Annette liked the idea of dating Jean Jausion. He understood art and Surrealism. He was well connected and respected in the art world. It would also prove her disinterest in Claude, while simultaneously making him jealous. Best of all, it would drive Bella crazy. A win-win for devious Annette.

They went to clandestine art openings, sat together at the Flore at a separate table from Claude and Bella, looked for used books along the quay. He read his poetry to her. She showed him her sketches. Something about Jean Jausion struck a chord deep inside her intellectual and spiritual being. She wasn't sure she was sexually attracted to him, though.

# A Chore Letter

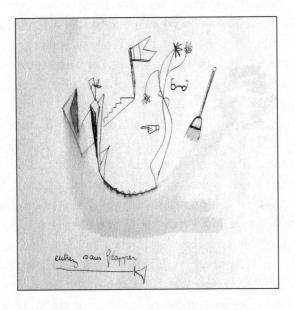

*To know Paris is to know a great deal.*

—HENRY MILLER

GATHERED AROUND THE ZELMAN DINING room table for tea
were Dora, her mother, and all of the "little darlings" (their

cousins), Annette wrote to Charles. "Dad told his legendary and memorable stories of our worthy family." He sang. He regaled them with tales of their Polish relatives, including their grandmother, who lived to the age of 110, "may her memory be a blessing." Amid family bliss, "Cami smashed a chair with Mom's umbrella or perhaps he smashed the umbrella on the chair. The umbrella is in as pitiful condition and Mother, whose tidy-tidy habits you know—ironic tone implied—was not happy. In a battle the winner is as bad as the loser."

Riffing on the comparison between chairs and umbrellas, in a kind of mini-homage to Dada, Annette notes "that the chair is superior to the umbrella because it could vigorously replace the latter, whereas you will never be able to sit on an umbrella, unless of course a new umbrella system is invented which could serve as a seat. Which seems unlikely to me because why sit on umbrellas when there are already chairs, folding armchairs, sofas, couches, poufs, Pullmans, stools, and folding seats?"

Imagining that Charles and she are having an actual conversation, Annette credits him for this "crazy idea! Replacing chairs with umbrellas! It really takes you to have thoughts like this....Ah, you will always be the same." The banter was the kind of silliness she and Charles engaged in when they were hanging out together. What sometimes appears as nonsense had themes that Charles would have picked up and served as their secret sibling code. "I can't wait for you to come back, my little *Chailo*," she wrote at the bottom of the letter. "Now that you've read Jean-Jacques Rousseau [part of the library she had sent him], very sacred, we'll act like little philosophers together and pay sneering irony on a bunch of stupid people.

"Basically, you're a tough guy.

"That does not prevent you from having bourgeois sides, which will have to be liquidated. We will see that.

"Your sister who loves you."

Finishing her letter to Charles, Annette wrote Guy in the Free Zone. The heading at the top of the page was "a Chore Letter." "That is to say that I see myself obliged by our tenacious father who refuses to transcribe this important letter, himself." That was her job.

"You are wise to stay in a small town," Maurice dictated to Annette. "Do nothing forbidden; do not buy cigarettes on the black market; do not go to Bordeaux; go to sleep early; send your health bulletin regularly to us." That was all Maurice had to say to his eldest son. In short, he was telling him not to end up like Charles.

So, what exactly was Guy doing for money? It seems not much. Work was hard to come by. When he begged his parents "to support [my] reputation," Kaila felt they should send money to him. Annette scoffed. Guy's "reputation" was about girls. "He has love conquests in every city and there are at least three women who want to marry him," she dished to Charles. "It's a good thing he still has some brains, because he would fall into the sin of bigamy, which is severely punished by the law."

While the younger children were busily writing their own letters to their brothers, Annette filled Guy in on the dramas his love life and hers were causing their mother. "Home is an environment that I escape with undisguised pleasure every day. Mom is in a charming mood, which translates into yelling at me about nothing and mostly behind my back. At the beginning I was very moved, but it has ended up becoming obsessive and it's embarrassing for the others." The broomstick, glasses and stern finger, in Annette's gouache and ink *"entrez sans frapper"* (enter without knocking) is an ironic tribute to Kaila's charming mood.

What was Kaila shouting about? Well, Guy had a beautiful blond shiksa girlfriend, Nicole, for one thing. For another, Annette was not only going out dancing, unescorted, she was getting more and more involved with goys. And it seemed the whole neighborhood on Boulevard de Strasbourg knew of the grief Annette and Guy were causing their parents. "What was especially unbearable is the endless parade of sympathetic women and professional weeping counselors" coming to commiserate with Kaila. "Madame Eva Singer comes every day with a new corkscrew hairstyle to accompany the watery grand symphony of a friendly little cry."

Advice from old biddies was more than Annette could tolerate. "What annoys me above all are the suggestions and the nonsense. It's all pointless!" When she did stick around long enough to overhear the gossip, she took pleasure in stirring the pot. She found their prejudices silly and laughable, which was probably why Annette delighted in putting "the eternal subject [of mixed marriage] on the table."

# Le Système D

The whole history of Poland resurfaces in a Jewish
grandmother's kitchen, where these women stood in
front of the stove, kneading their bread, making their
broth...food is the history of a people, of its culture,
of its religion, the table becoming a sacred place at
each feast.
——LAURENCE KERSZ, La Cuisine de Nos
Grands-mères Juives Polonaises

MAURICE AND KAILA HAD ALWAYS been tolerant, hands-off parents. Their relaxed attitude meant that the Zelman children enjoyed an unusual amount of freedom. Kaila's philosophy of enlightened non-intervention, her tolerant, unflappable attitude allowing her family's chaos to swirl happily around her, was now challenged by her eldest children's love interests. Kaila's standard response to problems—"It'll be better tomorrow"—evaporated.

Guy was still her favorite, but he was also hours away from her disapproval. Annette was not. Kaila was furious that Annette was still going out dancing at night and spending afternoons at the Flore. Exhausted from making weekly trips back and forth to Bordeaux to visit Charles and take him food, Kaila was reaching the end of her rope with her obstinate daughter. And as though that were not enough, she had to keep putting food on the table for her family. No easy task in occupied France.

The Wehrmacht had descended on Paris like a swarm of locusts, requisitioning food and unleashing on the market thousands of troops, who benefited from the exchange rate between franc and mark. The German invasion had disrupted the harvest and broken up delivery lines from the provinces. While the Germans indulged in *filet de boeuf* or champagne, the French were subjected to strict rationing. At the beginning of the Occupation, adults were allowed only 12 ounces of bread daily (a baguette typically weighs 8 ounces), less than a pound of meat per week, about a pound of sugar, 10 ounces of ersatz coffee, and less than 5 ounces of cheese per month, about a cup and a half. The French can eat that much cheese in one meal.

To get their rations, Kaila and other housewives had to use a *Carte d'Alimentation,* or a ration card. First you had to register with your butcher and baker. Then you must collect coupons, or *tickets* as the French called them, from your local *mairie,* or town hall. Long queues at the *mairie* were mostly made up of women collecting tickets for their families. Standing outside in the rain or snow, heat or cold, became a national pastime. And what if you had children at home? Who was taking care of them? People got up at dawn, risking arrest for breaking curfew, just so they could be the first in line. Wealthy Parisians paid others to stand in line for them.

Inside the *mairie* was a world of women who were in charge of different ration counters, and lines to get those precious tickets. Everything was a scramble. There was a line at the butcher counter, a line at the bakery counter, lines for vegetables and eggs, and clothing allotments. Everyone was underfed and stressed. The women handing out the ration tickets were rarely polite. And once the tickets were procured, you still had to head back out to the street to wait outside your local butcher and baker to get the food to put on the table to feed your hungry children.

To have to wait not just for food, but for lousy food, was yet another humiliation and a personal affront to French sensibilities. The queues were a place of quiet resistance and solidarity, though. Women exchanged news and gossip and whispered dissenting views. They had to be careful because spies and informants also stood in the queues, waiting for a loose word or anti-German opinion, that could be reported in exchange for extra rations.

In the fall of 1941, rations steadily declined to between 1,200 and 1,500 calories per day (from 2,500 before the war). France was one of the richest agricultural producers in the world, but her people were the worst fed of any country in Europe, except Italy. The meat shortage was the most severe. People resorted to keeping guinea pigs on their balconies to eat and killing pigeons in the parks. Cats and dogs weren't safe either. In October 1941, the Germans published a warning saying it was unsafe to stew cats.

The health effects of the shortages caused adults to lose anything between 4 and 8 kilos. Mortality rates from hunger increased by 40 percent. Visible signs of malnutrition, from boils to cracked skin, and swollen ankles and feet, were everywhere. The psychological effects of the shortages were subtler. Starvation partly explains reports of French passivity in face of the Occupation. When your biggest concern is putting food on the table, politics and resistance fade into the background. The real voice of France had become "the growling stomach."

To make up for the shortfalls, an ingenious system of bartering arose, known as *Le Système D*. The phrase comes from the French term *se débrouiller*, meaning "to get by or fend for oneself." The strategy involved everything from swapping ration tickets, which was illegal, to bartering foodstuffs you didn't need for ones you did. "You have to buy things you do not want to buy in order to buy things you want to buy," Gertrude Stein recalled. Everyone was obsessed with food.

Lucky Parisians who had family or friends in the countryside could receive what were called *colis familiaire,* or family parcels. But there was no guarantee the food would still be edible when it arrived. When Simone de Beauvoir received meat from a friend in Anjou, the beef was so hard that it had to be soaked in vinegar and boiled for hours; a joint of pork had maggots in it. She and Sartre cooked and ate it anyway.

*Le Système D* also meant being creative. Chickpeas or lupine seeds were used to make "coffee"; carrot tops or apple skins made "tea." Bread was baked with buckwheat, millet flour, and even chestnuts. The results were often unpalatable, but they stopped rumbling stomachs.

Despite all of this, the Zelman household always had a pot of chicken soup heating on the stove and an evening meal on the table. This speaks to Kaila's ingenuity and the fact that Maurice was able to trade the products of his sewing machine for eggs, a chicken, or some meat. They also had their friendly Algerian vegetable stand owner, Ben Guigui, who must have been very well-dressed in Zelman originals.

Sharpening Parisians' suffering, the approaching winter would be one of the worst on record. The snow started falling in November. No one had fuel for heat, so water pipes burst, creating ice waterfalls on the sides of buildings as temperatures plunged to freezing.

But throughout the autumn and early winter of 1941 neither food nor cold was Kaila's biggest concern: it was Charles.

Every Thursday night she caught a night train to Bordeaux, arriving on Friday to stay with her brother Leon and his wife Karolina Wilf. Early Saturday morning, she caught a tram or bus—perhaps several—in order to reach the prison for Saturday morning visitation. It was never long enough, but Kaila packed every minute full with news and family anecdotes, delivered fresh food to her starving son, and handed over a precious new collection of Annette's letters and a few books. Since the Gestapo made daily rounds weeding out Jewish prisoners, she and Maurice were probably bribing the guards as well. An hour later, she was heading back to Bordeaux to catch the night train to Paris. She got home on Sunday morning.

Keeping Charles's spirits up in his rat-infested jail cell was Kaila's sole goal in the autumn of 1941. That and making sure her daughter fell in love with a Jew.

# Laziness Mother of Lilies

*Whoever does not visit Paris regularly will never really be elegant.*

—HONORÉ DE BALZAC

**SATURDAY, NOVEMBER 1**

AS HER LOVE LIFE HEATED UP, Annette's commitment to daily letter writing waned. Still, every Saturday night the family gathered around the table to write "the petition of the family," as she called it. She doled out one piece of paper and told them to write to Charles. While Cami and Michele argued about who got to write first, their father slipped in a few lines at the top. Across the table, Annette eavesdropped on their mother and Madame Annie Bessarbie, who was sleeping in their apartment that week, and transcribed the dialogue for Charles's amusement (and her own). The subject was wigs and Lodz.

Among Orthodox women, wigs can be a true fashion statement, but they had become even more difficult to come by than food. Kaila was not a wig wearer, but Madame Bessarbie was. Thus the concern. It seemed wigs had been rationed, just like hats! Annette copied the rest of their scintillating conversation:

"The charm of the girls from Lodz in 1911," Madame Annie Bessarbie was saying.

"Remember Jorjet?"

"She was beautiful."

"She squinted a bit, but that chest, my dear!"

Madame Bessarbie was sharing the sleep pallet with Annette, and Annette feared it would "cost a few nocturnal hugs, which I hesitate to find purely friendly. But let's not be slanderous!"

As Cami finished his letter, Michele peered over at the paper. "Can I read what you wrote to Charles?"

"No." He covered it with his hand.

"Please..." Michele begged.

"It's private! I don't want you reading it."

"You're so...so...anti-Semitic!" Michele shouted.

"What does that have to do with anything?" Cami shouted back.

"Mrs. Grosoui, downstairs, said it's the very worst thing you can call someone!"

"*Les enfants* (these children)," Annette writes. "We are laughing out loud!"

**MONDAY, NOVEMBER 3**

Annette started frequenting the Café Capoulade, despite the twenty-minute walk from Café Flore. Capoulade had something the Flore did not. No Bella. Annette didn't want to sit across from her former friend while Bella "boiled with fury, like a miserable drunk sick with revenge."

Annette had another reason for heading to Capoulade more often: things had gotten complicated with Jean Jausion. They had gone on a couple of dates and she had enjoyed herself, but their budding relationship was causing a rift between Claude and Jean. Besides, Capoulade catered to some interesting characters.

ENTER: Mr. Suzanne. "Only you know his name," she reminds Charles. "He offered me a pack of cigarettes" and promised to bring some chocolate the next time he saw her. Only someone with black-market connections could get his hands on such valuable items and simply give them away. Almost certainly, the shadowy Mr. Suzanne was one of Charles's black-market connections—perhaps the only one. Annette was planning to make a trip to Bordeaux to see her brother, and she promised to bring Mr. Suzanne's gifts with her.

That Monday afternoon, she braved the Flore after classes and went in for a coffee. Salvatore was there and turned "pale when he saw me and began to stutter. Poor Salva!"

ENTER: Jean Jausion. He came over to her table but did not sit down. "I want to apologize at how awkward things have gotten between us," he said. Annette nodded. She was listening.

"I want you to know that I would like to be your friend and comrade, but I can't do that to Claude."

She raised an eyebrow.

"Claude is jealous," he explained.

"The boy barely says hello to me now!" Annette admonished. "I never see him, but if I go out with someone else, it hurts him?"

"Bella doesn't want me to talk to you either."

Annette burst out laughing. "And you obey? Do you people have nothing better to think about? What a bunch of pitiful hollow bases. And you call yourselves the elite of the Latin Quarter?" In a sputter of mirth, she stood up, gathered her sketchbook and pencils, and excused herself. "I have better things to do than deal with this nonsense."

Jean was left pondering this fearless and spirited young woman, who didn't take his situation, or Claude's, seriously. What had he hoped for? Some intimate commiseration? Bonding over the evil manipulations of Bella? Annette wasn't waiting around for anyone, least of all Claude or his scuba-diving friend.

"I cannot forget the confidences of jealous Jausion," she wrote to Charles that night. "I had to sit on the floor from laughing!"

# The Zelman Method

*The city, though still "heavenly beautiful," was war-worn and impoverished.*

—ANDRÉ SCHIFFRIN, *A Political Education*

**FRIDAY, NOVEMBER 7**

THERE HAD BEEN AN EARLY snow, barely an inch, but it clung in a thin layer of icy white. Pulling the collar of the new Scottish wool tartan coat that Maurice had sewn for her up around her neck, Annette wandered down the frozen streets of the Latin Quarter. Wisps of snow blew across rooftops and off gables. Snow snakes spun into mini-cyclones down the street in much the same way Annette's mind whirligigged around the Bella-Claude-Jausion dilemma.

"Please, write me about something else!" Charles begged.

But she could "only tell more Claudesques, Bellaesques, and Jausionesques stories."

When Kaila was home, Annette tried to spend as much time as she could in the art studio or cafés. That afternoon, at the

Flore, while sitting with her fake coffee, sketching the faces of her fellow Floristes, the *patron*, Boubal, beckoned. She had a phone call.

It was Bella.

BELLA: Is Claude there?
> *Claude sits with Jausion, on the other side of the café from Annette.*

ANNETTE: Yes.

BELLA: Tell him I am not coming! (*Slams the phone down. Dial tone.*)

"Talk about a surprise!" Her handwriting is so hard to decipher it suggests she is writing as fast as she's thinking. "At first, I did not understand, but I went to do the errand. Only then did I realize that Bella was punishing Claude because I was at Flore....Machiavellian, eh! Poor Claude. The Dish Cloth is punished without having sinned in the least."

And that was it.

Claude dumped Bella. Annette had won.


**THURSDAY, NOVEMBER 13**

Annette had devised a way of analyzing Guy's love life and her own. "It is called the Zelman method," she told him. "We substitute the people we love in our family for other individuals outside our family, in our band it is very well known. We really are innovators in the Zelman circus." She was going to have to be innovative if she was going to become embroiled in a love affair with a gentile.

Guy was as concerned about his little sister as their mother. What was she getting into with men like Mr. Suzanne and the other Rue Boissière riffraff?

"I am proud to have a virgin sister," he wrote, hoping for confirmation that it was still true.

"How touching. But you never know…" Annette taunted. "Virginity adds absolutely nothing to the value a woman represents as a human being, her vital point of view, etc. It is absolutely not taken into account." In her usual fashion, Annette stuck Guy on the teeter-totter of her mind and asked him right back if he was as concerned about his own girlfriends' purity. Finally, she acquiesces to telling him the truth, but "it is absolutely not due to a question of principle, but because a guy never liked me enough for me to give it to him!"

Annette adds at the bottom of her letter: "Dad wants you to write to him all by himself with health report, weight, and temperature sheet. Here are food cards, family hello, and branches. And here is my heart that beats only for you (Napoleon)."

This literary reference no doubt went over Guy's head, but Charles would have understood. The quote echoes Paul Verlaine: "Here are fruits, flowers, leaves and branches. / And here is my heart, which beats only for you. / Do not tear it with your two white hands." Guy was the Zelman method's emperor of love. Their own Don Juan.

A FEW DAYS LATER Interzone postcards, dated back to September, arrived from Jean Rouch's pig buddies, Ponty and Sauvy. They were "very nice and quite hypocritical cards… with tears in their voices…of the sweet time of our youth in Paris, student life, the madness of the Latin Quarter, etc., and very bitter regrets. It's quite funny, especially since I know perfectly well that they have absolutely no regrets. They have blue sea, spear fishing and a splendid canoe, a beautiful villa, and very pretty and very loving girlfriends of Surrealism," she confided to Charles, bitterly.

Neither Annette nor Bella knew that the pig buddies had received urgent news to report for duty as engineers for

French colonial service in Dakar and left for North Africa on September 23. The Interzone cards had been posted days before they left the continent. The friends would not return for years. Those innocent days in the Latin Quarter were gone forever.

Left behind by her lover, Yannick sent poignant letters to Rouch in North Africa. Rouch sent Yannick money, but the separation deeply affected the now seventeen-year-old Yannick, who felt adrift. She and Loleh found work in Marseilles at a cooperative called Croque Fruit, which had been set up by Sylvain Itkine, a French-Jewish theater director and former Floriste. But it was tough to survive on their own. They were only teenagers. For some reason, the girls didn't go home to their mother. Annette knew none of this. All she knew was that her former clique had abandoned her. At least she had won Claude back from Bella's clutches. The problem was that Annette was regretting Jean Jausion now. She was no more decisive than Claude had been a month earlier.

Her latest poem was titled "Indecision" or "Lamentation" or "Always More Beautiful" or "Still There Alone." She couldn't even make her mind up about its title.

> *The moon in its decline,*
> *Poisons the wedding*
> *And juicy at will*
> *Suspicion of lese-law*
> *The rites of the beautiful*
> *With its old tricks*
> *Old as cunning*
> *And hard begins the street*
> *The still trembling child*
> *Restarts the truce*
> *And the day by dreaming*
> *Corrects the House*

Under the poem, she added a note about their cousins in Bordeaux: "We have received a letter from the Wilf family. The devil be damned to them (gratuitous nastiness that is). All the more wicked as Joseph is in Pithiviers. It sounds crazy, but it's tragic...so Joseph is in Pithiviers where there's a camp." Joseph was Guy's age.

About an hour south of Paris, Pithiviers had been set up in the spring of 1941 as a concentration camp for Jewish foreigners living in France, most of whom were Polish. The first camp of its kind, Pithiviers was quickly followed by nearby Beaune-la-Rolande. Both internment camps were in the Loiret region and monitored by that prefecture.

The Wilf family had fled Poland after the German invasion and settled in Nancy near Kaila and Maurice. Under the new French laws, they were considered foreigners. During the invasion of Nancy, they fled to the southwest and ended up with the Zelmans in Bordeaux. They were the same cousins the Zelman children had shared mattresses and bomb shelters with—Joseph and Maurice, his seventeen-year-old brother, were with Kaila's brother, Leon, in Pithiviers. Their mother, Karolina, and the two other boys (Jean and Abraham) were still in Bordeaux.

The news alarmed Kaila and Maurice. At the family meeting that night, Maurice assured the children that they were safe from any roundups. "We are French Jews," he reminded them. The Nazis and Vichy government said immigrants were the scourges of society, not French nationals. He was overlooking the fact that he and Kaila were both born in Poland.

# Name of God

*All life rests on appearance, art, illusion, optics, the
need for perspective and for error.*
   —FRIEDRICH NIETZSCHE, *The Birth of Tragedy*

IT WAS MICHELE'S TURN TO WRITE the family's letter to Charles.
Now thirteen, she had little time or interest for punctuation or
other style points:

> Everyone loves Annette she is at school we received
> your good letter and we are very happy. We are
> going to see each other again soon, which makes
> me even happier. The lock, which is already not
> very good, as you know, broke again. Camille was
> carrying this key on him and as he wants to be
> clever he locked it with this key. As the key was
> broken, it stayed inside, well only a part of it, and
> we couldn't get in and it was already dark when we
> arrived home.

She was about to write that the locksmith had to break the door down when Camille grabbed her letter away and interjected with similar stylistic abandon:

> Don't listen to Michele she tells jokes every time I come in there's nobody home so of course I'm hungry and I stay for hours behind the door daddy gave me a bent key I thought I had it fixed at school. It broke in the lock so the locksmith broke the door down.
>
> I'm still going to school and I'm getting further and further ahead on my program. I'm a month ahead of schedule. I leave you with a kiss.

Michele grabbed the letter back in order to sign off with kisses and cuddles.

**MONDAY, NOVEMBER 17**

Annette had been following her brother Guy's burgeoning romance with Nicole and knew it would cause problems in the Zelman household if their parents found out. Nicole was not Jewish. That cold November evening, with a crescent moon hanging over Paris, she wrote to Charles to share her views on the subject of mixed relationships:

> My dear Brother,
>
> I am very happy to have received your fraternal and weekly letter. And I am also very satisfied that you received the visit of Nicole, who is a love. Which will make our worthy mother furious because after all Nicole is only a shiksa (in my eyes this fact alone makes her sympathetic) and Mama would prefer

that all the shiksas be execrable beings, which would make them more easily hated by your Guy and by all youth in general. Everyone knows that mixed marriages, so to speak, are the perdition of our sons and daughters. Cursed be they all. As for me, I might as well tell you that if there is a question of a marriage between Guy and Nicole, I will do my best and more for it to work.

### Probable

*Always give…*
*If I don't take, you laugh*
*We'll exhange*
*The luminous luxury*
*For poisonous ink.*
*Crisps the crunching sand.*
*Or bend a leaf that generates*
*Let it not matter*
*You have no others if you walk on the water*
*You have no fatigue*
*If you dance while dreaming*
*You do not have to laugh*
*If your lip no longer amuses you*
*Because I will not let a single word be traced*
*In the night hours*
*Or read…yes…take in your hand, the hands of se-*
*vere tenderness.*

It had been ten days since Claude broke up with Bella. Now Annette was stuck in another love triangle—between Claude and Jean. Her dates with Jean Jausion had intrigued her. He was patient. Attentive. Interested in moving forward to the next step. He kissed her hand and squired her along the quays looking at the book stalls, the Seine, the reflections of Notre Dame's spires in the moving waters, so free in their passing journey to the sea. After Claude dumped Bella, Annette began dating him as well as Jean Jausion again. She was a mess. Her entire letter is scribbled with "Name of God, Name of God," until she was printing it in all CAPS!

> I am in the process of becoming a woman in the full and beautiful sense of the word and that does not displease me greatly.
>     I kiss you.
>     Your sister yelling without knowing.

# Showdown at the Café Flore

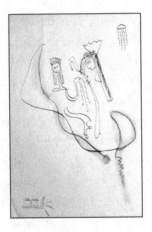

*What is hell? I maintain that it is the suffering of being unable to love.*

—FYODOR DOSTOEVSKY

**SATURDAY, NOVEMBER 22**

THOUGH THEY WERE NOT PRACTICING Jews in the traditional sense, both Annette's parents had been raised in Orthodox Polish-

Jewish households. They spoke Yiddish as well as Polish and ate pierogi, *klops*, and *golabki*, and, of course, kugel. The boys all had their bar mitzvahs. Both Maurice and Kaila were determined that, when the time came, their children would marry Jews.

Annette and Guy had other ideas. "You have to admit, it would be pretty funny to see Guy and Nicole get married," Annette gossiped with Charles. "Dad would hold his nose....But it wouldn't change his opinion [of gentiles]."

Of course, "the girls Guy knows do not know there are two to three others." But his shiksa, Nicole, had made it out of the slush pile and proven herself to be:

> brave, pretty, fine, elegant, and not nearly so stupid as I had thought. I have the damn prejudice of believing that a smart girl can't be in love with Guy!
>
> We pretty much know where we stand on the "love" chapter, when it comes to Guy and his romantic conquests, so don't get your hopes up. Nicole is far from being the first and even further from being the last....I pity her for having fallen into the paws of our faunistic sacrificer and Don Juanesque.

Annette had been careful to keep the two spheres of her life, her family and the Café de Flore, separate. She did not bring her boyfriends to the apartment on Boulevard de Strasbourg, preferring to conduct her relationships at the Café de Flore or on long romantic walks along the Seine or in art galleries. Then one bright fall morning in November her two spheres collided with a knock on the door. It was Claude.

"Fortunately, I was up. In my morning outfit. I sent him to the café downstairs to wait for me." Shutting the door behind her, she found the entire family looking at her in amazement.

Annette pushed past them and headed to the kitchen sink to splash her face with cold water and freshen her hair. Claude on her doorstep could only mean one thing! She dressed, put on her "dress for success" rabbit-fur coat, and went to hear what he had to say.

Maurice and Kaila watched as Annette primped, but said nothing.

Annette and Claude chatted at the café for two hours, nonstop. Claude wanted to be exclusive. Would she take him? Annette had a date with Jean Jausion in a few hours. She and Claude decided that she should be the one to break the news to Jean.

In the midst of their tête-à-tête, Maurice walked into the café. "You've been gone for two hours." He pointed to the clock. It was one in the afternoon.

"Claude turned red, like a red flower." Then he stood up and extended his hand to Maurice. Annette introduced the two men. Maurice was polite but escorted his daughter back upstairs without discussion.

That afternoon she met Jean Jausion at the Flore. Her planned destruction of Jean's hope took all of two minutes. She told him that Claude had come over that morning and bared his soul. "I don't think I like you," she said bluntly.

Jean stood up, took her hand, and kissed it. "Goodbye."

Five minutes later, as Annette left the Flore, she found the two friends sitting together on the terrace. Jean was crestfallen. Claude looked as if he were waiting for the results of an exam. She walked away without looking back. A block away, she slipped into the Saint-Germain-des-Prés church, crumpled into a pew, and "cried like a calf." Why was she crying? Was it just nerves? She had gotten what she wanted—she had gotten Claude. What was wrong with her? Maybe she was getting her period.

Wiping her tears, she returned to the Flore. Jausion waved shyly and left. When he returned, he sat with someone else and didn't look at her.

Dolf came over and sat down, shaking his head at her. "What are you doing?" he scolded. "I am sure you don't like Claude."

"That is exactly what I have been telling myself in the church," she confessed. "We had a long discussion about life in general, mine in particular, love in general and mine in particular." Maybe she didn't love Claude and this was really just about trying to get back at Bella. Annette left a note with Boubal for Claude: "Please meet me at 5 pm tomorrow."

When Claude got her note, he walked across the room without speaking to Jean Jausion. Then Bella arrived and sat at a separate table from Claude. The regulars and the waiters watched as the hypotenuse of the love triangle swayed precariously. Its apex, Annette, was not even present.

Annette spent the night weeping "for hours on end wondering why I was crying." Maurice worried about his little girl. What was wrong? he begged her to tell him. Did it have something to do with the boy who had showed up the other morning? Annette couldn't get the words out. But he didn't need explanations. Maurice held her in his arms and they wept together.

In *ROMEO AND JULIET,* the dusty streets of Verona are the backdrop for the deadly duel between Tybalt and Mercutio. In the Latin Quarter, the scene was the marble floors and imitation-leather banquettes of the Café Flore. At five that Monday evening, Annette left the art studio and arrived at the Flore to find Claude and Jean "quarreling to the death" in front of a crowd of friends and onlookers. Her tearful inner conflicts had brought the two friends to a breaking point.

"You have to choose between us," Jean Jausion begged. "We cannot choose between ourselves."

"I do not want to be upset in this way!" she yelled.

"You have to decide!"

Across the room, seated at her customary banquette with her own paramour, Simone de Beauvoir watched the altercation. The raised voices drowned out the murmured hum of conversation. Finally, the threesome's shouting subsided. The crowd held its breath.

Annette looked at the two men, both of whom she cared for, both of whom had wooed her. She pointed at Claude.

He beamed. Success. Just as he was about to take his place beside her, her heart caught. The tears of last night. The weeping in church. The what-ifs and sudden regrets. "After having decided on Claude, I was instantly in love with the one I didn't choose."

She held up her hand. "A moment."

Jean Jausion's abashed face rose slightly. Was there hope for him after all? Her heart was racing. She felt hot. Discontented. Uneasy. Dolf's criticism came back to her. "Name of God, Name of God," she swore under her breath. Something in the poet's eyes tugged at her soul.

"Jean Jausion."

The café erupted. Cheers and whistles. Tears and hugs. The waiters picked up their trays. De Beauvoir turned to Sartre. Such passion they themselves understood.

The stage was now set for Act Three.

ACT THREE

1941–42

# Happiness Illuminates
## My Future

*But the future is always a perfection, whatever it may be.*

—ANNETTE ZELMAN

MY SWEET AND PATIENT BROTHER,

You will say that your sister is very complicated, and you will not be wrong to say it. Everything is arranged between Jausion and me, and I don't care about Claude. He wants everything he wants with Bella Lempert.

She had had to explain her "gross error" in choosing Claude first, which had made Jean wary of her whims. They had several "long and interesting discussions" before he actually believed her initial dismissal was "out of fear, not dislike." Now they were together.

Claude had gone back to Bella.

I'm currently heavily involved in a Jausionesque story that only God knows if and how it will end. When you come back we will introduce you to the great Jean Jausion who wrote an article in Paris-soir about underwater fishing with a drawing representing him swimming with a very witty face and with his hand on a gun harpooning the most beautiful fish of the whole sea.

He is a writer, poet and currently a journalist. The latter not for taste but to earn a living (crust). In this sport it is necessary to wear diving glasses so advantageous to the physique, a clamp on the nose, and a pipe in the mouth. It is this same sport of which Jean Rouch and Sauvy also claimed to be champions. Wrongly and with great vanity.

Jean's article about scuba diving came out the week of the showdown at Café Flore, so she knew she had made the right decision. Here was her new lover's name in print, already (even if he had published it under the pseudonym of Jean Raymond, so as not to muddy his identity as a poet). It filled her mind with thoughts of the writing projects they might create together, and "as my sweet poet is not Jewish, nothing prevents him from succeeding."

The title of Jean's article has a pun in it, mentioning the "brothers Paradis," which is the name of twinned islands in Bandol Bay but also refers to the Trois Mousquemers (another pun as *mer* means "sea" in French)—Frédéric Dumas, Philippe Tailliez, and Jacques Cousteau—who were pioneering the new sport of scuba diving. "The first impression that we feel, when making contact with the underwater world is that of a continuous wonder," Jean begins. "These valleys, these plains of seaweed or sand, these deep caves, all of this bathed in a greenish, translucent atmosphere," are the divers' hunting grounds. Their equipment: an "underwater eye," or mask that had only recently been developed, and a harpoon modeled on the "terrestrial crossbow." It is not a benign world. "Everything here is a nightmare vision, not only these landscapes, but also the inhabitants, these silent, mobile fish, which show man a great distrust, due in part to the fact that they have already been hunted."

"Fear is the predominant emotion the underwater fishermen feel," he writes, describing the seaweed, a man-o'-war jellyfish, and a moray eel, "which bites your arm when you pass its lair, or attacks you in open water if it is big enough," and whose "teeth are arranged in such a way that it does not let go of its prey once it has it."

This was an underwater Darwinian world, "with its own laws, where the biggest eats the smallest." Much like the occupying forces in France. "A whole world in the image of ours, but where . . . everything happens in the greatest silence."

Many of the images Jean reports appear in *Par 18 Mètres de Fond*, the first ever underwater film, which was shot by Cousteau and Taillez at Sanary in 1941. It seems strange that Jean does not mention the filming of this historic event, if he was there.

Had he seen the rough footage when he visited Dumas in Sanary? We do not know. But it's striking that the film and Jausion's report are in identical order: the schools of silvery sardines, the dangerous man-o'-war jellyfish, the stingray, and the hunting of a grouper.

By letting her brothers know about Jean's success and slipping in a dig at Rouch and his pig buddies, who proclaim to be masters of sport fishing, Annette recovers completely from the slights she suffered from those former friends. Jean Jausion was one of just a few human beings in the world to experience this underwater world of scuba diving. He was an explorer, testing new inventions and on the cutting edge not just of literature and art but now of technology. What couldn't her man do?

> You'd have to be mad—or imprisoned!—not to see how I am in love with Jausion and how happiness illuminates my future. Quick, come back and let me introduce you. You will like each other. In any case, he will like you. I am sure of it. As for him, he is not

zany but he appreciates zaniness. At the moment he is writing a theatrical work which there is a good chance that it will be played at the Monceau theater in two or three days (which is not very compromising because it will only crush the dogs). [The daily paper *Paris-soir* had a "crushed dog column" that described news items of little importance that had no connection with current events.]

Of course, Dad doesn't know that I'm dating Jean, and I hope that you won't spill the beans. I think it will soon be cleared up, at least the mystery that hangs over this affair. That means that one of these days Daddy will be forced to face the facts and admit that his daughter loves a dirty goy.

Besides, I'm pretty sure he's not that opposed to mixed marriages anymore.

Nothing could have been further from the truth.

# *Blue Like All That I Love*

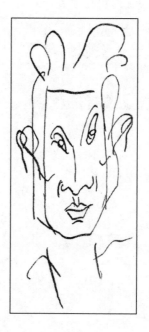

**TUESDAY, NOVEMBER 25**

THE PAPER WAS BLUE. The poem was blue. The letter was blue. "The blue attraction of this new wine blue paper" of her father's was so irresistible Annette had to take one for herself.

She decorated it with a cartoon of Charles and then launched into the topic closest to her heart:

> My Yannoush, I do not want to give myself up to the usual and banal declarations and oaths. I only wanted to talk to you....It is enough for you to know that if I have the desire to write to you it is because it represents an ersatz, a replacement for the more real, more precise desire that I have to talk to you and to be with you at this moment.

This was her first love letter to Jean and she writes longingly of her need to be cradled in his arms, spend all night making love and telling "dense stories" that would not be about love or proof of her love. She felt assured of her place in his heart and "the continuation of this thing that we will create every day a little more in that it is never entirely made never finished and never perfect because the perfection is in a future." Like her passion, her run-on sentences do not pause for breath or punctuation. Only when she catches her breath and slows down is there time to say what she means.

> Our love is like a painting that is always being retouched, but which is nevertheless satisfied, only more beautiful, and to which we continually give different and alluring appearances. This is obviously an ideal vision of a common future, a vision that we know as such. That is to say, as something dreamed of and almost unattainable.
>
> And what does it matter to you, apart from the fact that I'm saying it and I'm saying it with you in mind?
>
> Does this clumsy development replace for a single minute a single kiss or a single caress that you give me?

I am just a poor little philosopher who intended
to write a humorous letter with disconcerting drawings illustrating childish stupidities.

As for stupidities, we are not so far from it.

She signed her name and crawled onto the mattress pad she
was sharing with Madame Linger, who was still among the
stragglers, refugees, and friends needing a safe place to sleep
in the Zelman household.

### Blue Like All That I Love

*Blue like blue eyes*
*Blue like tenderness*
*Blue like the melting heart of love*
*Blue like the letters*
*We always expect too much*
*Blue like the ships that carry*
*Blue like the line of the Vosges*
*Blue like the hands hanging in shadow*
*Blue like mocking laughter*
*Blue like children's games*
*Blue like invisible sentences*
*Blue like immense agoraphobic places*
*Blue like fairy hair*
*Pinocchio's little mother*
*Blue like dark blue ink*
*Blue like the dress of the Arab dancer*
*Blue like amiable simplicity*
*Blue like all that I love*
*And all I know*
*That I don't like and don't know*
*When I sink my nails*
*Into my temples*

*And I close my eyes*
*And the blood beats me hard*
*Blue like the music that obsesses me*
*And that I don't like*
*Blue like pedantic conversations*
*Blue like mawkish literature*
*Blue like the hat of the coarse lady who passes*
*He saw the blue sky like a blue sky*
*The sky so blue, isn't it*
*And it was going to come out at last.*
*When a melodious and suave voice*
*Like Chantilly cream*
*Melodious like music that we have not yet dared to*
  *compose.*
*A melodious and sweet voice*
*A woman's voice sang in his ear*
*"Don't forget your umbrella"*
                              *—Annette Zelman*

# The Dress Chapter

*Sketch by Maurice Zelman*

*Style is something each of us already has, all we need to do is find it.*

—Diane von Furstenberg

In order to honor Charles's request to write about something other than her love life and the Flore, Annette decided to give him the "domestic details of family life" in a letter she called "The Dress Chapter." Their father had been making coats for everyone to fend off the plunging temperatures and early snowfall. Annette's new coat was a Scottish woolen tartan. Guy's coat was in a style known as rosewood, which was "a sensational revelation....As for you, you have a new navy-blue coat waiting for your return." She warned him that the coat was so nice that she might steal it from him.

"Dad is insanely stylish. He is very doctor-like. He looks very thin and ten or fifteen years younger." At least rationing was working in somebody's favor. "As for Mom, her age translates into disconcerting and other stylish eccentricities, such as a dress with a large hole that shows her skin, and the underwear elastic around her belly." To counteract her lack of new clothes, Kaila had taken to wearing an extravagant feather in her hat, which was "subject to the fluttering imposed by the wind or the movements of Maman in general. Each of her persuasive gestures is an expression of extreme spiritual agitation that contributes to convince others of the truth and that feather's assertions," Annette jokes.

"WITH ME AT home and next to me are Michele and Camille," Maurice scribbled quickly at the top of his stationery. "Your mother is with a chatty neighbor." He didn't like writing long letters though, so he handed paper and pen to Michele and told her to take dictation. She needed to practice her grammar too:

> Annette is not back yet, she'll be back any minute, she'll probably write you a letter too, I received your letter and I wasn't very happy because you say that the morale is not good and that doesn't make me happy, it should be the opposite; you have to have a lot of courage before the end.
>
> Now I'm going to write you a few words about myself.

I haven't worked for several weeks but this week I worked a lot and I am very happy and I hope to continue, but doesn't hurt me no bad luck for me, I hope to find work for next week. As you know, Uncle Henri is not in Paris and Aunt Hélène has left with Simone and Camille, to join him. I received a letter from them today; they write that they are very happy. They have a big house. I also received a letter from Henri Hecht [Theo's younger brother] who wrote that he is very happy in a youth camp. He has just arrived.

Madame Linger, she begins to disgust us with her absurd ideas and her friends whom she brings us. Now, I think you see that it is no longer Papa who writes but me (Michele) but it is Papa who dictates to me. Madame Linger naturally brought cards and always speaks with sadness when talking about cigarettes and crying about them. I leave you kissing you very hard

Michele

since I'm going to go out i kiss you, Papa

Since paper was scarce, every scrap and corner was utilized. Maurice told Michele to pass the letter to Cami, so he could fill in the bottom of the page with a note to his brother about attending a dental trade school. (Punctuation was not a concern.)

my dear charles

I'll give you a quick note I'm in the process of reviewing my lessons I will be, we will be very happy to see you out I am still advancing in my work in a few days I will start my first device with 7 teeth I kiss you

annette has just returned i kiss you, Cami

Annette stood in the doorway holding a large painting of abstract shapes in reds, oranges, and blacks, very avant-garde and a little disturbing. The children and their father looked at her in shock.

"What's that?" Maurice blurted.

"It's a gift from one of my friends at school," she said, telling the first of many lies to come. Her faux friend was none other than Francis Picabia, who had studied at the École des Arts Decoratifs in the late 1800s. The painting was a pre-consummation gift from Jean.

"Why don't we hang it over your bed?" Annette carried the canvas into the bedroom, and before anyone could argue, she nailed it up on the wall over the bed.

Maurice looked stunned. "It's going to give me nightmares."

# You Are the Man

*It's quite an undertaking to start loving somebody. You*
*have to have energy, generosity, blindness. There is even*
*a moment right at the start where you have to jump*
*across an abyss: if you think about it you don't do it.*
— JEAN-PAUL SARTRE, *Nausea*

"I HAVE DECIDED TO BREAK down all the ridiculous prejudices of
the previous generation and not be embarrassed by them. I'm
made of a different kind of flesh than that....That's what I tell
myself instead of biting my wrists in despair or shame," Annette wrote. No one was going to tell her how to live her life,
not the Germans and not her parents! And not his!

Like Romeo and Juliet, Jean and Annette faced fierce opposition from their parents. After Claude Croutelle had come to
the apartment on Boulevard de Strasbourg, Maurice was well
aware that Annette was going out with a gentile. Kaila had
sensed the direction their daughter was heading months earlier.
They were not happy about Guy's girlfriend either, but Guy
was a man. Annette was their precious daughter.

"I've never been so disgusted by the racial atmosphere in which we are locked up, voluntarily or not, and I am firmly determined to get out of it, in the name of God! Amen...," she wrote to Guy. "It must be the cause of all young people our age. I hope you will rally to my cause." Annette was prepared to fight against the traditional expectations of her Jewish family; Jean would take on his parents and his severe Catholic upbringing. Her mode of resistance lacked subtlety or maturity, but Annette was certain that love could and would conquer all. The young rebel lovers were going to change the system.

Amid the rush of new passion and purpose, the family was eagerly anticipating Charles's return home. Letters had kept them close, but she couldn't wait to hug him again and enjoy his quixotic mind. "We will probably go out a lot with Jean Jausion. And maybe with Claude if he is rid of his wound (in this case, Bella). She will hate me even more. What jealousy is."

Bella had started a smear campaign against Annette, using all sorts of insulting names, "the least of which was 'imbecile.'" Nothing upset Annette more than being called unintelligent, especially by a Sorbonne-educated young woman. "This superficial girl, whose exterior appearance is garnished (like a dish is garnished with an assortment that cannot be eaten) with a few well-known witticisms, successive gifts from previous lovers or friends (chilosa)— this girl who is content to be ironic and sing to me for the sake of intelligence asks Claude if I 'intellectually' sufficed him." That Claude shared these confidences with Jean Jausion, who then shared them with Annette, didn't help the girls' friendship.

Annette did not care about Bella anymore, though. Gone were the days of bonding over making original Zazou clothes and laughing together at the Flore. Annette had a man in her life. She didn't need girlfriends now. She was madly in love. Tongue in cheek, she tells Charles, "I still say that Jausion resembles Jean Rouch in some ways. To the point where I wonder if there is something serious about these first names acting on the personality of the individual. Obviously, Jausion doesn't look like Rouch physically, which is a pity. But he's not badly built at all and he has this very dark body with blond hair. As is well known, that is what I ask above all of a man, given my intellect."

She cleaved to Jausion's quirky take on reality, his hunger to challenge perceptions and societal norms. Hanging out with Jausion's friends Georges Hugnet and Michel Tapié meant that she was no longer a spectator on the fringes of one of the most exciting explosions of creativity of the twentieth century but at its center. Her own Surrealist writings and drawings reveal a dialogue between two kindred spirits. Jean Jausion was not just charming and well educated; he was a rung on the Parisian cultural ladder, her escort into the Surrealist art world.

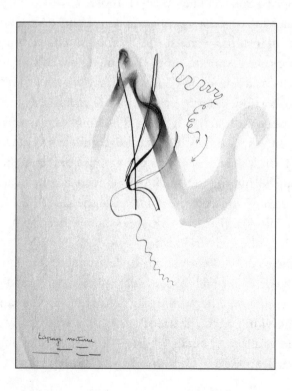

But what did Annette bring to Jean Jausion in return? She was a breath of avant-garde air: beautiful, sharp-witted, unconventional, a real "chilosa." Within weeks of declaring themselves, Annette and Jean were celebrities of the Café de Flore scene.

**FRIDAY, DECEMBER 5—AFTER MIDNIGHT**

Here is Annette sitting up late after everyone has gone to bed. Frost etches the windows; the last flames flicker in the stove. She blows on her fingers to warm them and starts her long looping cursive script across another stolen piece of blue paper: "How much I think of you, Jean...." She lifts the pen and looks around the dining room.

> Isn't it a bit ridiculous to write to try to explain something when if you were here, I wouldn't tell you anything...and if you were here, I probably wouldn't even realize how lucky you are to be here, how lucky I am to have you near me, looking at me, talking to me, and then I'm sure I'd even fulfill the most absurd of my desires.
>
> Don't you hate banality?
>
> I reread the first sentence of this letter and I remember an adorable song that the dancer at El Djazaïr [a cabaret club] repeats to satiety:
>
> *Cherie, Combien Je t'Aime "My darling, how much I love you,"* but so Parisianized that one is no longer surprised or charmed by its Oriental intonations. How I love these songs that also have bewildering lyrics where sometimes the answers precede the questions by a strange gift of divination and where the language mistakes are ingeniously

underlined to make the listener understand that it is Arabic. It should be appropriate to speak in poetry everywhere, shouldn't it?

I am in the ideal torpor which gives rise to sweet phrases...elegant expressions full of dreamy languor. Wouldn't it be better not to speak, not to write, rather to moan and groan while listening to yourself complacently, than to moan melodically and backward melodically and in verse?

Annette had a keen understanding of the Arabic style of Parisianized music that was quite sophisticated. She had never had formal musical training, but Maurice's penchant for performing traditional Jewish, Russian, and Polish songs gave her an ear and a deep appreciation for varied styles of music.

Jean, how much better it is that I have not written anything since I have known you, that contrary to what I thought, you do not inspire me, you do not write me any more poems, only the summer desire to be always with you and in you; the desire to see you always proudly carrying the trust I have given you, the desire of your severity as well as of your immense indulgence, the desire of your strength as well as that of a weakness that rests only on me.

The blue ink from her fountain pen covers the blue paper in bold lines, a looping hand, dotted here and there with inkblots and crossing outs. "How intoxicating and reassuring to know that I can be everything with you without ever surprising or displeasing you," she confides.

For a young woman who prided herself on her independence, this is a new subservient Annette who wants to commit herself to Jean, body and soul. I "must belong to you. You can form or reduce [me] at your will. I have no personality, I am a multitude of different personalities, sometimes odious, sometimes delicious, often silly. I am also a little girl who must be rocked and maybe beaten and I suddenly become a woman of great sensuality; as long as we want to awaken it.... If you knew how the simple gesture of putting my head on your shoulder signifies both trust and humility in front of you, tenderness and a kind of happy fear.

"I don't want to be your equal in anything except, my darling, in tenderness.

"You are Jean. Mine."

Annette was radiantly in love. More beautiful than ever. The baby fat was dropping from her face. She had cheekbones now, and there was a confident new sway of the hips when she walked. But she had shut her parents out of her life. And the duplicity ate at her.


**SATURDAY, DECEMBER 6**


There was something worrying Annette about her relationship with Jean. Something deeply personal. How would her sensitive, well-bred Catholic poet handle the Zelman chaos? If they were ever going to take their relationship to the next level, she would have to prepare him.

"I must also tell you that all the people of my family have thunderous voices," she writes her lover. "Half the apartment block seems to have taken up residence around the dining room table for the distraction of choice, a game of lottery, which is particularly lively tonight as money is changing hands—2.5 francs being the jackpot."

In fact, it was so noisy that Annette began to wonder if the neighbors would complain, but since the neighbors were all in the apartment, as well as being "damned descendants of my father," she needn't have worried. "I think with affection and a little disbelief of people who live alone [like Jean], who write in the silence of a room, who do not need to go begging the people next door to be silent, just a little, out of pity."

**FRIDAY, DECEMBER 12**

"A Year Rich in Big Decisions Is Before Us Declares the Führer."

That was the headline in *Paris-Midi* five days after the bombing of Pearl Harbor. "Germany is not fighting today only for itself, but for the entire continent," Hitler told the Reichstag. "It is this eternal Jew who believes that his time has come to set up against us....Never in the two thousand years of German history has our people been more united or more unanimous than today."

Seismic events shook the world as America entered the conflict and Germany renewed its offensives. Despite the threat of severe fines, Parisians tuned in to the BBC for news; Simone de Beauvoir read headlines about Japan's "shattering victories in the Pacific." On the Russian front, "the Germans began the battle for Moscow." For Parisians facing a second year of occupation, the free world and any hope of it seemed far away.

December was bitterly cold and the darkest, most oppressive month of the Occupation to date. As daylight hours shortened and the winter solstice neared, a new curfew was imposed. "As the result of some new outrage, the 10th arrondissement is closed at 6 P.M. until 5 A.M. as a sign of reprisals for an attack," it was reported. The curfews suffocated Paris's intellectuals, artists, and lovers. German officials changed curfew times for Jews at will, in order to catch them outside on the streets and arrest them. Paris jails were filling up with these "criminal" Jews. The rabidly anti-Semitic periodical *Au Pilori*

delighted in reporting how the streets emptied in the 10th arrondissement, as Jews scurried down the streets and into their
buildings like sewer rats.

THAT FIRST NIGHT of curfew caught Annette off guard. She
ended up sleeping on the floor with Jean at the Maillets' apartment, after enjoying dinner with Jacques and his pregnant wife.
The next day, after class at the Beaux-Arts, Annette met Jean
at the Flore for their customary coffee and stroll along the
frozen quays of the Seine. They ended up missing the second
night's curfew too and took refuge at the apartment of Michel
Tapié, "who is crazy about hot music and has an absolutely
magnificent record collection...some records of which are up
to 20 years old."

*A nod to Michel Tapié's style, 1941, by Annette Zelman.*

Browsing through Tapié's "very beautiful surreal and artistic library," she drifted into a state of euphoria. It was heaven to be in a home filled with jazz and stacks of art books. She felt like a grown-up. A real adult. Staying out late. Spinning discs of hot jazz. Talking about Surrealism. Free to experience this other world, so different from her life on Boulevard de Strasbourg, Annette fell asleep on the Tapiés' couch, in her lover's arms. Feeling Jean's breath on her cheek, she dreamt of the time they would always be together—no one, nothing, could keep them apart. She didn't really want to go home.

Annette returned home the following morning with a "stunning painting" by Michel Tapié, who was "an excellent painter but unfortunately ignored by the crowds." This one got hung in the dining room, over the piano, "surrounded by a luminous halo that created the admiring glances of competent visitors and others (who are more numerous)," Annette joked. "I told Familia that this painting was a gift from another friend-painter…but you have to be crazy not to see that a gift like this can come only from a man in love. Which man in love is absolutely not a painter (only loves painting). As for the painter, he is not enough of a friend with me to give me such a gift," she assured her brother. "Familia" was none the wiser.

Maurice arrived home not long after Annette. He had also been out for two nights in a row and looked a little chagrined as he tried to slip through the door unnoticed. "Where have you two been?" Kaila shrieked. "That's it! No more staying out all night!" She had been worried sick. It was bad enough that her husband had done it, but her daughter too? She put her foot down and demanded that Annette explain where she had been for the past two nights. It was time to tell the truth.

"With Jean Jausion," Annette said.

Kaila wailed. Maurice roared.

"It isn't like that!" Annette insisted. "We are in love."

Kaila collapsed into sobs. Maurice yelled that he would not accept a goy in his daughter's life. Annette begged him to meet Jean before he judged him. Maurice did not want Jausion in their apartment. Kaila agreed. Annette would not take no for an answer. Thunderous voices were raised.

"You are against him because he's not Jewish!" she cried. Why could Guy fall in love with a gentile but not her?

"Guy is older. He has more experience with love."

"You are a child."

"I'm twenty years old."

"I forbid it."

"We want to be together!"

"Never!"

Kaila and Maurice tag-teamed Annette with their prejudice. She threw back their dogma in their faces.

Michele and Cami watched their sister argue every point with the expertise of an attorney. Maurice changed tack. It wasn't because Jean was a gentile. There was a war on. She was too young.

"I've heard you use the phrase 'dirty goy'!" she flung back at Maurice. "You're as prejudiced as the Germans!"

A slap in the face would have stung less. Even Annette knew she had gone too far.

"I'm sorry, Papa. I didn't mean it."

"I'm sorry too."

They were all sobbing now, even Michele. "My father just wanted her to wait," Michele recalls. "It was harder on Maurice. My mother, well, my mother never caused any problems." That was Annette's role.

Maurice reached for his daughter. Annette collapsed into his arms like a little girl. Her chest heaved as if it might break in two from the power of this love and the pain it was causing. How could Maurice deny the child he loved so much the love she so longed for?

"If he loves you, he will wait."

"Wait until the war is over."

"The war may never be over! You can't put me in a cupboard and shut the door. I have to live my life now."

"Slow down. You barely know him. What about his family? Who are they?"

"His father is a doctor. Very well respected."

There was a pause.

"Please meet Jean."

Maurice acquiesced.

# The Ox Effect

*Paris would almost be a charming town, if signs pasted all over the walls with commands, lists of hostages and names of those executed, did not bring one back to reality.*

—PICASSO TO BRASSAÏ

**SUNDAY, DECEMBER 14**

ANNETTE ASKED PASCAL, THE HEADWAITER, if he would be kind enough to give her some paper, so she could write her last letter to Charles in prison on Flore letterhead. "I don't know at all what to write to you now! Since you are going to be free on

Friday and all the interesting or important things will be followed to you by mouth. Anyway, know that I am always assiduously Floresque. Besides, the paper bears the letterhead of this worthy place."

The mirrors on the walls of the Flore had eyes. Across the room Claude was sitting with Bella, who was giving Annette the stink eye and "doing lots of carnal seductions" on Claude. Annette ignored the "pinched airs" around her. "Never have I had such a fun life," she assured her brother.

Meanwhile, Zelman home life had been transformed. "Dad reads the same books as me. He understands me very well. And judges in a surprisingly sane and precise way." The airing of their grievances had brought them together. Like any good parent, Maurice had decided to try to understand his daughter rather than stifle her spirit. He wanted to bond with this new Annette. This grown-up. This young woman.

"At home, there is this painting which has an ox effect. You'll see it when you get home. It is amazing. I will introduce you to new types. But I don't know if you'll be here very long."

Maurice's sister, Hélène Goldman, had fled with Camille and Simone to Nice, where Uncle Henri had found a resort-like home for them. Guy had written urging everyone to leave Paris. The news of the Wilfs in the camp at Pithiviers and new threats against French Jews alarmed him. Under these new laws, Maurice and Kaila would be considered Polish foreigners; Guy was not propagating the Zelman myth that they were untouchable anymore. Even Aunt Alte and Aunt Deborah had left Bordeaux and were in Limoges now. Guy had already found a house for them.

"Talk about a joke. Especially since Christmas is approaching," Annette scoffed. There was no way she was leaving Paris. "Guy believes in Santa Claus!" For Charles's intellectual stimulation, she was referencing the film *The Assassination of Santa Claus*, which was the first film to be made in France since the invasion. On the surface it was just a mystery, but the film slipped a deeper meaning past German censors to the French public. The death of Santa Claus was a metaphor for the death of French ideals.

As ANNETTE RETURNED home that night, on time for once, the pale glow of menorahs flickered behind the window curtains of Jewish apartments above her. It was the first night of Chanukah. The next day nearly five hundred French police and operatives of the Nazi Sicherheitsdienst conducted a massive sweep of Jewish households. They arrested 743 affluent Jews, including some distinguished authors or citizens who had received medals from the French state; all were from wealthy or influential backgrounds, and sent them to Drancy. The following morning, Dannecker himself went to Drancy, selected three hundred of the most prominent prisoners, and ordered them transferred to a newly opened detention center in Compiègne, fifty miles to the northeast of Paris. Among those arrested and transferred was Pierre Bloch, the husband of a Sorbonne-educated marine biologist, Claudette Bloch.

The *chasse aux juifs*, the hunt for Jews, was well and truly on.

JEAN JAUSION WAS a regular visitor at the apartment on Boulevard de Strasbourg and spent most of his evenings with the Zelmans, their neighbors, and the rest of those "damn descendants" of the Zelman family. Here he found a home utterly unlike the austere household in which he had grown up. It was boisterous, fun, full of warmth, laughter, and music.

Sitting around the dining table on Boulevard de Strasbourg, Jean regaled the children with stories of his undersea adventures in Sanary. He described the limestone cliffs covered with delicate anemones, their bright yellow fronds and luminescent purples like a miniature of the sunflower and lavender fields of Provence. The schools of fish that swept past were silver filigrees waving in the current. Bands of light, refracting through the cerulean sea, cast muted beams into the deep where a great blue octopus curled in her lair. Emerald-green moray eels opened and closed their grinning mouths. Michele and Cami listened in wonder as Jean brought this magical world into their urban lives.

"He talked about books we should read, and we all listened to him," Michele recalls. "We read a book called *Mangeclous* by Albert Cohen, about Jews in Salonika, Greece, who were rather eccentric. It was a very important book for Jean—and for us. He was the one that gave it to us. Annette read it, too."

The young couple was careful not to be demonstrative in front of the family, but it was clear from the way they spoke to each other, the way their eyes held on to each other, that this was a real relationship. They had a bond that even the young Michele could sense. Bit by bit the opposition Maurice and Kaila had felt toward this goy faded, until one night Maurice gave Jean his seat at the head of the table, next to Annette. Jean Jausion was finally part of the Zelman circus.

ON THE OTHER side of Paris, Jean's parents were not as accepting of Annette. They were adamantly against the relationship and hoped their son's infatuation with the Jewess would run its course, like a virus, and die. Staunchly conservative Catholics, the Jausions were devoted supporters of the Vichy government and unashamedly anti-Semitic. They believed that Jews were a cursed race because of the ancient myth that the Jews had killed Jesus Christ, instead of the Romans. Ultimately, they believed their prejudice was patriotic. "State anti-Semitism," the term favored by *L'Action Française*, was in "the strict defense of the national interest."

The idea that the Jausions' adored only son was now in a relationship with the daughter of a Jewish tailor was anathema to them. However, like Annette's parents, they invited the young couple for dinner.

Rue Théodore de Bonville is an expensive street of imposing five-story houses, where many of the capital's top doctors and surgeons had their practices. There Dr. Hubert Jausion and his wife lived, just a few blocks away from their bohemian son's studio apartment. Annette and Jean thought the first meeting went exceptionally well. No neighbors barged in and out of the house and the family did not sing songs after dinner, but the Jausions were gracious and kind to Annette, if a little stiff and reserved. Annette felt very fond of Dr. and Mrs Hubert Jausion. She "loved" them. How could she not? They were Jean's parents.

PROFESSIONALLY, 1942 WAS an *annus mirabilis* for Dr. Hubert Jausion. At the peak of his medical career, he published more than a dozen scientific papers on his specialty, syphilis and ailments of the skin. An extract of his book on vitiligo, a disorder that results in the loss of skin color, was published in Paris in the *Annals of Dermatology and Syphilis*. Nazi pseudo-science regarded Jews as an aberration of nature. As Dr. Hubert Jausion peered through his microscope at infected skin samples, did he see the Jewish girl his son was dating in the same way— as a disease that needed to be cured? The thought of offspring from such a union was unbearable.

Like his son, Dr. Jausion was a well-regarded poet, though of a much more conventional ilk. He was friends with the collaborationist poet and playwright Jean Cocteau and had many contacts with the literati of Paris. Unlike his son, Dr. Jausion was doing well during the Occupation. He almost certainly attended the lavish events at the German Embassy, hosted by Ambassador Otto Abetz, where collaborationist writers and artists feasted on delicacies unavailable to the rest of the nation.

THE INTENSIFYING CAMPAIGN against Paris's Jews was aided and abetted by French collaborators. The pro-German journalist Lucien Rebatet used his weekly column in the virulently anti-Semitic paper *Je Suis Partout* (I am everywhere)—popularly referred to as *Je Chie Partout* (I shit everywhere)—to rail against Jewish artists and Freemasons. Camille Mauclair, a right-wing propagandist, attacked the artists of Montparnasse as "inverts, morphine addicts, alcoholics, and sex fiends." *Je Suis Partout* even published a weekly column that listed the names and locations of Jews trying to flee, while *Au Pilori* published the addresses of German agencies to which denunciations could be sent.

Reports poured into the German *kommandatur* in Paris at the rate of fifteen hundred per day. "*J'irai le dire a la kommandantur* [I'll go and tell the Germans about it]" became a dreaded catchphrase. Many denunciations were used to settle scores or to destroy a business rival, and the people who wrote them became known as *mouches* (flies) or *corbeaux* (crows), typically signing their complaints "A Good" or "Loyal Frenchman."

"Since you are taking care of Jews," one *mouche* wrote, "and if your campaign is not just a vain word, then have a look at the kind of life led by the girl M.A, formerly a dancer, now living at 31 Boulevard de Strasbourg. This creature debauches the husbands of proper Frenchwomen, and you may well have an idea what she is living off."

M.A. lived just a few doors away from the Zelmans.

AMID THIS DANGEROUS atmosphere, Charles was released into the arms of his mother outside the gates of Fort du Hâ. Somehow he had passed under the noses of prison authorities and evaded being rounded up with other Jewish prisoners, but he was so weak he could barely hold himself upright. Severely diminished, battered, and bruised, Charles leaned on Kaila as they made their way to the train station.

In Paris, Annette busily prepared a welcome home party for her beloved brother. But the man who stumbled up the stairs into the apartment on Boulevard de Strasbourg was barely recognizable. Michele gasped. Annette wept and fumed. Pulled into the arms of his family, Charles made his way to his pallet on the floor and fell fast asleep. Annette curled up with her dear brother and caressed his head with tears. There would be no party tonight.

All her plans to introduce Charles to the intellectuals of the Flore evaporated. Haunted by the possibility of being apprehended again, he refused to leave the apartment. He spent those first days sleeping, reading, and eating. Kaila and Maurice spent even more time trying to extend the family's meager rations, so Charles could regain his strength. His spirit would need more than food to recover, though.

At night around the dining-room table they weren't remaking the world anymore. They were remaking Charles.

Cue the piano and balalaika.

"We sang in chorus. Yiddish songs. Russian songs. French songs. Annette had a beautiful voice," Michele recalls.

Slowly, Charles's spirit rekindled. Jean Jausion swapped puns and stories with him. Despite himself, Charles found he liked his sister's humorous paramour. The two young men quickly bonded like brothers. Around New Year's Eve, Charles finally joined in the singing and serenaded everyone with a satirical song they had sung in prison: "At the *Fort of Ha* we entered by chance, the director, a very pleasant man." The director was infamously abusive.

# Escape to Limoges

*No one leaves home*
*unless home is the mouth of a shark.*
—WARSAN SHIRE, "HOME"

**FEBRUARY 1942**

HERE IS ANNETTE, PULLING UP the collar of her new plaid wool coat. Snow is falling again. Paris is a paper cutout of herself, flattened and two-dimensional as an unwritten letter. Draped in austere white, she is as cold and lonely as her people. What should be an artist's dream—snow clinging to the bare branches of the plane trees, filigree patterns carved in ice—goes unnoticed by a hungry, worn-out population. The porcelain-white basilica of Sacré-Cœur presses into a pallid sky; snowflakes cling to the metalwork of the Tour Eiffel. The crunch of a German staff car's tires, the muffled stomp of jackboots. Guttural orders are deadened by snowdrifts.

Annette is no longer allowed to go to classes at the Beaux-Arts. No Jew can get away with attending classes for higher education anymore. Landowski, the director, has turned a blind eye, but the SS keeps snooping around, looking for Jews, and he can't risk their lives or what is left of the school's autonomy.

As an act of resistance, Annette refused to register with the Union Générale des Israélites de France. The proclamation made on November 29 was aimed at isolating the Jewish population from the rest of France. Maurice and Kaila registered, but Annette would not submit to such terrorism. Instead, she chooses to avoid places where she might be questioned. She is thinking seriously about being a writer now. Maybe an illustrator. Her short stories are weird and wonderful. She enjoys the "bizarre, bizarre," as Jouvet (or Jacques Prévert) would say.

At the Café de Flore, Annette waits for Jean. Amid the crowd is Simone Signoret, who is bleaching her hair and using her mother's maiden name to hide Jewish roots (pun intended). Signoret has finally started to get small parts in films and is earning the much-needed money required to support her mother and two brothers. Her father is in London with de Gaulle's Free French resistance. Across the room, sitting at the table with her entourage, the captivating Sonia Mossé radiates a calm poise and grace toward the younger women. Perhaps they would like to join the lesbian corner today?

When Claude and Bella enter, they head to a banquette at the far side of the room and ignore Annette and Jean. Gone are the days of their camaraderie. When the brass doors open, Annette does not look up to see who has arrived. She is too cool to care. Only when Michele and Cami are standing in front of her table does she burst with delight and clap her hands.

"We've come to fetch you," they tell her.

Jean orders them lemonade and invites the children to warm their hands by the stove. Pascal, the headwaiter, serves them. Michele looks shyly around the room. Sipping her drink, waiting for their sister to say goodbye, Michele notes the hushed voices and hunched shoulders of patrons deep in conversation. When the Zelmans remake the world, they are loud and boisterous.

Floristes are quieter, steadier, but both kinds of family possess steely determination. When Jean and Annette cross the room to speak softly with de Beauvoir and Sartre, they gesture to Michele and Cami. Leaving the stove, the children come over to meet the philosophers at the corner table.

Outside, snow is still falling. Their footprints, etched into the white sidewalk, mark their passage to the Saint-Germain metro stop. Jean escorts them on the train ride home. Gentiles have a different curfew than Jews, so he can stay out later. Maurice and Kaila's animosity against the young man has faded. He loves their Annette, and that is all that matters. He is family now.

In 1940, THERE had been about 5,000 Jews on the other side of the Demarcation Line in the Free Zone. By early 1942, that figure had jumped to 150,000. No one knew the number of foreign Jews who had already been interned.

"Our family was very well informed about everything," says Michele. "We knew about the dangers from the Germans. We read the newspapers." Everyone on Boulevard de Strasbourg was discussing what to do. Should they send the children away? Should they all leave Paris? Was it easier to hide in rural France or the metropolis?

At night, Guy's idea of relocating to Limoges was the pivotal conversation topic around the dining table. There was less singing and more debating. Kaila adamantly argued that they should leave. In Limoges they could all be together again.

With his typical bravado, Maurice claimed, "We are Zelmans. And nobody touches the Zelmans!" Annette agreed with their father and was against leaving Paris.

Charles had been cured of that illusion. He wanted to get out of Paris and get out fast.

Around them, Jewish families felt their existence on tenterhooks. Would the end come with the ring of the telephone or a letter? Would it come with the terror of a knock on the door in the night?

YOU CAN TELL a great deal about the person on the other side of a door, simply by the sound of their knock. In the Zelman household, which had a barge-right-in-and-make-yourselves-at-home policy, knocking was a rare event. So, the knock—hard and authoritarian—gave Kaila pause. It certainly wasn't Madame Singer, from upstairs. A knock not followed by immediate entry meant whoever was out on the landing was neither friend nor neighbor.

Behind her the usual bedlam of the Zelman household was in a ruckus. Michele begged Cami to let her play the harmonica as Cami screeched and blew. Kaila checked her hair in the mirror, arranged the holes in her dress so her undergarments were not too visible.

"Who is it?" Kaila shouted as she flung open the door. Two uniformed gendarmes waved a document in her face. "Madame, we are looking for your husband, the Jew, Monsieur Maurice Zelman."

"That bastard?" She glared at them without blinking. "He left me and his damn brats a year ago for another woman!"

A Frenchman going off with his mistress was not all that unusual. And no self-respecting Frenchman was going to argue with an irate housewife who had children yelling in the background. Sheepishly, the policemen fled back down the stairs as Kaila hurled a tirade of imprecations on their heads. "If you find him, tell him he has a family to feed! The good-for-nothing, waste of a good skin…"

She shut the door and smiled, but she was shaking.

"Maman?" Michele queried.

It was time for the circus to get out of town.

When Maurice returned home, it didn't take more than a single breath for him to respond. "They'll be back. I'll take

Charles with me. It is men who are most in danger." He barely took the time to kiss them goodbye. "I'll send word when we're safe. You follow with the girls and Cami."

That fast, it was decided.

Maurice was always disappearing for days, slipping out to the country to bring back food or black-market items. "It was the way we lived," Michele says. "There was no crying." No cinematic goodbye scene. It was perfunctory and quite normal. "We said goodbye to our father in a very warm and affectionate way, like we always did. We weren't sad. Saying goodbye? That's just something we did. We lived our lives changing places and moving house. I was used to it."

AT THE BEGINNING of February, Dannecker passed a new decree forbidding any Jew from changing residence. That meant that it was also illegal for Jews to leave Paris. Maurice would have to use all of his tricks to save his family, but "he dressed half of Paris," Michele says. And that meant half of Paris owed him a favor.

Getting across the Demarcation Line was not as easy as it had been over the past summer. Authorized gentiles could cross, but only at official crossing points, and those were heavily guarded. To get an *Ausweis*, or pass, you had to prove urgent need: birth, burial, serious illness of a close relation. Passes required a raft of documents. No Jew could get one.

The network of *passeurs*, who had secretly facilitated crossings for English and French prisoners of war or downed fliers from the RAF, had expanded greatly since the invasion. Helping soldiers had been an altruistic way to help the war effort, though. Helping Jews was a different matter. *Passeurs* needed a reason to justify the danger to their own lives. They needed money. Fees for a crossing could run as high as 25,000 francs. And not all *passeurs* were honest. They might take payment and abandon Jews halfway to freedom, doubling their money by giving them up to the Germans. Trusting *passeurs* was a dangerous game, but fugitives had no other choice.

Charles donned his new navy-blue woolen coat, kissed Annette and Michele good-bye, ruffled Cami's hair, and followed Maurice downstairs. They carried nothing with them that would cause suspicion, just some money and a little food in their pockets. As soon as they were out the door, Kaila began to make plans for the rest of the family's exodus.

Despite his insistence that Zelmans were invulnerable, Maurice must have been working on an escape plan, because he knew where to go. In an unnamed village, he connected with a trustworthy *passeur* and set up arrangements for Kaila to use the same route. Snow was a curse for those fleeing across the border. Tracks were easily seen and traced. Charles was still weak. But Maurice was a fortress of strength and kept his son going until they were safely in the Free Zone.

IN PARIS, THE family waited impatiently for news. They went about their daily tasks and pretended nothing was out of the ordinary, but the delay in mail service had never been more inconvenient. It took two weeks for a coded letter to arrive saying Maurice and Charles were safe with Guy in Limoges. But the situation was changing fast. *Don't dilly-dally,* Maurice warned Kaila. *Come while the way is still open.*

This time the laundry tub was left behind. The children were not even allowed to say goodbye to their friends. Michele put on her favorite dress and then covered it with items that were warm and sensible—a woolen skirt, a sweater. Her mother had already sewn money into the hem of her skirt, and made her memorize the address of the new house in Limoges, in case they got separated. As Michele laced up her shoes, she could hear Annette and her mother arguing. Kaila was upset, Annette calm.

"I have work to finish for Eva. And we have to move the paintings to Jean's. We can't leave them here. They are too valuable," Annette was explaining. "I'll finish packing things up and will follow in a few days. It will be safer if there are only three of you. Four is too obvious."

As usual, Annette had an answer for every argument.

Kaila called to Cami and Michele. "Hug your sister good-bye," she told them.

"See you in a few days." Annette kissed them. "And don't argue and get caught!"

"There was no time for emotions," Michele recalls. "We did what we had to."

The Gare de l'Est was a stone's throw from the apartment, but it was also one of the biggest stations in Paris and full of Germans. Other main stations, like Gare d'Austerlitz, in the south of Paris, which would normally be the departure point for trains to Limoges, were also heavily patrolled. Michele does not remember which station they used, but almost certainly it was a small, suburban one. From there, to disguise their travel intentions, they took several more trains, all on country lines, zigzagging their way toward the border town where Maurice had arranged for them to meet their *passeur.*

Michele remembers a town called Cholet, but Cholet was still a hundred kilometers from the Demarcation Line—too far to walk in one night. The passage of time and perhaps the numbing of emotion have wiped away some of the details. But other memories are quite clear. "We had the address of a café where we were to meet the *passeur*," she recalls. "From there, we were taken to a farmhouse in the country, where we hid in the hayloft for three nights."

On the fourth night, they set off "in the middle of the night. I wasn't afraid. I was with my mother and Cami. So, I knew I would be okay. Anyway, we could not show any fear. We had to give our mother courage."

The *passeur* explained the best way to cross the barbed wire—by lifting it with a stick or a coat. Walking through a dark forest without a torch to light their way was not easy. They had to avoid stepping on branches that might crack and avoid saplings that whipped their faces and eyes. With so many Jews trying to reach the Free Zone, the Germans had stepped up surveillance. Dog patrols were the worst. The *passeur* made them pause often to listen for the sound of barking. Only owls spoke in the night. The sky was beginning to lighten when the *passeur* stopped and said, "It is just a kilometer ahead."

They thanked him and hurried into a gray mist.

At the coils of barbed wire, Cami used a stick and his coat to pull up the wire and let his mother and sister crawl under. Then he too ducked under the fence as the dawn chorus announced a new day.

Every afternoon since sending his letter, Maurice had gone to the Limoges train station to see if his family was on the train. So, it was with joy and relief that he saw Michele and Cami stepping out onto the train platform. They had made it. They were safe. Embracing Kaila and the children, he looked into the carriage and asked, "Where's Annette?"

# *Love Nest in Rue Laugier*

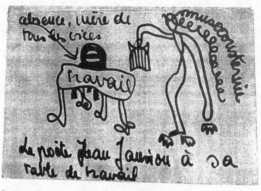

Spring in Paris: a promise, or a chestnut bud, is enough
to make your heart grow tender.

—Albert Camus

As soon as her family left Paris, Annette moved into Jean's
studio on Rue Laugier.

The packing up of the Zelman apartment had been part ruse. She didn't want anyone in the neighborhood to know her family had fled, so she kept her schedule. She left for the Flore when she always did, exiting the apartment with her bra, panties, and tights stuffed into her bag, her portfolio under her arm, and headed for the metro, as if nothing had changed. As usual, Jean met her at the Flore. From there, nearly bursting with anticipation, they departed for his apartment. Without guardians to monitor her behavior or watch the curfew clock, Annette would finally have the love life she desired.

Today the street where Jean and Annette lived is hemmed in by the river of metal that is the Périphérique, Paris's traffic-choked circular highway. But it is still a quiet, residential street running north–south from the Porte de Champerret to the Avenue de Wagram. In the 1940s it was even quieter. Jean's building was home to several other artists, including the actor and future director Robert Hossein. Their love nest was a one-room apartment with a small kitchen and a window that looked out onto a courtyard. Every surface was piled high with Jean's books and records. On the walls hung the art of Surrealists whom the respected poet knew. A small bed ran along one wall.

Breathing each other in, they fell upon this bed and made love. A tumble of lips and hands, thighs and waists, caressing, unbuttoning, this was their honeymoon. Through the open window, the lovers' chorus joined that of night birds singing.

EVEN UNDER THE Occupation, Paris in the spring was a city for love. In nearby Parc Monceau, the sticky buds of the chestnut trees were unfurling. Pink blossoms hung, like cotton candy, on the cherry trees. The air was warm and languid. These were happy days, idyllic times spent talking, reading books, writing, sketching, walking hand in hand along the Left Bank, and sitting at the Flore gazing into each other's eyes before hurrying back to the studio apartment to listen to jazz and a supper of meager rations, and then tear each other's clothes off to make mad, passionate love again. And again.

No one could stop them anymore. Not the Germans, not their parents; not Claude, not Bella. They had escaped them all.

Annette continued her routine, returning to her old neighborhood, picking up embroidery from Eva upstairs, and sorting the family's possessions. Every trip, she stuffed her bag with a few more of her things and returned to their new home. Over the next few weeks, she and Jean moved one painting after another to his apartment—carrying the canvasses of Tapié, Picabia, and Óscar Dominguez on the metro or by Velotaxi. One can't help but imagine them, leaning out the windows of a cab as they careened through the streets, clinging to the canvasses of "degenerate art" and laughing. The apartment soon looked like Bucher's gallery. From every wall, Surrealist images gazed down on the lovers' rumpled sheets.

Although she was not allowed to attend classes at the Beaux-Arts, the Spring Salon provided Annette with the opportunity to view the galleries with someone who loved painting as much as she did. On opening day, Jean Jausion squired her among the crowd of students, teachers, and German officials. There was the director, Landowski. There was her painting teacher, her life-drawing instructor. Taking Jean's hand, she led him down the hallways to the studio where she had spent so many hours working with what she called the "courage of Michelangelo."

The vaulted studio had paintings by the masters hanging high on the walls above them. Here was the easel; here, the vertical rack where her oil canvasses dried. Where they were now? She had no idea. She had to come back and get them, so they could hang in her and Jean's apartment between the Picabia and the Ernst. It didn't matter that she hadn't painted Surrealism in school. Jean wanted an original: A Zelman.

**WEDNESDAY, MARCH 18**

In this euphoric honeymoon state Jean and Annette swanned into the Flore to find Claude, weeping and distraught, surrounded by regulars. His fifth-floor walk-up had been invaded by police in the early hours of the morning. There had been a knock on the door. When he answered, gendarmes burst in, dragged Bella out of bed, and threw her into a paddy wagon outside with the prostitutes.

They called her a terrorist. A communist. A foreign Jew.

The news of Bella's arrest sent shivers down the spines of the Floristes. She was one of their own. How could this happen?

Annette and Jean sat down with their old friend. Bella's place at the table was a vacant reminder of what had been. They needed to strategize and act to save Bella. Together, they needed to help Claude.

Claude enlisted his father and together they worked to get Bella moved from Fresnes, an infamous prison where many British Special Operations Executive (SOE) spies would be tortured and executed in the coming years. The goal was to get her into Les Tourelles prison, which had a better reputation and allowed prisoner visitation. On April 11, Bella was finally transferred to Les Tourelles, and Claude began to visit her twice a week. He was part of a group of family and friends who waited outside the prison on Thursdays and Sundays, bringing food and clean clothes, comfort and care, and anything else he could provide to keep her spirits up. He and his father hired an attorney to get her released from the charges of terrorism. There was one problem. Even if Bella wasn't an active part of the resistance, she was a foreign Jew and could be deported.

At least Annette had been born in France. But if Bella could be a target, how safe was Annette? There was only one way to protect her. They had to change her name and make her Jean's legally wedded wife. With a new ID card, rid of the Zelman name, Annette would be afforded the full protections of the Jausion name, under his father's position as an esteemed physician and collaborationist.

**FRIDAY, MAY 15**

At the *mairie* in the 10th arrondissement, not far from the Zelman apartment, Jean and Annette filled out the necessary paperwork and published their marriage banns. An hour later, they walked out of the *mairie* with a small confirmation card; #42-N°144-1000: "Mariage: *Jausion–Zelman.*" The wedding date was set for May 24.

At the Flore, Boubal popped a bottle of bubbly and raised a glass to celebrate their brilliant maneuvering. Outfoxing the foxes, they were heroes of the Flore. Even Claude, despite his worries for Bella, was happy for them. Annette Zelman was about to become Madame Jean Jausion.

ON THE SAME day, a much-publicized exhibition of work by Arno Breker, Hitler's "official state sculptor," opened at L'Orangerie in the Tuileries gardens. Simone de Beauvoir noted in her memoir that "almost the entire French intelligentsia" snubbed the exhibition. But this did not stop a large number of Paris's high society and collaborationist artists and writers from flocking to the Hôtel Ritz to feast on canapés and champagne in the company of prominent Nazi officials. The collaborationist poet Jean Cocteau was present. Dr. Jausion probably also attended the *vernissage*.

To see Hitler's favorite artist feted in Paris was one more sign of how deeply the Nazis dominated French cultural life. Breker was everything that the Surrealists fought against. There was no playfulness or whimsy in his work, no sexual ambiguity or mystery of the human psyche. His oversized, mostly male,

figures, with their bulging pecs and forearms, were "the much talked about *Ubermensch* and his sanitized female companion," as Laurence Bertrand Dorléac writes in *Art of the Defeat*.

Five days after the opening of the Breker exhibition and the filing of their marriage banns, Annette submitted a request for vouchers to buy clothing and textile articles, including a suit and a tablecloth. The reason: a wedding. She signed the request: "*A. Zelman.*"

BUT MALEFICENT FORCES were mobilizing. In March 1942, Dannecker took a trip to Auschwitz to see how preparations for the Final Solution were advancing. Upon his return to Paris, he sent the first convoy of French Jews—all men—from Compiègne to Poland. Among those men was Pierre Bloch, who had been arrested in December.

On the heels of the secretive Wannsee Conference, the director of the Reich Security Main Office, SS-Obergruppenführer Reinhard Heydrich, Dannecker's chief sponsor in the Nazi elite, arrived in Paris that spring to discuss the escalation of Jewish deportations from France. And the Final Solution.

No sooner had Heydrich left Paris than Dannecker began overseeing the logistical details of trains, timetables, and guards for the deportation of five thousand Jews. The meeting with Heydrich was a prelude to a death kiss—for the SS-Obergruppenführer as well as France's Jews. Before the month was out, Heydrich would be fatally wounded from an assassination attempt in Prague. In the midst of Dannecker's busy plans, news of Jean and Annette's wedding landed on his desk at his headquarters on Avenue Foch.

Dannecker was horrified to learn that Dr. Hubert Jausion's son wanted to marry a Jew. He regarded mixed marriages as a "Jewish strategy" to insinuate themselves into non-Jewish circles, a travesty that must be stopped. He had already replaced the Commissioner of Jewish Affairs, Xavier Vallat, for being too "soft" on the Jews, with a virulently anti-Semitic French bureaucrat. By malign coincidence, the new commissioner lived at Number 12 Rue Laugier, a few hundred meters away from the future Monsieur et Madame Jean Jausion.

# Hitler's Parrot

*Most of those who died in Auschwitz were sent there
during Darquier's tenure. Almost all of the 11,400
children were sent there in his time.*

—Carmen Callil

THE STORY OF LOUIS DARQUIER, son of a well-to-do family in
Cahors, is one of venality, opportunism, and thuggery. A short,
thickset man with a pugilist's face, a squeaky voice at odds
with his bulk, and a monocle over his left eye, he was dis-
charged in disgrace from the French army in 1919 and spent
much of his twenties sponging off his parents. Eventually,
through family connections, he found work in the Alsace
wheat trade, run by Jewish businessmen. His work took him to
a number of European cities, including London. Habitually
living beyond his means, he acquired a reputation as a rake,
got into debt, and in 1926 quietly "resigned" for having his
hand in the company's tills.

Two years later, still with no prospects, he married Myrtle
Jones, a busty, dark-haired, wannabe singer from Tasmania. It

was a match made in hell. Like her husband, Myrtle was a fantasist and heavy drinker. She had left home to tread the boards at the age of twenty-three and married a British-born Gilbert and Sullivan trouper, Roy Workman. The only roles they were playing were those of Lord and Lady Workman-Macnaghten of Belfast, who scrounged off the unsuspecting rich as they flitted about Europe. Myrtle met Louis Darquier in London, dumped her actor-husband, and bigamously married her new French husband, becoming Madame Darquier de Pellepoix.

They spent four years in England, drinking, partying, and scrounging for money. By then, Darquier had adopted the aristocratic-sounding name de Pellepoix, grandly styling himself a baron. The reality of their lives in London was anything but grand. They lived in seedy hotels, from which they were often ejected for not paying bills. When they registered the birth of their daughter, Anne, Darquier gave his occupation as "landowner and French baron," while Myrtle signed herself "Myrtle Marion Ambrosene Darquier de Pellepoix, formerly Lindsay-Jones." Subsequently, and not merely to misdirect creditors, she answered to Sandra Lyndsay-Darquier, Cynthia de Pellepoix, and Myrtle Darquier de Pellepoix and was variously Irish, English, American, and the owner of ranches in Australia. She preferred the title baroness or *baronessa* to madame.

They were the parents from hell, drunk most of the time. Their infant child was farmed out to an English nanny, Elsie Lightfoot. When Louis was summoned before London magistrates for failing to register properly as an alien, the couple slipped back across the Channel to Paris, abandoning their daughter.

A photograph taken in Paris shows Darquier de Pellepoix standing, chest puffed out, with a monocle over the eye he had injured in World War I, and a homburg tipped at a rakish angle. Beside him Myrtle stands, feet splayed, in a matching calf-length skirt and a jacket cinched at the waist, with a chunky string of pearls around her throat and a black beret perched on her short dark hair.

Darquier's political rise began as a street fighter and rabble-rouser with fascist groups like Action Française, Croix-de-Feu, and Jeunesses Patriotes. By the late 1930s, he had become a prominent anti-Semite and was being funded extensively by Goebbels's propaganda office. He was even invited to Germany and became a devout propagandist for the *Protocols of the Elders of Zion*. As deputy secretary-general of the right-wing newspaper *Le Jour*, Darquier emerged as one of the main mouthpieces for Nazi propaganda against the Jews. His diatribes earned him the nickname "Hitler's Parrot."

Like Dannecker, Darquier saw in the Nazi crusade against the Jews an opportunity to make something of himself and exercise power over others. Both shared a taste for rich food, drink, and the seedier side of Paris's nightlife. But while Dannecker maintained the work ethic of a German, Darquier's time as Commissioner of Jewish Affairs was marked by venality, corruption, and sloth. He had a staff of one thousand and left implementation of his policies to colleagues and underlings, most of whom were criminals and sadists.

For a lazy man, he generated a great deal of activity. He organized roundups of Jews and their deportation, created an institute to provide a scientific basis for racial selection, and supervised the "Aryanization" of Jewish businesses and the confiscation of Jewish property. In all, fifty thousand Jewish businesses were redistributed to gentile owners and 12 million francs were stolen from prisoners held at Drancy. The camp's inventory even included eight thousand impounded pianos. The booty Darquier de Pellepoix extorted was spent in the best bars and restaurants of Paris, with his alcohol- and drug-addicted wife. Even Marshal Pétain despised Darquier, referring to him as "Mr. Torturer."

In a medium-sized three-story house on Rue Laugier with a bright blue door and solid bronze knocker, Darquier ran his anti-Semitic Club Nationale and the virulently racist newspaper *La France Enchaînée* (France in Chains). He held raucous meetings for his fascist supporters where the destruction of French Jewry was preached. "We need to urgently resolve the Jewish problem, either by expulsion or by massacre!"

THE FIRST THING Maurice did in Limoges was get a sewing machine. Within days of settling into the house, the rhythm of the treadle filled the air. Michele and Cami scoured the market for cheap secondhand clothes that Maurice recut and sewed into boys' shorts. Then they took the shorts to the market and sold them. Michele remembers it as a happy time.

Limoges had become a safe haven for Jews. The Zelmans had a ready-made community to plug into, as many refugees had come from Nancy. The main street had cobbled alleyways, timbered medieval houses, and was a friendly stomping ground, full of culture. A center of literature and art since the Middle Ages, Limoges was the birthplace of the painter Renoir and had been home to such giants of French literature as Balzac and Molière. The family knew Annette would love it when she arrived.

Of course, the anti-Semitic Vichy government was in charge of the Free Zone, but for the most part the Zelmans were safe. For now. And that meant Maurice was up to his old tricks of staying out all night.

A family of Russians he had known in Paris lived in a neighboring town. Maurice would disappear for days at a time, drinking vodka and singing Russian songs with them. At one point, he stayed away so long that Kaila took Charles with her to bring him home. They scoured the village until they found the Russians' home and knocked. As the door opened, Kaila could see Maurice sitting on a sofa with a beautiful young Russian woman, drinking tea from a samovar with several other Russians. It didn't matter that she had holes in her dress; she marched inside and took Maurice by the arm. "Come on, Maurice; we're going home!" Obediently, Maurice stood up, bowed to his hosts, and left without another word.

As usual, Kaila had her hands full, running the household, growing vegetables in the garden, and cooking meals, as well as keeping an eye on her husband. At least the children were old enough to help out now. Guy and Charles made friends with a group of wealthy young men and were soon in high demand for poker games. They were both card sharps and frequently returned home with their pockets stuffed with banknotes. Michele and Cami watched Guy do what he did best—chat up pretty girls—while Charles scoped out the local bookshops or sat in a café writing to their sister. When was she going to join them? She had yet to reply to his missives.

# A Zelman

*The real tragedies hadn't happened to me, yet they haunted my life.*

—Simone de Beauvoir

**FRIDAY, MAY 22, 1942**

HERE IS ANNETTE ZELMAN, IN the emptied apartment on Boulevard de Strasbourg. Her family is gone, but the walls still resonate with their colorful, chaotic lives. If she closes her eyes, she can hear the laughter. Open eyes reveal no trace of the Zelman circus. The walls are bare. Only the piano is left.

This is her last night as a single woman. She wants to say goodbye to the old Annette, the dance hall girl, the flirt, the insecure teenager. After working to finish some embroidery for Eva, she lies on the floor and sketches on the few scraps of paper she's found. She loses track of time. Curfew passes. Like a bride on the eve of her wedding, she wants to create space between herself and Jean so when they come together again it will be with all the swoon that twenty-four hours of separation can bring.

Tomorrow night will be their honeymoon, until Sanary-sur-Mer, the fishing town on the Côte d'Azur that Jean has raved about after his diving trip, can become a reality. She wants to express herself in a letter or a drawing. How does this transformation from child to woman express itself in line? In shape? What color is she becoming? She wants him to experience this moment of merging—the child, the teen, the blossoming woman. He has transformed her. Made her who she is. A work of art now. She is whole.

*Don't come to me, my sweet,* she sends him a message with her mind. *Stay where you are and allow me this last night to explore my solitude. That emptiness where thoughts expand without limitation.* Then she misses him. Wishes they were in their apartment making love and she had not decided to stay in the cocoon of childhood, beating her wings in the night until they are strong enough to carry her back to Jean's arms.

She can feel his thoughts press against hers. They touch through that mystical, silent communication of the mind. She caresses his musings. Tells him her heart. Then turns back to the sheet of paper on the floor to write more. There is so much more to say. She has all night to say it.

Falling asleep with her head on the pillow of her arm, she dreams of children running in and out of the apartment, the steady chug of the feed dog on the sewing machine, as it moves the fabric of their lives forward. As the needle pierces and the threads twist and loop and tighten, she hears Charles's voice warning her. And wakes.

There are footsteps on the landing. A pounding on the door.

WE MUST ASSUME that Annette had been followed for several days by gendarmes looking for the perfect opportunity to pick her up. An arrest on Rue Laugier would have caused an embarrassing scene for the Jausion family. Jean would have protected Annette and gone to his father, who lived nearby, for help.

Neighbors would have been alerted. No, Rue Laugier had to be kept out of all suspicion. Dannecker's Sicherheitsdienst agents knew what to do. They waited to pounce. Used their French collaborators to snatch her when she was alone. Defenseless. In the middle of the night. On Boulevard de Strasbourg.

Annette rubs her eyes. Blinks. Unlatches the door to the landing. Two gendarmes glare at her.
　—Papers, please, mademoiselle.
　—Why do I need papers? I am in my own apartment.
　They insist.
　She is in trouble now. Her ID card has expired. One look at the date is enough.
　—Come with us.
　—What have I done?
　—You are under arrest.
　Picking up her bag, she follows them outside. The concierge's door cracks open. Eyes peer out onto the darkened landing.
　"Tell Jean Jausion. Twelve Rue Laugier. Let him know I've been arrested!"
　The concierge locks the door.

WAITING OUTSIDE FOR Annette is the infamous *panier de salade,* "salad basket," the slang term used for police vans that is still used today because of the honeycomb-patterned grilles on the windows. Annette climbs into one of the narrow compartments. There are no seats, just a railing to lean against. Prostitutes mock the new arrival.
　—You don't *look* like a working girl!
　Jostled about as the cobblestones drum under her feet, the dimly lit, deserted streets of the Paris she loves slipping past in the dark. Down Boulevard de Magenta, one of the capital's main arteries, around Place de la République, where her brothers used to fight with fascist youths on Saturday morn-

ings, up Rue du Temple toward the heart of the sleeping city. Silhouettes of leafing plane trees are the sole witnesses to her passing. With each bump and pothole, the van rocks and sways. Her knees quiver.

The Seine is black as gunmetal as they cross the Pont au Change and head down the Quai du Marché Neuf. Ahead of them rise the turrets of the vast fortress that is the Palais de Justice. Bound by the Seine on two sides, the menancing, six-story-high limestone walls with towers on each corner occupy an entire city block. In the distance, the shadowy form of Notre Dame rises into the night.

For centuries, the Palais de Justice has been—as it still is—the nerve center of French justice. During the French Revolution, it was used for tribunals. This is where Charlotte Corday was tried after assassinating Marat in his bath and where Marie Antoinette was held before being guillotined. In a famous scene in Victor Hugo's *Les Misérables,* the police inspector, Javert, leans on a parapet over the Seine looking across to the Palais, whose forbidding towers he calls the "lineaments of the night." Above an ornate door on the corner of Boulevard du Palais and Quai des Orfèvres is the Latin motto *Gladius Legis Custos:* "Might must be at the service of the law," literally "The sword is what protects the law."

The main entrance on Rue de Harlay is a monumental flight of steps half a block wide, leading up to a vast portico and the watchful gaze of neoclassical statues representing clemency, justice, and truth. But this is not where Annette will be brought, and she will find none of those qualities here. Prisoners destined for the underground holding jail inside the Palais are smuggled in through barred iron gates at a side entrance on the Quai de l'Horloge.

Disembarking from her cage in the "salad basket," Annette enters this tenebrous, new world through the vaulted interior courtyard. A hefty bronze door towers over her head. Under the sickly light of flickering lanterns, Annette follows the other prisoners into the bowels of the Depot.

THEODORE DANNECKER'S MEMO to Darquier de Pellepoix was short and to the point:

## Marriage between Jews and Non-Jews:

It has come to my attention that the French citizen (Arien)[sic], Jean Jausion, philosophy student resident at 58 Blvd. Strasbourg, intended during the Whitsun holidays to marry the Jew Anna Malka Zelman, born 06.10.1921 in Nancy....I have therefore ordered the arrest of the Jewess Zelman and authorized her detention at the Tourelles camp.

# The Depot

*All those who pass through the Depot...and they are
legion, describe it in roughly the same terms as a sor-
did place filthy and stinking of stagnant water.*
—FRANCE HAMELIN, *Femmes dans la Nuit*

IT WAS ONE O'CLOCK IN the morning when Annette was strip-
searched with the "turfs," or streetwalkers, of the Bois de
Boulogne and Rue Saint-Denis. Her purse was plundered of
nail files, scissors, anything sharp that might be used to deliver
her from life in prison or harm someone else. Colorless nuns,
dressed in gray and wielding rings of clanking keys, wrote
Annette's name in a thick, yellow-paged book. Since the nineteenth century the Sisters of Marie-Joseph and Mercy have
lived with female prisoners in the Depot's cells, where those arrested are held between custody and possible incarceration.
With residences above the inmates, on the second level of a
large communal sleeping chamber, referred to as the "oratory,"
the nuns looked down on the female prison population like unforgiving angels from on high. "The most cruel people I ever
met," Claudette Bloch called them.

The prostitutes filed into the drafty oratory with the click-clack of high heels and sharp-tongued, rough banter. Their stockings, torn fishnets, and stained lingerie smelled of semen and lust. Change jangled in their purses. They complained about their bad fortune and the cold, then flopped onto rank straw mattresses with the practiced air of the previously initiated.

Annette recoiled at the filth of the straw pallets and worn wool blankets that stank of cheap perfume and sweat. Heart-sick and panicked, she looked into a stygian darkness as the flickering light of a nun's lantern was snuffed out behind the clank of a metal door. The barrel-vaulted ceilings overhead were supported by a honeycomb of pillars holding up the gothic arches where one bare light bulb dangled like a withered body on a wire.

The sounds of slumber among strangers sent shivers down Annette's spine. A snort. A snore. Sniffling. Inconsolable, she curled up in a fetal position and wept. What was she doing in this hellhole? What crime had she committed? None! As soon as Jean heard what had happened, she had no doubt that he would get her out. It was all a mistake. A small detail—no ID in her own home? It was not like she had been out in public.

A couple of hours later, a list of women's names was called out in the dark. "Claudette Bloch, Josette Delimal…" Shadowy figures stood up and picked their way among the sleeping women on the floor around them. A door opened to swallow their departure.

PALE GRAY LIGHT shifted through the windows high above their heads. Annette's fellow inmates were not just working the streets—they were women from all walks of life, young and old, well-dressed and undressed. Many were Jewish. On a pillar in the center of the vast communal dormitory was a rendition of the Mother Mary and baby Jesus. Beneath this visage of mercy, strewn about on dank and dirty straw mattresses, girls of all shapes and sizes slept. On one side of the room was a wall of toilets. On the other side, a small chapel had washbasins where some women were washing their naked bodies from head to toe. While some of the women bathed without modesty, others were less interested in hygiene and simply flicked water under their armpits and gave a halfhearted splash between their legs. Annette let the water wash her tear-stained face and hoped she wouldn't stink too awfully when Jean came to rescue her.

Breakfast was half a cup of lukewarm Viandox—a soy, yeast, beef- and celery-flavored enhancer used in cooking. Here it was served as a broth with a few leaves of cabbage added. It was disgusting. After this so-called refreshment, the nuns ordered the women into a section of the men's prison for roll call and cell assignments.

Cell 13 had just been added to the roster of holding cells for political prisoners: communists, terrorists, resistance fighters, and Zazous. Prior to that, only Cell 14 had been used for this purpose. Because of overcrowding, a group of about ten women, including Raya Kagan, Sonia Gutmann, and Masha Lews, were moved to a new cell.

Their former cellmates, Claudette Bloch and Josette Delimal, had been freed in the middle of the night. There was gossip about their release, a sense of relief and hope. Claudette's arrest was well publicized among the women prisoners. After months of hearing nothing from her husband, she had taken the day off from work, left her young son with his grandmother, and gone to Gestapo headquarters to start an inquiry.

"What is this Jew doing here?" Theodor Dannecker began shouting. With his narrowed eyes filled with disgust, he erupted into a fury of obscenities: "*Juden! Juden!*" If a Jewish woman could be arrested for asking "Where is my husband?" what couldn't she be arrested for?

In Cell 8, where Claudette had spent her first days in prison, "there was hardly room for lying down," she recalls. It was a much smaller cell than the others, had no skylight, and the women were stacked almost on top of one another. They had to wedge themselves tightly onto metal-framed beds or make do with the cold stone floor. As a result, they formed close relationships and got to know one another quickly, but two of their cellmates were gone now. Two new ones were in their place.

A few doors away, in Cell 13, Annette did not acknowledge the presence of any of the twelve other women in her cell. In despair, she sank into a corner and wept. What Annette did not know (and no one bothered to explain to her) was that publishing her intention to marry a gentile had made her a political prisoner.

At around nine in the morning, the spyhole on the cell doors flipped open and the women were allowed to visit the prison canteen. Since prisoners were only given a piece of bread twice a day to eat, going to the canteen was the highlight of their routine. There they could get a cup of ersatz coffee or a cup of beans, even a glass of wine, but nothing was free. If you didn't have any money on you when you were arrested, you couldn't afford the fifteen francs for a bite of gristly meat or overcooked lentils.

There was no habeas corpus. No phone calls were allowed. No one had visiting privileges. No contact with the outside world was permitted, except through censored letters and parcels. Annette received neither. As the day waned, she fell into a torpor. What she really needed was a pencil and paper. She needed to draw. She needed to write. She did nothing but stare into space.

By the second day, Annette was a bundle of nerves and tears. She fretted that the hasty message she had left with the concierge had not been delivered to Jean. She obsessed over possible explanations for his silence: Perhaps he was abandoning her? Perhaps his parents confiscated her message and hid the truth from him? Or forbade him to contact her? Perhaps something terrible had happened to him? There was no way to find out. In a sweat she wrote to the concierge to see if there was any news of Jean.

No one responded. She cried a lot.

## MONDAY, MAY 25

They were supposed to have been married by now. Last night should have been her honeymoon. Instead she was in prison and had not heard from Jean in four days. She found a utensil to write with and some paper. Though unsure he would ever be allowed to read it, she began a long epistle to her future husband. "The bed is a straw mattress, which is not always the same," she wrote. "Every night we have to fetch it ourselves and a blanket. Everything gets mixed up during the day and the next night we hesitate to get blankets from mattresses that have been used by the tramps or prostitutes. Who knows what they carry on their bodies?

"I miss you so. This evening I have the blues. Darling, I'd like to give you courage, to show you how I am confident, but today, waiting for something new to happen, nothing occurred. Dearest mine, Jean, look after yourself, don't forget to eat, don't run too much. If I don't have news of you, I know that means you are very busy, my very own. My letter cannot replace my tenderness, my darling, my happiness, my gentle one. I feel a bit desperate tonight. I am your very own little one. I miss you so much. There is no freedom, my love. Tell me you will be more courageous than me."

As letters were censored, she couldn't give Jean any negative information about prison conditions. Instead, she decorated the envelope with a collage of ideograms and coded political symbols.

At the top are the words "*Annexe de la Maison MP* [Annex of the MP house]," a reference to Marshal Pétain, the head of the

Vichy government; the man ultimately responsible for her imprisonment. Next to a childlike drawing of a house are the words
"*Pavilion de la famille Zelman* [the pavilion of the Zelman family]."

A second, more pointed reference to Pétain occurs in
another boxed text: "*Et sur les marches tutumulbants…les trois
mousquetaires avec le quatrième supplément, tous quatre abbayi que
le Maréchal Pétain a visité hier la fondation des orphelins exécutés*
[And on the tumultuous steps…the three musketeers with the
fourth supplement, all four amazed that Marshal Pétain visited
yesterday the foundation of executed orphans]."

The word "orphan" occurs frequently, suggesting how Annette felt. Is the phrase "*orphelins neant l'évidence* [orphans
denying the evidence]" a reference to Jewish prisoners like her?
Elsewhere, in typically allegorical language, she refers to "*la fondation des Orphelins Examateux* [the foundation of the orphans
suffering from eczema]"—perhaps a reference to Dr. Jausion's
specialty in skin ailments.

Next to another drawing of a house she writes the words
"*Le Pavillon des Nanceans* [the pavilion of the people from
Nancy]." In the window are four figures: three boys in hats and
a girl, representing Michele and her brothers.

Annette's language is surreal but not playful: "The moon
is wide and pale / The Snake Man / Ironic fingerless claws /
to make sure he doesn't sleep / The fickle Moss multiplies his
incandescent glances / the Flower of the elite [Annette] / Erot-
ically calm / for it carries within itself the Annette Zelmans."

Is the Snake Man a reference to *The Snake Charmer* painting by Le Douanier Rousseau?

She makes a reference to the painter Watteau, referring to herself as his *Orphelin Admirateur* (an orphaned admirer). She also
makes a literary reference to "Uncle Tom," a metaphoric Christ
figure who, like her, is condemned though he is innocent, and
draws a cross on top of an apple: "*La Pomme Crucifie* [The cru-
cified apple]".

Confronted with these oblique texts and images, the censors must have dismissed them as the demented products of a lunatic mind and let them pass. The letter and its envelope reached Jean. Taken together, the inked drawings and phrases add up to a vivid, coded description of Annette's life in jail; a condemnation of her persecutors, and a longing for her family.

THE DEPOT WAS supposed to be a clearing house for prisoners, a stopover. But with so many new arrests all over the city and overcrowding in other prisons, it was packed to bursting. Holding cells were at most 32 square feet, and women prisoners spent half the day in these cramped cubicles. Once a day, inmates were taken outside for thirty to forty-five minutes of exercise in isolated outdoor cells. Women used this time to play games or dance. They even sang to each other, their voices flitting like winged birds over the concrete barriers that separated them physically, but not spiritually.

A petite curly-haired brunette, twenty-nine-year-old Ida Levine, would soon become one of Annette's closest friends, but initially Annette bonded with no one. There was no reason to. Once the authorities learned of their mistake, she would be released. Jean would see to that.

MANY OF THE new prisoners had committed only minor infractions—like being out after curfew or not having their identity card with them. These girls weren't fraternizing with bomb makers or the underground. They should have been in and out of prison in a few hours, instead of locked away for weeks. What had these girls done that was so reprehensible? Their plight attracted both the attention and concern of older detainees.

One of the political prisoners in Cell 8 was a keen observer of the new Depot detainees. In Cell 13 "was a delicate, very feminine blond girl who had been arrested because of a denunciation.

Her boyfriend was a French Aryan, whose father was a professor." And so Raya Kagan met Annette Zelman.

## THURSDAY, MAY 28

It took almost a week for Annette to receive any news from Jean. After receiving a small parcel that lacked even a note, she became petulant and critical, admonishing him that he hadn't sent more. "When you bring a package, you can, I think, take a letter to the office." A letter would get through censorship more quickly and arrive in a few hours, while a package took a whole day. If he had only done that sooner, she would not have been in such a state of tears and terror. Anything would have been better than nothing. Even a sentence would have helped break the isolation.

"Perhaps he did write," someone in her cell suggested. "If he doesn't put his address on the letter, they won't deliver it." That was probably the truth of it. Either that, or the censors had gone on strike, because no sooner had his parcel arrived than she received "3 letters in order I used for the concert in D-minor, 3-2-1!" She referred to the Dorian jazz scale, and the prompt jazz leaders give their bands. Jean's letters ignited the spark and spirit of our Zelman spitfire. The real Annette emerged from her puddle of tears.

She begged Jean for news of home and her parents, but she did not want them to know where she was or what had happened. She was supposed to be safe in Limoges by now. Her father would be angry that she had turned down her chance to escape. If he knew she and Jean had published their marriage banns, he would blow a Zelman gasket! "Tell them I'm fine and I'm too lazy to write. If there isn't anything new by next month, I'll tell them myself." As if anyone in the family would believe that Annette was too lazy to write a letter!

"Love mine, this morning, I am very well, and I have good hope. I would like you to bring me hairpins and two pieces of soap and panties, one or two coveralls, two bras and something else to wear." While the women were allowed to wash, they had access only to cold water and had to have their own soap. Without soap, she felt like "a wandering bundle of filth, a packet of dirt."

No sooner had Annette sent her litany of requests, than "ten minutes later a package of bra, soap, etc." arrived. Having anticipated her desires, Jean had not only sent every item she had listed, but the bundle had been delivered along with freshly baked rolls and "that special cut of butter from the bakery" she liked on Rue Théodore-de-Banville, where his parents lived, "and sausage from the Jausion warehouses. It made me very happy because I imagine the money supply is diminishing."

Like any wife running a household while away, Annette gave Jean instructions for keeping their home in order and reminded him who owed them money—Lussac, a saleswoman on "La Rue Gay, owes us 200 francs"—and addressed the issue that he was receiving her ration cards, as well as his, and she wanted him to use them. Since she had been arrested with all the meat ration cards in her pocket, she worried that Jean was getting less to eat than she was in prison. Somehow he managed to send her a roasted chicken, though. "Did you at least taste the chicken you sent me?" As for the "grape sugar, I order you to keep half of it. The same goes for chocolate in the month of June. Please don't deprive yourself of the things you love. My darling, keep half of the chocolate and sweets. Send me a few pieces of sugar. Just a few."

Annette tried to avoid any direct reference to the trauma her situation was causing her—since she tended toward the dramatic she didn't want her suffering to be misinterpreted as histrionic—so she only casually mentions that since her arrest, "I don't dream at all."

Surrealist Annette was devastated by the loss of her night-time "royal road to the unconscious." Dreams were important to her, both literally and metaphorically. In an undated "Imaginary Letter or Short Scene," she wrote about a couple "who dreamed of each other and continued to talk and see each other, each dreaming the other's dream and visiting each other in their sleep," a reference to *Peter Ibbetson* by George Du Maurier, which was later made into a film by the same name, starring Gary Cooper and Ann Harding. When the film was released in France in the mid-thirties, it became a touchstone for the Surrealists. In the film the male character, Peter, is in prison, and dreams of time with his lost love, until their deaths.

She had loved the film then. She was living it now. The only way she could touch Jean was in her dreams. Sometimes those watching her sleep noticed the faintest shadow of a smile cross Annette's face and would muse that she was dreaming of her lover. Losing that rich dreamworld was taking a psychological toll. Modern-day research shows that REM sleep helps prepare the brain for normal daytime stress. Without her vibrant dream life, Annette felt increasingly overwhelmed and dejected. "I miss it very much. I would especially like to dream about you, but I sleep like a stone."

No one intended at the Depot could receive visitors; even attorneys were barred from speaking with their clients. The inmates were solely dependent on correspondence and packages, and those could only be delivered once a week, on Mondays. If nothing was delivered on the designated day, prisoners were reduced to eating nothing but tasteless, dry bread.

PRISON WAS A seesaw of emotion—every extinguished flight of fancy sent her crashing back to the reality of her situation. As her diary of letters expands, her paragraphs become pages packed with incongruous snips of daily life, meditations, and rage. Meanwhile, Jean was dealing with a guilty conscience. He felt responsible for her predicament. If he had only insisted she leave Paris with her parents instead of marrying him. It was his fault she was in prison.

"On the contrary," she assured him, "I suffer knowing that you are worried about me and that you are unhappy."

Jean had decided that he had to tell the Zelmans in person that Annette had been arrested. He sent a letter assuring Annette he would be gone for two days, three at the most. Today, the train to Limoges takes on average four hours. In occupied France, it would have taken longer, especially as identity cards had to be verified before crossing into the Free Zone. We do not know if Jean was allowed to cross legally, but with his father's influence it is probable he was able to get a pass.

**FRIDAY, MAY 29**

One week after Annette's arrest, an onerous new law for Jews was announced: the mandate for wearing the yellow star. The star was not just about identification and isolation; it was dehumanizing and created inner turmoil for young and old alike. "If I do wear it," the young Jewish diarist Hélène Berr wrote, "I want to stay very elegant and dignified at all times so that people can see what that means. I want to do whatever is most courageous." The law equally distressed another teenage girl, who would become known as a "friend of the Jews." Her name was Alice Courouble.

JEAN JAUSION'S ARRIVAL in Limoges was a complete surprise, especially as the Zelmans had been expecting Annette. Seeing the young poet walking up the path was not a positive sign. One look at his face and Kaila knew something was wrong. Emotionally and physically exhausted, he delivered his solemn news, then broke down and wept. "We were devastated," Michele recalls. "We were like a closed circle. Now, one element was missing. Worst of all, we did not know why she was arrested."

Maurice decided to find a lawyer and immediately began developing a plan of action for Annette's release. A high-profile Parisian lawyer named Maître Juliette Goublet came highly recommended. Jean was instructed to hire her when he returned to Paris.

Goublet was the daughter of a *préfet,* the French equivalent of a governor. She had graduated with a degree in law and philosophy and been admitted to the Paris Bar at the exceptionally young age of twenty-two. In 1938 she had traveled to Spain to support the Republican cause in the civil war. She was also a prolific author who published numerous children's books and textbooks, and had a mystical side, frequently departing Paris to go on pilgrimages to purify herself spiritually. As a lawyer, Maître Juliette Goublet was best known for her work representing poor clients, communists, and other left-wing militants. Maurice agreed to help pay the fees.

The next day, Jean was supposed to take the train back to Paris but fell ill with tonsillitis and was rushed to a nearby hospital. Having tonsils removed is a simple enough operation today and usually involves a diet of ice cream. In the 1940s it was more complicated, and Jean was already run-down. In the middle of the night, he woke up choking on blood. Kaila tried to stem the hemorrhaging, but he was feverish and needed to be hospitalized again. It took three days for him to recover. He probably needed more time to heal, but he had to get back to Annette. Kaila handed him a thermos of chicken soup and a few items to give Annette, and he caught the next train to Paris.

Without Jean bringing her food, Annette was doomed to eat "only bread." She was hungry and grumpy, and chided Jean. No more cabbage, which "I do not like. Meat is what I'm asking for, and a few more sweets. I know I've already had a ration of chocolate, but s'cusez moi, I would like more! Please allow me to be difficult," she teases, and then adds that of delicacies she longs for "fruit—a packet of cigarettes—very hot and sweet coffee in that pretty Thermos."

The poor diet, along with the beginning grind of yellow star arrests, made her feel demoralized, and she begged him to make compensations on her behalf. It was not easy to be at the mercy of the police, the guards, and the law. Uncertainty abounded in the dank Depot darkness. She wanted Jean's arms around her. She missed him so much she felt ill and in very un-Zelman style began to succumb to the despondency of the doomed. She also wanted a hairbrush.

Jean did not mention his health issues or why he had been delayed. He didn't want her to worry. He told her to write an explanation of her side of the story so their attorney could begin working on her behalf. The narrative should include how she was arrested in the middle of the night and how the gendarmes treated her, he explained. This letter was important because Maître Goublet could not meet Annette in person. All correspondence, even from attorneys, had to go through the censors.

The response from Maître Goublet was quite positive. She was sure she could secure Annette's release but warned that the authorities might demand some concessions. In the meantime, Goublet would work to get Annette transferred to Les Tourelles, a barracks prison in eastern Paris, "a relative paradise, compared to the Depot." Best of all, visits were allowed, so the lovers would be able to see each other again. Goublet had seen the arrest warrant and knew the *mouche* who had denounced Annette. Jean sought the responsible party out and begged them to retract their complaint.

IT WAS ALSO Jean's task to raise funds for Annette's defense and subsequent release. Annette suggested that Jean "go to the dental school (in the 9th arrondissement) and *Mer Anvers* [Sea

Antwerp]." The instruction makes no sense, if deciphered literally. In order to give any information with an address and
protect the individual at that destination, Annette used wordplay and puns to slip this information past the censors. She was
telling Jean to "see the Belgian" and get the dentist tools that
the Zelmans had purchased for Cami's dental classes. "There
is one for 2000 francs. It would be a shame to lose them. I think
one of my brothers-in-law [code for Jacques Maillet] will either
give them to you or send them to you." Then she asked, "What
did you do with your TSF?" *Télégraphie Sans Fil* was code for
the couple's radio.

With their finances secured and hope of her release or transfer now a reality, Annette's next concern was clean clothes:

> Here is what you should take out of the trunk. My
> skirt with big stripes, my beige jacket, the wooden-
> soled shoes, my red bag, and my navy blue or light
> blue shirt, for you.

She wanted to look like a free woman when she saw him
again.

> My dark brown skirt and the blouse I returned, my
> red belt, my blue jumpsuit and bras, rusks, panties,
> butter in a small glass jar, and a hand towel.
>     My darling, I'm in better spirits but I've been
> missing you since Tuesday and don't do so well
> when I don't hear from you.

Annette's melancholy receded when drawing utensils and
books arrived, securely packed next to tins of sardines and
Spam. Using the paper and pencils Jean sent, she began practicing what she called "street art in the place where we sleep

with a great girl who is an excellent model." "I read *Nausea*, which is an infinitely intelligent book. Sartre perfectly succeeds in making himself as obnoxious as he wanted. Sartre is an awkward character but so deep. I find him terrifically strange and endearing. I hate him at the same time and that is not paradoxical." Perhaps Annette felt a kinship with the self-taught man of letters in Sartre's novel.

Other books Annette devoured included Jaroslav Hašek's *Good Soldier Schweik,* as well as Kafka's "hallucinating and very beautiful" stories. Jean delivered parcels for the body as well as the mind. The woman who delivered the post remarked that Annette received more packages than anyone else.

Jean's gifts helped her feel important, raised her profile, and allowed Annette to be generous with her compatriots. "Don't be mad if I gave one of your books to my girlfriend from Colline as a present. I have already read it. As for *Choléra*, which I have also read, I will leave it in the library that the prisoners have organized, which is extremely eclectic!"

Annette's altruism did have some limits. The political prisoners intended to create a prison library, which Annette wanted to support, but she did not want "a bunch of ignorant and dirty girls" reading Jean's precious first editions. "I sent *Manhattan Transfer* back to you because I don't want it damaged. [It] would take a hell of a beating." Any future volumes, she suggested, "should be very cheap editions. It pains me to see the books you had such a hard time finding treated like this."

One gets a sense that the political detainees felt intellectually superior to their less educated fellow inmates. Certainly, many of them were students or graduates of the Sorbonne, but autodidactic Annette was not impressed: "99 percent of these politicals would understand nothing if they read Pierre Benoit (*L'Atlantide*) or even Henry Bordeaux."

Then she reached a point where she was not in the mood to read:

I draw, I dance, I sing. Dearest, I know you love and
care about my intellectual evolution, but I already
have too many books. But do send me another block
of drawing paper. I'm distributing my works to the
others! I will kiss you a thousand times for that!

Send me some biscotti. I love it! I love you, mine!

Annette began to open up and make friends. The petite,
dark-haired pixie Ida Levine, with her seriously quizzical face,
would become one of her closest confidantes. Their other cellmate, Tamara Isserlis, whose long dark tresses twisted like rope
wrapped around her head, would tell Annette she was "the
best dressed" of all the prisoners. "I see that I am admired,"
she told Jean.

"Paula, very sixteenth [Paris's wealthiest arrondissement],"
was a German Jewish girl who Annette used to see every day
at the pool last summer. "Guy liked her very much. We had
never spoken to each other much because once while playing
ball, she broke Guy's record. She is pretty and very childish.
We talk about jazz and she says that I should help her artistic
education because she finds me very knowledgeable, especially
in painting. She heard my eclectic discussion the other day
with the other German Jew, Anne-Marie, who knows all the
Surrealists, and since that day Paula has had a boundless admiration for me."

Anne-Marie had been married for two years to a gentile
when her in-laws denounced her. In some ways, her situation
was similar to Annette's. "She is very touching because her
grief is very fresh and I, who am seven or eight years less than
she, pull her up." They talked about "Erskine Caldwell, Max
Ernst, Breton, Fra Angelica and Paul Uccello" and had mutual
friends from the Flore. "My darling, I assure you that our conversation yesterday, all intellectual and full of useless
refinements for a prison, was such an astonishing diversion that

our grief was gone. We went to bed laughing our heads off and being called names by the others because our unquenchable laughter kept them awake. But I didn't care.…Today I am in a good mood and don't care about anything. I love you my darling husband. My own."

IN ADDITION TO the communists and the terrorists, there was a third group of political prisoners, the innocents—those who had been denounced or committed minor infractions, like being caught after curfew or without an ID, that in a normal world would have been cause for a warning at most.

The political prisoners who had been in the Depot for longer than most realized that new detainees arrested straight off the street needed help. Without any money, they were doomed to eating nothing but two pieces of bread per day and a cup of Viandox broth. They couldn't even purchase a cup of coffee. To help, those with communist sympathies encouraged everyone to create money and food pots in their cells. The money went to purchase food from the canteen, so the whole cell could eat. Collected foodstuffs were divided equally. These acts of solidarity fostered a sense of community, improved circumstances, and demonstrated human compassion. They were stronger together, and deep bonds formed among many of the women.

Almost everyone pitched in to help those less fortunate. However, parcels of food often created tension among prisoners who received nothing. There was never enough to go around and everyone was hungry, so having food packages created an ethical dilemma for recipients. Did you hide something for yourself? Share it with a friend? Or dole out every morsel equally and remain hungry?

Other issues in communal living also required solidarity— the chamber pots in the day cells. The cells were small and crowded, and there was no ventilation. If women agreed to use the pot only if necessary, the cell wouldn't smell like a sewer.

But some women just couldn't help themselves. "We are 12 in a tiny cell where there is no air but no end to unpleasant odors," Annette tells Jean. "There are the toilets first and a neighbor who gives off a foul odor with every movement. There must be a very intense swarming and fermentation under her skirts. She is also the same who snores at night like a throat slap!"

HAVING STUDIED AT the Sorbonne, Masha Lews outlined a program of intellectual stimulation to keep her fellow inmates' spirits up and their minds strong. She organized language classes, including Yiddish and Russian, got newspapers from the canteen so the women could discuss headlines, and invited others to give classes in their expertise.

Thanks to Jean's book deliveries, Annette began a book group and helped the others discuss and analyze their readings, just as modern-day book clubs do. In addition to literature, they discussed films and art. They even organized a chorus. "And I have fun drawing," Annette adds.

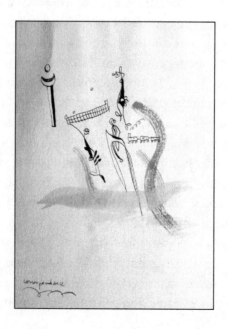

Trying hard to maintain her spirits by writing to Jean, Annette knew the importance of having a connection to the outside world. That she was now in the same situation that Charles had been in was a cruel irony. She wrote so many letters that the prison began to limit her correspondence to twice per week. So her letters became epic diaries of day-to-day activities, dreams, and desires:

> Darling, we lead a hard life here. At night we sleep in a huge and dirty room (nice!) where all the cells meet. At least there I can meet Anne-Marie, who is in the 7th cell. I am in the 13th. She would like to read *Odal* [written by linguist and scholar Otto Behaghel; the rune Odal is associated with Nazism]. Do you still have copies? You have to take care of them, as it would be a shame to lose them and I won't always be in prison—I hope to get out soon.
>
> My love, I know you have heard that I am in very good spirits and that I sing. That's true. I am. I have a company, a band, that loves me very much and that I lead and that agrees with me, as my little brother, Cami, would say.

Annette was a natural leader.

AIR-RAID SIRENS shattered the night's peace or the torment of dreams. Furious at the loss of sleep and the fact that they had to secure their prisoners, the nuns flung open the door to the oratory and bellowed for the women to hurry into the shelter.

Voices hoarse with sleep and panic shouted in the passageway, "*Vite! Vite! On y va! Allez!* Quickly! Let's go!"

Jarred by the roar of airplanes overhead, the prisoners felt a flood of joy. With the skies above them abuzz, they hoped the British bombs would land on Gestapo headquarters or some other important Nazi building. It did not matter if they were locked up in the basement of the Depot; the planes were the sound of a world still at war, not the occupied world that imprisoned women for infractions of love or dancing after curfew.

Half-awake, the women scurried down to the bomb shelters deep in the bowels of the Depot, where they were locked in tiny cells and left for up to two hours. The closeness. Their body heat. The stifled tears and sweaty flesh. The panic in the dark. All was suffocating. The detonating of bombs overhead deafened their ears. There was no light. The air was heavy and got heavier. In a space that should have held no more than three or four women, they were crammed in on top of one another. Annette's cellmates were "spiritual prostitutes, full of tact, as you can imagine." They made crude attempts to lighten the women's collective fear of being crushed to death underground. "I resisted having a nervous breakdown with some difficulty."

FOLDING DAYS UPON days, Annette's monologues have no date references because dates were meaningless. Life was unending routine. Utter drudgery. Rare sunlight. No calendar. The more confused and detached from reality, the more docile detainees were and the easier to control. Only two days stood out on the prison calendar: Tuesdays and Fridays—Parcel Days. The end or beginning of some week. The challenge was not to keep track of time but to remain creative and organized. Their fundraising efforts had met with some success. Jean was able to secure 300 francs and included it in a letter to her. There was a trade-off between the money and one of her parcels. Some of the things he sent her had not made it through the censors. "I regret the records, the books," Annette wrote. "The water that was refused in the package. I regret Sanary, the sea, the fishing."

The phrasing here is peculiar, as it sounds as if she and Jean had traveled to Sanary together, but that was simply not possible. For Annette to have gone south past Marseilles

would have meant traveling to the Free Zone and then returning to Paris, between the time her family fled for Limoges and
her arrest. Jean so loved the region that he told Guy he had
purchased property on the island of Levant, one of the four
islands that make up the Hyères, for himself and Annette.
There was a well-known nudist colony (it is still there today)
on the island. He dreamed of a day when he could take Annette there and together they could live out a Gauginesque life,
walking on the sandy beaches, making love under the stars, as
naked as Adam and Eve.

Annette was superstitious about that dream, though. "My
darling, you talked too much about the sea and Sanary-sur-
Mer for that to happen. I should certainly have had an
indefinable premonition of this misfortune. Do I have no intu-
ition? We were too happy." Thwarted from the dream of living
on the sea, Annette now focused on the dream of being transferred to Tourelles. She dreamt of being able to see and touch
Jean again.

As ANNETTE'S INCARCERATION moved into its third week, Maître Goublet warned that Annette was in danger of being made
an example of by Dannecker. All he had to do was invoke the
new law he had introduced the day after Annette's arrest, which
made intermarriage between Jews and gentiles illegal. Alarmed,
her parents and Jean wrote letters encouraging Annette to
maintain a "submissive appearance," while Goublet tried to get
her transferred to Les Tourelles. Jean assured Annette that both
of their families were working on her behalf but cautioned that
she had to be careful. "Don't make waves or bring notice to
yourself. The guards are watching. Dannecker has spies," he
warned.

The advice made the free-spirited Annette cringe. "I hope
your parents are truly trying to help me and that they have not
told us stories. I am thinking about the freedom we have been

promised. And Les Tourelles is presented to us as Eden compared to the Depot. Are your parents taking care of me?" Prison had made her suspicious of motive. What would be demanded in return for her release? She was about to find out.

Annette knew that Dr. Jausion and his wife were anti-Semitic and disapproved of her. To them, Jean was marrying not only beneath himself but beneath their race. Despite that, Jean went to his father to beg for help. His assistance was not

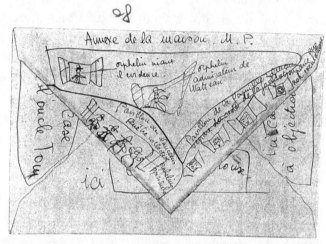

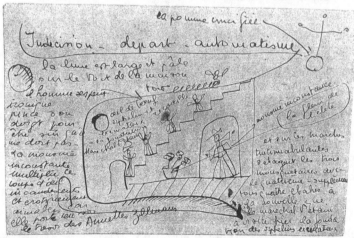

immediate, but finally, Dr. Hubert Jausion relented and asked his friend, Georges Scapini, the Vichy government's ambassador to Berlin, to intervene on Annette's behalf.

The tactic worked, but the next letter was a hammer blow. Maître Goublet explained that leniency would only be granted if Annette annulled the marriage banns and signed a statement ensuring she would never marry Jean Jausion. That was the only way to secure her release. As part of that condition, as soon as she was released, Jean would take her to her parents. There would be no wedding.

> I am absolutely devastated and my heart is in terrible pain. I am writing to you but every word causes me excruciating pain. You will make a poor girl of me. My elbow hurts. I cannot stand it anymore. You must explain to me quickly. I don't believe this thing is possible. Is this the submissive appearance that I must maintain that you were talking about? I won't be able to live without you and since my stay here (which is, I didn't want to tell you, actually excruciatingly depressing) I will have to go back to my parents. Without you. And you imagine that as possible Jean?! You hurt me horribly—I'm really at the end of my rope and my heart is getting weaker and weaker. Don't hurt me. You are my whole life. Quick, explain to me. I do not live until your next letter.

She did not sign her name.

# Yellow Stars

*Don't worry, after the war you can make us wear false noses.*

—JEAN COCTEAU TO A JEW WHO COMPLAINED
ABOUT WEARING THE YELLOW STAR

## SATURDAY, JUNE 6

"IT WAS A HAPPY SATURDAY, lit by sunlight," young Alice Courouble recalled of the morning she took to the street arm in arm with her best friend, Suzanne, who was Jewish, to protest the newest anti-Semitic laws. It had taken a week to organize the protests, but finally the streets of Paris were alive with protesters and students. By 8:00 A.M. the first group of "yellow stars" demonstrators began arriving at the Depot.

Arrested for wearing the yellow star while not being Jewish, Alice Courouble was thrown into a "salad basket" with a number of other protesters. Among them she noted a teenage girl who had been arrested for going to the post box in "her dressing gown." Who wears a yellow star on their dressing gown? A woman named Lillian had a yellow cockerel—symbol of the French resistance—pinned with an effigy of Jeanne d'Arc, and another "created a belt made of eight stars made out of yellow cardboard, each decorated with a letter of the word Victory." Elise Mela and her daughter, Franceska Mela, were arrested while walking down the street on their way to purchase their yellow stars. No excuses were accepted from the Jews. Nor were any accepted for friends of Jews. One woman had even been arrested for putting the yellow star on her dog. The dog remained free.

Energized by the fact that the Germans were arresting and beating demonstrators, prisoners shouted, "Courage!" as the yellow stars and newly christened "Judenfreunde" (friends of Jews) filed into the Depot. The new detainees were immediate celebrities.

Being arrested and arriving in the dark fortress that was the Depot was a frightening experience for adults. For a teenager like Alice Courouble, it was terrifying. She was called a political prisoner, a serious offense. A nun told Alice she could expect to be in prison "perhaps until the end of the war, or for life, we don't know!"

Terrified by her surroundings, Alice Courouble stayed close to the other yellow stars. However, no sooner had they been secured in a holding cell than a rotund, aristocratic woman, who was "further enlarged by two enormous fox furs, collapsed on the bench like a ball of cotton...let out a deep sigh and said gravely: 'Shit me!'"

Alice and the women around her burst out laughing.

The teen was taken under the wing of Josepha, another political prisoner, who had been picked up three times for saying "*les Boches*" to a German. Josepha called Alice her "little chicken" and introduced her to a few of the other political prisoners, who quickly took Alice under their collective wings.

———

"HONEY," ANNETTE WROTE to Jean:

I would so like to know what's going on with these star stories. In the quartier there were student demonstrations. There are students who have been arrested here for having carried the stars in parody. There is a little girl near me who was shamefully beaten by the Germans on the Champs-Élysées in front of everyone for carrying a little yellow star with "Christian" instead of Jew in the middle. She's covered in bruises. "They pulled me by the hair along the sidewalk to the German car," she told us. According to her there were at least 200 people watching and no one moved. It is more and more edifying. There are a lot of women here who have been beaten up by the Germans. They washed themselves naked in front of others, and I could see their buttocks or backs entirely streaked with blue. It even seems that I was lucky to escape it. And you know it's true.

More and more people are being arrested. Every day women arrive in large quantities. Jews who did not wear the star. A medical student who wore it but with a small tricolor cockade underneath. Another for going to the police station to look for someone was stopped on the way because she was not wea-ring the star in public. It is complete madness. From all the arrests there seems to be an incredible panic outside. On the other hand, I know that people still walk in the streets unsuspecting or really caring. As proof of this cowardice of the French, no one reacts to the spectacle of a young girl, blond, frail, beautiful, elegant, beaten in the middle of the street by two enormous Germans.

My darling, I prefer to be locked up right now. I'm not an ass licker. What a show, what an experience. Your father should be here and see these women who have been beaten for nothing. Aryan or Jewish...My adored, I embrace you with all my fervor. I love you. Your wife.

THE NUMBER OF protesters who arrived that weekend tipped the Depot from full to bursting. Early Tuesday morning, June 9, the nuns called out a select few prisoners' names. In the near-darkness of their communal sleeping area, Annette watched her cellmates Masha Lews and Tamara Isserlis depart out the oratory doors. The friends beseeched one another with questioning eyes. Would they ever see one another again?

That day she wrote, "My adored, I embrace you with all my fervor. I love you. Your wife. I no longer believe in my release."

# Les Tourelles

*Even though the Germans scream at you, "You will
stay here until your heart breaks!" it has not broken.*
—RAYA KAGAN QUOTED BY
ALICE COUROUBLE

**WEDNESDAY, JUNE 10**

THE WOMEN WERE AT THEIR morning toilette, washing their
private parts at the communal sink, checking the bruises of the
new detainees. They were comforting one another after a restless night, when the door of the oratory opened and a guard
began shouting names: "Gutmann, Litvax, Levine, Kagan,
Mela—both of you—Zelman! Follow me." Elise Mela and her
mother gathered their few belongings from the corner of the
oratory, where they slept, and lined up next to the other women
whose names had been called. Annette picked up a few of her
favorite books, all of her drawing pads, and the charcoal and
pencil set Jean had delivered. Standing beside Ida Levine and
Sonia Gutmann, she cast her eyes around the oratory for the
last time as the doors opened.

256

nnette manipulated a photo negative to create a marriage of classicism and surrealism. "I've just painted a 'cure of youth' in the buff (very good)!" she wrote. "I am literally in awe of myself and my talent."

Outside the Zelman clothing store in Nancy, the Zelman children were posed
on a ladder in order of age: Guy (at the bottom), Annette, and Charles.
To their right, Maurice leans on the ladder and stands beside Kaila.
To the left of the ladder is his sister, Hélène. Others are unidentified. (circa 1924)

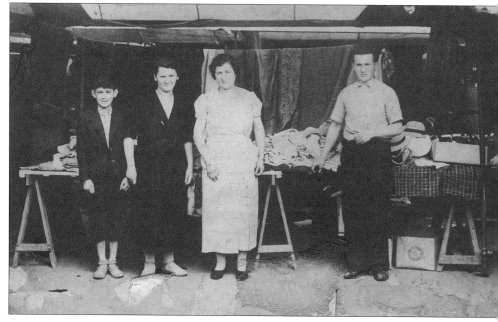

At their clothes stall in the Nancy market, near the Jewish quarter.
From left to right: Pierre Sierpinski; unidentified woman; Kaila's sister, Eso Sierpinski; and Henri Sierpinski

Zelman children were lined up a photo studio in Nancy for their portrait. From left to right: y, Annette, and Charles.

And then there were five. From left to right: Michele, Camille, Charles, Annette, and Guy. (circa 1930)

With his business flourishing, Maurice bought an automobile and took the family on vacations with their cousins. From left to right: Robert Sierpinski, Guy, Annette, Charles, Max Wilf, Ginette Wilf, and Camille. Michele is the baby.

Michele Zelman as a schoolgirl in 1937 (age 9), proudly showing off her book.

the seaside in Paramé, ittany, 1936. From top left: y (age 16), Annette (14), Charles (13), mille (8), and Michele (7).

A local Jewish organization organized camping trips in the mountains near Nancy. Annette is the second from right, and to her left, posing with his pipe, is Guy. (Summer 1939)

At the beginning of 1941, Annette enrolled as a student at the prestigious École des Beaux-Arts in Paris. Here she embraces the *Discobolus* statue she had to draw for her entrance exam.

In the depths of teenage despair, Annette took her school photo, tied a thread to a pin that she stuck on her nose, and drew circles.

The winter of 1940–41 was one of t coldest on record. Annette, wrapp in an overcoat, poses in the courtya of the École des Beaux-Ar

Yannick Bellon, the daughter of famous photographer Denise Bellon, was one of Annette's first friends at the Café de Flore. Here, Yannick contemplates the *Discobolus* statue at the Beaux-Arts.

uy and Annette loved dancing in Nancy. Here they are dressed up for a Saturday night out. (circa 1938)

Annette, in the center holding her dance card (No. 17), with other Jewish girls at a dance in Nancy. Friend Paulette Matusiewicz is to her right.

After fleeing Paris the Zelman family celebrated
Christmas 1942 in Limoges in the Free Zone.
From left to right: Cami Zelman, Kaila, and
Jean Jausion. (This is the only surviving photograph
of Jean we could find.)

Annette (age 19) strikes a p
in Paris, soon after ente
the Beaux-Arts acade

The Café de Flore came to define
Annette's life, as it had for so many others.
Here, the exterior is shown just after the war.

Jean Paul Sartre and
Simone de Beauvoir upstairs
at the Café de Flore, where
they wrote and held court.
Michele and Cami often came
to pick up Annette from the
café and take her home for
dinner. From left to right:
Jacques-Laurent Bost and his
wife, Olga; Jean-Paul Sartre
and Simone de Beauvoir.
Jean Cau and Michelle
Léglise-Vian. (1950)

Jean Rouch snapped this
photo of his "pig buddy"
Jean Sauvy (left) and his
new lover, Yannick Bellon
(right), in Poissy, near Paris,
September 1941.

Actress Simone de Signoret,
one of the Café de Flore regulars,
promenades along the quays
of the Seine with her husband,
Yves Montand.

Michele spars with
her adored brother, Cami,
at the family's new apartment
in Paris in 1945.

Les Bains Deligny was the best
place to cool off in the summer.
The Zelman children spent many hot days
there with friends from the Flore.

"My neighbor on Rue St. Jacques. Dead after deportation," Jean Rouch wrote on the back of this photo of Bella Lempert.

Bella Lempert's arrest card. She would later be imprisoned with Annette and Raya Kagan in Auschwitz.

Bella's lover and Jean Jausion's best friend, Claude Croutelle with his dog, Struppi. (Paris 1939)

Sulamitte Frajlich was arrested on a scorching hot day in June. She did not survive Auschwitz.

Syma Berger was 22 when she was arrested and had been in Les Tourelles since February 18, 1942. Neither she nor her 14-year-old sister, Hélène, would survive

Annette Steinlauf was born in 1914. She did not survive Auschwitz.

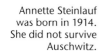

Rosette Idzkowski, née Bark was born in 1902. She did not survive

Eva Szuberski was from Belgium and was 28 when she was deported. She did not survive.

Annette's friend, Raya Kagan Rapoport. Raya's memoir gave Michele some closure and Annette's last known words.

In their cell at the Depot, the Algerian, Alice Heni, also known as "Couscous," taught Annette and their friends how to belly dance. Her talent helped her secure work from an SS officer. Nonetheless, she did not survive Auschwitz.

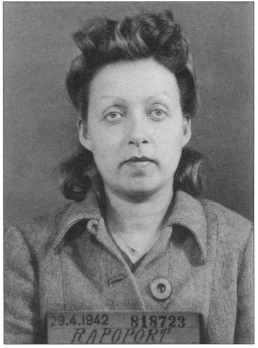

In the Depot, 29-year-old Ida Levine was in the same cell as Annette, Raya, and Sonia. One of Annette's closest confidantes, Ida and Annette were together the last time Raya saw them alive. Ida died on September 1, 1942.

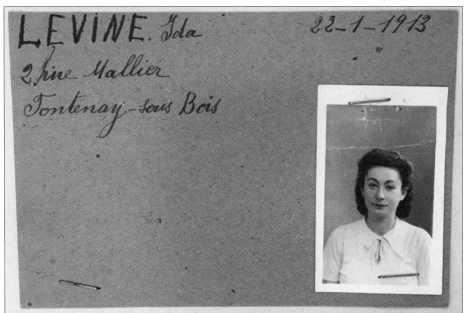

TOURELLES

ISSERLIS , Tamara ( 26 Ans )

HABITANT : IO Rue Buzanval

PARIS ST CLOUD

*pointage*
*41816*

Tamara Isserlis was arrested for getting onto the non-Jewish metro car.
One of the "Friends of Jews" incarcerated in Les Tourelles with her wrote,
"Tamara is a flower in the grayness of the camp."

This is Szajndla Nadanowska's mug shot. She was 28 years old. She did not survive Auschwitz.

Rachel Zalnikov was
24 years old.
She did not survive.

ka Goldstein was
ears old when
was deported.
did not survive.

Syma Sylberberg
was from Belgium
and was arrested on
November 8, 1941.
She was transferred
to Les Tourelles on
February 18, 1942.
She was 40 years
old and would not
survive.

arah Gesik, born in 1909,
d not survive Auschwitz.

Cypa Gluzmann
was 21 years old
and was transferred
to Les Tourelles
in March 1942.
She did not survive.

Chana Grinfeder was transferred
to Les Tourelles on April 20, 1942.
She was 26 years old.
She did not survive Auschwitz.

Pesia Gromann was born in 1920.
She did not survive Auschwitz.

Emilie Soulema was born in 190█
She did not survive Auschwit█

Sara Tassemka ("Boubi") was arrested
with her mother. In Les Tourelles,
she cut her hair short and wore shorts like a boy.
Neither survived Auschwitz.

A "rare beauty," Elise Mela was arrested with her mother on June 8 for not wearing their yellow stars. Elise and her mother died together on September 15, 1942, most likely selected for the gas. Father and husband Richard Mela survived.

After marching from Marble Arch to the German embassy in London, Claudette Bloch Kennedy, one of the few survivors of the third convoy, protests the resurgence of Nazism in Europe while wearing her Auschwitz prisoner uniform. (1960)

Another Empty Seat: Sonia Gutmann was ill the last time Raya Kagan saw her with Annette on August 18, 1942. She did not survive and, like so many others who died in Auschwitz, has no surviving photograph.

First postwar beach photo with the Zelman Circus sans Annette. From left to right, standing in the back are Michele and Guy with his arm around his mother, Kaila. Sitting are Cami; Maurice; and Guy's wife, Madeleine. Charles took the photo.

In 2020 we accompanied Michele on an emotional visit back to the Café de Flore, along with her twin daughters, Laurence (left) and Valerie (right). There we saw the banquette where Annette and Jean and their friends sat in 1941.

Michele Zelman married Gaston Kersz in 1951. Walking arm in arm into the synagogue with her father, she passed Dr. Hubert Jausion's wife (with glasses on). The Zelmans would not discover the Jausions' dark secret until years later

Michele's three daughters, Annette's nieces (from right to left, eldest to youngest): Jocelyn, Valerie, Laurence

On the Quai de l'Horloge, white buses were waiting. Different from the "salad baskets" the women had arrived in, these buses had seats and did not separate the prisoners from one another. At least they were afforded that bit of comfort.

Advancing south across the Seine to Boulevard Saint-Germain, where Annette had known so much happiness at the Café Flore, she must have peered out the window, longing to pass just one familiar face.

A breeze wafted off the Seine, a comforting urban briny smell, tinged with pine, cedar, and lavender. The morning hustle was in full swing. Shopkeepers swept sidewalks, unfurled their awnings, or pushed crates and carts along the road. Women carried baskets of wilted vegetables and a precious baguette.

The buses swung north onto the Îsle de la Cité and crossed back over the Seine at the Pont d'Arcole. As the Gothic arches of Notre Dame came into and then out of view, it began to rain.

Passing through Rue Oberkampf, a semi-industrial area where metal- and leatherworkers plied their trades, they climbed the hilltop neighborhood of the Belleville district, where the Zelmans had briefly lived.

About an hour later, the buses turned right onto Boulevard Mortier, not far from the famous Père Lachaise Cemetery, where the bones of the star-crossed lovers Abelard and Heloise are purported to lie buried. And so Annette and her companions arrived at Les Tourelles, a gated barrack of bleak four-story brick buildings, which are today the headquarters of Direction Générale de la Sécurité Extérieure, France's Secret Service.

Herded into an administrative building, the women were registered and searched. Valuables and weapons were confiscated, as was cash. Escorted across the prison yard to one of the four-story buildings, the new arrivals entered a large room full of their friends and cellmates, who they thought had been released already. The reveal was brutal.

The Depot was a one-way conduit to Les Tourelles, not freedom.

Among the women scanning the new arrivals' faces was a scowling Bella Lempert. Having arrived on April 15, eight weeks before Annette, Bella was already well ensconced in Les Tourelles and had a clique of friends. She looked at her former Café de Flore companion with all the friendliness of a cat cornering a bird. With a cool and knowing smile, Bella ruffled Annette's feathers. In one year, they had descended from bosom buddies at the heights of intellectual society and Latin Quarter chic to archenemies and prison mates.

"I won't be friends with her," Annette wrote Jean later.

For Raya Kagan, finding Bella Lempert at Les Tourelles was not an unpleasant surprise. The two women knew each other from the Sorbonne, where they had studied philosophy together. Paris was a small-town kind of city.

LES TOURELLES WAS "pretty good," Claudette Bloch recalls. Not only were the sleeping arrangements better, but the rooms were larger, and women could move about within the building to visit one another. "It was more like a strict school than a prison. There were about one hundred women. Divided into two. Those who had been arrested, like me, for nothing, so to speak, except being Jewish." There were also communists, "pullers" or pickpockets, black marketeers, and terrorists guilty of espionage, like cursing a German or falling in love with a gentile.

> Jean, my darling,
>
> I'm at Les Tourelles. They brought me here today. Try if you have time to come and see me. Visits are on Thursdays and Sundays for 1/4 to 3 hours. If you receive my message in time you can see me tomorrow. I hope so with all my heart. I am very sad, I don't know why. There are too many people here

and too many busy people. The Depot made me feel numb; here I feel even more confined. It would seem unbelievable to everyone here that Les Tourelles is a paradise compared to the Depot.

If you could come tomorrow (Thursday). I don't have any hope of getting out soon. I would like to see you tomorrow. Otherwise, it will be Sunday,

she warned.

A strict protocol required submitting a written request to the director of the prison before a prisoner could receive visitors. If someone came to see a prisoner who was not on the permission list, they were barred from entry. Annette immediately wrote the director, so that Jean could visit.

Well before 1:00 that Thursday afternoon, the women began assembling on the landing outside their rooms. No one was allowed down the stairs unless the guard called their name. They jostled one another with anticipation, waiting impatiently. Trying to see if Jean had gotten her message, Annette climbed onto the window ledge and clung to the railings with a few of the more agile young women. Because of the chestnut trees outside the front gate, it was impossible to see who was waiting in the queue, but those standing outside would press their faces between the bars of the fence and wave up at the windows, so their mothers, lovers, sisters, and friends might catch sight of them.

Annette fluttered with nervousness. The silhouette of a young man cast his shadow across the stairs.

"Zelman!" the guard bellowed.

Annette flew down the stairs and flung herself into Jean's arms. Pressing her body against his as if to merge into his being, she clung to him and he to her. The women who knew their story watched through tears as Annette and Jean walked into the dining area without taking their eyes away from each other. The bond between them was so powerful that it felt like an electric current of silent communion that no outside force could break.

Drifting upstairs from the refectory were the "bubbling sounds of joy" as families were reunited. Among them were Alice Courouble and her parents, and Claudia Bloch with her son. Caresses and kisses. Laughter and tears. Children's voices. In the visitation room, Claude sat with Bella. He and Jean were friends again, even if their girlfriends were not. Together the young men were fathoming the deep seas of the French legal system and trying to keep each other going while putting on brave faces for their lovers. Minutes ticked down the end of the hour. "Silence stifled reunions as the dread of separation approached," Alice Courouble recalls. "The threat of the gendarmes' whistle neared. …Furrowed brows and worried faces replaced joyous ones. Prisoners and visitors could no longer hide their concerns."

When the whistle blew, Annette clung to Jean and kissed him desperately, until the guards threatened to pry them apart. She wrapped her arms around the package he had brought her—foodstuffs, hairpins, a change of underwear, and the precious pages of his love letter, full of poetry, longing, and encouragement. They turned their heads to gaze into each other's eyes until the last moments of severed longing, then raced back into each other's arms for one last caress, in a pas de deux worthy of Fonteyn and Nureyev.

Upstairs, those who had been lucky enough to have visitors spread the contents of their parcels on their beds and doled out what they could share. Yellow star protester Jo Massey had homemade tarts from her mother that she shared with Bella and Tamara Isserlis. "Big Alice," the rotund aristocrat who had so amused everyone with her "shit me" statement over the weekend, "received suitcases from her husband filled to the brim—cooked meats (a whole kilo!), dozens of eggs, pounds of butter, all this at a time when everything was rationed and often unavailable, even on the black market." Alice Courouble was astonished by the feast, and the fact that Big Alice shared it with everyone. There was even honey and spiced bread.

For Annette Zelman, the few things that Jean had brought "were the only thing in the world that mattered for her. And kept her going," Raya observed. The women had begun to call Annette "the Bride." Everyone knew about her case and was "surprised and also indignant" that she should be treated so badly, "which is as it should be," she told Jean.

SEEING AND TOUCHING Jean transformed Annette's demeanor:

> Since yesterday I have been in a total euphoria and particularly useful to cheer up the others. There is also here in my cell a girl I knew because she worked at Eva Singer's house. Tell Eva that this girl has become huge and she only eats and sleeps. She is a disgrace to the community. Especially since she receives parcels that are absolutely gigantic to the point that the guy in charge of bringing them [up-stairs] can barely carry them and she doesn't share them with anyone. Amour, I don't care because I have more than enough. You are a love who thinks well of me and I adore you. As for my friends, Anne-Marie (the Surrealist) (the other one called Elise [Mela], it's lovely), she is more and more touching. It will be hard for me to leave all these girls when I'm released. Here each one tries to be kind and gentle because it is the only way to have a life. Our parcels are divided between two or three. Me, I have another close friend (Erna, a physical education teacher). That is to say that we eat together from her parcels or from mine.

When I go to bed, I feel you close to me, and I
moan softly to please you.

I love you so much my sweet little child. I kiss you!

T'Annette.

TO KEEP THE girls from languishing with the monotony and
ennui of prison life, Masha Lews had already reinstated the curriculum she started at the Depot and created a pop-up women's
college inside Les Tourelles. Their long days were full of Russian
and Yiddish language lessons, lectures by former professors,
and classes in art and singing. They taught one another songs
from their varied childhoods: Russian and Polish songs, German and even Algerian. Annette sang songs she had learned in
Nancy, including a song that Jean disliked because it was so violent and repetitious. "The story of the girl and the brother who
arrives, who arrives, who arrives and who throws three stab
wounds, stab wounds, stab wounds." Erna continued to lead the
gymnastic exercise classes she had held in the Depot, only now
recreation time took place under the leafy shade of a lone
centuries-old oak standing in the prison yard.

Here is the coltish companionship of young women—some
still teenagers, others new to womanhood, some mature—scam-
pering about in the grass. Tapping one another's heads, chasing
one another in circles. Playing games of round robin, chain of
checkers, king's knight. Leaping into the air for jumping jacks,
swinging their arms like helicopters. Running in place. Holding
their breasts to keep them from jiggling too madly. Laughing.
Squealing. Here are the delights of summer air. Of golden light
and soft breezes. Of a madeleine's crumbs in an empty teacup.

A FEW DAYS after their arrival, Anne-Marie asked Annette and
Raya if they would like to join her for a lecture by a marine
scientist in one of the "conference" rooms. Sitting among the
audience was Jo Massey, one of the yellow star protesters, who

immediately recognized Professor Claudette Bloch from her college classes. The biologist spoke about her research to her captive audience. Annette couldn't help but think that Jean would love meeting Claudette and learning more about marine science.

After the lecture, Annette turned to the very attractive young redhead, dressed in a silk evening dress and fur, who was sitting next to her. "What happened to you?" Alice Heni explained that she had gone into a bar to make a phone call when Captain Dannecker walked in and began demanding IDs. Huddling in the corner, Heni slipped the phone back onto the hook, but his eagle eyes had seen her. Jews were not allowed to make phone calls.

"You telephoned?" he barked. "Off to the concentration camp!"

She was still traipsing around in her evening gown because no one had yet brought her a change of clothes.

Dubbed with the nickname Couscous because she was an Algerian Jew, Heni began teaching belly dancing in the afternoons as part of their curriculum. Adorned with heavy rings and bangles that jingled as she undulated her hips and waist, she bent backward to touch her head to the floor while waving her arms above her lovely chest. It was Annette's favorite class.

Among the internees in the women's dormitory were at least two mother-and-daughter pairs: Elise and Franceska Mela and Hara and Sara Tassemka. Sara, who was lovingly referred to as Boubi, wore her hair cropped like a boy's and always wore shorts.

There was also a countess among the women. She was most likely Alice Cahn, who had been married to a member of the Gestapo for ten years when her husband denounced her for being Jewish. It is not clear what he did with their children. Anne-Marie and Annette were not alone in having been betrayed due to love.

The new routine at Tourelles included visits, a biweekly shower in the men's section, and Catholic communion on Sunday, Alice Courouble explained. "Each day also had its regular cadence. Roll call by the gendarmes, lunch in the refectory, a walk, supper at six o'clock, then roll call again," which was always at the foot of their beds. At least they had beds now, but the lack of hygiene continued. They were allowed to bathe, but their soap had been confiscated when they arrived, as had all sanitary napkins and washcloths. It is hard to comprehend why women were prevented from simple hygiene. "It was impossible to get warm water even for our intimate needs," Alice complained. In contrast, Annette thought it was divine to be allowed to shower twice a week, after the filth and stench of the Depot.

Laundry was another problem. Between menstruation and bad food, clean clothes were impossible. "Every day we had cabbage. For months, cabbage in the morning, then cabbage in the evening. This became a collective disgust," Alice Courouble says. Of course, cabbage causes gas and, when eaten in excess, bloating. With only one communal toilet downstairs, referred to as "the Village," their cruciferous diet caused serious problems. It was "our biggest torment," Courouble recalls. Meeting urgent needs was not always a matter of respect by the gendarmes, who had other things to do at night, like sleep, and another woman's urgency could impede your own. "As a result of the cabbage and the rotten bread, we often had to spend the whole day and night queuing up at the Village."

VISITATION DAYS WERE the one "great event of our reclusive lives," and preparations began the evening before, Alice Courouble writes. Those who had more than one outfit spent the evening helping one another decide what to wear. For the teenager, who was just expecting her parents, Alice watched the fluster of activity and joyful preparation with delight. They fussed over one another like schoolgirls at a slumber party. They dampened their tresses and helped each other roll their hair with pin curls or used socks to create long, soft waves.

The moment Annette awoke, she started getting ready for Jean. She washed her body with fresh water, laid her outfit out on her bed so the wrinkles might fall out. Slipping into fresh underwear, she buttoned the waist of her brown skirt and tucked in her blue blouse, before unpinning her hair, so a delicate wave undulated across her shoulders. She ended with a primp in the reflection of the window. There were no mirrors.

Big Alice—lovingly called that because of her rotundness and furs—would do her hair so tightly that she looked like "an English magistrate" and then dressed up "like a coquette" for her husband, donning "a summer frock decorated with multicolored flowers, white shoes, and a fox fur stole." The women loved Big Alice's eccentricities.

Incarcerated mothers, like Claudette Bloch, dressed for their children, trying to make sure that they looked happy and healthy, confident and secure. With curly black hair and brilliant dark eyes, like his mother, Claudette's little boy was a touching presence in the gallery and delighted everyone. Her tears fell only when she was alone again.

**THURSDAY, JUNE 18**

The line outside was thinner than on Sundays, but Jean and Claude were there. No one could help but watch the way Jean and Annette clung to each other, oblivious to the fact that their caresses and kisses were public. This devotion was so sincere, this separation so cruel, that everyone felt their pain.

Imbued not only by a sense of virtue but ethics, Annette had struggled with the concession required of them by the court. She—they—had been wronged. How could anyone be punished for love? Despite her misgivings, Annette had signed the petition promising not to marry Jean Jausion. So why hadn't Goublet secured her release?

*Any day now,* they assured each other. *Don't give up hope. We will get out of this and flee south to Sanary. We will climb the limestone bluffs of the Calanques and plunge into the sea. We will don masks and snorkels and visit the tiny anemone fields that cling to the rock and hold hands underwater, as the miniature yellow ones shaped like sunflowers and the bright purple so like blooming lavender undulate in the current, as above the sea, so below. We will be free. We will live as husband and wife, even if we cannot marry. Our love will vanquish all.* Longing to possess every molecule of her being, to slip her in his pocket and secret her away, Jean kissed her lips. Her cheeks. Her brow. "Write me," he whispered, slipping her his pages of love to feed her lonely nights without him. She slipped him her letter. Their hands intertwined like vines.

As the hour for departure neared, Annette felt her courage wane. She had seen him three times in the space of eight days. It was not enough. She could not let Jean go. The gendarmes tore them apart once again. Annette returned to her bed and collapsed into tears.

ANNETTE AND ALICE COUROUBLE were in the refectory, finishing their meager meal of cabbage à la water, when the guards bellowed, "Everyone outside!" Standing up warily, Annette headed into the courtyard to stand under the old oak.

Raya Kagan had been getting ready for bed and came outside in a dressing gown. No one hurried her or noticed her pause on the edge of the group. It was odd to her that Jewish women, as well as the yellow star protesters, were being forced to line up.

In front of them stood three uniformed SS and other German officers.

Heni hissed Dannecker's name under her breath.

Dannecker did not have the face of a human being. His eyes were cloaked, like he was wearing a mask of hatred for every woman standing in front of him.

"All Jews between eighteen and forty-two go to one side!" Dannecker barked. "Stand in a row!"

"The rest turn your backs!" the commandant shouted.

Standing on the edge of the group, Erna instinctively reached out and clasped Raya's hand. They were close to a narrow, unguarded passage between two buildings, which led to another courtyard, and a brick wall to freedom.

Erna looked at the passage and suggested in the barest of whispers that they escape. In a dressing gown, without ID or money? Raya didn't move. Erna did. She squeezed Raya's hand and slipped into the shadows.

The commandant ordered the rest of the women to return to their rooms.

Nerves jangling, Alice Courouble and her remaining roommates headed upstairs, where they were ordered to stand next to their beds.

"Not a cry, not a word, not a sign or a movement!" one of the guards yelled. "Remain standing in front of your beds. The first person to move will join the other women and leave with them! Understood?"

Leave? Where were they taking them? Alice looked at the empty beds, trying to count the absences, as the gendarmes marched past and formed a human barrier from one end of the room to the far wall, where there was a door. One of the guards opened the door. It was dim, but Alice could see mattresses on the floor, no chairs or beds.

The young Alice Courouble watched Annette and the column of women enter the room. "Our silence formed a kind of wall around them. All were calm. Here is Sonia, Raya, here is Elise, so blond, then a mother, then a daughter. We wept, while trying to stifle our sighs, not even daring to wipe away the tears."

The door slammed shut behind them and was locked. A gendarme turned to look at the remaining women standing in front of their beds, all gentile or older Jewish women, whom Dannecker had not selected. Lifting his chin with a jerk, he released them from their positions. He did not leave his post.

Inside the room, Annette and the others took measure of their predicament. Along with two small adjoining rooms, the space was worse than the Depot, if that was possible. Filthy straw mattresses strewn on the floor. Not a single chair or bench. Tins served as makeshift toilets. A few bottles of water. Raya went to the window just in time to see Erna throw her coat over the barbed wire and climb over the wall. She had a sinking feeling that she had made the wrong decision.

A gendarme came in and called out each woman's name, checking them off. When he came to Erna's name, the guard shouted it over and over in the dimming light. No one said a word. Annette searched the room for her athletic friend; she was gone. They were forbidden to speak to one another as the gendarme exited. Outside the escape alarms began to wail.

For the rest of the night, the gendarmes stomped across the creaking floorboards in their heavy boots, making regular bed checks with their flashlights.

When morning broke, Alice and the remaining women in the outer room took a chance to implore the nightguard to open the door. "Monsieur, monsieur! Be kind, monsieur. We know you are a good man." They had a plate of biscuits and a few tarts they wanted to give their friends. Their sisters. Their daughters. Food is love in any culture.

"I don't have the right. Orders are orders," he said.

Franceska Mela fell to her knees on the floor and pressed her mouth to the lock in the door. "My daughter, my little one, my Elise!"

On the other side, Elise's voice broke with tears. "Maman! Maman! My dearest."

"Mon Dieu, my daughter!" Franceska collapsed on the bed near the door. Her bitter moans were as low and sonorous as a man's.

The guard relented and opened the door a crack. The women poured forward, pressing against his arms. Alice could see their distraught and tearstained faces. There was Sonia, Raya, Ida, and Annette; the beautiful countess, and raven-haired Bella; Dvora, the ethnographer; Couscous, the belly dancer; the teenage girls, Elise and Boubi; the medical student, Tamara, and Professor Claudette Bloch, whose adorable son had delighted them so.

Alice Courouble was devastated by the scene inside the room. "In the bright light, there was a multitude of faces, some with red hair, some black, their mouths open, crying, begging, their hands held out in supplication. There were so many, it was impossible to know which face belonged to which hand. A tangle of human bodies, a chorus of supplication: 'Water! Call my mother! Pass my handbag, quick! Hurry!'"

Tears and hysteria. Weeping and moaning.

"*Ça suffit!* Enough!" The gendarme pushed them back and slammed the door shut.

LOCKED IN, THE women realized that if they spoke softly the guard couldn't hear them, and so they began to get to know one another. They were a mix of cultures, from Algeria, Egypt, Italy, Greece, Lithuania, and Romania, as well as Germany, Poland, Czechoslovakia, and Ukraine. Not everyone had been in the Depot together. Some of them, like Bella, had been in Les Tourelles for months. Two women, thirty-two-year-old Chaya Messer and forty-year-old Syma Sylberberg, had been incarcerated since 1941. A brilliant ethnographer, Dvora Lipskind, had studied ethnography with Professor Marcel Griaule of the

Musée de l'Homme, the same professor with whom Jean Rouch had studied. A few of the women spoke in Russian so the others could not eavesdrop. Bella and Annette kept their distance, but in such cramped quarters they could not avoid each other completely. Women paired up, like sisters. Raya and Sonia had been bonded since their arrest together. In the shadows, Annette and Ida leaned on each other for support. It was a forever four days. Isolated together, their moods rose and fell with exhaustion of the unknown. Hope and despair. Singing and grieving. Staring at the nothingness.

FRIDAY AND SATURDAY night came and went. There was no outside exercise. Alice Courouble "was queuing for the 'Village'" when she saw "three stinking tins full of excrement balanced on a plank, with bits of paper swimming in them." Her mind and heart reached out to their beautiful "countess"; she could feel the hurt and humiliation of her friend, so betrayed by her husband that her fate was to stand in that fetid chamber, defecating into a public pot. She couldn't shake the thought of her "enormous eyes and tears running down the countess' face."

Once per day, the sequestered women were allowed to go down to the basement for a cold bath, without soap or a sponge. Even that activity was heavily regulated. When Annette and the others were brought out to wash, the gendarme gave a piercing blow on his whistle to send the other female prisoners back to their rooms. Once inside, the guards locked the doors, "barricading them from their former roommates," Alice remembers. "This interdiction against seeing the [Jewish] girls made it seem as though they were already dead."

On Sunday morning a guard burst through the door and shouted a name. That woman scuffled to her feet and practically ran out of the room. "The rest of you should prepare for a journey."

The women begged to know where they were going. He would not say. The door latched behind him.

In a flurry of supposition, they tried to guess why she was suddenly free. They concluded that someone outside had paid off the guards with expensive bottles of wine

Was it that easy to buy freedom? Annette's family had hired an expensive attorney, but Goublet had done nothing but take their money. Why hadn't she and Jean thought of bribery? She sent him a psychic message and prayed he could hear her voice in his head.

The guards returned a little later, this time to search the women's belongings.

They warned the women that the Germans would take everything and to leave anything of value behind; they promised to give all valuables to their families.

So they were going to Germany! Finally, some idea of what was to befall them.

Not one of the women trusted the French any more than the Germans, though, and most refused to leave any items of value behind. The guards handed aluminum drinking cups out to the remaining sixty-eight women, and large yellow cloth stars, which they were to stitch over their hearts. Silence was no longer the order of the day. They worried out loud.

As visiting hours neared, Sunday became a torture. Annette paced the rooms. She had no way to tell Jean she was locked up. Bella was in a similar state of agitation. Torn from her baby son, Claudette fretted. Through the one small window, they struggled to see visitors walking or waiting outside, but the line was on the other side of the compound. All they could hope for was that their friends who could receive visitors would carry a message, so their loved ones would know something had happened. What had happened no one was sure.

———————

ON THE STREET outside nothing was normal. Tormented by the unknown, barred from entry, Jean and Claude must have fumed and argued with the guards. Why couldn't they see their girlfriends, their fiancées? Where were they? Were the young men full of bluster and bravado? Did they threaten to retaliate and drop the names of Dr. Hubert Jausion and Maître Goublet? Or did they pace and storm in futility, shouting the names of their hearts to the heavens?

—*Annette!*

—*Bella!*

Visitation hours passed with no one the wiser. Cut off from the love that had buoyed their spirits, Annette and Bella were shattered.

AS THE LIGHT outside faded into evening, the door opened. One of the gendarmes told the women to say their goodbyes to their friends and mothers, then stepped back. The women tried to maintain their composure. But it was a cacophony of voices. What do you say in the face of the unknown? Bon voyage? See you soon? No platitudes sufficed. The women in the dormitory tried to comfort the others as best they could, but there was an overriding sense of doom around them. Annette and the others begged their friends to get word out to their loved ones. We imagine their pleas:

—*Tell Jean what happened,* Annette must have begged. *His father is Dr. Hubert Jausion.*

—*Tell my son and mother-in-law,* Claudette would have asked.

—*Claude Croutelle, please get word to Claude Croutelle,* Bella surely pleaded through tears.

—*We will write,* they probably promised. *As soon as we arrive and know where we are, we will write.*

Hara cradled Boubi in her arms.

"That's it," the guard whispered, urging them to step back. "Hurry up."

Franceska Mela wrapped Elise in her arms and wept. "We'll see each other in the morning," she promised.

IT WAS A long night. To dispel the darkness descending upon their souls they sang. Not a single guard complained. When the singing paused, Annette surely serenaded them with Maurice's lament, "Ochi Cherny."

IN THE PREDAWN, headlights streamed across the courtyard of the compound, illuminating the ceiling and the watching faces of Alice Courouble and those sleeping outside of the locked chamber. The door opened like a wave of nausea.

Once again, Annette and the others walked silently through the room between rows of gendarmes, separating them from their friends. No last communication attempts were possible. This time they were leaving.

Ushered outside, they shivered in the chilly dawn. Lights came on inside the men's barracks as women on the other side of the compound pushed open the windows. The summer smell of moss and leaves, dew and dirt, filled the room. And then, through the graying light of dawn, the women heard the voices of their male compatriots singing the Marseillaise. The voices of their friends joined the men's voices.

Annette and the others took courage and raised their own voices in the French national anthem, until even the birds seemed to be singing along. Their voices resounded between the prison walls. Then there was a deep and somber quiet, as prisoners sent prayers to uncaring deities. "One gendarme was weeping," Claudette Bloch remembers.

The women locked inside the dormitory picked up the traditional song of "Auld Lang Syne," singing the French version, across the compound. "It's only au revoir, my brothers; it's only au revoir," their lilting voices drifted down from the open windows like a blessing upon their friends, and the men answered,

"It's only au revoir, my sisters; it's only au revoir." In unison, they sang, "Do we have to leave without hope, / Without hope of returning, / Do we have to leave without hope, / Of seeing each other someday?"

| | | | | |
|---|---|---|---|---|
| | | - 4 - | | I8 JUIN I942. |
| √4 | SYLBERBRG Syma Ketsnenica | I5.I2.I902 | polonaise | 8.II.4I |
| √5 | SYMCHOWIEZ née Rotenig Elsa Varsovie | I3.I.I92I | polonaise | 27.4.42 |
| √6 | SZEPSHAN Ryuak Bedow | I0.I.I9I2 | polonaise | I.I2.4I |
| √7 | SZUBERSKI née Sylberberg Eva Londres | 25.I0.I4 | belge | I.I2.4I |
| √8 | TASSEMKA Sara Hayange | 2I.2.2I | française | I7.6.42 |
| √9 | TRAISTER Fredel Berlin | 28.8.I922 | polonaise | I9.2.42 |
| 60 | WEILER née Ulmann Andrée Dijon | I2.I.I908 | française | 27.3.42 |
| 6I | WEIL Janine Paris 9º | 3.I2.I9I5 | français* | I7.6.42 |
| 62 | ZAJB née Berber Zysa Strynov | I5.2.I9I0 | polonaise | I7.6.42 |
| 63 | ZALKINOW Rachel Tours | I6.6.I9I8 | française | 26.3.42 |
| 64 | ZELKOWICZ Jacheta Belsin | II.6.I909 | polonaise | 26.3.42 |
| 65 | ZELMAN Annette Nancy | 6.I0.I92I | française | I0.6.42 |
| 66 | ZIMMERHANN Esther Paris XI | 24.8.I92I | française | I7.6.42 |
| 67 | ZLAMARBUN Yvonne Varin | I2.3.I909 | française | 5.5.42 |
| 68 | ZYCKIEWICZ Cécile Kolossen | 25.5.I9I4 | polonaise | 22.4.42 |

68

gi long - ≠ 29
+ 66

66

Blinded by tears, serenaded as if by angels above, the women hesitated.

The gendarmes were in a bad mood now. The prisoners had exposed them as collaborators in the crime that was about to occur. They shouted and hustled Annette and the others, pushing and shoving them onto the buses. The buses sputtered and spewed blue exhaust smoke into the crisp morning air. No sooner had they settled into seats than one of the guards stomped onto the bus, looked down at the list he was holding, and crossed two names off. "Lempert! Zimmerman!" he shouted. "Off!"

Twenty-one-year-old Esther Zimmerman stood up and pushed her way past the others with whom she had spent the past four days. Bella followed. Annette must have watched Bella's back as she exited the bus and wondered how she had managed to escape their fate. Wondered if Claude had saved her at the last minute. Wondered if Jean would be able to do the same for her. Wondered if she would ever see her nemesis again. As the buses crunched across the gravel courtyard and onto the road, the dawn chorus grew gradually fainter and then the world was empty.

—*Where are they taking us?* someone whispered.

A gendarme told them they were going to Drancy first.

Josette Delimal perked up. Her brothers were in Drancy, and she hoped she'd get to see them.

# The Third Convoy

HALF AN HOUR LATER, THE BUSES pulled up outside the
Bourget station in Drancy. Through the grimy bus windows
the women looked out at the drab surroundings. Gone, the
Latin Quarter and the Eiffel Tower, the beauty and the light.
Gone, Cami and Guy, Michele and darling Charles. Her
father's blue eyes. Her mother's steady comfort. Gone, Saint-
Germain-des-Prés and Sacré-Cœur. Gone, the Beaux-Arts
and Café de Flore. Here in the mean-spirited suburbs, men
with hard hearts read that vile rag *Je Suis Partout* and children
spat at Jews.

Arriving at Le Bourget, the women were ordered to disem-
bark and stand on the train platform. Looming over them was
the weathered Gothic form of the station building. On the
tracks was a long train of livestock wagons. Hundreds of men
with backpacks were being loaded into the cars. The men were
carrying blankets; the women had not been allowed to bring
theirs. All were wearing yellow stars with the inscription *Juif* on
their chests. On the outside of each livestock car, the words *8
chevaux* were stenciled. Eight horses.

The policemen separated the women into two wagons. Each was handed a baguette, some cheese, a slice of meat, a tin of sardines, and a tin of apricot conserve. They were still French, after all, even if they were Jewish. It would be uncivilized to send them off without a bit of *pain et fromage* and a little something sweet. They were also allowed to bring whatever food had been delivered during visitation.

One of the French guards explained that the two buckets in the car, especially the one full of water, should be carefully hoarded. The other one was empty, its designation clear. This was the only sign they had that they were going on a long journey. The doors to the wagons were left open while the men were loaded over the next couple of hours. When the guards were not looking, the women arranged themselves so they could be with their friends. Finally, the doors were pulled closed and sealed with an iron bar.

Fifteen hundred kilometers away, in Poland, the commandant of Auschwitz, Rudolf Höss, received notice that one thousand Jews with sixty-six women on board the train had left Le Bourget, Drancy, at 9:20 that morning.

"THE ATMOSPHERE IN this train you cannot imagine," Claudette Bloch says. The women who had been incarcerated for political reasons were more stalwart and calm. Others were shrieking hysterically. Some were semi-catatonic. The strongest sang for a while. Claudette found the singing unbearable.

It was one of those cloudless days when the sky seems infinite and war seems impossible. Rays of sunshine slipped through the barred windows, striping their faces and bodies. It was stifling hot, and someone realized that the chain was loose and they could slide the door back to get a breeze and look out from their moving cell. Quieter now, they watched the French countryside slip past.

The train was long and cumbersome on turns and moved laboriously under bridges and past forests. As the locomotive reduced speed to head into a tunnel, gunshots rang out. Grinding to a stop, the train rocked on its tracks. The weight of its cargo was so light—humans weighing less than cattle or horses—that they tumbled against one another. Sonia fainted. Then another girl dropped to the floor.

—*We need a doctor!* the women screamed. Outside, a German soldier barked orders. Soon a young French doctor, his head shaved in a militaristic crewcut, opened the padlock on their wagon and dislodged the iron bar. He set his medical bag inside and jumped in. The women crowded around him as he bent over Sonia and checked her eyes and pulse.

They wanted to know what had happened and learned that one of the men had leapt out of the train. He had been shot. The women stared at the doctor in disbelief. Did he know where they were being taken? Did he know what was going to happen to them? Their voices were many, but they all asked the same question.

The doctor was clearly wondering the same thing. He was courteous and typically French. Holding out his hand, he helped Sonia to her feet. Her skin seemed translucent in the cattle car. He tried to assure them. It would be something like expatriation, he tried to explain. Some of us were born in France, they told him. He was only a doctor. All he could do was encourage them to be brave. Then he jumped out of the cattle car with his bag and saluted.

German soldiers came down the tracks, shouting and slamming doors shut, tightening the chain locks so there was no way to open the doors even a crack. The heat of the day increased, and the air grew stifling inside the wagon. A minimal breeze crept through the tiny overhead window. The train chugged forward and shifted to another track. As the day lengthened and the towns slipped past, someone suggested that they write cards or letters with their families' addresses on them. Annette had paper and a pencil. Claudette used a nail file they hadn't taken away and dug through a burl in the side of the train until they had a hole big enough to throw their notes onto the tracks.

When the train paused at a station, soldiers came to empty the refuse bucket and refill the water. As the train started again, the women slipped their missives onto the tracks. They had courage now and wrote more notes. Maybe they would get picked up by a kind Frenchman and delivered by post. Every station where the transport slowed, the women sent notes out of their car. Claudette heard French being spoken outside as she threw her note:

"We are heading for an unknown destination, somewhere east...." she wrote. Her parents were addressed on the fold.

Amazingly, Claudette's parents received her note, which was probably passed on by one of the French railway workers, many of whom were sympathetic to the resistance. Annette's note to Jean was never recovered.

Night descended as they crossed the border into Germany. Curled up like kittens, they lay against one another for comfort and warmth. One of the women told Raya that she could lay her head on her shoulder. The woman murmured about her husband and son and how they had escaped to the Free Zone. She had been captured at the Demarcation Line and ended up on this train.

Night was long and uncomfortable. Glazed eyes shone like onyx in the murk. When dawn came, it cast a radiator grille of crimson light on disheveled hair and mascara-streaked faces. They had no more food. No water. Their stomachs ached. Their throats burned. To break up the monotony, they took turns watching out the little window. Beautiful fields of Saxony passed by. Towns of German inhabitants looked at the train with curiosity. The women were now in the land of their persecutors. Did the Germans they passed even know there were humans in the train's cattle cars?

Now when the refuse buckets were dumped, the water bucket was not refreshed. At one stop, a group of German Red Cross nurses was standing on the station platform, neatly dressed in their gray-and-white uniforms. The women shouted desperately in French and German, *Water! Water! Please! De l'eau, si'l vous plaît! Wasser, bitte!* Even the Red Cross ignored their pleas.

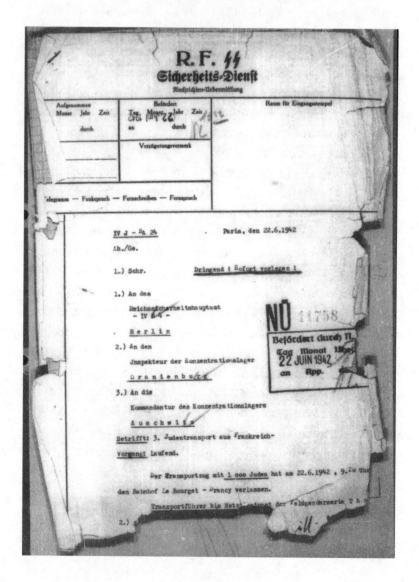

Darkness descended as a second night claimed their dreams.

Morning was muted with mist. They had no ersatz coffee or baguettes, no apricot preserves. But there was one ritual that the Frenchwomen could perform. They opened their handbags and tissued away the black circles under their eyes from too much crying. They reapplied mascara, powdered their noses, dappled color on their cheeks and lips, pursed their lips, and blotted them. No sense in looking pale as well as hungry. They brushed and pinned their hair. They had painted their nails in preparation for visitation days, and a few now fixed the chips, while the others chuckled. Nothing like a little freshen-up to make one feel like a woman again.

The train heaved and swayed through pine and birch forests. It passed factories and chimneys puffing black smoke into the skies of occupied Poland, now known as Greater Germany. "I think we are in Upper Silesia," Claudette said. "My husband was sent to a place called Auschwitz. If only I could get there."

Anya Litvac wondered what they would be doing when they arrived, wherever they were going. Other voices joined hers. Wondering. If the men worked in mines, would the women's jobs be to clean and cook? The doctor had suggested that they would remain together. They were relieved by that thought. If they could just stay together, it wouldn't be so bad.

# *Auschwitz*

OUTSIDE THE TINY TRAIN WINDOW WAS a stone-gray sky. Tattered villages speckled flat plains. The women longed to stretch their legs and breathe air that was free of the stench of excrement and urine sloshing on the floor.

The train slowed and swayed. Its human cargo bumped against one another. It was eleven in the morning when the brakes ground the train to a stop. Steam hissed. They had been traveling for two days.

Outside, German orders were being shouted. Dogs barked. Iron bars clanked as they were lifted off their locking cradles. Metal wheels ground as the sliding doors were pushed back. A rush of air. Not fresh. Stale. Heat. Sweat. The women struggled to maintain their balance. Their eyes squinted and blinked rapidly. Pain and light.

Faces, gaunt and pale, looked up at the new arrivals. Guard dogs, huge and dangerous, barked from the perimeter. The men in the neighboring cars clambered out of their wagons. They halted and stared at the scene around them.

Peering through the slats of the wagon, Annette and the others saw scarecrow-like creatures shoveling coal. Scrawny and sunburnt, with tufts of hair sprouting out of their heads and bald patches covered with blisters, they barely looked human.

This was not the Auschwitz of movies. No death gate towered over new arrivals; no chimney stacks belched smoke. Instead, the Frenchwomen beheld a drab landscape bereft of lush summer green. A featureless plain stretched in every direction. It should have been farmland for potatoes and other root vegetables. But there was no vegetation here. Russian POWs had eaten the grass. The French girls didn't know that kind of hunger yet.

"Out! Out! *Raus! Raus!*" The SS held their rifles, butts ready to pulp any disobedience. "Leave your bags!"

To leap out of the wagon was no easy feat. They suffered from *mal de debarquement* and nausea. With the floor beneath them no longer swaying, they stepped unsteadily forward. The railway embankment was steep to prevent flooding and there was no ramp. No assistance. One or two braver women jumped from the open wagon doors and then turned to help the next, who turned to help the next, until they were all on the ground. Smoothing their skirts, fixing their hair, they were slow and polite, unresponsive to the barking, the shouting, and the whips the SS were using on the French male prisoners. When one of the women stumbled against the wagon, an SS pointed to a truck and suggested if she was ill she could ride in the flatbed to camp.

The bizarre, scarecrow-like creatures began babbling in barely audible voices. "*Za každú cenu chod'.*" They looked like men, but their voices were high and sweet. When the Frenchwomen ignored them, one of the scarecrows spoke in German. "*Gehen Sie! Geyn Sie! Auf Jeden Fall Gehen!*" Quickly, the German speakers, perhaps Heni or Raya, translated for the others. They were being warned to walk. *Marchez!* No matter how tired or sick they felt. Walk!

Those who had headed toward the trucks turned back and joined the others. Their lives had just been saved from a trip to the only currently functioning gas chamber in camp.

"*STELLT EUCH IN Fünferreihen auf!* Line up in rows of five! *Schnell! Schnell!* Quick! Quick!" Orders were shouted in German. Slow to react, the confused Frenchwomen felt the stings of whips cracking across their shoulders.

"We have to line up, in rows of five," the German-speaking women translated. These were not French gendarmes; they were SS—hard-eyed and hardhearted—and looked at the new arrivals with hatred and disgust. At least in France they had still been treated as human beings. Now they weren't sure what they were. Annette and the others lined up in rows of five.

"*Abmarsch!* March out! *Raus!* Out!"

With guns aimed at their faces, nine hundred and thirty-three Frenchmen and sixty-six women began a dusty march across fallow fields, where stooped human beings tried to break up clods of hard-packed clay and push cartloads of dirt across dry-crusted earth. Despite being two days in a railway car, the Frenchwomen still looked French. Their hair was in place. Their lipstick was fresh. They carried the remaining traces of their femininity with lifted chins, walking past the mesmerized faces of dispirited, disheveled observers.

It was a mile's hike toward a tangle of barbed wire encircling brick buildings. At a guarded gate the men were separated from the women and taken beneath an iron archway of welded German words that made no sense to the French. Did the Frenchwomen who understood German whisper the meaning to the others or were they too afraid to speak? *Arbeit Macht Frei.* Work makes you free.

As they watched the men head down a dust-strewn road hemmed by brick buildings, they did not know that in less than eight weeks, only 186 of those men would still be alive. Not knowing that her own husband, Pierre Bloch, was already dead, Claudette looked for his beloved face amid the gaunt forms and striped uniforms of male prisoners watching them from behind barbed-wire fencing.

The women were taken around the perimeter of the men's camp, past what looked like an underground factory, with a smokestack rising out of the baked ground, and turned right. Here was the entrance to the women's camp.

Annette and the others remained in rows of five as the male SS handed them over to a homely middle-aged woman dressed in an SS uniform, skirt below the knees, sensible shoes, a capped head with tightly bunned hair. She accepted the detainees with a nod and instructed her crew of stern-eyed female *kapos* adorned with colored triangles on their chests—green, red, yellow—to take over.

Whips cracked. German orders, harsh and staccato, struck the Frenchwomen's ears. This foreign language didn't just confuse; it terrified. The gestures were obvious, though. *Go inside. That building. Through the doorway.* Annette's eyes darted toward Raya's, then Ida's. The women who spoke German told the others to merge into a single file. They pushed into line, clinging to one another's eyes when they couldn't cling to a friend's hand as they entered a claustrophobically small room. Under a low-beamed ceiling, amid washbasins and tables, they were told to strip.

—*Setzen Sie Ihr Geld und Wertvolles her!*

—*Entkleiden!*

Translations were simultaneous whispers. They had to leave their money and valuables here. They had to disrobe. That was the last straw. Tears ran. Black mascara streaked down carefully made-up cheeks.

Young adolescents wearing cotton trousers, their heads shaved and topped with colored caps, came up to the women and studied them as if they were not just from a foreign country but another planet. Had these boys never seen a mature woman before? But they weren't boys! Now that the Frenchwomen could see them close-up, they could see the scarecrows were in fact teenage girls without hair, skinny urchins with no semblance of breasts. Annette and the others removed their dresses, their slips, as these children swarmed around them. Wielding shears, they razed the Frenchwomen's beautifully coiffed hair from their heads and private parts, where only lovers or husbands had ventured. Annette and the others yelped and wept unabashedly as their hair was yanked from the roots by blunt shears. Elise's lush curls tumbled to the floor. Heni's red tresses draped her feet. Annette was no longer blond, no longer feminine.

The baritone laughter of braggarts outside caused the shaving to pause. Stomping into the room to gloat at the naked frailty of these new women, Commandant Rudolf Höss and a few of his SS cronies entered the processing chamber to peruse the latest shipment from France. Their very own strip show. Paris had finally come to Auschwitz.

The commandant and his SS men pointed at the women's pedicures and roared with laughter.

Covering her breasts with her hands, Alice Cahn sidled up to Höss and spoke softly in German. He waved her away but then gestured to the shaving girls to leave her hair. Everyone else was quickly shorn bald as a baby. If they hadn't watched the transformations themselves, they wouldn't have recognized one another afterward. The female *kapos* now shouted at them to climb into a large vat of cold, dirty water that was supposed to be for disinfecting. There was no soap. The water stung the girls' shaved and nicked flesh.

Dipped and shorn like sheep, they were sent to a final room where men's uniforms awaited. Bullet-hole-ridden Russian coats, bloodstained blouses, and trousers smeared with feces were tossed at the naked women, who clung to these filthy garments to avoid the prying eyes of Höss and his voyeurs. The

soldiers' uniforms were for big men, not petite women. Neck-
lines billowed off their narrow shoulders. Baggy and gaping,
the jackets hung off their bodies like sacks. They were given no
undergarments. No bras. No panties. No feminine hygiene products to stanch menstrual blood. No socks or hose. Footgear
called clappers were flat wooden slabs with a single leather
band over the toe or arch, made by men, for men. Not women's
delicate feet.

Annette and the others stumbled out of the gray room of
drab olive uniforms back into a bright summer day. On the *lagerstrasse,* or camp road, they were told to line up again and led
to a brick building where they were given red bowls of tepid, un-
identifiable soup. It smelled so rancid that most of them handed
the slop to the hungry scarecrow-girls, who greedily slurped it
up and then returned the bowls to their new owners.

—*Don't lose your bowl,* the bald teenage girls warned. *You'll
starve if you lose your bowl.*

Between the brick buildings were prefabricated Nissen huts.
The Frenchwomen were instructed to enter one of the huts,
where they found bunk beds lining the cramped quarters. Exhausted, Sonia crawled onto a bunk to rest. Ida and Annette
curled up on a neighboring shelf. No sooner had they lain their
heads down than Roza Zimmerspitz, the Slovak block elder in
charge, announced the new arrivals had to report outside. She
spoke orders in German.

At the administration office, the new arrivals were given or-
angey-yellow star badges and four-digit numbers. Moments
later, they were lined up in front of emaciated men in striped
uniforms and tattooed with sharp needles, which inserted blue-
black ink under the flesh of their left forearms. These numbers
supplanted their names. Henriette Bolotin was #8004; Claudette Bloch was #7963.

The rest of the afternoon, Annette and the others were
forced to carry large sacks of laundry up and down stairs and

across the camp. As the sun slanted toward the horizon, *kommandos* of the Slovak urchins began to arrive. The scarecrows and Frenchwomen lined up in rows of five. Waiting. Waiting. The *kapos* and SS women strutted up and down the rows. Counting. Counting.

The teenage girls around them were like something from a childhood nightmare—black and blue from beatings, swollen from starvation, shorn like lambs, their eyes as wary as a deer's. The Frenchwomen reached to squeeze each other's fingers or hands, seeking comfort and reassurance. Deep inside they knew that soon they would look exactly like the Slovak girls around them.

THE MOMENT THE prisoners were released from roll call, Annette and the others were surrounded by and bombarded with questions in German, Slovak, and Polish. Those were the only languages spoken in the women's camp in June of 1942.

What is happening in the world? Do people know about the calamity that has befallen us? They begged to know. Despite their desperate faces and starved bodies, their eyes lit up. The Frenchwomen were proof that the world still existed, proof that a war was being fought. Proof of life outside Auschwitz. "In our imagination, the term 'Frenchness' is associated with refined grace," Júlia Škodová, prisoner #1054, writes in her memoir. "These tiny cuties look extremely miserable. We pity them more than ourselves."

Without any language but French and some Yiddish, Annette floundered. Her love of words betrayed her without a multilingual hope of communication. Her other language, art, was not spoken here. And after the mutilation perpetrated upon them, they were rendered asexual and bereft of their feminine wiles.

A few of the Slovak girls had been to Paris. Their eyes teared at the thought of it. They had never thought women from other countries would come to Auschwitz. They thought the camp was only for Slovaks and Poles. Someone mentioned that they had heard there had been a couple of transports of Frenchmen, but most of them had already died. Claudette heard those words and wondered if their son would be an orphan soon.

The girls and women jostled in a line for bread, the only supper they would receive for the day. One of the Slovaks warned that they should save half for the morning, as they'd have nothing more to eat until the next evening.

A kind-faced blond Aryan, wearing a red triangle, watched the Frenchwomen with a certain sympathy in her eyes. The *kapo* introduced herself as Annie in heavily accented French, but at least she spoke French. Now it was their turn to ask questions:

*Where are we? What is this place? Where are our things? How long do we have to be here?* Annie Binder, whose kindness is recorded by many survivors of Auschwitz, spoke French with a German growl. She answered their questions while directing them to the Nissen hut where they would sleep. Another French-speaking Slovak, by the name of Lison, also introduced herself. She had come on the second Jewish transport, on March 28. Having lived in Paris for a couple of years before the war, Lison had recently been chosen for office work because she spoke German.

The Nissen hut quickly filled up with young women, climbing onto the hardwood shelves as if they were beds. They had no mattresses, sheets, or pillows. After twenty-four hours of no food or water, barely any food the day before, and only cabbage à la water in Les Tourelles, the Frenchwomen were already wasting away. It seemed like a month had passed since Erna snuck down the alleyway, and they were locked apart from Alice Courouble and their friends. It had been less than a week.

# Roll Call

FOUR A.M. *"RAUS! RAUS!"*

"Get up! Roll call!" Roza and Frida Zimmerspitz shouted as their other two sisters banged on the shelf beams with sticks, swatting the hips and shoulders of reluctant risers. The Frenchwomen were used to prison but not to this kind of cruel awakening in the predawn hours perpetrated by other prisoners, just like themselves. Teenage Slovak girls and young women scurried past. In Les Tourelles one toilet had served one hundred women. In Auschwitz over a thousand women per barrack were queuing and jostling for a chance to relieve themselves. "It was impossible to squeeze into the washroom," one survivor recalls. All this chaos took place in a foreign language Annette did not understand. She stuck close to Raya and Sonia. Ida never left her side.

At the door of the hut was a large cast-iron kettle, where two skin-headed girls ladled something that looked like tea into their red bowls. On first sip, there was a gag reflex. This was worse than the Viandox at the Depot. Not tea. Not coffee. Laced with bromide, this foul smelling liquid was used to sedate prisoners' libidos, reduce hunger, and cause brain fog. Thirst won over disgust, but newbies were rewarded with diarrhea after they drank it. Old-timers sipped their "tea," preparing themselves for what was to come. Thirst. Hunger. Exhaustion. Two to three hours of standing at attention for roll call in the dark until sunrise. Work.

Following the line of young female prisoners out to the *lagerstrasse*, the Frenchwomen blinked back at the searchlights that blazed overhead and cast light on the meshed shadows of the wire fences enclosing them. Some mornings charred bodies clung to the electric wires around the perimeter of camp.

Thousands of women dressed in their ill-fitting Russian uniforms streamed out of the surrounding brick barracks and Nissen huts to line up in orderly rows of five. On the other side of the fence, thousands of male prisoners dressed in striped uniforms were performing the same ritual. The Frenchwomen caught one another's eyes. Clung to the hands of their friends. *Quelle horreur. Mon dieu* [What a horror. My god], they whispered.

SS women paraded past the rows of female prisoners. Counting. Counting. Always counting. The countess stood beside the belly dancer, who stood behind the Surrealist artist and next to the biologist, in front of the beautiful terrorist who was next to the polyglot. The SS women stopped and looked searchingly at the Frenchwomen. As the commandant and his SS men had done before them, they pointed at the Frenchwomen's feet and laughed. Red nail polish peeked out from under the tattered men's pants. If Annette still had nail polish, she would paint every woman's toenails in the camp. She would give them manicures and red fingernails. Red, a political statement against oppression. If only they had lipstick, too.

ROLL CALL WAS dismissed with a whistle and shout. The Slovak girls, many barely sixteen or seventeen years old, rushed around in the mayhem.

—*What do we do?* the Frenchwomen asked one another.

*—Join a work detail. Be quick! Get a good one,* a Slovak girl mumbled in German as she fled past them toward her target group.

The Frenchwomen tried to scurry as well but did not know where to go or what "work" meant. Wanting to stay together, they moved as a unit toward where a group of prisoners were standing.

The *kapo* shouted and pushed them away. Her work detail was full already. They had to find an empty detail that could take all sixty-six of them. An impossible task.

Only one *kapo* had barely any prisoners lined up behind her. There was a reason for that.

Similar to Hester Prynne's scarlet letter, the system of triangles designated a prisoner's crime for all to see. Prostitutes wore black triangles. Political prisoners, meaning communists or anyone opposed to the Nazi regime, wore red. They were often the best *kapos* to work under. Ironically, murderers were given the life-affirming color of green. As *kapos*, these sociopaths had been given carte blanche to do what they liked to their charges. No one cared if they killed Jews. Auschwitz was a serial killer's idea of heaven. "The 'green' female prisoners were of a special sort," Commandant Höss divulges in his diary. "They far surpassed their male equivalents in toughness, squalor, vindictiveness and depravity."

"*Raus! Raus!*" the SS women and *kapos* yelled.

Every order is a shout and every shout means "*Now!*" There was no "later" or "in a little while." "*Schnell! Vite!* Hurry up!" Whips are out. The Frenchwomen separate, rushing to join the only *kapos* without workers lined up around them, the *kapos* wearing green triangles, already serving sentences for murder.

ORGANIZED INTO WORK details, thousands of women filed through the gate at the far end of the *lagerstrasse*. Then something strange happened; as they neared the guard gate, the girls quickly removed their footgear, flicking the "clappers" off their feet.

The SS guard bellowed at the Frenchwomen, *"Aus! Aus! Off! Off!"* One hand flew to his ear while the other waved his rifle in the air. He looked like a rabid dog. The *kapo* raised her stick, striking blows at any offending shoe wearers. Later they would learn the reason. The sound of the wood thwacking against the backs of their heels hurt the guard's ears. If they didn't remove their shoes, he would shoot them.

The Slovak girls had been marching out barefoot since March, even in the snow and ice.

An antiphonal chorus of far-off birds accompanied the seven thousand shuffling steps of tender female feet across baked ground, still warm from the previous day. In a few hours a harsh summer sun would beat down on their newly shaved heads. Winter-heavy wool and roughhewn cotton scratched flesh more familiar with silk lingerie. Raw and painful nipples scabbed without any bra to protect them. Sweat formed beneath sagging breasts. Between the wool and the bites of fleas or lice, which had already found homes in their underarms and crotches, everything itched. In a few days when their pubic hair began to grow back it would itch even more. It wasn't legal to scratch.

THE INHOSPITABLE SOIL around Auschwitz varied between two extremes: deep mud and hard clay. Basically, it was good for growing potatoes and making bricks. Some of the Frenchwomen marched to an area designated for brick making. The others were in a detail for *Planieerung,* or the leveling of ground. Both details would have to use tools to work. They stopped at a shed on the way; here the Slovak and Polish girls picked up the smallest tools. Spades disappeared first, then hoes and claw rakes. Shovels, mattocks, and pickaxes were left for the French.

In March 1942, when the first Jewish transport had arrived in Auschwitz, their main work had been demolishing Polish houses, confiscated by the Germans, who forced the residents to abandon their homes and farms without compensation. After those homes were blown up with dynamite, the teenage girls had been forced to dismantle them, pushing brick walls over and gathering the bricks below. It was a dangerous job that claimed many lives. Bricks fell on their heads. Walls collapsed on the unfortunate. They fell off rooftops. How many died we do not know. No one recorded the deaths of women or girls in the spring and summer of 1942. Only men's deaths were recorded.

The bricks from the demolished houses were used to build new prison blocks. Not only were more bricks needed but the land needed to be brought back to its original flatness. That meant that both work details were required to dig. The soil was as uneven and hard as miniature mountain ranges. Wielding a pickaxe was no job for a frail city girl, but that was what Claudette and the others ended up doing.

Standard army pickaxes in 1942 were no different from today's run-of-the-mill gardeners' pickaxes. They had a forged iron head with a pointed pick on one end and chisel on the other. The mattock has a pick and an adze or flattened horizontal end. Both are used for grubbing soil and had regulation wooden handles of 3 feet in length, which the toiler is supposed to swing overhead. The weight of the toiler, combined with the centrifugal force of the axe, loosens unforgiving soil. Mattocks, pickaxes, and spades had been widely used in World War I for trench warfare. But these were tools for strong men who were close to double the size of the mattock's handle and capable of swinging the 2.5-pound iron blade overhead without losing their footing—something neither Claudette, Annette, nor anyone else from Paris could do.

Most of the young women in camp were about 5 feet tall, give or take an inch or two. Annette was 5'4". The only way they could wield these tools was to hold the axes at their hips and strike the dirt. In a matter of minutes their soft hands were blistered. Sweat poured into their eyes. What was left of their mascara stung their eyes. Their throats grew parched. Their lips cracked in the dry heat.

Hours later, as the sun reached its zenith, men arrived carrying heavy metal kettles of standard Auschwitz fare: foul-tasting soup of sour cabbage and rotten horsemeat. If you were lucky, you got a piece of potato skin or meat. There was no water to drink. Sunburned. Sore. Palms sticky from broken blisters and blood. Nipples and crotches rubbed raw from the rough woolen uniforms. This was not the Vendanges of the previous year. This was brutal forced labor, ungodly work. There was no toilet break.

No sooner had the newcomers had their first taste of soup than the first cramps of diarrhea arrived. To ask to go to the latrine was reason for a beating. It only took one of them to discover that fact. Watching their compatriot get flogged was as painful as being struck themselves. But the rest held their guts or hid their shame as bowels loosened and let go.

The sadists in charge delighted in every opportunity to torment the Ooh La Las, be it with the back of a hand or the sting of a whip.

—*Soon les Parisiennes will be one woman less than their original number,* the *kapos* taunted.

—*Who will be first to die?*

HEAVE A PICKAXE over your head. Swing it down onto the hard soil. Over and over, thunking metal on the hard clay until clumps of dirt dislodge and luckier women with spades can lift those clods into wheelbarrows, which must then be pushed across the uneven land to cart away without the ease of temporary railway ties. The only relief is to push that wagon with others and hope that someone else will do the work while you rest your cramped hands; to lick the blood from your blisters before you pick up a shovel and unload the wagon onto a growing pile of hard clay and dirt, which another work detail will break apart and sift through wire mesh, so the dust can be mixed with water to build barracks to house more prisoners, more Slovak Jews, more French Jews, more unknown numbers to arrive.

It is an endless day. There is no siesta or moment of relief or rest. "We won't make it," one of them whispers.

Twelve hours pass. Only when the summer sun finally tilts toward the horizon do the *kapos* bark the call to line up in rows of five. The Frenchwomen can barely lift their sore and aching legs. They shuffle-march back to camp. Separated from one another since morning, they are so drastically transformed by the filth of sweat, dust, and hunger that they barely recognize one another. At the moment of dismissal they make a desperate dash for the Nissen hut where they grab a jug of water and take turns glugging it down. They collapse on the bunks that they now think of as beds.

"Roll call! Line up!" *kapos* shout. Block Elders bang on bunks, rousing the exhausted.

The women return to the *lagerstrasse* and line up on the dust-filled road, still thirsty. Still hungry. Still in need.

Despite the dehydration, bladders leak. Hunger gnaws. It is nearly dark when the *kapos* sputter, "*Hau ab!* Scram! Disappear!" and thousands of exhausted girls and women rush for the blocks, where each retrieves a piece of bread the size of a woman's hand. Supper. And claim a straw mattress to sleep on.

Day One over. Day Two a few hours away.

ON THE SECOND morning, the SS picked "200 female Slovak and French Jewish women" to be transferred to the Budy Penal Colony. There was no way those who were chosen could change places with others, and no chance to say goodbye.

At first glance this relocation might seem to be a positive move that could improve life expectancy. Auschwitz I was about to suffer a serious typhus epidemic that would kill SS and prisoners alike. Overcrowding is a friend to disease. The Budy sub-camp would separate the female prisoners from the disease, at least for a while. But the Budy *kapos* "were soulless and had no feelings whatsoever," Commandant Höss wrote in his postwar confession.

We do not know which of the Frenchwomen were transferred to Budy on June 25, but their work details included wading into the fishponds, scooping out muck, cutting back reeds with sickles, and digging drainage ditches to keep fresh water moving through the ponds for the livestock. However, a few months after their transfer, the "'greens' [*kapos* with green triangles serving murder sentences] knocked the French Jewesses about, tearing them to pieces, killing them with axes, and throttling them…" Commandant Höss wrote. Even he was disturbed by the massacre. "The Budy blood-bath is still before my eyes."

The remaining women of the third convoy headed out to the fields for a second day of pickaxes and digging. It was clear to Claudette Bloch that none of them could live very long under this regime. They rushed to work, rushed for food, and were afforded only minimal hours of sleep. Prison life was a brutal routine that ground down well-educated intellects, reducing them to basic survival. Philosophy student Raya Kagan was more familiar with analyzing Kant's *Critique of Pure Reason* or Descartes's famous dictum "*Je pense, donc je suis* [I think, therefore I am]." Now she was faced with a far more existential dilemma. The need for food.

One evening a Slovak friend pointed to some small boxes where she thought they might be able to hide their bread, so it wouldn't get stolen in the middle of the night by a starving block mate.

Prisoners generally did one of two things with their food. They devoured it immediately or ate half at night and saved half for the morning. Of course, if you saved it for the morning, you risked having your bread stolen while you slept. "You had to sleep with your bread in your hand, like a pillow," Judith Spielberger Mittleman, of the first Jewish transport to Auschwitz, recalls. "But we stole them from each other!" It was a Shakespearean "to be or not to be" question.

ON THE LAST day of June, the SS recorded that 2,289 Jewish men had been killed in the camp complexes. In addition, 1,203 Polish gentile prisoners had been shot or gassed, after being "declared incapable of working." There was no record of how many women died in the same period. But die they did. Annette, Ida, and Sonia soldiered on. Elise Mela, Sara Tassemka, and Tamara Isserlis were still alive. But "every day some of us had already died," Claudette states.

**SATURDAY, JULY 4**

The first selection of Jews was "performed on the train platform by the camp administration," was a transport from Slovakia. In what would become standard protocol they were separated from one another—men and boys to one side, women and girls to another. Then came a second winnowing by a reception committee made up of the camp doctors and high ranking SS, who evaluated the age and physical condition of the new arrivals. "Young, healthy and strong men [264 in this instance] and women [108] were led off to the camp. Old people, children, mothers with children, and pregnant women were told that they would be driven."

Full of hundreds of families, the trucks trundled off across the fields, past a large, mostly empty, fenced-in complex of rectangular buildings, to a "house" referred to as Bunker 2, which was newly operational. Under the shade of birch trees, the new arrivals climbed out of the flatbed trucks and were invited to enter a communal shower. This was not unusual in 1940s communities. Most towns had bathhouses where hot water was available for bathing. After a long train journey, who didn't want to get clean? The outer chamber was for disrobing. Women helped their children undress, hung their own dresses and underwear up on hooks, and entered the shower room.

This was the first mass gassing recorded immediately after the arrival of a Jewish transport. The number of men, women, and children executed was not recorded. However, on that same day a new *Kommando* was formed. Made up of Jewish men, the *Sonderkommando* was forced to dig a mass grave to bury the bodies of the Slovak Jews who had just been gassed. When the work was completed, these men were separated from the rest of the prison population and isolated from camp, so they could not report what they had witnessed.

# Operation Spring Breeze—
# Paris

*Something is brewing, something that will be a tragedy, maybe* the *tragedy.*

—HÉLÈNE BERR

**PARIS, THURSDAY, JULY 16**

BEGINNING AT FOUR O'CLOCK IN the morning, a group of some nine thousand Frenchmen, made up of police and members of the Parti Populaire Français (PPF), divided into 880 separate teams of six men each, began combing the city district by district for Jewish families. The Vichy authorities had identified Jewish households through mandatory registrations and restrictions on location passed that February.

It was six o'clock in the morning when fourteen-year-old Sarah Lichtsztejn-Montard and her mother were forcibly removed from their apartment and the door was taped shut. Outside, in the 20th arrondissement, hundreds of other Jews were herded out onto the streets. "Some people put their things in sheets, others carried children's mattresses. Parents were completely panic-stricken and looked haggard. They were holding little children, who were awake, crying, surrounded by policemen. It was a terrible shock."

Safe for the moment in her suburban, middle-class neighborhood, Hélène Berr wrote furiously in her diary, trying to record the horrors that friends reported to her. One woman had gone into hiding but returned to see the concierge of her building "just when the policeman was coming to get her....In Montmartre there were so many arrests that the streets were jammed. Faubourg Saint-Denis has nearly been emptied. Mothers have been separated from their children....One woman lost her mind and threw her four children out of the window." Another woman jumped herself. One family turned on the gas and died in their apartment together. It was almost as if they had foreseen the end planned for them and used the same means that the Nazis would have but were able to hold one another as they died by their own hands. Jewish districts like Boulevard de Strasbourg had become their own Masada.

Directed by Theodor Dannecker and carried out by his cronies—Darquier de Pellepoix, the new Commissioner of Jewish Affairs, and Rene Bousquet, secretary general of the French police—Operation Spring Breeze was the German code name for what is now known as the Vélodrome d'Hiver Roundup. A sports arena situated near the Tour Eiffel on Boulevard de Grenelle and Rue Nélaton, the Vélodrome had once hosted the original Tour de France on its indoor cycle track. It was a well-known venue for sporting events and had what Hemingway described as a "smoky light" in the late afternoons.

In 1940 the roof had been painted dark blue to help camouflage the complex from bombers and now "gave off a glaucous light," so "the people who sat there had a greenish look about them," the young Sarah recalled. From a fence at the top of the stadium, German soldiers looked down on the people milling below. Some lay or sat on the ground; many were screaming. One young Jewish survivor remembers that every once in a while he would "see something flying out over the balconies. I didn't realize it at the time but they were people…committing suicide, leaping to their deaths."

In the stifling July heat, people needed air, but all the windows had been secured, and no one could escape. Police were positioned at the entrance. Sarah Lichtsztejn-Montard's mother told her daughter that they had to escape. Sarah did so by walking backward through the crowds coming in; her mother linked up with a street sweeper and was escorted out on his arm. For those remaining inside, the Vélodrome became a holding cell with no ventilation, only five toilets, and little food and water. One person claimed that the Germans even cut off the water and gas mains.

Held for five days in such unhygienic and inhumane conditions, this mass of humanity was relieved only when overcrowded buses carted them off to Pithiviers and Beaune-la-Rolande in the Loiret, or to nearby Drancy, and over the next few weeks transported them on to Auschwitz. Of the nearly thirteen thousand Jews arrested, four thousand were children. Only a few survivors escaped because of a kind policeman turning a blind eye, or some other act of courage that allowed them to slip through Dannecker's net.

IN THE MIDST of this hailstorm of arrests throughout the city, Claude was left with no one at Les Tourelles to visit. Bella had once again disappeared. He was now in the same position as Jean had been a month earlier. He continued to make trips to Asnières, where he begged Bella's parents to flee to the Free Zone. They told Claude they would wait for Bella to return before they fled. One day, they were no longer there when he came to visit.

Driven by their desire to save Bella and Annette while lacking power to do so, Claude and Jean sat at the Café Flore, their nerves raw with the pain of loss. Returning to their respective apartments, they were confronted by the missing girls' clothes still hanging over a chair or wall hook, the fragrance of their perfume, combs with strands of hair still tangled in their teeth.

On Rue Laugier, Annette's pen and ink diary, *Les Solutions Tardives*, lay open on the table of Jean's studio apartment.

# Himmler Inspects Auschwitz

A CONVOY OF BLACK MERCEDES flying swastikas from the hoods rolled up in front of the *Arbeit Macht Frei* gate of Auschwitz I, and the glossy boots of the head of the SS, Reichsführer Heinrich Himmler himself, stepped onto the dusty camp road to be saluted by the guards on duty. This was his second visit to his favored camp. His first trip had arranged the creation of the women's camp, in preparation for the first official Jewish transport that arrived on the twenty-sixth of March with 999 Jewish teenage girls and young women from Slovakia.

The purpose of this midterm inspection was to further his operational interests in the eradication of European Jewry and oversee the latest architectural designs and expansion plans for the ultimate death camp. Himmler wanted to make sure that all the elements were working together as efforts were made to ramp up the efficiency of the killing machine.

His visit would last two days. The itinerary was packed full, marked by the arrival of the first two transports from Holland. The SS had been practicing the selection of Jews on the train ramp for two weeks and performed the protocol for the

*Reichsführer's* approval. No doubt Himmler participated in his own thumb waving—to the left, to the right, gas or hard labor. Of the 2,000 Jews from Westerbork and Amersfoort, "1,251 men and 300 women were registered in camp." The other 449 men, women, and children were taken to the gas chamber, where Himmler witnessed their disrobing and gassing and assessed the *Sonderkommandos'* clearing of the gas chamber. Due to the difficulty of burying so many bodies in a short period of time, he encouraged Commandant Höss to get the crematoriums up and running. After a busy day, a reception was held in the *Reichsführer's* honor.

THE NEXT MORNING, as usual, Annette and the rest of the women lined up for roll call. Nothing else would be usual about that day. As the scorching sun rose, they were not released from the lines.

"Take off your uniforms!" SS women and *kapos* ordered the thousands of female prisoners standing at attention.

Their first reaction was disbelief. They were standing outside. In front of the men's camp. Easy targets for ogling eyes. For those already beaten into submission over the past four months, this latest order was no more shocking than any other. The new arrivals were aghast. Slowly, the women unbuttoned the jackets or blouses of the Russian prisoners and unknotted the ropes holding up the trousers until they were naked to the elements. The sun beat down on the delicate skin of their scalps, the backs of their necks, their breasts, shoulders, and pale buttocks. Most of the girls kept their eyes on their feet. Like mice in an experiment, they had no choice but to do what they were told. The heat was stifling.

Around midmorning the camp gate opened and an entourage of SS, flanking their *Reichsführer,* escorted Himmler into the women's section of the main camp. With the SS men strode SS-Oberaufseherin Johanna Langefeld. Dwarfed by the men,

Langefeld was nevertheless an imposing woman with white hair. In a rare photograph of the elusive SS woman, taken in Ravensbrück a year or so earlier, Langefeld's hair was dark. Auschwitz had made her hair prematurely white.

Having done her best to organize the women's camp, Langefeld was working under the difficult circumstances of not realizing the true scope of the Final Solution. A devout Lutheran and Nazi, she was not soft on Jews, but neither was she comfortable with mass murder. Perhaps because of that moral reluctance, Commandant Höss undermined her authority as director of the women's camp.

As Himmler strode in a parade of SS, he appraised the women *kapos* first, before turning his attention to his female Jewish prisoners. The SS woman barked orders, forcing the young women to march past Himmler, Höss, and the other SS men and women, while holding out their arms in a Hitler salute. It is hard to imagine strong-willed and independent Parisiennes succumbing to such debasement without defiance, but hunger and exhaustion can coerce the strongest spirit. And the "tea" served every morning had already befuddled their brains. Barefoot, bare-legged, their most private parts exposed, Annette and her friends trudged past the SS. The red varnish on their toes was still chipping away.

THE NEXT MORNING, fourteen of the women from the third convoy were told to line up in front of the SS offices rather than march out to work. They stood outside in a windstorm for three hours. Occasionally SS peered out of the windows at them. When Langefeld finally came outside, she interrogated the Frenchwomen and chose Henriette Bolotin; Heni (Couscous); Leonore Kaufman; and Raya Kagan for office work. All four of the women spoke German.

They were given blue-and-white-striped dresses, black aprons, and white caps to adorn their recently shorn heads.

Luxury of luxuries, they were also given underwear, leggings, socks, and shoes.

For the others, the routine of hard labor continued.

Now at 4:00 A.M., Annette dashed for the toilet, then tea. She lined up for roll call and stood beside Ida and Sonia, Tamara, Claudette and Anya. Released from roll call, in the hope of escaping the "greens" they had suffered that first day, they ran to the "safer" *kapos* wearing red or black triangles. They watched strangers and friends get hit, beaten to death, and shot for the slightest infraction. They lined up for a thirty-minute lunchtime break of rotten soup, worked or were killed working, marched back to camp, stood in line for roll call, stood in line for bread, went to sleep. At 4:00 A.M. they were awakened and it all began again.

"The French women were unable to grasp the filth, the cold [and heat] and the terrible hunger here. The clogs fell off their feet," Júlia Škodová recalls.

Who ever would have thought that the Depot would be missed? What they wouldn't have done for some Viandox broth and a day of sitting in a cell with only the briefest bit of exercise outside. The monotony of prison life was enough to drive anyone to throw themself on the constantly buzzing electric fence around the perimeter. Its siren call promised relief from pain and hunger, debasement and sorrow. To resist this dark night of the soul took willpower and faith that there was something beyond the fences worth living for. Annette clung to her love for Jean. Someday, they would be together again.

**TUESDAY, JULY 21**

Three days after Himmler departed Auschwitz, Bella arrived on the seventh convoy from France. Of the 879 men and 121 women on her transport, 375 men were immediately

selected to die in the gas chambers; all of the women were registered in camp. Prisoners' tattoos designated their arrival date
and the transport they arrived on. Bella's four-digit tattoo
would have been between 9703 and 9823. With Bella on that
transport was Elise Mela's mother, Franceska, and Syma
Berger's little sister, fifteen-year-old Hélène. Syma had been on
the third convoy with Annette. Her sister would last but one
month in Birkenau. There is no death date for Syma, but she
did not survive.

Of the nine thousand women who had arrived in Auschwitz
since March, those still alive were crammed into a space that
should have held no more than five thousand. "People were living outside," Linda Reich Breder, #1173, says. "It was so
crowded that we had to step over people who were sitting outside." It wasn't easy to recognize friends or enemies among the
new arrivals. Shorn of her inky black mane of hair, Bella was
just a slightly tall young woman with creamy skin. Gone were
her signature sunglasses and Zazou suits. Instead, she was
dressed in an ill-fitting Russian uniform. In the leveling field of
Auschwitz, Annette and Bella were no longer rivals. They had
only one common enemy—death.

# Birkenau

**THURSDAY, AUGUST 6**

IN THE THREE WEEKS AFTER Bella's arrival, over six thousand additional women arrived in Auschwitz—from France, Holland, Slovakia, and Poland. Without death records it is hard to know how many women were actually in the overcrowded camp, but they were being numbered in the fifteen thousands. Male prisoners were being numbered in the forty thousands. Annette and Bella's four-digit tattoos were a thing of the past. New arrivals were forced to sleep outside on the ground. Lining up for morning roll call was almost impossible.

At 4:00 A.M. August 6 that all changed. Instead of being released for work details, a portion of the women in camp were syphoned off from the rest and marched out the gate. Friends and cousins were suddenly separated. Panicked, they called out to one another and risked a baton beating to remain together.

—*Where are they taking them? Where are they going?* the girls asked the *kapos*.

The answer was unhelpful.

—*To another camp.*

Five kilometers away, across hard-packed, dust-choked roads, girls and women marched past fields where Poles had once grown potatoes and cabbage. Not a solitary tree or plant survived on this vast plain. Marshaled behind more electric fences, the first group of women was assigned to single-story, brick blocks—bricks taken from the houses the Slovak girls had demolished or made with their bare hands. The blocks had dirt floors and wooden planks stacked in three tiers. These sleeping shelves were sandwiched between brick walls the size of a horse stall. There were no mattresses. It was claustrophobic, stuffy, and unhygienic.

In Auschwitz I there had been toilets inside the barrack. In Birkenau one communal latrine stood at the far end of the camp. This excrement ditch was covered by cement cast molds with large holes for toilet seats. Some of the holes were so large that small women fell through and drowned in the sewage below. Beside the latrine was another trough, supposedly for washing, but the water was polluted. Soap was handed out once every few months and only lasted a few days.

Birkenau swallowed up the thousands of women who filed through its gates. A new set of rules was shouted overhead: anyone caught outside their block after dark would be shot. *What if I have to go to the bathroom? What if I am sick?* This was not the kind of place where you could raise your hand for clarification. Gunshots and beatings were the only way questions were answered.

Of the surviving Frenchwomen of the third convoy, we know that Annette, Ida, Sonia, Claudette, and Elise were in the same block together. In the "new" blocks, they inherited threadbare blankets, worn out from the twenty thousand Russian POWs who had been worked to death or executed over the past two years. It was those men's uniforms the girls were wearing.

That first day in Birkenau, the girls cleaned the newly constructed sleeping quarters, tried to find where their friends' blocks were located, and wandered around this new hell in stunned silence. The next morning a few thousand more women and girls arrived from the "mother camp"—Auschwitz I—to Birkenau. Relocating all the women would take four days. By August 10, Auschwitz I was a men's camp again. The wall dividing the men's and women's camps was torn down.

IN BIRKENAU THE women's uniforms were changed to striped dresses. No longer having to suffer the scratch of wool on their bare skin was only a temporary relief. They were still not given underwear and with no easy access to toilets, soiling oneself was impossible to avoid. Transports delivered thousands of Jews to Auschwitz/Birkenau. New arrivals suffered so terribly from dysentery that diarrhea streamed down their legs. The SS took particular delight in observing the elegant city girls from Paris and Amsterdam and speculating how long they would last.

"The Slovaks and Poles were tough," Linda Reich Breeder explains in her USC Shoah testimony. "They were more familiar with the dehumanization. The Dutch and French girls, coming from cities, did not have the physical strength of peasant farm girls. The shock of Auschwitz hit every woman who arrived, but to have suffered years of anti-Semitism as the Poles [and Slovaks] had, we were more prepared."

Annette and the first Frenchwomen faded into the masses now arriving daily from all over Europe. The sixty-six girls of the third convoy were vanishing fast. Their red nail polish was gone.

WHILE THERE EXIST no accurate death records for women who arrived in early 1942, we know those records once existed because of the secretarial pool, where death cards were filled out and filed. Júlia Škodová and Lenka Hertzka worked with Raya Kagan recording prisoners' deaths. These secretaries were more than just witnesses to the mass extermination as the murder machine accelerated toward its Final Solution. They were its record keepers.

In 1961 Raya Kagan gave essential evidence against Adolf Eichmann in a particularly damning witness account of her time in Auschwitz. Hers was a gruesome job, seeing the names of friends and family crossing her desk. Prisoners who were injected with phenol were listed as "deceased." Those who were selected to die in the gas: "deceased." In January 1945, as the Russian front crested the snowy horizon after the liberation of Kraków, that evidence and most of the death records for women were destroyed in bonfires, making the eyewitness testimony of Raya Kagan all the more important.

THE FIRST "SELECTION" of female prisoners was on August 15. The word "selection" meant nothing that morning. By the end of the day it was the new horror everyone dreaded. Lining up for roll call, the women stood in their lines of five waiting for the SS and *kapos* to count them and release them for work. Instead, they were ordered to remove their clothing and stand naked, just as they had when Reichsführer Himmler had inspected the camp a month before. Slowly, their lines moved forward, until those in the back rows could see their fellow inmates stepping in front of a group of SS men, one at a time, being directed to the left or the right.

Dr. Manci Schwalbová (from the second transport, #2675) witnessed "the first ruthless, terrible selection [of female prisoners]." Prior to that, condemned prisoners were only taken to the gas chambers from Schonungsblock, the so-called prisoner hospital. Despite the purposeful lack of women's death records, Dr. Schwalbová reports: "Eighty percent [of the girls in camp] were sentenced to death, in addition to all older women in the camp." There is no formal statement in the archival record of the first selection of women prisoners in

Birkenau, but we know the date from the few surviving death records that reveal twenty Slovak girls from the first transport died on that day.

Of the Frenchwomen, we know that Annette, Ida, Sonia, Heni (Couscous), Sara (Boubi), Tamara, Dvora, and Claudette survived the first selection. So did Bella Lempert.

By now, seventeen transports from France had arrived in Auschwitz and a little over 3,200 Frenchwomen had been admitted into camp. In all, over fifteen thousand had been tattooed and registered. Of course, not all those fifteen thousand-plus were still alive.

The women's camp in Birkenau was divided by a camp road, or *lagerstrasse*. Jews working hard labor lived on one side in brick blocks that were more like stables than housing. Gentile prisoners and Jewish functionaries, who worked in the SS staff quarters, lived on the other side of the camp road in green barracks. They were given more bread—two pieces per day rather than one—and their soup was not the dreck doled out to the slave labor force. Every morning, the secretaries and other functionaries marched five kilometers back to Auschwitz I, where they worked in the large three-story white building that made up SS staff quarters.

Other work details returned to the "mother camp" each evening, as well. One was a sorting detail called the white kerchiefs and red kerchiefs because the girls and young women were allowed to wear scarves on their heads that identified them. The sorting detail was one of the best details to get work in. Not only was it under a roof, rather than outside in the elements, but the job entailed standing and sorting underwear, sock, and blouses, instead of thrusting pickaxes into unforgiving soil. Often food tidbits could be found in the pockets of coats. Daring girls knew how to slip morsels into their mouths or pockets to eat later, after roll call. Anyone caught eating was beaten, but starvation was more powerful than fear. Eventually the sorting detail would be referred to as "Kanada," a tribute to that distant country and dream of freedom.

The sorting detail was full of Slovak girls who knew each other from home and had been in Auschwitz since the beginning. The Frenchwomen had little hope of forming friendships with these teenage old-timers. Necessities like shoes or a luxury like underwear required something to trade, as well as having the contacts to trade with. If you couldn't communicate with someone, how could you trade? Yiddish was the one common language, but many urban dwellers had never learned that language.

Then there was the question, what did you trade? Bread was worth gold, but it was also the only staple. To give up your slice of bread meant you might be too weak to work the next day and that meant you might get beaten or, worse, injured, and that could mean death. Every action could be fatal. Every inaction could be fatal. That was the Auschwitz dilemma.

## MONDAY, AUGUST 17

Annie Binder, known as the "kind *kapo*" by many female prisoners, let Claudette and Raya know that their fellow deportee Anya Litvac was in the prison hospital. A few days later Anya was dead. With a heavy heart Raya marched back into camp as the last rays of scarlet swept a dramatic sky. Across the *lagerstrasse*, she saw Ida and Annette.

"Sisters!" Annette called out. From the mass of women, Ida, Sonia, and Elise stepped out. Dirty and exhausted from hard labor, they embraced their friend.

Sister, they named her. Sisters they were.

"You know," Annette began. Tears poured from her eyes. "It's not the pain [of hunger]....That's okay."

Raya choked back her own tears, struggling to speak through the tight-fisted sorrow squeezing her throat. Ida sobbed on Raya's shoulder and clung to her dear friend. Ida's bones protruded from beneath her prison clothes. Sonia was ill, her beauty stolen by the filth and starvation, disease and brutal labor. She looked terrible. Elise looked haggard and worn-out.

Why hadn't Annette gotten a job in the seamstress detail or in the laundry? She certainly had the training and skill for such work, but would she have left Elise, Ida, and Sonia behind? Annette never compromised.

OVER NINETEEN THOUSAND women were in Birkenau by the middle of August. This fresh labor force had not been beaten and starved to uselessness. They weren't too ill to work. Every selection took another one or two thousand worn-out girls and women to the gas chamber to make room for new arrivals.

At roll call one morning, SS Elizabeth Hasse pointed to the smoke billowing from the now functioning crematorium on the edge of Birkenau. In that smoke were Anya and so many others. "Look." Hasse pointed at the smoke and hissed at Rena Kornreich, #1716, "The French models are burning."

## TUESDAY, AUGUST 18

After work Raya hurried across the *lagerstrasse* to where Annette was already waiting at the door. She had soup in her red bowl for Sonia. It was still warm. "Come in." Annette beckoned. "All our friends are here." She followed Annette into another world—a world of the doomed.

The block was somber. It did not matter that an August sun angled its harsh light and caused long shadows at the end of the day. No light found its way inside. No air. The bricks of the outer walls baked all day in the August sun, creating a kind of kiln. Exhausted bodies lay on inhospitable shelves. Sweat pervaded the heavy air.

Like the big sister she was, Annette had been caring for and comforting her friends since they arrived. Sharing what little she had, she supported her *lager* sisters, and her spirit shone amid the dark foreboding of their lives.

Sonia was feverish and thirsty. Raya wanted to help her dear friend and asked Annette to join her. The two women hurried outside. Desperate to find something, Raya burst through the door of her block. It was no mystery what was going to happen if she didn't help. *Water for Sonia. Something. Anything for Sonia.* The morning kettle of tea sat in the shadows. She dipped a gourd into the stale liquid and hurried back across the *lagerstrasse* to where Annette waited, hands open.

As they rushed back to the block where Sonia and Ida were waiting, the *kapos* bellowed: "*Appell!* Roll call!" Up and down the camp, prisoners hurriedly shuffled out of their blocks to line up. Raya was always on the lookout for her friends from the third convoy, but it wasn't easy to find people among the many thousands of sunburnt faces. When she walked past a row of women already lined up for roll call, she stopped. Ruth and Nadine were standing before her. She ran to embrace them and was immediately surrounded by a group of women whose hair had just been shorn—pale figures from the third transport from Malines, Belgium.

Hearing French being spoken lit the hearts of the new arrivals, and they barraged the old-timers with questions and begged for help. Helpless herself, Raya was about to turn away when she felt the eyes of a woman deep back in the row looking intently at her. It was almost impossible to recognize the "slightly tall young woman with creamy skin" from the Sorbonne. Bella Lempert was in Auschwitz. She had arrived on the seventh transport on July 21. It had taken almost a month for them to see each other. The old friends clung to each other. The *kapos* shouted, "*Appell!* Roll call!"

The *lagerstrasse* was a sea of thousands of women lining up to be counted. Raya didn't have time to get back into the block and see Sonia. She had to get back to her own roll call. Outside of Block 2, Annette traded Raya's red bowl for the gourd. Amid the bedlam, the two friends clung together holding in their arms the gift of day-old tea between them.

"*Merci,*" Annette whispered before being swallowed up in the sea of lost women.

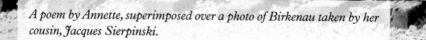

Je fais avec tous les regards
une couronne tiède
je la pose sur ton front
et t'admire de loin.
Je versifie les fleurs
et harmonise le ciel
et je peins sur tes lèvres
la forme de mes lèvres.
je danse avec les arbres
à un rythme de folle.
et je repose en ta bouche
mon haleine épuisée.

*A poem by Annette, superimposed over a photo of Birkenau taken by her cousin, Jacques Sierpinski.*

# ACT FOUR

## 1944–45

# The Empty Seat

*Sadness*
*Shelters a flat ice floe calm*
*Suffers from sentimental bigamy*
*Rancid star of death*
*Star rot*
*Spider stars*
*Baritone without seams on the back*
*I'm hungry*
*Homeless cruelty*
*Possesses my languid soul*
                    —JEAN JAUSION

THE CAFÉ FLORE BECAME SOMBER when Claude and Jean came in and sat at their old table. From across the room Simone de Beauvoir felt their loss and suffered with them. "The way these gay and beautiful girls simply vanished into the blue, without a word, was terrifying enough in itself. Jausion and his friends still came to the Flore..." she wrote. "But there was no mark on the red banquette to indicate the empty place at their side. This was what seemed the most unbearable thing about any absence to me: that it was, precisely, a nothingness. Yet the faces of Bella and the blond Czech girl were never erased from my memory: they symbolized millions of others besides."

Among the thousands of French deportees who would not return to Paris or the Café de Flore was Man Ray's friend, the designer and model Sonia Mossé. She had avoided the Vélo-drome roundup that July, but by February 1943 she and her sister were denounced for refusing to wear the yellow star "and frequenting public places." Simone de Beauvoir thought Sonia was probably the "victim of another woman's jealousy." Typical of Sonia, she managed to send a message via the Flore asking for someone to bring her a sweater and silk stockings to Drancy, where she was interned. Frenchwomen always want to be well-dressed. Even in prison.

On March 25, 1943, Sonia and her sister were sent from Drancy to the Sobibor concentration camp, near the Polish city of Lublin. Sobibor was already liquidating its prisoners, using a different execution style than the Zyklon B that was used in Auschwitz. Instead, carbon monoxide was pumped into a tube. Women had their heads shaved just prior to execution. Varying death dates are reported in multiple sources for Sonia, but none suggest that she survived the month of March. The beautiful lesbian model, who had inspired the masters of Sur-realism, supped with Picasso and Dora Maar, and been loved by so many, died in brutal agony.

JEAN TRIED TO keep busy, writing articles for the periodical *Le Rouge et le Bleu* and working on his novel, *The Man Who Walks in the City*. But his heart was not in it. In August, he wrote to Guy in Limoges:

> My dear Guy, still no news of Annette. I did every-
> thing humanly possible to get her out of there and
> to find out something. I found the door closed and
> their faces closed. People are afraid to act. I drag my

carcass. Work doesn't distract me. I am horribly unhappy, and it doesn't get any better. I buy books. I'm
making a library for Annette when she comes home.
I also prepare a pleasant environment for her. As
soon as I have some money, I will buy furniture for
a nice apartment. But all this without her is nothing.
If you only knew how much I love her, my dear Guy.
You don't tell me if you received the wicker trunk? I
will not send the TSF through the zone. It's very
fragile. I will come to the Free Zone at Christmas
and take the opportunity to bring it [his radio] then.
I kiss you, my dear Guy. Your unhappy brother, Jean.

Equally distraught, Claude took a different tack than Jean to assuage his broken heart. Like Georges Hugnet, he was already
forging identity papers, but his shock and anger at Bella's arrest
made him want to take more decisive action to defeat the Germans. He became a courier for the Maquis, the guerilla fighters
in the French resistance. It was a dangerous job. Carrying messages back and forth between Paris, Nice, and Marseilles, he
risked arrest and even execution. Without Bella, he had nothing
more to lose. Like all resistance operatives, he was given an alias
and a new identity: Claude Loursais. It would remain his name
for the rest of his life.

As LEAVES LITTERED the streets of Paris and the days shortened,
Jean decided to leave for Limoges earlier than he had planned.
He missed the Zelmans and thought being with them would
bring Annette closer, if only in spirit. He carried the radio and
the beginning of his novel with him.

The Zelman circus was more sedate than usual. Very little
was said about Annette, but her spirit hung over the family's
gatherings like a mist that would not clear. In the mornings,
Jean worked on his novel and then delivered his pages to his
amanuensis, Michele. Typing Jean's handwritten pages on an

old typewriter someone had lent her made Michele feel a little bit closer to her sister. Jean adored Michele and doted on her. It only took a little prodding for him to recount his underwater adventures or wax eloquent on the nudist colony off the coast of Sanary. Someday, she would visit Jean and Annette there, though she wasn't so sure about the nude part.

A photograph taken at the house in Limoges shows Jean Jausion standing next to Kaila and Cami. Dressed as ever in a suit and tie, with a crisply laundered handkerchief in his breast pocket, Jean leans against a weathered shutter with his left hand in his pocket. Shadows from an overhanging vine partially obscure his face. Kaila smiles under a cap. Her short-cropped hair is graying. Cami looks full of teenage impishness, as though he knows the punch line to a joke. He usually did.

Jean's novel was a bleak, metaphorical meditation on his own experience of loss, with several elements from his and Annette's story transported into the narrative. Set in the cobbled streets and smoke-filled bars of the port of Le Havre, against a gritty, social-realist backdrop, it recounted a love triangle among a brutal, hard-drinking port worker, who has lost his job, his unfaithful wife, Madeleine, and his friend, a lonely man significantly named Jean, who is having an affair with Madeleine. The husband is killed in mysterious circumstances when he falls into a dry dock. Madeleine denounces her lover in an anonymous letter and then commits suicide by opening the gas tap of the stove. While the police investigate, the fictional Jean remains alone in the city, walking the streets, thinking of his deceased lover and the meaning of existence.

The Zelmans had become Jean's surrogate family. He even began to learn Yiddish with Maurice. When he was not writing, his days were filled with Cami's shenanigans or hanging out with Charles and Guy. They were truly brothers now. Charles had recovered his sense of humor and tried to make Jean laugh by dressing up as a clown and dragging him out to cafés.

Annette never wrote.

All they knew was that she was somewhere in Eastern Europe, perhaps working in a German factory. Charles hoped the work would not be as unforgiving as the Vendanges. Jean promised them that as soon as he could find a way to travel east, he would set off to find her. The absence of her laugh and bright voice hung over the family as the days shortened and darkness fell ever more completely over France.

Michele was typing Jean's manuscript when news broke that the Germans had occupied the Free Zone. Two days earlier, on November 8, Allied troops had landed in North Africa, threatening France's Mediterranean coast, which was part of the Free Zone. The Germans couldn't allow the Allies a foothold in Europe, so they eradicated the Demarcation Line. France was immediately divided between Italy and Germany, with a border running roughly from Marseilles northward toward Lyons and then northeast to Switzerland. Grenoble and Provence fell under Italian jurisdiction. Everything west of that newly created border was under German control. The Vichy government remained in place but had no power. Its strings were pulled by the puppet masters of the Third Reich.

Limoges quickly began to echo with the stomp of jackboots and the rumbling diesel of military vehicles. As the year drew to a close, snow blanketed the fields around the town and settled on the stone mitre of the statue of Saint Michael in the Place Saint-Michel.

As he did every year, Maurice made everyone winter coats. Jean's was a brown leather bomber jacket with a fleece-lined collar, better known as a "Canadian." Soon after the New Year, Jean decided to return to Paris. His novel was almost done and he had work to do. "I have to go back," he told Kaila and Maurice. He kissed Michele on the cheeks and embraced his brothers. In her letters, Annette had written: "I am your wife." They didn't need a ceremony to conclude their commitment. He carried her words in his heart. Taking his beloved in-laws' hands, he looked into their eyes. "I am going to search for Annette. And I will find her."

# Dispersal

AFTER JEAN'S DEPARTURE, THE ZELMANS' situation became increasingly precarious. The Germans were ramping up activities against the Jewish population of Limoges, so the family moved to an apartment in the center of the city. As they had done in Bordeaux, they hoped to blend in with the one hundred thousand other urban inhabitants.

The apartment was cramped. Along with the six Zelmans, their cousin, Ginette Wilf, and her sixteen-year-old brother, Max, were taking refuge. Three years older than Michele, Ginette had been so traumatized by the arrest and deportation of her parents in Bordeaux that she rarely spoke. When Kaila discovered different-colored inks, paper, and stamps hidden under her bed, she went ballistic. Quiet Ginette was forging identity documents for a local resistance cell.

"What are you doing, endangering us all?" Kaila yelled. "You cannot do that here!" Ginette left the apartment and formally joined the resistance. Her bravery did not go unnoticed by the Zelman boys.

The Gestapo intensified its roundups of Jews once again, using the lists that had been compiled with the help of the

Vichy authorities. They searched addresses where Jewish families lived or had lived. Questioned neighbors and shopkeepers, café owners and waiters. Informants were everywhere.

The Zelmans rarely went out, but with every passing week their situation became more untenable. It was time to act. Guy decided to escape through the Pyrenees to Spain and, he hoped, to catch a ship to Casablanca, where de Gaulle's forces were assembling. He made it across the Pyrenees but was captured in Spain and interned in a camp. He told the authorities that he was a French Canadian and wanted to return to Canada. They didn't believe him and shipped him out to Casablanca. As usual, Guy got what he wanted!

Charles was the next to leave. He crossed the Pyrenees successfully, avoided capture, and also shipped out to Casablanca. There, by a twist of fate, he found his brother in the warrens of the Kasbah. "Charles walked around the streets of Casablanca using the family whistle," Michele says with a laugh and then performs the whistle that they used all their lives to find each other. "That is how he found Guy!"

The brothers reported for duty together. When asked what he wanted to do for the war effort, Guy said, "I want to join the air force." He was sent to the United States to train with the USAAF, as part of the Free French army in America. Charles was sent to England to train with the RAF as a rear gunner.

Cami was also eager to do his part, but the border crossings across the Pyrenees were becoming too dangerous. So, like Ginette, Cami joined the resistance.

Limoges and the surrounding region of Limousin were a center of operations for the Maquis. The group was active in helping Jewish children escape. Its well-organized efforts were funded by Œuvres de Secours aux Enfants (OSE), which relied largely on money raised by American Jews. Each resistance network had key local personnel, who were aware of the lay of the land and what towns and crossings to avoid.

Ernest Balthazard, aka Saint-André, was one of the men who helped children escape into Switzerland from the village of Annemasse, on the Swiss border. He ran a reception center for "holiday camps" that served as a front for *passeurs,* men and women from the underground who secretly shepherded Jewish children across the frontier. But first the children had to get to the border.

It was a dangerous job. If caught, *passeurs* could be executed, but that threat did not prevent a host of brave young men and women from trying to save Jewish children from the Final Solution. When Mila Racine, one of the female *passeurs,* was caught twenty meters from the frontier and sent to Ravensbrück, another young woman, twenty-two-year-old Marianne Cohn (aka Marie Colin), stepped up as a *passeur* for children.

Notices were posted in local synagogues, informing parents whom to contact if they wanted their children to leave France. Kaila was terrified to lose sight of another daughter, but when harmonica playing Camille Goldman abruptly disappeared, she became more afraid of keeping Michele in France. "My mother came to me and said, you have to go," Michele recalls. "She put me on the list that was circulated at our school. It was meant to be children aged eight to fourteen. I was fifteen, but I lied and said I was fourteen."

The Zelmans were told to bring Michele to the synagogue wearing nothing but the clothes on her back. Michele was used to this protocol by now, but it was early spring and still could be cold at night. To keep her warm, Kaila dressed her in layers. "I had two skirts on. A blouse, sweater, and coat. None of us had bags or suitcases, because that would have aroused suspicion."

From the synagogue, they walked to the train station. "Our cover story was that we were going on a school trip to a holiday camp. There were ten other children. Nearly all the rest were little ones, much younger than me. So, Marianne (Marie Colin) said to me: 'As you're older, you will help me with the younger ones.'"

It was Michele's turn to be the big sister and she took to the role: "I wasn't afraid because I had to look after the younger children and have courage for them."

To avoid suspicion, they took a circuitous route toward Toulouse. They used regular passenger trains on local rails. Smaller stations were used to avoid detection. Michele does not remember the full route. If anyone asked them, "we had to say we were going on holiday. Even the little ones said that."

One little girl kept blurting, "We're going to Switzerland!" blithely unaware that they were trying to be unobtrusive. Thanks to Annette and Charles's babysitting expertise, Michele had an arsenal of games in her head and came up with original Zelman amusements to entertain the children, as well as the old standards of I Spy and Twenty Questions. Her games calmed everyone's nerves. It wasn't until they were I-spying mountains that Michele knew that their journey was ending.

ANNEMASSE WAS A beautiful village, with plane trees lining the sidewalks and a tram running up and down the streets. Everything was clean and orderly, displaying the best of French and Swiss influences. But 150 SS were stationed at the border. Regular sweeps of local hotels, the train station, and the surrounding forests were conducted. Posters warned of severe punishment for crossing the border. Tanks patrolled the roads and barbed-wire fences protected the frontier. But the town also had a network of resistants and sympathizers. Even the mayor of Annemasse was friendly to the resistance and had managed to save a few of the children who had been arrested with Mila Racine.

DISEMBARKING FROM THE train, Michele and the other children maintained their appearance of going on holiday by singing the Vichy national anthem. Marianne told them to lift up their chins and march while they sang. Swinging her arms in time with the song, Michele led the parade of proud little Vichy French children down the street, singing at the top of their lungs, if a little off-key.

Saint-André met them with food and drinks at the reception center and let them play games and run around, just as children should who were going on holiday. At "about nine P.M., we started out for the forest," Michele remembers.

"We have to be quiet now," Marianne warned. Then they took one another's hands and walked under the dark canopy of trees. Michele felt the first squeeze of her hand a few feet into the woods. Then she felt a second. Marianne was sending little pulsing squeezes down the line of hands of her charges. It felt like a game, but it helped them all feel safe and assured.

In the dark, another *passeur* appeared and whispered, "Send the children."

Marie let go of the hand she was holding and whispered farewell. The new *passeur* took Marie's place and led the children deeper into the forest. "We walked for about an hour," says Michele. Single file. Holding hands.

Finally, the *passeur* gestured for Michele to come forward. "Only fifty meters to go," he explained in a whisper. "When you get to the barbed-wire fence, climb over, and help the little ones cross. The village lies straight ahead. Walk there." She paused and looked at him. "Go." He pointed and turned to leave them on their own.

She headed into the dark, hoping not to get lost. Michele helped the children over the fence. On the other side was a steep gully. Michele clambered down into it, reached behind her to help the littlest down the embankment, and then had to push each one up the other side. Once the children were safe above her, she climbed up the embankment to join them. She had just crested the ridge when she saw two soldiers standing in front of them.

Panicked, Michele grabbed the nearest children by the hand and tried to flee.

"*Komm! Komm! Ici Schweiz!*" the soldiers shouted. "Come! Come! This is Switzerland!"

She paused. Her heart raced. The children clung to her.

"*Suisse?*" she asked in French.

"*Ja! Ja! Schweiz!*" the men answered in Swiss German.

Finally, they were safe.

The children were taken to a camp, where "we had to register our names, ages, and addresses," and were given warm milk before being bedded down for a well-deserved sleep. In the morning, "we were divided up and put into different buildings according to our gender and age." Michele was in a dorm for teenage girls, all of whom had crossed the frontier and left their families behind.

IT IS ESTIMATED that between February 1943 and April 1944, one thousand Jewish children were smuggled across the Swiss border. Michele and her group were lucky to have arrived when they did, on April 29, 1944. One month later, Marianne Cohn was arrested with almost thirty children. They were imprisoned in the Gestapo's Prison du Pax, which was known as one of the worst prisons in Haute-Savoie. The children were questioned, but not one ever admitted to being Jewish, even though they were beaten.

"Every morning, Marianne was taken away for questioning, returning each evening with a red and swollen face, having been subjected to hot and cold baths, amongst other forms of torture," recalls Renee Bornstein, née Koenig, who was among the children who were caught. "Her face became more deformed as time went on. Marianne never faltered or relented. She had the opportunity to leave us, to save her own life, and to reveal our true identity, but she did neither." Jean Deffaugt, the mayor of Annemasse, tried to help Marianne, but she forbade him from divulging her secret status in case it endangered the children. Marianne died of her injuries on July 7, 1944. Two weeks later, the mayor was able to free the children and get them safely to Switzerland.

MICHELE ADJUSTED TO her new life in Switzerland. As one of the older children, she helped with administration, washed the corridors, and cleaned up after meals, duties that helped her feel normal and a part of the community. The house where she slept included "girls from all over Europe, who were my age. Many of them didn't even know where their parents were." Michele had that bit of comfort. At least she thought she did.

In fact, Kaila and Maurice had fled their apartment in Limoges and taken refuge in a barn loft in the countryside. The farmers hiding the Zelmans must have known Maurice. Michele guesses that they were promised free trousers for life.

It was a challenge to raise that much food on the farm without the authorities being alerted. The adults depended on the children to carry it off. One of the children would go to the market in town and barter for food, perhaps in exchange for some Zelman clothing, and return to the loft. The adults rarely went outside, except at night, and always with extreme caution. There was no revelry, but there was storytelling, along with Maurice's Russian songs, sung sotto voce. "They were not unhappy," says Michele. "They were there with other family members and everybody adored my father."

They hid for nine months.

# To the Barricades!

*On the water, whitish, the fog was beginning to lift.*
*There was not a breath of wind. The foghorn began to*
*blow at regular intervals.*

—JEAN JAUSION

THE PEOPLE OF FRANCE HAD been robbed of their most essential freedoms: to eat, live, love, and speak their minds. Informers and denouncers had infected the cafés and streets of Paris. But the evil spell that had been cast over the city was finally being lifted. By 1944, the French resistance had an estimated one hundred thousand members who were actively blowing up railway lines and attacking German forces.

At the Café Flore, patrons who had secreted radios away continue to share the latest developments from the BBC's daily broadcasts. The Germans were also coming under increasing pressure as Allied troops landed at the Anzio beachhead in Italy. American and British airplanes pounded German cities from the air. There were rumors of an Allied invasion. Paris held her breath.

**TUESDAY, JUNE 6, 1944—D-DAY**

In the largest amphibious landing ever undertaken, more than seven thousand naval vessels landed on the beaches of Normandy with 150,000 British, Canadian, and American troops. It was the first time the Allies had a military presence in northern Europe since the evacuation at Dunkirk in 1940, and it would mark a decisive turning point in the war.

In Paris, Simone de Beauvoir celebrated D-Day at a fiesta hosted by Charles Dullin, the director of the Théâtre de la Cité. Partying with her were Sartre and other artists and writers, including novelist Albert Camus, who danced a paso doble. "We played records, we danced, we drank and soon we were wandering all over the place as usual," she recalled.

Liberation was still months away, but it was only a matter of time. By mid-August, the Allied forces were advancing on the capital and the Germans' viselike grip on Paris loosened. On August 17, the Wehrmacht began its withdrawal from the city. Convoys of tanks and trucks headed east. As a group of bathers on the Seine watched the panzers pass, a mood of jubilation prevailed. "Are they finally leaving?" the student Yves Caszaux wrote in his diary. "We dare not believe it is true. We have been waiting for this moment for so long, dreaming of it."

On the outskirts of Paris, the sadistic commandant of Drancy, Alois Brunner, deserted his post with one last trainload of prisoners.

That night the Vichy government also fled.

In the morning, crowds defiantly sang the Marseillaise on the streets of Paris. Striking postal workers marched down Rue de Rivoli, shouting, "Bread! Bread!" On the Champs-Élysées, where Hitler had strutted triumphantly in June 1940, defeated German soldiers fled from the approaching Allied armies. Finally, it was the French uncorking bottles of champagne, not Germans.

Plenty of Wehrmacht troops remained in the capital and the fighting continued. During the night of August 18, Free French resistance forces seized the *mairie*, a stone's throw from Jean's studio. Jean had always avowed a pacifist philosophy. Poets were not meant to take up arms. But now was not the time for aesthetic debates. It was a time to strike a blow against the forces of evil that had taken Annette from him. The next morning, French tricolor flags were hoisted back up on public buildings and the swastika flags were ripped down. Jean joined the hundreds of resistants, journalists, and other Parisians marching to occupy the Prefecture.

The fighters were a motley crew. Sporting armbands and French berets, they hung confiscated German guns from their belt loops. Weapons ranged from submachine guns and hand grenades to broom handles and everything in between.

At the Prefecture, Jean and his compatriots were plunged into a fierce battle, firing on German tanks from the parapets of the Quai Saint-Michel. Fighting erupted all over the city, as the remaining German forces tried to maintain cruel control of the city. Simone de Beauvoir saw twenty German soldiers fire into the crowds on Rue de Seine, hitting two women. After they were hauled away on stretchers, a concierge came out onto the street with a bucket and a mop to clean up the blood. "The sound of revolution is in the air," one witness wrote. "Dogs are barking, whistles blowing everywhere."

In the mayhem at the Prefecture, Jean was captured. It's not clear how or what happened next, but it is likely that Dr. Jausion went into overdrive, leveraging his many influential contacts among the Occupation forces to release his son. According to Michele Kersz, he offered himself in Jean's place. Whatever the case, Jean was quickly released and soon helping build the barricade on Boulevard Saint-Michel, not far from the Café de Flore.

"The whole neighborhood is here," poet Camille Villain wrote in his diary. "Determined men in shirtsleeves rip up the paving stones, women and children form a human chain to pass the stones along....I can see local shopkeepers, office workers, laborers, the boss of a biscuit factory, women of all classes." The crowds felled plane trees and dragged furniture, scrap metal, burned-out cars, and even kitchen stoves to erect rubble mounds of more than six hundred barricades across Paris.

On the night of August 22, the French resistance broadcast a call to arms on the radio every fifteen minutes, ending with the Marseillaise. At the Palais Royal, where horses from the Houcke circus were temporarily stabled, French policemen fired at a passing German convoy. The Germans retaliated by sending in two Tiger tanks, an armored car, and two unmanned Goliath tanks, which detonated seventy-five kilos of high explosive. Smoke billowed from the roof and windows. As the performers led the horses outside, one horse was hit by bullets and collapsed on Avenue Montaigne. Starving Parisians rushed over and chopped it into pieces until all that remained, according to a witness, was "a pile of innards and a head with milky, staring eyes."

The city was in an uproar for days, but finally on August 24 Notre Dame's bells spoke after four years of silence. Across the city, "churches rang out, drowning the sound of cannon fire. Liberty and France are beginning again," the essayist and resister Jean Guéhenno penned in his diary.

Two days later, under clear skies and hot sunshine, General Charles de Gaulle led the Free French forces into the city with General Jacques-Philippe Leclerc's French Armored Division and the U.S. Fourth Infantry Division.

———

A VAST SEA of humanity, twenty people deep, lined the Champs-Élysées. Girls wore red, white, and blue dresses and flowers in their hair; children were hoisted on their fathers' shoulders; people hung out of windows and climbed on rooftops to watch the tricolor flag hoisted atop the Eiffel Tower, replacing the Reich's detested swastika. At the Arc de Triomphe, General de Gaulle stood on a podium and saluted the crowds. Waves of voices rose into the air as the Marseillaise rippled down the Champs-Élysées. "The kissing and shouting and autographing were almost overwhelming," wrote veteran American journalist Ernie Pyle. "The pandemonium of a free and loveable Paris reigned again."

The long nightmare of occupation had ended. Paris was free.

Twelve days later, Jean set off to find Annette.

# The Road to Lorraine

*There was no grave, no body, not even so much as a*
*bone. It was a though nothing had happened, abso-*
*lutely nothing.*

—SIMONE DE BEAUVOIR

**WEDNESDAY, SEPTEMBER 6**

"ALL FIRE, ALL FLAME, COVERED with revolvers and armbands," that was how Jean Jausion was dressed. Standing
outside of Bucher's gallery, his dear friend Georges Hugnet
wished Jean luck in finding Annette. Leaning "on the side of a
car, his hair blowing in strands over his forehead," Jean Jausion
radiated confidence and determination, Hugnet recalled.

Little remained of the smartly dressed son of a bourgeois
doctor. Jean was now a full-fledged resistance fighter and war
correspondent, having landed a position with the newspaper
*Franc-Tireur*, the newspaper of the resistance. His hair was now
shaggy and long. He sported a blond beard and the "Canadian"
brown leather jerkin that Maurice had made him in 1942.
Standing next to two other resistance fighters and a female re-

338

porter, Jean waved goodbye to Hugnet with "a huge smile on his face."

To identify the group as press, the reporters stuck a *Franc-Tireur* placard on the back of their black Citroën 11. Patton's Third Army had already marched out of Paris. The Citroën headed down the old Route National 4, via the Marne Valley and the medieval town of Provins, in hot pursuit. Today, traveling east toward Metz and the German border via the same route—without tanks and trucks clogging the way, or on dirt or gravel roads—would take five and a half hours, give or take a picnic on the lake at Château de Baye, or stopping for a champagne tasting in Épernay. In 1944 it was a long, hard slog.

Caterpillar tracks creased the verges, proof that Patton's troops had stormed along the route a few days earlier, in their lightning run chasing the retreating German troops. Roads were clogged with backed-up U.S. Army vehicles. Out-of-gas trucks were pushed to the sides of the road. Petrol was in chronically short supply.

Much of the country lay in ruins. In towns and villages, survivors picked through the rubble of their shattered homes. Freshly dug graves of German soldiers were marked by rows of helmets. In Provins, a line of burned-out German vehicles had been abandoned after being hit by American fighter planes; their contents—documents, ammunition boxes, guns—had been looted by Free French fighters. German soldiers were reported to be "fighting among themselves for transport.... Bicycles, horses, carts, anything that moves or can move, is at a premium." A sense of euphoria and relief prevailed. Joyous locals greeted Allied soldiers and reporters alike, handing out previously hidden stores of cognac, fresh flowers, and even fresher kisses. France was French again.

The countryside around Provins is as flat as a billiard table. Church steeples pierce the horizon; farms with red tiled roofs stand among the fields. It was the start of the wheat and hay harvest. Horse-drawn wagons vied for passage with tanks and trucks, trying to get stores into barns before rain ruined the crop. As the weather deteriorated, heavy downpours turned the dirt roads and ditches into quagmires. Past the eleventh-century Église Saint-Ayoul, the Citroën's tires drummed against the cobbles of the main street, which today is called the Voie de la Liberté. Provins had been a center of the resistance, and the cellars of some houses had been used to hide both Maquis fighters and Jews. A network of tunnels connected some houses to provide escape into the forest.

AFTER CLIMBING A steep hill from outside the town, the travelers might have seen lush green meadows open up again if it hadn't been for residual tank tracks chewing up the landscape. American GIs crouched exhausted at the sides of the road, rifles over their shoulders, smoking Lucky Strikes or Camels. Some trudged forward, carrying their kit bags, many with masks over their faces, as armored cars, gun carriages, and tanks headed east. Vast piles of gasoline tanks and oil drums dotted the fields. "My men can eat their belts," Patton is reported to have shouted in exasperation. "But my tanks have gotta have gas!"

The Citroën 11 in which Jean and his group were traveling had a spacious trunk, as well as front-wheel drive. Mud was not an issue. They probably carried an extra can of petrol in the trunk.

As a war correspondent, Jean would have had a notebook to scribble scenes of the war for the article he was expected to file. Perhaps he had a camera. To navigate, they probably used the *Michelin Guides*. Publication of the "Little Red Book" had been suspended in 1939, but the Allies had it reissued for military use in 1944. So, Jean and his comrades probably had a map. The names of roads were German now, so maps were essential, especially where devastated landmarks no longer served as clear signposts.

From Provins the Citroën headed east to Épernay, the largest and wealthiest town in the region. Sitting atop a hill overlooking acres of golden vineyards, it is a city of grand bisque-colored limestone buildings, the epicenter of the champagne region, home to Perrier-Jouët, Moët & Chandon, Veuve Cliquot, Dom Pérignon, and smaller family-run vineyards. The main road through the town is still called the Avenue de Champagne.

Production had continued during the Occupation, despite the shortage of male workers, who had been sent to labor camps in Germany. To keep this liquid gold out of the hands of the Germans, much of the champagne was hidden in walled-up cellars. At the end of 1943 the Maquis became active in the region. Having been tipped off that there was a resistance group within the Moët & Chandon winery, the Germans arrested the ringleaders. Paul Chandon-Moët was deported to Auschwitz. Count Robert-Jean de Vogüé was condemned to death and, incarcerated in a fortress, only narrowly escaped execution. Numerous other merchants and vine growers were deported. In the cellars of Piper-Heidsieck, Hemingway's favorite tipple, the Germans found discarded British army parachutes.

Patton's army had liberated Épernay the week before Jean and his group passed through but boobytraps had been left behind by the Germans. The local resistance network guided American troops around these sections, thereby saving time and lives. And so it was with joy and relief that the townsfolk welcomed the Americans and probably Jean's small party of French journalists as well.

From Épernay, the Citroën bumped across the Marne and headed for Reims, close behind the American convoys. In 1942, whole Jewish families from the Marne region had been sent to Drancy and from there to the death camps in the east.

The magnificent thirteenth-century Notre Dame cathedral of Reims is one of France's most iconic and grandest examples of French Gothic architecture. The sweeping flying buttresses along the sides of the cathedral are "topped by slender booth-like tabernacles [and] spires." And the rose window creates a bath of indigo glass and light that will make one's breath pause in wonder and awe. Today, visitors can stand beneath the Chagall windows and feel awash in his tribute to spiritual beauty, far removed from the violence and strife of the wars that have scarred this town and its cathedral. It had almost been destroyed in the First World War after the wooden roof caught fire and the heat shattered the cathedral's precious stained-glass windows.

IT IS POSSIBLE that Jean and the other journalists stayed in Reims for the night or perhaps bivouacked with Americans or French compatriots at an inn or in the hayloft of a spare barn. On the night Jean and his group stopped to rest, Patton made his move south, circling Metz and liberating Nancy, where Annette had been born. By September 7 the Third Army brigades were moving up the west bank of the Moselle River toward Metz, where pockets of SS *Panzergrenadier* divisions engaged in battle across the last great barrier before the German frontier.

Jean woke to heavy rain. As the Citroën pushed toward Verdun, vineyards gave way to forests and the architecture became more Germanic, with gabled roofs and *Zwiebelturm* church towers. Echoes of the Great War were everywhere, from the massive defensive walls of Verdun to the Ossuaire de Douamont, the tomb of thousands of men's bones and bare-eyed skulls—French and German—who died in *die Hölle von Verdun,* the Hell of Verdun.

The recent German retreat reverberated in a community devastated by heavy fighting. Numerous buildings had been destroyed and bridges had been detonated by the German army, the town's archives were burned, and sixteen men were hanged by the Gestapo in the town square. Only the Beaurepaire Bridge was still usable. Compatriot Fernand Legay had taken on the mission of singlehandedly throwing the Germans' explosives into the Meuse River before they could be detonated. His act of bravery was critical to Patton's ability to continue east.

Fifty miles away was Metz, the most heavily fortified city in all of Europe, the site of Hitler's key defensive: the Siegfried Line, or West Wall. This last German stronghold in France was protected by a line of tank traps, dragons' teeth, and forty-five thousand German troops positioned in and around the city. Hitler ordered that Metz was to be held "to the last man."

"German High Command is preparing to contest any further advances into Alsace Lorraine by Patton's armor," war correspondents cabled to British news outlets. Amid the excitement of war reports, one small item, center-column on the front page in the *Daily Herald,* posted a message that was being broadcast by the BBC calling for "enslaved foreign workers in Germany to take action both to hasten the defeat of the Nazis and to save your own lives." It was a naïve call to revolt, and yet the call may have been heeded as far east as Auschwitz, where the prisoner underground was devising a plan to blow up the gas chambers. Meanwhile, Anne Frank and her sister, Margot, had arrived on the last transport from Westerbork, Holland, to Auschwitz, where over eighty thousand women and two hundred thousand men, Jewish and gentile prisoners, had been registered for slave labor and untold numbers murdered.

LARGE EXPANSES OF hay and wheat fields stretched along both sides of the Citroën, as it traveled along the D603 road toward the village of Gravelotte. Fighting had been intense in the area. Numerous American tanks from the Seventh Armored Division had been destroyed. Human casualties were also high. One of America's most popular baseball players in the minor league, Les Wirkkala, would be killed here when his unit encountered German forces. Jean Jausion and his comrades were on the front line.

MOGADOR FARM SITS on a sweeping rise above Gravelotte. Patton had holed up here for two weeks, after his tanks ran out of fuel. The day before the Citroën drove past, his troops had re-mobilized and headed south to liberate Nancy. The farm was now abandoned.

In peacetime this nondescript village surrounded by rolling fields has little to distinguish it. But in wartime, Gravelotte has always been the scene of bloody battle. It's the geography. Set on the top of a steep escarpment thirty miles from the German border, Gravelotte guards the road to the Moselle River, which descends through narrow gorges to Metz. In chess parlance, it is the pawn guarding the queen. During the Franco-Prussian War in the late nineteenth century, the fields were watered with the blood of thirty thousand soldiers.

The road into Gravelotte curves down a hill, with open fields on either side. It was this road that the Citroën traveled down in the late afternoon of September 7. As storm clouds banked east, a rainbow arched over the sky. Surely a good omen for what lay ahead. Road-sore and tired, Jean was buoyed by the realization that they were close to the German border. Somewhere behind it, he was sure, he would find Annette and they would be reunited.

Disengaging the clutch and coasting down the hill to save gas, the Citroën's driver passed an ancient oak on the right, silent witness to two world wars. In the tree's shadow was a gravestone dating back to 1870. On the left, Mogador Farm lay empty, except for the abandoned corpses of German soldiers. Ahead, out of sight, at the bottom of the hill, was a platoon of one of the most battle-hardened units of the German army.

Here is the rat-tat-tat of machine gun fire. The shatter of glass. The crunch of metal. The squeal of brakes. A woman's screams. Here is a rush of blood. Its spatter across a worn-out land. The crush of last breath. Then nothing.

> The editors of *Franc-Tireur* appeal to anyone with information about the disappearance of one of our collaborators, Jausion. Jausion was born on the 20th August 1917 in Toulouse, the son of doctor Jausion, of 21 Rue Theodore-de-Banville, Paris 17th. He fought with the FFI on the St. Michel barricades during the week of the liberation of Paris. He left on September 6th, as a reporter for *Franc-Tireur*, with a young band

of old resistance fighters, Les Leconte, in a black Citroën 11, with front-wheel drive, reg. no. R.N 6283, with a white sign on the back reading: Franc-Tireur. Since that time, he has not reappeared nor given any news of his whereabouts to his family or friends.

He was dressed in a dark blue outfit, over which he was wearing a beige "Canadian" jerkin with a fur collar. He was wearing yellow shoes. In the fold of his elbow, he had a long transverse scar. He was carrying diverse identity papers, including a testimonial from the FFI St. Michel and a confirmation of his assignment with *Franc-Tireur*. On the eve of his departure, he told his parents he was headed for northern France and the front.

## ON RECHERCHE

La direction de *Franc-Tireur* serait reconnaissante à toutes personnes pouvant donner des nouvelles sur la disparition d'un de nos collaborateurs, Jausion.

Jean Jausion, né le 20 août 1917, à Toulouse, fils du docteur Jausion, 21, rue Théodore-de-Banville, Paris (XVIIᵉ), était F.F.I. de la barricade Saint-Michel, où il a combattu pendant la semaine de Paris.

Il est parti, le 6 septembre, comme reporter de *Franc-Tireur*, avec un jeune ménage d'anciens maquisards, les Leconte, dans une Citroën 11 noire, traction avant, immatriculée R.N. 6283 et portant à l'arrière l'inscription blanche *Franc-Tireur*. Depuis cette époque, il n'a pas reparu et n'a donné de nouvelles, ni au journal, ni à sa famille, ni à ses camarades.

Il était vêtu d'un complet bleu marine et d'un survêtement genre canadienne, en drap beige, avec col de fourrure. Il portait des souliers jaunes. Il avait au pli du coude (droit ou gauche) une longue cicatrice transversale.

Il était muni de divers papiers d'identité, dont la carte réglementaire, d'une attestation du P.C. F.F.I. St-Michel, et d'un ordre de mission de *Franc-Tireur*.

Il a dit à ses parents, la veille de son départ, devoir se diriger vers le Nord de la France et le front.

# *Return to the City of Light*

*You have no idea how sad Paris is, how depressing,
worn out....You would find us all aged by twenty-five
years. We have not completely lost the feeling of being
an occupied country.*

—LETTER FROM ROGER MARTIN DU GARD
TO JACQUES SCHIFFRIN

**MONDAY, SEPTEMBER 11**

"THE LIBERATION OF LIMOGES WAS a glorious operation," the
newspaper *Combat* reported. "The FFI [French Forces of the
Interior] completely surrounds the city and they only have to
tighten their grip when the order to attack arrives. The fights
in the suburbs are hard; finally, the defeated Germans propose
surrender.... An Allied officer arrives by car in front of the German AHQ hotel. Under the eyes of the enemy sentries at
attention, the crowd, overflowing with enthusiasm, threw themselves on the car, hugged and kissed the envoy, who only with
difficulty emerges."

And so the extraordinary Zelmans emerged from hiding.

*Kaila and Maurice, circa 1950.*

The Red Cross helped Parisians return to their homes or find new ones. Maurice and Kaila found a new apartment on Rue de Cléry, in the Sentier quarter, the center of Paris's rag trade. Many surviving Jews, mostly of the Sephardic tradition, were settling in this readymade community for the war-weary and grief-stricken. A bit like Venice's Jewish ghetto, the quarter had four- and five-story buildings that offered space for workshops, as well as family accommodations.

Another attraction was the quarter's geography. Boxed in on all sides by large boulevards, the Sentier was a warren of narrow, twisted streets famous for their bottlenecks. Having been chased from one place to another for much of the last five years, prey to the Nazis and the vagaries of fortune, a Jewish family could find no better place to set down new roots than among their own people, in the almost hermetically sealed world of the Sentier.

With its high ceilings and spacious rooms, the apartment on Rue de Cléry was the best accommodation the family had ever inhabited in Paris. Where Maurice got the money is not clear, but once again he had pulled a rabbit out of the hat to ensure that his family began a new chapter of their lives in style.

Cami was the first of their sons to return home. The boy who had left his family to fight was now a man. A photograph of him was featured on the front page of a local newspaper in the South of France to celebrate resistance fighters. Dashing and ruggedly handsome, he has a cap on his head and a machine gun in his hand. The headline read: "*Ils ne sont pas morts en vain* [They did not die in vain]."

Dutiful son that he was, he helped his parents set up the new shop and home. After years of fabric rationing, everyone needed new clothes. Maurice and Kaila were soon pumping the treadles of a new sewing machine. Zelman Vêtements was back in business.

Snow fell in meters across Europe that January. Belgium had seven-foot drifts. The Allies fought in three feet of snow at the Eastern Front. Despite blizzard conditions, the Russians took Kraków and on January 27 liberated seven thousand sick prisoners—four thousand of whom were women—from Auschwitz. Ten days earlier, the secretarial pool of Auschwitz had been forced to burn masses of documents, including death records. Then they were forced to join the regular prison population and death-marched to Germany. Among the thousands of women sent out into blizzard conditions on the night of January 18 on that march were the only four remaining survivors of the third convoy.

IN FRANCE, NEWSPAPERS posted a daily map of the changing front lines. Most of Poland and the Czech and Slovak Republics were free or would be in a few days. Like other Parisians, the Zelmans read the headlines and listened to BBC correspondents reporting from their locations embedded with Allied forces.

Winter was cold and fuel was short, but at least there were no more Germans on the boulevards of Paris.

ONCE THE SNOWS cleared, Jewish parents who were still alive sent word to their children in Switzerland. Michele was one of the lucky ones to be repatriated with the help of the Red Cross. Other children remained behind, waiting for news of their relatives.

On Rue de Cléry, Cami found his little sister all grown up, but their bond was as strong as ever. The two siblings worked together to help their parents and the business, all the while waiting for the war to end. Maurice got a phone line, but the real reason for the phone wasn't business. He was hoping to hear something. Anything. About Annette.

And then the phone rang one day.

Michele stopped what she was doing and moved into the hallway to listen.

"Dr. Jausion." Maurice sounded a little surprised. "How are you? Your wife? Jean?" There was a pause. A gasp. Michele came to the door. Her father had tears in his eyes. "I'm so sorry for your loss." Michele felt the sting of her own tears.

"Yes," Maurice said, "he was often at our apartment on Boulevard de Strasbourg. We all liked Jean very, very much." He must have said more, but she couldn't bear what she had heard already.

Michele turned to see Kaila's crushed face.

The last time she had seen him, Jean had been full of life and hope, working on his novel and planning his search for Annette. Michele had hidden and escaped, been scared and courageous, but she hadn't really fathomed the idea of death. Dead seemed so foreign. So final.

Stunned and silent, Maurice hung up the phone.

**FRIDAY, APRIL 20, 1945**

The newspaper *Combat* reported that Buchenwald, the camp "where there were the most heroes," had "more than 6,000 French deportees awaiting repatriation." Many of them were sick, requiring treatment and care. Lists of names were being compiled and once "complete, they will be communicated with the public. However, due to the state of transport in this sector of the front, it is not possible to achieve a rapid return of those liberated." Among those who were liberated was Claudette Bloch, who had recently escaped from a satellite camp in Leipzig, near Buchenwald. Raya Kagan was in the same camp, along with two others from the third convoy, Rachel (possibly Szepsman) and Dvora Lipskind.

The end of the Thousand Year Reich, when it finally arrived, came fast. As Jean had witnessed six months earlier in Lorraine, Patton's Third Army swept all before it, knocking over cities like Darmstadt and Mannheim like dominoes. Wheeling south, Patton then stormed through Bavaria, capturing Munich, the city where Hitler began his murderous rise to power.

On the same day that the German army surrendered in Italy, Mussolini and his mistress, Clara Petacci, were executed and their bodies hung upside down in Milan's central square, to be spat at and attacked with hammers and knives by an angry mob. The next day, hiding in his bunker, Adolf Hitler shot his beloved German shepherd and slipped his mistress, Eva Braun, some cyanide pills before turning a gun on himself. A week later, Germany surrendered unconditionally.

**TUESDAY, MAY 8**

For many Jewish survivors of the camps, the days leading up to May 8 were more than a prelude to VE Day; they were new birth dates the survivors would honor for the rest of their lives.

A reception center was set up at one of Paris's grandest hotels, the luxurious Hôtel Lutetia, to receive the thousands of deportees now returning to the city. An elaborate tribute to Art Nouveau architecture built in 1910, the Hôtel Lutetia was one of the first in Paris to have running hot water and telephones in all the rooms. The Roaring Twenties found numerous writers and artists hanging out in its lobby and bar. James Joyce played the lobby piano and wrote sections of *Ulysses* in the hotel. Picasso and Matisse both stayed there in the 1930s. Hemingway drank in the bar with Gertrude Stein. Other guests included Charlie Chaplin, Henri Matisse, Josephine Baker, Isadora Duncan, and Pablo Picasso. Charles de Gaulle spent his wedding night there.

Its resplendent history had been sullied when the Germans requisitioned it for the Abwehr (counterespionage) department and interrogated suspected members of the French resistance in a room overlooking the Cherche-Midi prison. Perhaps that was why de Gaulle chose it as the venue to accommodate his compatriots. Spread over seven floors, the Lutetia's 350 rooms now housed the very people the Nazis had tried to exterminate.

Eager to find Annette, Michele and her mother joined hundreds of other hopeful families waiting every day outside the revolving doors. Among those waiting was a battle-fatigued Claude Croutelle, now going by Loursais, and Richard Mela, looking for his wife and daughter, Franceska and Elise.

What began as a hopeful occasion soon shifted, as gaunt and half-starved survivors exited into the crowds.

Thousands were arriving by bus, many still wearing the striped uniforms they had worn in Buchenwald and Bergen-Belsen, which were among the first of the death camps to be liberated. On arrival, the former prisoners were disinfected and checked by medics, then interviewed about their experiences, so that their torturers could one day be brought to justice. Officials were on high alert for collaborators or former SS trying to pass themselves off as victims by hiding among the refugees. Already many (like SS concentration camp guard Irma Grese) had been caught trying to impersonate prisoners. Heinrich Himmler was arrested after using a British Military Intelligence ID.

The irony that this luxurious establishment now hosted resistance fighters and Holocaust survivors was not lost on those returning home, who often found they had no homes or families waiting for them. Patrons of the Lutetia were more familiar with tuxedos than prison garb. Photos of former prisoners show haunted faces among guests unsure how to act when being served a full tea service. After they had depended on only a red bowl to eat and drink from and often use as a toilet, fine china was a foreign object.

Every morning, French radio "read out this long list of deportees who'd arrived at the Lutetia," Christiane Umido recalls in a BBC interview. When she heard her father's name among those on that list, she hurried to the hotel. Arriving at "this huge square" outside the hotel, she waded through the crowds "of families all waiting. I just remember this great building in front of me and this silence. It was very emotional and sad."

A FEW WEEKS after the liberation of Europe, Charles arrived from England in a smart RAF uniform. No longer the broken, scared prisoner from Fort du Hâ, he had fought the enemy and reclaimed his spirit. He was punning again too.

He joined Michele and his mother on their vigil at the Lutetia. They had just returned one afternoon when a large car pulled up outside the Zelmans' building. Its driver honked madly. Racing to the window, Michele and Cami saw Guy step out of the car and wave up at them. He looked even more handsome than ever in his American airman's uniform. From the fifth-floor window, Michele watched excitedly as a vast pile of suitcases, full of American clothes, jazz records, and even a pair of cowboy boots, were unloaded from the trunk of the car. In typical Guy fashion, he had won lots of money playing poker.

For days the family swapped stories of their experiences around the dining-room table. Charles paraded up and down the apartment in his RAF uniform or recited the names of all forty-eight American states, which he had learned to pass the time while in prison. He was funny again, entertaining, and desperate to find his big sister among the returning refugees. Guy described life in America as "huge cars and chewing gum, Tennessee whiskey and speakeasies." Cami talked about the fearful retributions carried out against collaborators. On one occasion, his Maquis platoon entered the château of an aristocratic woman, a well-known collaborator, and executed her in cold blood.

THE ZELMANS WERE not just a family. They were also a firm. So, once everyone was settled, Maurice called a family meeting. Seated at a long table, they came up with a plan of action. Maurice and Kaila would continue the family tailoring business. Charles and Cami would work in the fashion business with their father. Michele would return to school. Guy said nothing.

"Guy," Maurice asked, "what do you propose to do?"

"Oh, you know, Guy doesn't like to work too hard," Kaila said, smiling at her favorite son. "Let's leave him."

Guy shrugged and smiled. Everyone laughed.

One person's laughter was still missing.

FROM APRIL THROUGH May 1945, between eighteen and twenty thousand concentration camp survivors arrived at Hôtel Lutetia, some on stretchers, most skeletal and ill. One photo shows male survivors sitting on gilded velvet chairs in the fine dining room, looking out of place amid such luxury. They were served "meat, butter, bread, lime-blossom tea, coffee, jam, cheese and gingerbread," and some photo captions claim that champagne was poured.

But the disassociation between this luxury and their lived experience was a chasm many psyches could not cross. "Many found themselves alone for the first time in years and could not sleep in a bed after years of deprivation," wrote Charlotte Delbo, who was on the first transport of French female resistance fighters deported to Auschwitz in January 1943. She found the seclusion of Hôtel Lutetia soul-crushing. "I had dreamed of freedom during the whole deportation. That was freedom, that intolerable loneliness, that room, that fatigue."

Maurice Cling was sixteen when he was deported with his parents. When he returned to France he weighed just 28 kilograms, half the weight of a normal sixteen-year-old boy. Entering through the revolving doors of the grand edifice that was the Lutetia, he was immediately doused with DDT dust to kill any typhus-carrying lice or fleas. Hundreds of photographs of missing family members lined the walls.

Every day Kaila and Michele searched for Annette among the returnees. They walked past desperate families who repeated the names of their loved ones to survivors, begging for information. "Did you know so and so?" they asked, over and over, holding up photographs of "normal people with chubby faces, with hair....We only recalled empty faces and shaved heads," a young returnee, Joseph Bialot, recalls. No one had any idea how many millions of Jews had entered the camps and died. Those who did return were sick at heart, repeatedly telling desperate families, "No, I didn't see him. I didn't know her. I never saw them."

In the Jewish community in Paris, the death camps became the number one topic of the day. People shared information, showed one another photographs, and listened aghast as survivors shared horror stories. The news was so far outside any reality anyone had ever experienced, or could imagine, that it was hard to believe. The full scope of the Nazis' genocide took time to digest. No one wanted to believe that their loved ones had been gassed. No one wanted to believe that human beings could perpetrate genocide on such a mass scale or that humanity had allowed such monstrous crimes to occur.

The Lutetia was the site of miracles, as well as heartbreak. Every day brought scenes of both reunion and disappointment. Among those lucky enough to come through the hotel's doors were the mother and sister of singer Juliette Greco; Marceline Loridan, who went on to become a well-known writer and filmmaker; and her friend Simone Veil, who would become one of France's most revered postwar politicians.

Among the crowds of survivors streaming into the hotel every day, Annette's mother found one of her Wilf cousins. Just one. One day, the Zelmans were sure, Annette would walk through those revolving doors and back into their arms. The Zelmans refused to give up hope. Days turned into weeks. The weeks turned into two months. Charles, Michele, and their mother went every day. Hoping.

This plaque in memory of writers who died for France during the Second World War is located in the Pantheon in Paris. Jean Jausion's name appears below that of poet Max Jacob, a friend of Picasso.

J. GOSSE...
OLGA GOUTWEIN
P. GRANIER DE CASSAGNAC
DR. L. GRAUX
J. GROU-RADENEZ
NANNIE GRUNER
B. GUEGAN
J. HACK...
M. HALE...
P. HOLY...
R. ISSA...
E. JACOB
MAX JACOB
J. JAUSION
A. JAVAL
H. DE LAGARDE
R. P. DOM LAMBERT
M. LANGLOIS
G. DE LARIGAUDIE
J. LAURENT
A. LAUTMAN
T. LEFEBVRE
L. LE...

A.R. MOS...
R. NAVI...
IRÈNE N'Y...
R. PET...
G. PE...
A. PE...
P. PE...
G. PO...
J. PO...
R. P...
J. P...
J. ...
P. ...
Y. ...

**ACT FIVE**

*1942*

# *Poland*

FOUR DAYS AFTER RAYA TOOK the tea to her friends, she and the other secretaries and functionaries were sent back to live in the "mother camp" at *Stabsgebaüde* (the basement of the SS headquarters). No longer able to keep a caring eye on the women she left behind tortured her. Her friends from the Depot and Les Tourelles were "condemned to disappear," she wrote, "and nothing could save them." The young women of *Stabsgebaüde* were considered an elite group of prisoners. They had access to a shower and two toilets. They received an extra portion of food and slept on straw mattresses on shared bunk beds. No one was trying to steal their blankets or their bread as they slept. They were even allowed to grow their hair. Most important, they were not faced with random selections.

Birkenau was another world.

Losing contact with their friend from the third convoy had to have been a devastating blow for Annette and the other Parisiennes. Seeing Raya cross the *lagerstrasse* had given them some shred of hope. Even the comfort of tea had meant the world to them, as they tried to save Sonia from death.

359

**TUESDAY, SEPTEMBER 15**

When Elise Mela's mother, Franceska, arrived in Birkenau, she was lucky to find her daughter amid the thousands of other scrawny-faced teens who filled the women's camp. Franceska did not last long, but she died with her daughter. On the same day that the beautiful Elise Mela and her mother were selected to die in the gas chambers, Claudette Bloch was moved to *Stabsgebaüde*. She had been working in Rajsko, the plant-breeding station and laboratory, where experiments were being conducted on dandelions to increase the elasticity and durability of rubber in tires. The job was considered one of those plums that allowed workers a modicum of safety and perhaps survival, but typhus was still rampant.

One of the Polish prisoners working with Claudette was Janina Kukowska, #7453; she died of the dreaded disease, as did the wife of the agricultural director, Joachim Caesar. To prevent further infection, Caesar had his lab workers relocated to *Stabsgebaüde*. His action may very well have saved Claudette Bloch's life. It was here that Claudette found her former cellmate, Raya Kagan.

The two Frenchwomen struggled to face the reality of their friends' fates. Having been in Birkenau longer, Claudette had seen their friends go to the gas or die in Block 25. Josette Delimal was gone.

Couscous, the belly dancer, had gotten a job as a maid for one of the SS. Despite the release from hard labor, she would not survive. Twenty-one-year-old Boubi, Sara Tassemka, had gotten a job sorting clothes with the white kerchiefs in Kanada. She would not survive either.

Ethnographer Dvora Lipskind had gotten work outside of Birkenau, perhaps in Harmenze, the farm where food for the kitchens was grown. This was another fairly safe detail, run by an SS woman who was considerate to prisoners. Why were

Dvora, Raya, and Claudette so lucky? Did such a thing as luck even exist in Auschwitz? Some survivors believe in the Jewish concept of Bashert, predestination. In truth, there was no answer.

The rest of the survivors from their convoy could be counted with one hand, Claudette states. And that was in the fall of 1942.

Of the women who died in 1942, only a few records survived. Tamara Isserlis, of whom Hélène Berr wrote, and who had been Claudette's best friend, had gotten work in the hospital ward "where life was more possible for the doctors," Claudette recorded in her postwar testimony, but the young woman who had gotten into the wrong metro car "caught typhus and suffered the same fate as the other prisoners or victims of the disease." She and Ida Levine died on the first of September. Bella Lempert died in September as well, but no death date was recorded. There is no death record for Sonia Gutman. That means that only Annette may have still been alive in camp, and she was all alone. "Nobody survived Auschwitz on her own," Edith Grosman, #1970, says. "You had to have a *lager* sister to help you keep going."

WE DO NOT know what Annette's last moments were. Was she laid low by typhus and left to wither in Block 25, riddled with fever and too delirious to know if her last breath would be dirt or gas? Was she beaten to death by a *kapo* or SS guard? Did she look at the electric wires around the perimeter of camp and walk to her death, her last dance a solo? Was she selected for the gas, among the one thousand on October 1, or two thousand on October 2, or in the historic "Big" selection of Shabbat Chanukah that sent ten thousand women to the gas chambers and left Birkenau practically empty and bereft of its sisterhood on December 5? Or did she go willingly with her lager sisters, Ida and Sonia, to comfort them in death?

What were the circumstances around Annette's death?

If only we had a date. If only we knew. But we don't. So, we must pause here to reflect on Annette herself—the girl who began this story and the woman who ended it. She had more to do. She knew it. We know it. And that is why we cannot let the figure of Annette Zelman dissolve into nothing. Nothing Annette did was empty.

# *Epilogue*

*I am not dead. We are only separated.*
—BOURLA, QUOTED BY SIMONE DE BEAUVOIR

**CAFÉ FLORE, SUNDAY, JULY 26, 2020**

"THAT IS WHERE ANNETTE USED to sit." Michele points to a red banquette to the right of the side entrance of the Café de Flore. "Simone de Beauvoir sat there." She points to the corner across the room.

It is a hot summer day, the kind of weather that wilts flowers, but not Michele. At ninety-two, she is vibrant, active, and beautiful. And, like all Parisiennes, elegantly turned out, in a bright red trouser suit. Her identical twin daughters, Valerie and our dear friend Laurence, have met us at the Flore to tour it with their mother.

We peer inside the diorama created by Charles Matton on the stairs. It features miniature photos of the Flore's famed artists and writers, dated newspapers folded on tables or tossed on the floor, and of course the red banquettes. As we listen to the sounds of the bustling waiters, still dressed in their black-

and-whites, only the ceramic stove in the center and the patron, Monsieur Boubal, behind the counter, are missing. There are too many empty seats to count.

From the Café de Flore we drive across Paris to Boulevard de Strasbourg, where the Zelmans lived before fleeing to Limoges. The configuration of the building has been altered, the entrance has an automatic locking system, and the concierge does not answer the buzzer. Standing outside on the street, Michele points out where she and Cami roller-skated, where Ben Guigui, the Algerian, sold fruits and vegetables. Except for the brightly colored awnings and the range of produce, the market barrows and stalls are much as they were in the 1940s. Michele smiles fondly. "The apartment, the street, and the school, that was my world."

As she is speaking, someone exits the building. Heather performs her infamous New York City move, slipping her toe into the door before it can close. Michele claps her hands delightedly as we hold the door open for her to enter. The hallway is mirrored and modern, but the marble stairs are narrow and worn in the middle. One can almost hear the Zelman circus racing up and down them. The past echoes around us. Upstairs, we knock on the door of Michele's former apartment. A little boy about Marcel's age in 1942 opens the door. Michele smiles.

The little boy's mother, an African woman dressed in a brightly colored robe and headscarf, has her hands full with children playing inside and looks suspiciously at the Covid masks covering our smiling faces. She does not allow us inside. Considering we are in the midst of a pandemic, that is not surprising.

In the courtyard outside, Michele points up at the open windows of the flat. "That was the dining room. That was my parents' room." The high-pitched voices of happy children come from above, and one can almost hear Camille blasting Cami's harmonica. There is no smoke billowing from one of Annette's forgotten meals, though. As we are about to exit the courtyard, Michele points to a utility closet. "That was the latrine."

Farther down the street we stop outside the public bath-house where Annette and the rest of the family took their weekly showers. Opposite it is the school Michele attended. It is still a school for girls. Next to its sign, *Ecole de Filles,* is a plaque commemorating the more than five hundred Jewish schoolchildren from the 10th arrondissement who were deported to their deaths. Fighting back a tear, Michele says, "I find it very moving coming back here."

OUR LAST STOP is 31 Rue de Cléry, where the family lived after they were reunited in Paris. The building the Zelmans lived in still has a textile business downstairs, but there are twenty-four apartments upstairs.

"After the war, every Saturday night young, Jewish people went dancing," Michele recalls outside the Zelmans' former atelier. "That's how I met my husband." Gaston and Michele raised three daughters in the same apartment that she lives in today, where we have spent over a month listening to her tell the story of Annette and the Zelman circus. From two huge windows opening out onto the Square de Clignancourt, a light breeze caresses our Dalmatian's fur. It is a quiet, elegant part of Montmartre, one of the Jewish neighborhoods obliterated in the Holocaust.

On the walls around us are framed photographs of the family: Maurice in full Cossack uniform; Kaila and her sister, Loupa; Grandpa Wilf, with his bright blue eyes; photos of Michele's children and numerous grandchildren. Her long dining-room table is covered in files and documents—Michele's archive of Annette—diaries, paintings and drawings, and letters.

AND WHAT OF Jean Jausion?

In August of 2020, we leave Paris to meet Michele's nephew, Jacques Sierpinski, in Nancy. Our plan is to retrace the route Jean and the Citroën took from Paris in the wake of General Patton's advance. Today, that route is known as the Voie de la Liberté, or

Liberty Road. In Nancy, we meet Jacques and visit the city's memorial to Annette Zelman and then find the old storefront for the Zelman clothing shop. Down the street, the apartment where they lived has a plaque to Annette hanging above the mailboxes. The next day, we drive to Gravelotte with Jacques and his wife.

MOGADOR FARM IS still there. When we knock on the door, an elderly woman, dressed in the traditional black clothes of French countrywomen, answers. She explains that she and her husband were not the owners in 1944. But some years ago, she tells us, a Canadian historian researching a book about General Patton's Lorraine campaign told her that the American general had stayed at Mogador Farm for almost two weeks.

She points to a pile of rusting U.S. Army equipment by the gate. "We found those in the courtyard and in the fields." There are two exploded M42 tank shells, a U.S. Army water canteen, a collapsible shovel. She knows nothing about Jean Jausion.

Over the centuries, the fields around Gravelotte have been doused with the blood and bodies of thousands of soldiers. But the bodies of Jean and his comrades were never recovered. The only information about the circumstances around Jean's death comes from an investigation conducted by Dr. Hubert Jausion, which he shared with Guy in February 1945. "Jean, seriously injured at the farm, would have collapsed on the spot," writes Hubert Jausion. "The Mogador farm was littered with German corpses. But all we found of Jean was his jacket, full of holes and blood. His right lung had been punctured. Was he killed? Or was he evacuated to Germany, as the abandonment of his jacket for a bandage would lead one to believe?"

That was the hope that Mr. and Mrs. Jausion clung to for months.

But Jean never returned home after the war, and his death remains a mystery. Some thought he may have intentionally driven into the German patrol in an apparent suicide. Even

Simone de Beauvoir suggests this melodramatic notion. But would Jean Jausion really have committed suicide, as well as the vehicular homicide of his compatriots? No. Jean believed in his cause. He was going to find Annette and to be reunited with the woman he loved. He had everything to live for.

AFTER THE WAR, Dr. Jausion continued his distinguished career at the Franco-Muslim hospital, as a specialist in the diseases of the skin. And though the Jausion and Zelman families had never met when their children were alive, their lives intersected in the postwar era. When Guy got married, Dr. Jausion offered Jean's studio on Rue Laugier to the newlyweds. A year or two later, Maurice developed a skin condition and went to see the specialist.

"That was when Dr. Jausion asked if he could attend my wedding," Michele says. "We were all pretty surprised, but we said yes." Two photographs taken at the synagogue show a sour-faced Madame Jausion, watching the ebullient Michele, dressed in white, on her father's arm.

Two years later, Maurice was diagnosed with stomach cancer. "I was pregnant when he went to the hospital," Michele says. "He touched my stomach and said, 'Oh, my daughter is pregnant. I am so happy.'" He was sixty-two when he died. Nine years later, Dr. Jausion would die. His terrible secret almost died with him.

"ONE DAY, IN the early 1960s," Michele recalls, "a woman came into the shop and said: 'You know who betrayed your sister? It is in a book by historian Henri Amouroux.' So, we went to buy the book. And that's how we found out."

*La Vie des Français sous l'Occupation* contained original documents written by SS-Hauptsturmführer Theodor Dannecker discussing Annette's arrest, which the family had never seen. In a letter to Darquier de Pellepoix on May 23, one day after Annette was arrested, Dannecker writes under the heading:

## Marriage between Jews and Non-Jews.

Jausion's parents wanted to prevent this marriage at all costs, but up until now had no opportunity to do so. I have therefore ordered the arrest of the Jewess Zelman and have authorized her detention at the Tourelles camp.

What began as disbelief quickly turned to shock and disgust. The man who had betrayed Annette to the Nazis was not some random "*mouche*" or crow taking revenge on a neighbor. Annette had been given up by the man who should have become her father-in-law, the very man who had asked for an invitation to Michele's wedding, the father of the man she loved more than anyone in the world; Dr. Hubert Jausion had denounced her.

IT IS NOT clear if Dr. Jausion went directly to Dannecker to denounce Annette or just filed a formal complaint. But he and his wife precipitated the lovers' tragedy, and perhaps most painful of all is that Annette knew it. "Ah! Your father, your father!!" she wrote Jean from the Depot. "I hate your parents copiously and be certain that I will never want to see them and that I will remember this cowardice all my life....How I hate them! I hate him all the more since I know that I loved him, and I will not be able to take revenge on him."

Jean must have been devastated by the fact that his parents had betrayed Annette. How could he ever face them again? And yet he did try to get his father to retract his complaint, so Annette could be freed.

A note in the archives of the General Commissariat for Jewish Questions reveals that while Dr. Jausion may have retracted his complaint, he also made sure that the lovers were forced to do everything Annette had protested so ardently against.

[The] two fiancées have declared in writing to abandon any plan of union, in accordance with the wishes of Dr. Jausion, who wished that they should be dissuaded and that the young Zelman be simply handed over to her family, without any further consequences.

Of course, Dannecker was not about to hand Annette over to anyone but the Nazis.

After the war, Boris Vian, the famous jazz trumpeter, author, and friend of Jean and Annette's, wrote, "Poor Jausion, whose girlfriend…was deported at the request of Jausion's father, who said to the Germans: 'Scare this girl, otherwise he will marry her.' So they scared her to death."

ALONG WITH THE revelation of the Jausions' betrayal, the Zelmans discovered that Annette's high-profile lawyer, Maître Goublet, had also double-crossed them. Goublet was infamous for defending enemies of the Nazis on the one hand and acting as a Gestapo informant on the other. While she professed to be fighting to save the Zelmans' daughter and took their money, she knew full well that Annette was doomed.

"THE REVERBERATIONS OF Annette's arrest and disappearance were very powerful in our family," Michele says. "Each had his own feelings. But I didn't see us talking about Annette. We went on as before, always the Zelman circus, but without Annette. Sadness is not an emotion that our family does much. Sometimes, we would mention her. But it was a closed affair. I think it was too painful. My father suffered the most, because he had stood in the way of their marriage."

A rare faraway gaze crosses her eyes. "My father was an upbeat, joyful man. He still went on playing the piano and singing. But there were moments when he seemed far away and filled with melancholy. I think he felt guilty that he had stopped her from becoming Mrs. Jausion. If he had let her get married, perhaps she would still be alive. But those things he kept private in his own mind. It was too hard for him to talk about it."

Guy's first wife, Madeleine, didn't have a father and became a kind of substitute for Annette. However, when Maurice died, ten years after Annette disappeared, the Zelmans all said, "*Il va chez Annette* [He has gone to join Annette]."

After Maurice's death, Kaila moved into an apartment near Michele in Montmartre. "She was with us every evening for supper," Michele recalls. "My sisters-in-law used to buy her beautiful clothes. She was a princess." Like her husband, Kaila died of stomach cancer, in 1967. The starvation of the war years had taken their toll. She was seventy-seven.

Dr. Hubert Jausion let Guy inherit the contents of Jean's apartment, including all the art that Jean had collected and given to Annette. At today's market prices, the canvasses that Annette and Jean schlepped down the streets between Boulevard de Strasbourg and Rue Laugier would be worth millions of dollars. At some point Guy must have given Annette's love letters to Charles, which he kept with his own letters from Annette.

The Zelman children stayed close. Guy's business as a textile importer flourished. But, ever the *bon viveur,* he spent most of what he earned on restaurants, clothes, and trips abroad. In 1970 he bought a large country house in the north of Paris, which became known as Maison Zelman. At the huge dining table, the ever-expanding family celebrated birthdays, holidays, and Yom Kippur.

Charles continued to work in the fashion business with his father, supervising the atelier and the staff until he married a beautiful, wealthy woman who set him up in his own clothes shop with Cami. "It was called Sidur," says Michele. "Charles became rich. He used to go skiing in winter and lived on Rue Pelouze in Paris in a big apartment, full of antique furniture and mirrors." But his eccentric side never left him. At family weddings he would sometimes get up and dance all alone. In front of the bandstand, moving in time to the music, completely lost in his own world, he would cradle a rose in his hands. That rose was Annette.

WHILE HE WAS in business with Charles, Cami decided to move one floor above Michele's apartment and became sandwiched, as he had been growing up, between Guy and Michele. "Everyone loved Cami. He was handsome and kind, and used to come down and see us every evening with Guy."

Like his elder brothers, Cami rose to a high position in the Freemasonry movement. But even in the twilight of his life, he retained his childlike spirit. "Cami bought a motorbike, when he was already quite old, and one evening, we were eating here, and he said, 'Come on, Michele, let's go for a spin.' It was nine o'clock, but off we went, all over Paris, with me sitting on the back behind him, holding on. He was like a little boy that way."

Though Michele says the family rarely spoke about Annette, in 1992, on the fiftieth anniversary of the day she and Jean filed their marriage banns, Cami took up his sister's case again. Writing to the Contemporary Jewish Documentation Centre, in Paris, he asked why Dr. Hubert Jausion had never faced justice for his part in her deportation to Auschwitz, and her death.

ONE BY ONE, Michele's brothers followed Annette and their parents to the grave. Cami was the first to go, at age seventy-two, in 1996. "He was about to retire," says Michele, with a tear in her eye. "He dreamed of all the things he was going to do, but he died of a brain tumor before he could do them. I went to the hospital every day. I looked after him until the end with his wife."

Charles followed him in 2008, at age eighty-five. The last to go was Guy, who died in 2013, at the age of ninety-three. "I buried my three brothers with whom I had shared all those experiences," Michele says. "I think of them all the time, I look at their photos. I always think I will be reincarnated as Cami. But I never think about death. I haven't time!" She has a bridge or golf game to get to.

For seven decades, Michele had almost no records or mementos by which to remember Annette. That all changed after Charles died. "His daughter, who is also called Annette, found boxes full of documents and gave them to me. That's when I discovered that they existed. She brought me a package and said, 'I think this is meant for you.'

"Why did he never tell us about the letters?" Michele asks. She holds her hands up in a gesture of incomprehension. "You have to imagine, he left prison in Bordeaux and carried them with him back to Paris, then Limoges, and kept them for the rest of his life. Without telling any of us, even though we saw each other all the time." She shakes her head. "And they were only copies. Where are the originals? That question I have never been able to answer. Charles was always a bit odd."

One theory is that he kept the letters in a safe-deposit box and never shared the location. Maybe he took them to Sanary and gave them to the sea. Whatever happened to them, they have disappeared, like his sister. But the sudden discovery of Annette's nearly eighty photocopied letters transformed Michele's understanding of her sister. "I got to know her truly when I received all these papers," she says, patting the stack of pages protected in plastic sleeves set before her. "Before, I didn't know her. I was a child. Now I found out who she was. And I got to know Jean, as well. This was a new Annette. It amazed me. How did she write these extraordinary letters at our dining table? It made me think she was with us, and yet not with us. She had all these things in her head, a second Annette, a secret Annette."

Along with her letters, Charles had hoarded a treasure trove of Annette's drawings and paintings, many of which appear in this book. Despite attempts to find remnants of her portfolio from the Beaux-Arts, we could find no trace of the paintings that she did there. Perhaps Paul Landowski stashed them away; perhaps they were discarded when she did not return to her studies.

What happened to Jean's papers and personal effects is equally obscure. His books, letters, and paintings were still in his apartment when Guy lived there. Michele saw them when she visited Rue Laugier. When Guy moved a few years later, he took the paintings, but none of Jean's papers were ever found. And Dr. Hubert Jausion's archives are medical, not personal. Family members who visited Guy in Saint-Raphaël, on the Côte d'Azur, remember a "Jean Jausion corner" in Guy's library. But when we reached out to Guy's widow in 2020, she insisted there were just a few books and nothing else.

Claude Croutelle's (aka Loursais's) widow, Claire Jortner, confesses that when she and Claude fell in love, he asked her to clean out his apartment in the Latin Quarter. He had not been able to go through anything since the war. To help him, she threw loads of papers and mementos, including his Resistance Medal of Honor (by accident), out the *chambre de bonne* window. "Every so often," she recalls, "like out of a fog, when he couldn't sleep at night, I could hear him calling the names of 'Bella' and 'Jausion.' They were like phantoms haunting him."

As a result, we have been unable to locate any personal documents relating to Jean, except the few letters that Michele has in her archive. Other than the photo snapped in Limoges in 1942, there does not seem to be a single surviving image of Jean, and none of the couple together.

"It's difficult to know who Annette would have become," Michele says. "Certainly, something in the arts. She wrote all the time. She drew all the time. She practiced automatic writing. She never spoke about wanting children. Perhaps she thought about it." She smiles. "She would certainly have married Jean. I always regarded him as my brother-in-law."

ON OUR LAST afternoon in Paris, we took Raya Kagan's memoir to Michele's apartment to pore over those sections where Annette and Bella are mentioned. We worried about the emotional impact these revelations might have on her, but Michele insisted she wanted to know the truth.

Immaculately dressed in a white T-shirt and white cotton pants, Michele sat down at her long dining table. Neat stacks of thick family history folders—Wilf, Zelman, Annette—are lined up on the end. To memorialize the moment, Heather set up her camera to film Michele reading the carefully marked pages. These are the last known moments of Annette seen alive. Heather explains that the date had to have been "a few days before August 22, when Raya Kagan was moved to *Stabsgebäude*." Up until now, the family always thought that Annette had died on the day she arrived in Auschwitz. However, there were no selections of arriving prisoners in June of 1942, so we knew that date was inaccurate. Kagan's memoir proves that Annette was alive for at least two months, and probably longer.

"I accompanied Annette down the *lagerstrasse,*" Michele reads out loud. "She holds me in her arms. 'Merci,' she said before she disappeared into the crowds of women." A shadow passes over Michele's eyes, but she does not cry. Sadness is not an emotion the Zelmans do much.

"How could such a beautiful, creative girl die like that?" she asks with a deep sigh. "She was twenty years old. She wasn't even able to reach twenty-one. It's more than anger I feel. It's a sense of injustice." Laying her hands on the table, Michele looks directly at us. "She had so much ahead of her. But she never had the chance to construct her future. This book will be a memorial to Annette."

# A Biographical Roundup of Some People Mentioned in the Book

## Rue Strasbourg

**Camille Goldman,** the harmonica-playing, handsome redhead, was picked up by a train on his way to Limoges in 1944. He was going to visit a girl. Our charming young flirt was deported to Auschwitz, where he died on May 20, 1944. The rest of the Goldman family—Hélène and Henri, and their daughter, Simone—survived.

**Ginette Kobrinec,** her husband, Henry, and their daughter, Eliant, survived.

**The entire family of Leon Wilf died in Auschwitz.** Leon, Karolina, Jean, and Abraham were sent on the thirty-first convoy from France on September 11, 1942, and were murdered in the gas chambers upon arrival on September 16, 1942; Leon and Kaila's sister, Lejbas, was with them. The other two boys were deported to Auschwitz on the eighth convoy from Pithiviers. Twenty-two-year-old Joseph went to the gas with his seventeen-year-old brother, Maurice, on July 25, 1942.

**Ginette and Max Wilf,** the children of Sruel and Louba Wilf, survived. Their parents died in Auschwitz.

**Surèle and Marcel Singer,** the Zelmans' upstairs neighbors on Boulevard Strasbourg, survived. So did their mother, Eva. **Theo Hecht** survived.

**Hélène, Alte, and Dora Zelman** (Maurice's sisters) survived.

375

**Eso** (Kaila's other sister) survived. Her other brother, Israel, did not. There is no death date for him. In all, Kaila lost eleven family members in the Holocaust.

## Jean and Annette's Circle

**Yannick Bellon,** Annette's Café de Flore friend and the amour of Jean Rouch, went on to become a well-known filmmaker. She began her career during the war in Nice, in 1943, at the Centre Artistique et Technique des Jeunes du Cinéma (CATJC). To gain entrance she had to disguise her Jewish origins, omitting her mother, Denise Bellon's, maiden name, Hulman, and registering instead under the name of her grandmother's second husband, Lemoine. Her first solo film, *Goémons,* won the Grand Prix for documentaries at the Venice Biennale in 1949. She went on to make numerous other films, mostly with a women's liberation theme, including *La Femme de Jean, L'Amour Nu,* and *La Triche.* "If through my works, you conclude that injustice revolts me," she said in an interview in 1961, "and dignity seems to me to be the most important virtue, so much the better." She died in 2019, aged ninety-five.

**Loleh Bellon:** After the war, Yannick's younger sister, Loleh, who had shared that idyllic summer in Brunet in 1941 with Jean Rouch and his pig buddies, went on to become an acclaimed actress and playwright. After making her stage debut in 1945, in J. B Priestley's *Dangerous Corner,* she went on to act in numerous films, including *The Perfume of the Lady in Black* (1949), *Quelque Part Quelqu'un* (1972), and *Jamais Plus Toujours* (1976). She also became a well-known playwright, winning the 1976 Ibsen Prize for *Les Dames du Jeudi.* She died, aged seventy-four, in Paris in 1999.

**Claude Croutelle:** After the war, Claude retained the alias he had been given when working for the resistance, Claude Loursais, and became a well-known TV director and writer. The detective series he created in 1958, *Les Cinq Dernières Minutes,* became one of the longest-running shows on French TV.

He remained haunted by the events of the war, but never talked to his wife, Claire Jortner, about those memories. Toward the end of his life, Claude suffered from bipolar disorder as well as insomnia and began to drink heavily. He drowned in a hotel swimming pool in Avignon, in 1988, after a sleepless night, while attending the theater festival. He was sixty-eight years old.

He never spoke about Annette.

**Georges Hugnet:** After the war, Georges Hugnet went on to have a fascinating career as an author and a dealer in rare manuscripts and books. He also continued to create collages and photomontages of (mostly) nude women, insisting that "a woman's nudity is wiser than a philosopher's wisdom." In 1950, he married seventeen-year-old Myrtle Hubert (Hugnet was forty-four). They had one son, Nicolas Hugnet. In 1969, he published *Huit Jours à Trébaumec*, an imaginary erotic travel story based on photos he had taken in Brittany in 1947. He died in 1974, aged sixty-eight, in Saint-Martin-de-Ré, on the west coast of France.

**Pierre Ponty:** Pierre Ponty, whose family estate in Brunet was the setting for Yannick Bellon and Jean Rouch's idyllic summer, remained a lifelong pig buddy of Rouch and Jean Sauvy. In 1946, they traveled down the Niger River by canoe and raft while shooting a documentary film together. Ponty went on to become a children's book author and writer. He died in Paris.

**Jean Rouch:** "I think of my friends from that cruelly eccentric period," Jean Rouch tenderly recalls. "Anne or Bella, you are no longer here to remember those shirts with pockets on the sleeves and those multicolored ties, which you invented for us before disappearing, as we were leaving for Africa and the war. They were arrested and disappeared in the concentration camps."

Rouch remained in Africa for the rest of the war, serving in a sapper unit in the French Army of Africa and putting his engineering skills to good use designing and building floating pontoons. He then served briefly in Germany, arriving in Berlin in August 1945.

In 1946, Rouch returned to Africa with his pig buddies from the Café de Flore, Jean Sauvy and Pierre Ponty, to descend the Niger River in a dugout canoe. Rouch, who had always been passionate about cinema, took along a Bell and Howell 16mm camera; the footage would become his first film, *Au Pays des Mages Noirs* (In the Land of the Black Magicians).

Rouch went on to become one of France's most distinguished filmmakers, using his ethnographic studies in Africa to create what he called ethno-fiction, in which authentic ethnographic footage is combined with staged scenes employing actors. His inventiveness and cinematic innovations, like the use of a handheld camera, influenced the filmmakers of the French New Wave, like Jean-Luc Godard and François Truffaut, and a new generation of African filmmakers. In 1960, Rouch coined a new term for his method: "cinema verité."

He and Yannick Bellon remained friends. He never spoke about Annette. He died in 2004, at the age of eighty-six, in a car accident in Niger. He is survived by his second wife, Jocelyn Rouch.

**Jean Sauvy:** After traveling down the Niger River with Rouch, Sauvy went on to become a successful journalist and author. Among his numerous books were *12 Aventures Qui Ont Forgé Mon Caractère* (12 Adventures That Shaped My Character) and *Mon Parcours dans le Siècle* [My Journey through the Century]*: 1947–2001*. In 2013, at the age of ninety-seven, he also published a memoir, *Maladie d'Alzheimer Vécue à Deux* (Alzheimer's Disease Lived Together), recording the ten years his wife suffered from the illness. He died in Paris in 2014.

**Michel Tapié:** Jean's close friend from the Réverbères, and later Annette's, became one of the most celebrated French artists and critics in the postwar years. In his book *Un Art Autre* (A Different Art), he espoused the notion of "informal art," which sought to make a radical break with traditional forms of composition. He developed the practice of *tachisme,* a French style of abstract painting, which deployed splotches or dabs of color and many saw as a European answer to abstract expressionism. He also became a globe-trotting promoter and broker of art. Sporting his trademark pipe and his monocle, he traveled the world, organizing exhibitions and promoting the work of other artists, including Willem de Kooning, Jackson Pollock, and Alfonso A. Ossorio. The love of jazz he shared with Jean Jausion continued throughout his life, as did his clarinet playing. He famously said, "In the words of Saint John of the Cross, 'To reach the unknown, you must pass through the unknown.' Academicism—finished for good, isn't it?" He died aged seventy-eight in Paris in 1987.

## The Enemy

**Theodor Dannecker:** In August 1942, three months after sending Annette to her death, Dannecker was dismissed from his post in Paris for a trivial offense: not switching on his sidelights, as demanded by the German military police, when he parked his car late in the night on the Champs-Élysées. The real reason was that Helmut Knochen, the head of the Security Service and Dannecker's boss, had become exasperated by someone he regarded as troublesome and insubordinate. Shortly afterward, Dannecker quit Paris to continue his genocidal policies in Bulgaria, Italy, and Hungary, where he oversaw the deportation of more than eleven thousand Jews. Then, as the Thousand Year Reich began to implode, Dannecker himself became the hunted one.

He was in Budapest with Eichmann as the Soviet army surrounded the Hungarian capital. The two Nazis changed out of their SS uniforms into ordinary Wehrmacht ones and slipped back into Berlin. Ilse Dannecker had heard nothing of him since February 1945, so she decided to go and look for him, traveling to Berlin with her two sons, where she made inquiries at Wehrmacht HQ.

Rumors swirled through the German capital that the Russians had reached the outskirts of the city. With them came stories of rape and revenge killings. Fearing for her safety and having failed to locate her husband, Ilse Dannecker departed for Munich on one of the last trains out of the city.

Dannecker was also on the run. Since mid-March, he had been in Berlin. Helped by his adjutant, he cleared out the family apartment on Müllerstrasse, hiding the family's possessions in the cellar. But on March 18 the house was bombed in an Allied air raid and most of his possessions were destroyed. Dannecker informed his wife of these events in a letter. It is the only personal artifact of him that survived the war.

For the next few months, Dannecker remained in hiding. But in December 1945, having learned from his sister of his wife's whereabouts, he traveled to Bad Tölz where the couple was reunited. But it was to be a brief reunion. The couple living next door to the Danneckers in the boardinghouse did what he had done to so many others: they betrayed him to the authorities. The next day, Dannecker was arrested by the American military police and incarcerated, with instructions that he was dangerous and should be closely guarded.

On December 10, 1945, he was interrogated and given a typewriter and paper to write a detailed account of his life. He also wrote a last note to his wife. He signed it "in endless pain and greatest love." The next day, when he was visited by the head of the prison and a doctor, he was found hanging in a standing position from the bars of his cell, with the cord used to open and close the window tied around his neck.

Ilse Dannecker tried to follow him into death when she attempted to poison herself and her two sons. But the screams of the younger son, Bernd, alerted the neighbors. The younger boy survived, but his older brother, named Theodor after his father, died. Ilse Dannecker was arrested and accused of murder. But she was freed on the ground of diminished responsibility due to her mental state. In February 1949, she married a Hungarian businessman named Vilmos Bernath and immigrated to Australia with her surviving son, Bernd, who changed his name to Ben and still lives in New South Wales.

**Maître Juliette Goublet:** In 1942, after she had double-crossed the Zelman family by pretending to help Annette while being an informant for the Gestapo, Goublet became head of the women's section of Jeunes de l'Europe Nouvelle, a group that encouraged collaboration between French and German youth in support of the Nazi war effort. In May 1943, she even traveled to Germany to volunteer for work as a metallurgist apprentice. A photo taken by Roger-Viollet shows her being waved off by a French policeman at the station, dressed in a military-style outfit, with a backpack and bedroll over her shoulders. In March 1945, she was sentenced to five years of forced labor and national degradation for life for her collaboration with the Nazis. She was released in 1947 and subsequently rehabilitated.

**Louis Darquier de Pellepoix:** Darquier de Pellepoix was dismissed from his post as Commissioner of Jewish Affairs in 1944, after his Nazi bosses had grown tired of his laziness and corruption. By then, he had assisted Dannecker in the transport and murder of tens of thousands of Jews. In all, between 1941 and 1944 seventy-four convoys were organized, deporting 73,853 Jews, mostly to Auschwitz. A tenth were children and more than half were gassed on arrival. After the end of the war, fewer than three thousand survivors returned to France.

By then, Darquier de Pellepoix had escaped to Franco's Spain, where he lived in Madrid until his death in 1980, eking out a living as a freelance translator. He was sentenced to death in absentia but never extradited. In 1947, he was joined by his wife, Myrtle, who bore him a second child but sank further into alcoholism. She died in 1970.

In 1978, Darquier de Pellepoix gave an interview to a French journalist in which he reiterated his venom against the Jews and denied the existence of the Holocaust. When asked whether he had any regrets, he replied dismissively, "Regrets for what? I don't understand your question."

**Xavier Vallat:** After being replaced by Darquier de Pellepoix as Commissioner of Jewish Affairs, Xavier Vallat was appointed head of Vichy Radio, which he used as a platform to broadcast his anti-Semitic views. He was arrested in Vichy in 1944 and transferred to Fresnes Prison, where numerous Jews had been incarcerated. In December 1947, he was tried and sentenced to ten years in prison, after unsuccessfully seeking the removal of one of the judges because he was Jewish and disclaiming any responsibility for the deportation of French Jews. He received amnesty in 1954 and returned to anti-Semitic agitation, becoming editor of the extreme right publication *Aspects de la France*. At his funeral, in the South of France in 1972, the legendary French Nazi hunters Serge and Beate Klarsfeld caused a sensation when they arrived in the church carrying a huge wreath in the shape of a yellow star, the symbol Xavier Vallat and the Nazis had forced French Jews to wear.

# Acknowledgments

Our heartfelt thanks to Michele Zelman Kersz for the many hours she spent sharing her sister's and her family's story with us, during two heat waves and a pandemic. Though she is now in her nineties, Michele's memories were remarkably detailed; she never invented or embellished and always told us when she could not remember something. The numerous documents and images from her archive, above all nearly eighty of Annette's letters, were the treasure trove of this book. Without Michele's willingness to sit and carry us through her memories, Annette's story would still be just a story, though. Michele, you have done a service to your sister's memory and your family's.

We would also like to thank Michele's daughter Laurence, for patiently telling us for years to write a book about her aunt, Annette. Laurence's book *La Cuisine de Nos Grands-Mères Juives-Polonaises* is a marvelous addition to anyone's kitchen, should you wish to cook like Michele and Kaila. To Laurence's partner, Ronald Crooks, one of Heather's oldest and dearest friends, and their sons, Elliot and Gregory, who have been a part of our lives since they were infants, blessings to you all. We look forward to spending many more summers on the beach together. And thanks to Gregory, who deciphered his aunt's cursive script and typed all of her letters, so we could translate them more easily, on his phone, of all things! *Merci!*

We first met our brilliant agent, Scott Mendel, by chance at the five-hundred-year anniversary of the Jewish ghetto in Venice—a fortuitous meeting—and we are so grateful to his commitment to our work. We would also like to thank our excellent editor at Kensington Citadel, Michaela Hamilton, who always worked tirelessly to make *Star Crossed* the beautiful book it is; the production team, including Arthur Maisel, Rebecca Cremonese, and

Sherry Wasserman; and our publishing team at Kensington: Lynn, Jackie, Vida, Ann, you deserve another bottle of our favorite tipple, Writer's Tears.

To Michele Kersz's nephew, Jacques Sierpinski, and his wife, Hélène, thank you for spending a few days walking the streets of Nancy and exploring Gravelotte with us. Jacques, your beautiful photomontages create such a powerful testament to the Zelman and Wilf families and our star-crossed lovers, Annette and Jean.

Writers need support and I am sincerely grateful to Caroline Moorehead for spending an afternoon over tea and helping me with 999 and to envision the career path of my dreams. To my writer's group, Suki and Felicia, I love you and can't wait to see where we go next.

A special thanks to Raphael Villaneuva, our on-the-ground researcher in Paris, whose indefatigable investigations in the National Archives and elsewhere yielded invaluable information about Annette at the Beaux-Arts, after our own attempts failed.

For his brilliant analysis of Annette's writing and letters, we would like to thank Andrea Paganini of the Jean Rouch Foundation, who was able to unravel complex, sometimes lapidary French literary and cultural references in Annette's letters that often eluded us.

Jocelyn Rouch, the widow of Jean Rouch, generously shared with us her memories of her late husband. Thanks also go to Barberine Feinberg of the Comité du Film Ethnographique/Festival International Jean Rouch.

Claire Jortner spoke to us from her lovely house in Brittany about her personal recollections of her ex-husband, Claude Loursais (Croutelle), and his role in the lives of Annette, Bella, and Jean Jausion.

Dear friend Akiva (whose mother and aunt were on the first transports from Slovakia to Auschwitz) and Sara Ischari helped Heather with Hebrew translations of Raya Kagan's testimony at the Eichmann trial, and it was during that Zoom chat that they mentioned Kagan's memoir. That book changed everything for the Zelman family and their knowledge of what happened to Annette in Auschwitz and allowed us to share the truth of Annette's disappearance with Michele.

Among the many historians whose work helped and inspired us, we would like to recognize the celebrated Nazi hunters and French authors Serge and Beate Klarsfeld: their work is seminal as is their deep knowledge of the persecution of the Jews in France. We also owe a special debt of gratitude to French historian Laurent Joly, who was one of the first writers to investigate Annette and Jean's story and whose book *Denonciation des Juifs sous l'Occupation* was a key text for us.

Thanks to Eric Le Roy, whose work on Yannick Bellon and Jean Rouch helped us pin Annette into that circle; Claudia Steur and Rachel Century gave us valuable insights into the life and career of Theodor Dannecker; and Dannecker's surviving son, Ben, who shared his own memories of his father via email.

We would also like to thank Juliet Everzard, who generously shared a chapter of her forthcoming book about Michel Tapié and the Réverbères; and Annette Finley-Croswhite, who sent us her article about the Paris synagogue attacks of October 1941.

To Dr. Colin Roust, musicologist at the University of Kansas, that was probably the most fun we have ever had on an interview! Musical accompaniment included. *"Clopin! Clopant!"*

For the photos and documents relating to female prisoners in Auschwitz, including Bella Lempert, we would like to thank Alain Alexandra and Florence Letablier at the Département des Fonds d'Archives/Services Historique de la Defense, Caen. What would we do without the wonderful researchers who helped us along the way? Dorothie Boichard, at the Paris Mémorial de la Shoah, who gave us the copy of Alice Courouble's testimony, as well as helping us find photographs of a few women on the third French transport, whose faces and names were all but lost until now; *merci* to Cecile Lauvergeon, as well. As always, thanks to Georgiana Gomez, the USC Access Supervisor, and Stephen Vitto at the United States Holocaust Memorial Museum for helping me conduct research from a distance, while the archives were closed. Your support, encouragement, and emails were so helpful! *Aussi, merci à vous*, Anais Depuy-Olivier, at the Bibliothèque Richelieu, who helped us navigate the Jean Rouch archive and make one of the most exciting discoveries of our research—Bella's photograph.

Valentine Gay, at the Louvre, shared with us her Ph.D. thesis on the École des Beaux-Arts during World War Two, which gave us invaluable information about the director, Paul Landowski. We would also like to thank Sophie Boudon Vanhille and Alice Thomine-Berrada, at the Beaux-Arts; Veronique Flambard-Weisbart of Loyola Marymount University, who helped interpret Annette's letters; Jordan Walker, for helping with footnotes; Sara Gordon, for her valuable insights on the first part of the manuscript; Boris Khalvadjian, our lawyer in Paris; Adriana Getler, of the Bibliothèque Kandinsky, Paris, for her help in locating images relating to the Réverbères; and Ali Rhabri, of the Office du Tourisme, Saint-Germain-de-la-Riviere, for information about La Lande-de-Fronsac.

Last minute gratitudes to Zvi Erenyi at the Gottesman Library, at Yeshiva University, and Elliott Wrenn at USHMM, Library and Archives Reference Desk, thank you both for such prompt responses to last minute source note queries. Thank you to Madene Schacar, at the Ghetto Fighters' House, and their "Talking Memory" lecture series, and to Dr. Hanna Yablonka for bringing Júlia Škodová's memoir back from obscurity. Serendipity seems to follow this story, and we are forever grateful to the testimonies of survivors—like Júlia, Raya, and Claudette—who give Annette and the other young women of the third convoy the chance to be remembered in memorium.

*Merci, mon "pote,"* Serge Alonso, for hosting our research trip to Sanary-sur-Mer—it was tough going, but someone had to go to those beaches! Heather would also like to thank Cassis Calanques Plongée for introducing her to the underwater world of the Calanques that Jean Jausion dove in and wrote about, a world just as vibrant as Provence. And to Vlado, Serge's son, who helped us with several technical issues on the BnF archive.

For renting us their wonderful garden and art studio in Montmartre in the summer of 2020, thank you, Karin and Erik Blum. We could not have stayed in Paris for two months during a pandemic without your olive tree to calm our nerves and some very nice bottles of rosé.

To our Dalmatian, Dylan Thomas Waggle-Bottom, who has traveled the world and escorts Heather to and fro across the Big Pond and beyond, thank you for your patiently waiting for your walks and not getting into too much trouble in Paris. A big "woof" to all our friends—canine and human—at Les Poilus de la Butte Montmartre dog park, where we have spent many happy hours in the shadow of Sacré-Cœur over the years and hope to spend many more.

John and Janet Macpherson, our Covid parents in England, who gave us a safe space to work and kept up our spirits (literally) with G&Ts, we adore you both.

We would also like to thank Nick Worrall, Simon's son, for his support and belief in the project, and Josephine Perl and Donna Snyder for their continually talented young lives.

Finally, the authors would like to say a big thank-you to each other for avoiding any homicidal impulses (there were moments) and making this a murder mystery rather than a love story. Please keep in mind that any errors in this book are our spouses'.

# *Archives*

AA        Arlson Archive
AGRB      Archives Générales du Royaume Bruxelles
AN        Archives Nationales (Pierrefitte-sur-Seine)
AU        Państwowe Muzeum Auschwitz-Birkenau
BNA       British Newspaper Archive
BNF-G     Bibliothèque Nationale de France—Gallica
CAEN      Caen Centre Historique des Archives/Service Historique de la Défense
CDJC      Centre de Documentation Juive Contemporaine (Mémorial de la Shoah, France)
FFA       Frank Falla Archive
RB        Archives générales du Royaume Bruxelles
STIWOT    Stichting Informatie Wereldoorlog Twee
USC       University of Southern California Shoah Foundation Visual Archive
USHMM     United States Holocaust Memorial Museum
YV        Yad Vashem, the World Holocaust Remembrance Center, Jerusalem

# Photo and Art Credits

p. 10      Sulamitte Frajlich, Syma Berger, Annette Steinlauf, Rosette Idzkowski, and Eva Szuberki were found at CDJC, @Mémorial de la Shoah.

p. 11      Raissa Rappoport (Raya Kagan) was found at CDJC, @Mémorial de la Shoah.

p. 12      Alice Heni was found at CDJC, @Mémorial de la Shoah; Ida Levine and Tamara Isserlis were retrieved from CAEN; Szajndla Nadanowska was found @Mémorial de la Shoah; all rights granted.

p. 13      Rachel Zalnikov and Molka Goldstein were found at CDJC, @Mémorial de la Shoah; Syma Sylberberg, © National Archives of Belgium. All rights granted.

p. 14      Sarah Gesik, Cypa Gluzmann, and Chana Grinfeder were found at CDJC, @Mémorial de la Shoah.

p. 15      Pesia Gromann, Emilie Soulema, and Sara Tassemka were found at CDJC, @Mémorial de la Shoah.

p. 16      Elise Mela's image was retrieved from YV @YadVashem. Photo of Claudette Bloch Kennedy was taken by Albert Strobel. Photo credit: Albert Strobel/Alamy Stock for Süddeutsche Zeitung Photo.

## In-Text Art and Photos

Act One      Photo by Salvatore Baccarice; montage © Jacques Sierpinski.

Act Two      Zazou © Albert Harlingue/Sonia Mosse © Gaston Paris—Roger-Viollet.

Act Three      Annette Zelman and Jean Jausion, photographers unknown; montage © Jacques Sierpinski.

Act Four      Birkenau photograph by Jacques Sierpinski, writing by Annette Zelman, © Jacques Sierpinski.

Act Five      Photograph by Jacques Sierpinki © Jacques Sierpinski.

3      *Café de Flore*, gouache and ink, 1941, by Annette Zelman.

10      *Three Faces*, charcoal pencil, 1941, by Annette Zelman.

16      Monoprint by Aline Gagnaire. *Les Reverberes* © CNAC/MNAM, Dist. RMN-Grand Palais/Art Resource, NY.

20      *Abstract*, gouache and ink, 1941, by Annette Zelman.

43      *Conversations*, gouache and ink, 1941, by Annette Zelman.

66      Ration card for fabric, June 19, 1941, with grateful permission from Michele Kersz.

72      *Moon Doodle*, pen and ink, 1941, by Annette Zelman.

76      *Buddha Doodle*, pen and ink, 1941, by Annette Zelman.

92      *Automatic Drawing—Charles Prison*, pen, 1941, by Annette Zelman.

99      *Peche Sous Marine*, gouache and ink, 1941, by Annette Zelman.

*Cent ans de modestie francaise,* 1941, Cornil, Cent *Ans de Mode Francaises 1800–1900,* and author, Annette Zelman.

110     *La Luxure* or *Lust,* gouache and ink, 1941, by Annette Zelman.

118     Pablo Picasso, from Bucher Editions, *Head* from the illustrated book *Non Vouloir,* 1942 © Succession Picasso/DACS, London 2022; © ARS, NY, 2021.

127     *On ne badine pas avec l'amour,* or *Love is no joke,* gouche and ink, 1941, by Annette Zelman.

134     *Monsieur Suzanne,* 1941, print published in Cornil, *Cent Ans de Mode Francaises 1800–1900,* and writing by Annette Zelman.

A surreal story by Annette reveals not only her sense of humor but her political astuteness as she mocks Marshal Petain and Cocteau as being in bed together; mentions Tchang-Kai-Tchek in China; and gives a nod to her soon-to-be lover. She ends by blasting Cocteau for embracing the Nazis' new version of France's independence in a mixed metaphor connecting "Marianne" to the virgin Mary.

> The stubborn modesty of Louis Philippe transmits itself 76 times a year. The 18 horse-like butchers with their autistic mares' profiles meet the dithyzautic musician, who compresses the beats of his panicked heart at the sight of these horse charms. Mr. Philippe Pétain, very eager and very French gallantry, offers at his own risk and peril a ring to the blushing young girl. Coup de theatre! This young girl is Jean Cocteau in disguise, who to seduce Zepuelly has adopted a tender and frightening air. However, it happens that Mr. Tchang-Kaï-Tchek, leader of the revolts of the central post office of Nancy and ready to play a role in history, rushes to meet Francis Crémieux, who has come in the hope of getting to know Parisian fashion. His passion for Berthe, dressed in white taffeta, and composed of little ones to shape it, Jean Jausion offers. In the end, the same Jean Jausion is confused, because a rolling stone does not guarantee impurity. As for Jean Cocteau, he rushes from the top of the rock of the Virgin.

137     Jean Rouch and Yannick Bellon in Brunet, August 1941, photo probably by Jean Sauvy or Pierre Ponty, permission granted thanks to Yannick's biographer, Eric Le Roy.

140     *Femme Fidele* or *Faithful Woman,* gouache and ink, 1941, by Annette Zelman.

141     Cover for *Solutions Tardives* (*Annette's art journal*), gouache and ink, 1941, by Annette Zelman.

143     *Entriez sans Frapper* or *Enter without knocking*, gouache and ink, 1941, by Annette Zelman.

152     *Paresse Mère des Lys* or *Laziness Mother of Lilies*, gouache and ink, 1941, by Annette Zelman.

165     *Olympia*, gouche and ink, 1941, by Annette Zelman.

173     *Menage Heureux* or *Happy Household*, gouache and ink, 1941, by Annette Zelman.

175     *Paris Soir*, © BNF.

182     Dress design by Maurice, 1938, by Maurice Zelman.

188     *Tapage Nocturne* or *Nocturnal disturbance*, gouache and ink, 1941, by Annette Zelman.

197     Flore letterhead, doodle by Annette Zelman, 1941.

212     Absence, Mother of all Vices envelope, 1942, by Annette Zelman.

217     Marriage banns of Annette Zelman and Jean Jausion, 1942, Kersz Family archive with grateful permission from Michele Kersz.

246     *Correspondence*, gouache and ink, 1941, by Annette Zelman

250     The Depot envelopes, 1942, by Annette Zelman.

274     Transport list for the third convoy, Zelman Annette, June 22, 1942, VCC 87b ordner Nr 24/BB11179563_0_1.jpg/ \Accessed at AA,18 Nov. 2020.

280     Memo from the Sicherheits-Dienst (Security Service–Intelligence Agency of the SS) office, Zelman Annette, June 22, 1942, /BB11179555_0_1.jpg/ Accessed at AA,18 Nov. 2020.

345     *Franc Tireur* © BNF

347     Maurice and Kaila Zelman, 1950, photographer unknown, probably one of their sons, with grateful permission from Michele Kersz.

# Source Notes

## Annette

Michele Kersz's recollections of her sister, combined with her copious archive of Annette's letters, drawings and diaries, form the backbone of this story. We also consulted numerous historical works, biographies and memoirs from the period, to enable us to set Annette's story within its social and political context. Where there are occasional gaps in Annette's writings, we improvised scenes in keeping with the genre of literary nonfiction, based on our knowledge of her character, her wit and way with language, fieldwork and historical context.

3    **Here is Annette.** We use the phrase "Here is" as a literary device to introduce characters and create scenes based on research, historical fact, and fieldwork. Some of these scenes have been further constructed through improvised imagination, to create a vibrant palette illustrating these real people and their lives. You will also find several quoted instances of the phrase, "Here is," in Annette and Alice Courbouble's writings, so our creative device has historical authenticity, as well.

       Was the day Annette was accepted into the Beaux Arts the same day that Salvatore took his photos? We cannot be sure. We know the acceptance was in the winter of 1941 though and recreated this scene based on the photos, Annette's letters, bibliographical and historical research of the area, Michele's memories, walking the route Annette took every day to the Flore and improvised imagination.

6    **Green Beans:** Ronald C. Rosbottom, *When Paris Went Dark: The City of Light under German Occupation, 1940–1944* (New York: Back Bay Books, 2015), p. 111.

7    **"celluloid bell":** Simone Signoret, *Nostalgia Isn't What It Used to Be* (New York: Penguin Books, 1979), p. 15.

7    **Being cold is as common:** Christophe Durand-Boubal, *Café de Flore: L'esprit d'un Siècle* (Paris: Éd. Lanore, 2004), p. 44.

## Petit Matin du Flore—In the Small Hours at the Flore

Details about Jean Rouch come from the memoir *Jean Rouch tel que je l'ai connu*, by his fellow student at the École Nationale des Ponts et Chaussées and later explorer, Jean Sauvy, as well as a personal interview with Rouch's widow, Jocelyn, at her Paris apartment in July 2020.

10   **One of the new realities:** Ian Ousby, *Occupation: The Ordeal Of France 1940–1944* (New York: Cooper Square Press, 2000), p.109.

13   **Zazou men:** Alan Riding, *And the Show Went On: Cultural Life in Nazi-Occupied Paris* (New York: Alfred A. Knopf, 2010), p. 102.

13   **slathered brilliantine to shine and shape it:** Simone de Beauvoir, *Prime of Life: The Autobiography of Simone de Beauvoir*, translated by Peter Green (London: Andrea Deutsch and Weidenfeld and Nicolson, 1963), p. 279.

13   **"Our only weapon":** Jean Sauvy, *Jean Rouch tel que je l'ai connu* (Paris: L'Harmattan, 2006) p. 59.

14   **looks more like a bookworm:** At the Rouch archive at the Biblio-thèque Nationale de France in August 2020, Photo 8c NAF 28464 A (3)-Bela Lampert [sic]. Looking as surprised to find us as we are to find her, Bella's face looked out from the bottom of a 1940 box of pho-tos in the Jean Rouch Archive at the Bibliothèque Richelieu. She is cool. Waiting. Knowing. Full of self-confidence as if she knows that some-day someone will find her here, that someone will care. I burst into tears. My sobs rack the silence of the library. To my right a woman looking at an illuminated manuscript looks up, concerned. "Bella!" I cry. "Bella!" My husband races over to see what I have found. There are no tissues anywhere. I am a mess. You would think that I would be used to this, unearthing photographs of lost girls, but I never get used to it. We were looking for photos of Jean or Annette. Until that moment we had no idea that Bella and Jean Rouch were even friends. The narra-tive of the story we are uncovering shifts beneath our feet. Bella is not just a love rival. She is one of the group at the Floré. She was a friend of Jean Rouch.

14   **"blonde Czech":** Simone de Beauvoir, *The Prime of Life* (Harmonds-worth, England: Penguin, 1986), p. 401.

14   **"the Shock Brigade":** Ibid, p. 278.

## Les Réverbères

Images for this chapter come from Michele Kersz's cousin, the photographer Jacques Sierpinski, the Kandinsky Library at Centre de Georges Pompidou, and the Graphic Arts Collection of the Firestone Library at Princeton Uni-versity. We also had a delightful Zoom interview with Dr. Colin Roust, director of graduate studies in music at the University of Kansas, who played musical selections for us, while vividly explaining the jazz techniques and syncopations of the time and performing an original score of "The Pelican Dance."

17    **"took on the appearance of sarcasm":** Georges Ribemont-
      Dessaignes, *Deja Jadis: Ou Du Movement Dada à l'Espace Abstrait*
      (Paris: Rene Juillard, 1958), p. 74.

19    **"The Virgin with a white smile":** Jean Jausion, *"Polypheme" Ou l'Es-*
      *cadron Bleu* (Paris: Les Réverbères, 1939).

20    **"Suddenly, all had disappeared":** Quoted by Andrea Paganini in
      Jean Rouch and Andrea Paganini, *"Saluts d'Irrémédiable!" & Autre Sa-*
      *luts, Homages, et Portraits* (Montreal [Seine-Saint-Denis]: Editions De
      Loeil, 2021).

20    **"The syncopated rhythms":** Letter to Michel Tapié, quoted by Ju-
      liette Evezard in her forthcoming book, *Un Art Autre: Le Rêve de Michel*
      *Tapié* (Paris: Les Presses des Réel, 2023).

21    **Genevieve La Haye:** M. Michel Fauré, *Histoire Du Surréalisme Sous*
      *l'Occupation: Les Réverbères, La Main à Plume* (Paris: La Table Ronde,
      2003), p. 11.

22    **German propaganda team applauded:** Ibid and Arthur Rimbaud,
      Paul Schmidt, and Robert Mapplethorpe, *A Season in Hell* (New York:
      Little, Brown, 1997). After this failed show, at a raucous meeting at the
      Cafe de Flore a new group split off from Les Réverbères. The Main à
      Plume was opposed to the Dadaism of Les Réverbères. "La Main à
      Plume vaut la main a charrue" ("The hand with a pen is as good as
      the hand on a plow").

## Hitler and Annette

Our portrait of the city of Nancy is based on material we gathered during a
trip in 2020. Aided by Jacques Sierpinski, Michele Kersz's cousin, we visited
the sites associated with Annette's childhood, including the apartment in the
Jewish quarter where her family lived.

23    **as in a bad novel:** Albert Speer, *Inside the Third Reich—Memoirs by*
      *Albert Speer*, trans. Richard and Clara Winston (New York: Macmillan
      Company, 1970).

24    **decadent art:** Laurence Bertrand Dorleac, *Art of the Defeat: France*
      *1940–44* (Los Angeles: Getty Research Institute, 1949), pp. 9–11.

25    **Just three hours:** Maksym Chornyi, "War-Documentary—Travel
      Your Own History," *War Documentary—Travel Your Own History*
      (blog), April 4, 2021.

30    **Edith Piaf:** Jürgen Brendel, "Édith Piaf: The Dark Life of the Singer
      of Love," Deutsche Welle, December 2015.

34    **Small rural communities felt inundated by outsiders:** Shannon
      Lee Fogg, "Denunciations, Community Outsiders, and Material
      Shortages in Vichy France," *Proceedings of the Western Society for French*
      *History* 31 (2003).

37    **apprentice seamstress:** Laurent Joly, *Dénoncer Les Juifs Sous l'Occu-*
      *pation: Paris, 1940–1944* (CNRS, 2017), p. 88.

37　**Statut des Juifs:** Michael R. Marrus and Robert O. Paxton, *Vichy France and the Jews*, 2nd ed. (Stanford, CA: Stanford University Press, 2019), p. 3.

38　**December 8, 1941, a massive squadron:** Cristiano D'Adamo, "Bombardments of Bordeaux," www.regiamarina.net (Direzione Generale del Personale Militare—Regia Marina Italiana, 1996).

## The Circus Comes to Town

For details on weather we used multiple sources from memoirs, newspaper articles, and the online historic weather (https://www.infoclimat.fr). Our description of the Zelman apartment on Boulevard de Strasbourg comes from the memories of Michele Kersz and touring the district with her in the summer of 2020.

44　**Colette praised the heat-giving:** Ousby, p. 122.

44　**Collaborationist papers:** Riding, *And the Show Went On*, p. 60.

44　**Judisches Gesellschaft and Enterprise Juive:** Ibid.

44　**I thought it repugnant:** de Beauvoir, *Prime of Life*, p. 381.

45　**Cross of Lorraine:** "What Is Cross of Lorraine—History and Meaning," Symbol Sage, August 2020.

45　**For the first time:** de Beauvoir, *Prime of Life*, p. 376.

45　**tiny tricolor flags:** Ousby, pp. 207–8.

## A Surprise Visit

Due to Covid restrictions we were unable to have a personal tour of the Beaux-Arts and had to use personal interviews and online images. All scene and dialogue material came from Landowski's diaries, quoted in Valentine Gay's PhD thesis, "La Défaite Récupérée Nationale Supérieure des Beaux-Arts."

51　**the Seine froze over:** Bernard J. Toulgoat, "Life in Paris under Nazi Occupation (May 1940–August 1944, Part 2: 1941)," HubPages, December 2012,

51　**Captain Heinrich Ehmsen:** Armin Zweite, *Fritz Hofmann und die Städtische Galerie 1937—Eine nationalsozialistische Museumskarriere, ihre Vorgeschichte und Konsequenzen*, in Ausst. Cat. *The 'City of Art' Munich, National Socialism and "Degenerate Art"* (Staatsgalerie moderner Kunst, Munich, 1987), pp. 262–78.

52　**great hall of the Palais des Études:** Lee F. Mindel and FAIA, "Tour Paris's École Des Beaux-Arts, the Venerable Art School That Trained Some of History's Top Artists and Designers," *Architectural Digest*, December 2014, https://www.architecturaldigest.com/gallery/tae-ecole -des-beaux-art-slideshow.

54　**The mission of the Nazi Propaganda Department:** Julian Jackson, *France: The Dark Years, 1940–1944* (New York: Oxford University Press, 2003), p. 199.

55    **German ambassador, Otto Abetz:** Riding, p. 52.

55    **Théâtre Sarah-Bernhardt:** Ousby, p. 171.

55    **"Are your fellow students patriotic?":** Valentine Gay. "La Défaite Récupérée Nationale Supérieure des Beaux-Arts." PhD thesis, 2011, p. 90.

57    **Landowski raised funds:** Ibid., p. 101.

57    **Jewish students like Annette:** Ibid., p. 80.

57    ***auditrice libre*, or visiting student:** email from Raphael Villaneuva, October 12, 2020.

57    **64 percent of students:** Gay, p. 99.

58    **3 percent of the student body:** Ibid., p. 79.

58    **"chase out all Jews":** Ibid., pp. 61–69.

## Becoming a Floriste

In 2020, we also visited the café in the company of Michele Kersz, who shared her memories and showed us the banquette Annette and Jean had sat at all those years ago.

60    **The Paris café has a special culture:** Riding, *And the Show Went On*, p. 18; Carole Seymour-Jones, *A Dangerous Liaison: A Revelatory New Biography of Simone de Beauvoir and Jean-Paul Sartre* (New York: Overlook Press, 2009).

61    **"never to compromise":** de Beauvoir, *Prime of Life*, p. 381.

61    **"dog-ends and dottle":** Ibid., p. 400.

61    **smiled at the new girl:** Signoret, *Nostalgia Isn't What It Used to Be*, p. 57.

62    **"All of the men":** Signoret, *Nostalgia Isn't What It Used to Be*, p. 57.

62    **Paul Boubal, owner of the Café de Flore:** Christophe Boubal, *Café de Flore, l'Esprit d'un Siècle* (Paris: Lanore, 2004), p. 52.

62    **"resolutely hostile":** Frederic Spotts, *The Shameful Peace: How French Artists and Intellectuals Survived the Nazi Occupation* (New Haven, CT: Yale University Press, 2008), p. 22; de Beauvoir, *Prime of Life*, p. 376.

## The Zazous

Though we were unable to unearth the exact exercises Annette and her fellow students followed as part of their curriculum at the Beaux-Arts in 1941, we used exercises that students at the Pratt Institute were assigned in 1978, our source being Michele's son-in-law and dear friend of Heather's, Ronald Crooks. Michele did not remember all the sewing techniques she used when helping her sister, so we asked professionals for help on understanding pleating, including Donna S. Vassalotti, Heather's cousin. Scenes of catching the late train come from personal experiences on subways and metros in New York and Paris, after hours.

67    Using the tape measure: Donna Vassalotti, Personal Interview. Dela-
      ware, March 20, 2022; and YouTube Videos by Kim Dave, "How To:
      Make Full Circle Skirt Pattern," February 2018, and "How to: Draft
      Box Pleated Circle Skirt Pattern," March 2018.
67    circumference of her waist: Courtney Nicole, "DIY: How to a Sew
      a Pleated Skirt!" YouTube. June 2015.
67    "Think of A": Ibid.
69    "Zazou hey hey!": Paul McQueen, "Remembering the Legacy of
      France's World War 2 Punk Culture," *Culture Trip*, August 6, 2017.
69    "the decline of critical faculties": Larry Portis, *French Frenzies: A
      Social History of Popular Music in France* (College Station, TX: Virtu-
      albookworm.com, 2004).
69    "Scalp the Zazous!": Ibid.
70    Eddie Barclay: David Drake, *Paris at War: 1939–1944* (Cambridge,
      MA: Belknap Press, 2015).
70    The hottest sound in town: Michael Dregni, *Django: The Life and
      Music of a Gypsy Legend* (New York: Oxford University Press, 2006).

## The Moon Prepares Her Nightly Toilette

73    "Rouch liked strong": Jocelyn Rouch, personal interview, Paris, Au-
      gust 20, 2020.
74    "The person I am today": Signoret, *Nostalgia Isn't What It Used to
      Be*, p. 55.
74    "Surrealism suggested": André Breton, *Le Surrealisme Au Service de
      La Revolution: [Numéros 1 à 6, Juillet 1930 à Mai 1933: Collection Com-
      plète]* (Paris: Jean Michel Place, 2002); *Surrealism and Manifeste Du
      Surréalisme—Poisson Soluble* (Paris: Éditions du Sagittaire chez Simon
      Kra, 1929).
74    "oppressive rules of modern society": Elena Martinique, "The
      Avant-Garde Nature of Surrealist Manifesto," *Widewalls*, December
      18, 2016, https://widewalls.ch/magazine-Surrealist-manifesto.

## Flea in a Glass Cage

The sketches and paintings were among Annette's archive, in Michele
Kersz's possession. Information about the Bains Deligny comes from Michele's memories, several online articles, and archival photographs.

77    Rouch became adamant: Under the terms of the armistice signed
      in June 1940, France was divided into two zones, the Zone Libre (Free
      Zone) and the Zone Occupée (Occupied Zone). In December 1940,
      the Germans then changed the name of the former to Zone Non Oc-
      cupée. The French nicknamed them the Zone O and the Zone Nono.
78    The most famous of the pools: "The Swimming Pool That Sank and
      Other Watery Tales," *Paris Is Invisible*, January 2013, http//parisis

invisible.blogspot.com/2013/1-the-swimming-pool-that-sank-and
-other.html.

79 **"Dirty, cloudy, often foul"**: Eugene Briffault, *Paria dans l'Eau* (Paris: 1844; repr., France: Collection XIX, 2016).

82 **"it was not so very difficult"**: de Beauvoir, *Prime of Life*, p. 389.

83 **Annette and Bella sewed:** Jean Rouch, preface, in Justin-Daniel Gandoulou, *Entre Paris et Bacongo* (Paris: Centre Georges Pompidou, Centre De Création Industrielle, 1984).

83 **"Toward evening a woman"**: Ibid.

83 **measures were taken:** Ministry of Defence, "The Demarcation Line Ministry of Defence General Secretariat for Administration Directorate of Memory, Heritage and Archives," p. 7.

## Eichmann's Man in Paris

Our primary source was the deeply researched German book on Theodore Dannecker by Claudia Steur. We also interviewed Rachel Century, author of *Female Administrators of the Third Reich*, who provided us with valuable information about Ilse Dannecker nee Warnecker and Theodore Dannecker's only surviving son, Ben.

87 **"They were material:** Claudia Steur, *Theodor Dannecker: Ein Funktionär der "Endlösung"* (Cologne: Klartext-Verl, 1997), p.157.

87 **"parasites" and "scum"**: Ibid., p.156.

87 **Anti-Semitism was a route:** Ibid., p. 40.

88 **"Nisko Plan"**: Ibid., pp. 30–33.

89 **Ilse Warnecker:** Interview with Rachel Century, April 2021.

89 **Ilse would remember:** Interview with Ben Dannecker, September 19, 2020.

90 **Reichsbräuteschule:** Interview with Rachel Century, April 2021.

90 **esophageal sphincter:** Steur, p. 45.

91 **Other anti-Jewish measures:** Ibid., p. 58.

91 **"elite troop"**: Ibid.

## Family Crisis

We have not been able to definitively establish a date for Charles's arrest, but details in Annette's letters suggest it was in August 1941. Information about his black-market activities comes from our own deductions and interviews with Michele Kersz. Photos by Roger Berson of anti-Semitic propaganda at *Le Juif et la France*, an anti-Jewish exhibition at the Berlitz palace in Paris, 1941, were used to describe scenes. Annette's letters: 1.

95 **"an iron and hell constitution"**: Annette is playing on the French *fer* (iron) and enfer (hell), punning.

97 **Le Juif et la France:** Rosbottom, *When Paris Went Dark*, p. 245.

98   **photo by Roger Berson:** Roger Berson/Roger-Viollet/Granger 0764193.

98   **The Jewish art dealers:** Camille Mauclair, "Our Artists Must Rediscover the Common Faith and Sense of Craft Solidarity," *Le Matin*, September 18, 1941.

98   **Fort du Hâ was infamous:** Jacky Tronel, "Au Sujet des Atrocités Commises par les Allemands à la Prison Militaire de Bordeaux…" *Histoire Pénitentiare et Justice Militaire*, July 2010.

## Dangerous Liaisons

Simone de Beauvoir mentions crossing the border in 1941 with Jean Jausion and the "pretty Czech girl, blonde also," but we know that is impossible, as Annette was busy writing letters to her brother from Paris at that time. We must keep in mind that her memoir was written almost twenty years after the events of the war and some memories may not be completely accurate. For instance, she is incorrect about Bella's arrest date, which was before Annette's. We believe Jausion traveled with Claude because Annette mentions that they came back together from a trip in the fall of 1941. Annette's letter: 40.

## Topography of Terror

This chapter pulls from the resources of Annette Finley-Croswhite and Gayle K. Brunelle, "Creating a Holocaust Landscape on the Streets of Paris: French Agency and the Synagogue Bombings of October 3, 1941," *Holocaust and Genocide Studies*, as well as Steur, *Theodor Dannecker*.

106   **That evening, Himmler scribbled:** Steur, p. 62.

## Detox

Annette's letters vividly describe her trip to the *Vendanges*. For the conditions and work details of the grape harvest, we drew on Simon's own memories of working at a château near Bordeaux, when he was a student in the 1970s. After contacting the Chamber of Commerce in La Lande-de-Fronsac, we established that, most likely, the priest Annette befriended was Father Jean Maurice Lamarque, the pastor at the church of St. Pierre. We could not find any information about him, but we know he was at the church throughout the Second World War and remained there until his death. Annette's letters: 9, 17b, 22b, and 23.

## I'm Feeling Extremely Kittenish

For the analysis of Annette's writing style, we are indebted to Andrea Paganini, the biographer of Jean Rouch. Annette's letters 2b, 19, 23, 24.

113 **Les Caprices de Marianne:** This classic of French theater was the inspiration for Jean Renior's film *La Règle Du Jeu (Rule of the Game,* 1939) which was banned by the Vichy government.

115 **Andrea Paganini:** Paganini email correspondence, July 2021.

117 **"Entartete Kunst" or "degenerate art":** Anne Sebba, *Les Parisiennes* (New York: St. Martin's Press, 2017), p. 312. In defiance of the Germans, over the next four years, Bucher would curate twenty exhibitions for artists like Picasso, Miró, Kandinsky, and other modernists whose work had been dubbed "degenerate art."

118 **one medical student:** Ibid., p. 286.

118 **Non Vouloir:** The poem by Georges Hugnet was on the left side; an untitled Picasso print faces the poem. We think the print looks very much like a photo of Hugnet taken by Man Ray in 1934.

## I'm Afraid of Becoming a Woman

We have not been able to establish the exact identity of the mysterious Mr. Suzanne, who crops up several times in Annette's letters, but from references to Charles and his friendship, we assume he was a black-marketeer and the man Charles was working for when he was arrested. Annette's letters: 95, 18.

## I'm Only Good When I Have a Boy in Mind

For information about the fall salon at the Beaux-Arts, we went to the BNF-Gallica Newspaper archive. For other reference material about the Beaux-Arts, we are indebted to our intrepid researcher in Paris, Raphael Villaneuva. Annette's letters include: 8, 22A, 23.

128 **prizes had been awarded:** *"L'Information Universataire: Journal Hebdomadaire,"* BNF-Gallica, 18 Octobre 1941, p. 6.

129 **Le Misanthrope:** Robert Le Vigan, one of the most celebrated actors of his generation, would later be a well-known collaborator, who denounced colleagues to the Gestapo. After the war, he fled into exile, first in Spain and then Argentina.

129 **"The Heron and the Fish":** de La Fontaine, "La Fille, Le Héron."

## Re-Enthusiasm for a Boy

For the analysis of the cult film *Drole de Drame,* we are indebted to Andrea Paganini, biographer of Jean Rouch. Annette's letters 41, 16, 17a, 92, 54, 96.

131 **commissions for art:** Michele was unaware that Annette was getting commissions for her work, and no record of those commissions or who commissioned them survives.

132 **a popular Zazou hangout:** Nick Heath, "The Zazous—1940–1945," *Organise! The Theoretical Journal of the Anarchist Federation,* p. 59.

132 **Michel Simon:** Paganini email, July 12, 2021. "Michel Simon was one of the best actors ever.... For Jean Rouch, the films (which were soon to become classics) of the late 1930s by Carné, *Drôle de drame,* and the following ones, Le quai des brumes, Hôtel du Nord, Le jour se lève, up to Les visiteurs du soir (in which Jouvet is very present), were fundamental," Andrea Paganini writes.

133 **Interzone card:** Ministry of Defence, "The Demarcation Line Ministry of Defence General Secretariat for Administration Directorate of Memory, Heritage and Archives."

## I Rejoice Like a Thief

The description of Rouch and his friends' visit to Brunet with Yannick and Loleh Bellon comes from *La Mirada de Frente,* by Eric Le Roy, who also gave us rights to the photo of Rouch holding Yannick in his arms; we are indebted to Eric Le Roy. Annette's letters: 21 and 39.

137 **"Yannick for Rouch and Loleh"** Annette gets her details wrong here. The "family park" was at Pierre Ponty's family château in Brunet; and it was Jean Sauvy, not Pierre, who fell in love with the sixteen-year-old Loleh Bellon.

## Solutions Tardives—Late Solutions

Annette's art journal, entitled Solutions Tardives, and her letters 17a, 19, 54, 96.

141 **Very strong never missed:** Based on an Old French Proverb; Rouch quoted in Paganini email, July 5, 2021.

## A Chore Letter

Untangling the other obscure references contained in Annette's letter fell to Heather Dune and Andrea Paganini. Annette's letters 2c, 5, 12, 29, and 90.

143 **"little darlings":** Annette is making a reference to the sleepy-eye dolls popular in the 1940s. The dolls had eyelashes and glass eyes that closed when they were placed down for a nap and opened when they were upright.

## Le Système D

Details about the weather in the winter of 1941 come from *Dora Bruder,* by Nobel Prize–winning French author Patrick Modiano. Details about prison conditions in the Fort Du Hâ, in Bordeaux, where Charles was interned, come from the Frank Falla archive.

148 **Inside the mairie:** Ousby, p. 117.

149 **also stood in the queues:** Rosbottom, *When Paris Went Dark*, pp. 192–94.

149 **between 1,200 and 1,500 calories:** Ousby, p. 118.

149 **unsafe to stew cats:** Ousby, p. 127.

149 **the growling stomach:** Marrus and Paxton, *Vichy France and the Jews*, p. 238.

149 **Mortality rates:** Ibid., p. 125.

150 **"You have to buy things":** Quoted in Ibid., p. 128.

150 **When Simone de Beauvoir received:** de Beauvoir, *Prime of Life*, p. 413.

150 **the approaching winter:** Patrick Modiano, *Dora Bruder* (Paris: Gallimard, 1999), p. 61.

151 **rat-infested jail cell:** Roderick Miller, "Bordeaux Fort Du Hâ Prison," Frank Falla Archive, n.d.

## Laziness Mother of Lilies

The vignettes and direct quotes of family life on Boulevard de Strasbourg, and Annette's frequenting of the café La Capoulade, come from letters 30, 31, and 90.

## The Zelman Method

Annette's letters: 26, 2a.

159 **"but the separation deeply affected":** Ibid.

159 **Croque Fruit:** Eric Le Roy, *Yannick Bellon: La Mirada de Frente* (San Sebastian: Euskadiko Filmategia-Filmoteca/Vasca, D.L, 2019), p. 43.

160 **"Joseph is in Pithiviers":** At twenty-one years old, Joseph was imprisoned with his younger brother, Jean (eleven), and their father, Leon. His mother, Karolina, and his other two brothers, Maurice (seventeen) and Abraham (fourteen), were later imprisoned in Drancy.

## Name of God

Material for this chapter comes from Annette's letter 20.

## Showdown at the Café Flore

Annette's wonderful descriptions of this decisive moment in her life are taken from her letters. After months of prevarication and rivalry with Bella, she had finally chosen the man she loved and would plan to marry. Annette's letters referenced in this chapter include: 15, 20, 25 and 37.

168 **"imitation-leather banquettes":** Signoret, p. 57.

### Happiness Illuminates My Future

Jean's article for *Paris-soir* was found in the French archive, Gallica BNF. In the summer of 2020, we visited the Museum Frederic Dumas in Sanary-sur-Mer, which provided source material here. Heather Dune went diving along the Calanques to see the underwater world Jausion experienced and describes the underwater limestone cliffs and rich sea life she observed. There is also valuable information in *The Silent World* by Jacques-Yves Cousteau and Frederic Dumas. Material for this chapter also comes from Annette's letters: 93, 14, and 45.

177     **"crushed dog column"**: Paganini, email August 7, 2021.

### Blue Like All That I Love

Among Annette's letters in Michele Kersz's archive 93, 14 and 45, Number 100 is Annette's wonderful poem.

### The Dress Chapter

Material for this chapter comes from Annette's letters 7 and 13b.

### You Are the Man

Details about the paintings that Jean Jausion gave to Annette come from Michele Kersz, who remembers them hanging on the walls of the apartment on Boulevard de Strasbourg. We do not have a full list, but they included works by Óscar Dominguez, Francis Picabia, Michel Tapié, and Max Ernst. At today's market prices they would be worth millions of dollars, but at the time they were simply gifts for Annette from painters in Jean's circle. The details about the plot of land Jean may have bought on the Ile Du Levant comes from Michele Kersz. After the war, she visited the island with her brother, Charles, to try to find out details of the purchase, but they were unsuccessful. Letters 4, 15, 47.

189     **El Djazaïr:** Opening in the 1930s, El Djazaïr was one of the first cabarets to perform belly-dancing shows in Paris. More clubs soon followed, including: "La night," the "Tam-Tam," the "Bagdad." These exotic cabarets quickly attracted artists and musicians. More posh clientele followed as "rich representatives of the Arab diaspora, Parisians, or European tourists, and, after the invasion, Nazis" frequented the clubs where exotic fantasies and sexual allure were served amid food and drink. Annette is fully aware of the musical influences that the cabarets introduced, mentioning the poetry of the "oriental" sound. In fact, these influences, largely coming from French Algeria, "gave rise to a new generation of singers, who did not hesitate to combine the musical stylings of songs

mixing French and Arabic on Latin rhythms (rumba, cha-cha-cha, tango, etc.) or even jazz songs described as 'Franco-Arab,' 'Franco-Arab,' or 'oriental'—or covers of French variety." Paganini, "Analysis," August 7, 2021.

192    **"A Year Rich in Big Decisions"**: *Paris-Midi*, December 12, 1941, p.1.

192    **December was bitterly cold:** Modiano, *Dora Bruder*, p. 55.

192    **Au Pilori:** Spotts, *The Shameful Peace*, p. 54.

195    **"You are against him"**: This argument is pulled from the letter describing the incident and Michele's own recollection.

## The Ox Effect

197    **"Paris would almost be a charming town"**: Spotts, *The Shameful Peace*, p. 11.

199    **Santa Claus was a metaphor:** James Travers, "Review of the Film *L'Assassinat Du Père Noël* (1941)," frenchfilms.org, 2002.

199    **Three hundred of the most prominent prisoners:** Marrus and Paxton, *Vichy France and the Jews*, p. 226; Claudette Bloch Kennedy. (2 of 6) "The Living Memory of the Jewish Community—Jewish survivors of the Holocaust," Oral history, British Library—Sounds, interview by Natasha Burchardt, Sounds.bl.uk, December 7, 1988.

200    **"State anti-Semitism"**: *L'Action Française*.

201    **Annals of Dermatology and Syphilis:** Dr. Hubert Jausion, *Annals of Dermatology and Syphilis* (1942).

201    **Nazi pseudo-science regarded Jews:** Henri Nahum, "2013/1 the Annette Zelman Affair or the Dramatic Consequences of Ordinary Anti-Semitism," *Cairn* 46 (May 2013). Other information about Dr. Hubert Jausion comes from Renee Birman's *Memoir de Mon Bonheur* (Paris: L'Harmattan, 2004) and from documents consulted at National Archives in Paris.

202    **"J'irai le dire a la Kommandantur" (I'll go and tell the Germans about it):** Ousby, p. 146.

202    **anti-Semitic paper *Je Suis Partout*:** Marrus and Paxton, *Vichy France and the Jews*, pp. 43–44.

202    **"morphine addicts, alcoholics, and sex fiends"**: Dorléac, *Art of the Defeat*, p. 54.

## Escape to Limoges

Michele's memories of escape are enhanced with the help of additional source material, as some details are now hazy. This is a rough itinerary and timetable based on her recollections. Details about Simone Signoret's father comes from her memoir. The story of the arrest of Hélène Berr's father comes from *The Journal of Hélène Berr*.

205     **Union Générale des Israélites de France:** Marrus and Paxton, *Vichy France and the Jews*, p. 109.

205     **"We've come to fetch you":** Michele Kersz, personal interviews, Paris, July–August 2020.

206     **5,000 Jews on the other side:** Marrus and Paxton, *Vichy France and the Jews*, p. 103.

207     **the terror of a knock on the door in the night:** *The Journal of Hélène Berr* (New York: Weinstein Books, 2008), p. 67.

208     **Getting across the Demarcation Line:** Ousby, p. 69.

208     **network of *passeurs*:** French Ministry of Defence "Remembrance and Citizenship," Demarcation Line, Series 7, Directorate of Memory, Heritage, and Archives, n.d.; and Vincent Dozol, "Annemasse, Ville Frontière 1940–1944," Institut d'Etudes Politques de Lyon (Lyon: Université de Lyon, 2010).

## Love Nest on Rue Laugier

Our portrait of Rue Laugier and the surrounding area comes from our tour with Michele Kersz in the summer of 2020 and additional source material. Biographical details about Dr. Hubert Jausion come from a memoir by one of his colleagues, Renee Birman, and periodicals discovered at the National Archives in Paris. The description of Bella's arrest is based on Simone de Beauvoir's account in her memoir, our interview with Claire Jortner, Claude Croutelle's ex-wife, and documents obtained from the archives of the Service Historique de La Defence, in Caen. The documents recording Jean and Annette's wedding banns, and the request for wedding clothes come from Laurent Joly. Because Annette wrote about longing to go to the Beaux-Arts salon with someone other than Dora, someone who loved art as much as she did, we surmised that Annette took Jean to the spring salon and from there we imagined that she would have brought him to the art studios.

213     **future director, Robert Hossein:** Michele remembers Hossein living there when Guy was in the apartment. Attempts were made to reach Robert Hossein in 2020; unfortunately, he died of Covid before we could reach him.

214     **Velo taxi:** Archival photos of Velo taxis were found taken by Robert Doisneau and the Ministry of Information—photography division. 1945. "Parisian Traffic, Spring 1945: Everyday Life in Paris, France, 1945." Imperial War Museums. 1945, which reveals these were "homemade bicycle taxis . . . with cellophane windscreen, makeshift hood, two old bicycle wheels and wooden box body," although there are also many factory-made versions in circulation. The fare for a trip in a Velo taxi is about 400 francs or £2 per mile, roughly equivalent to a motor taxi: "Motor taxi drivers, reproached for high charges, answer that they have to buy their petrol on the black market, Velo taxi riders say that they have to buy their food there too."

215 **Wednesday, March 18:** de Beauvoir, *Prime of Life*, p. 423. We did not quote part of this section, because de Beauvoir was confused about the order of the girls' arrests. Bella was arrested almost two months earlier than Annette, on March 17, 1942. The description of Claude's apartment comes from an interview with Claire Jortner, Claude's second wife.

215 **They called her a terrorist:** Bella Lempert's Dossier comes from *Caen Archives et collections du Mémorial* and states that she was arrested for being "part of a resistance group." Bella was probably first taken to the Depot before being transferred two days later to the prison at Fresnes (famous for housing Allied agents and members of the resistance). It is clear that Bella and Raya Kagan knew each other from the Sorbonne; both studied philosophy. They would not have crossed paths at the Depot before Bella was transferred to Fresnes and again to Les Tourelles on 15 April. Raya Kagan was arrested not long after, on 29 April.

215 **Fresnes, an infamous prison:** Ben Macintyre, *Double Cross: The True Story of the D-Day Spies* (New York: Random House, 2012).

217 **bulging pecs and forearms:** Dorléac, *Art of the Defeat*, p. 117.

217 **The reason: a wedding:** Joly, Dénoncer Les Juifs Sous l'Occupation, p. 92; and Kersz Family Archive.

218 **"Jewish strategy":** Joly, Dénoncer Les Juifs Sous l'Occupation, p. 231.

## Hitler's Parrot

In 2020, we visited Rue Laugier to see Jean's studio, and found Darquier de Pellepoix's headquarters at No. 12. The brass door knocker is still there. Michele Kersz is the source for the family's arrival and lives in Limoges.

219 **Most of those who died in Auschwitz:** Carmen Callil, *Bad Faith: A Forgotten History of Family and Fatherland* (London: Jonathan Cape, 2006). p. 303–4.

221 **Protocols of the Elders of Zion:** This is a notorious anti-Jewish tract that blamed Jews for all the ills of the world. It is believed to have originated in Russia in 1903, but in 1921 the *Times of London* exposed it as a crude plagiarism of a French book (that did not even mention Jews). In the 1920s, chapters of the *Protocols* were disseminated in America by Henry Ford's newspaper, *The Dearborn Independent*. Later, it was taken up by Hitler and Goebbels and widely disseminated in Germany, where at least twenty-three editions were published by the Nazi Party between 1919 and 1939. USHMM.

221 **Commissioner of Jewish Affairs:** David Coward, "Monocled Baron Charged," *London Review of Books*, June 8, 2006.

222 **anti-Semitic Club Nationale:** Callil, . 145.

222 **"We need to urgently resolve":** Nicholas Fraser, "Toujours Vichy: A Reckoning with Disgrace," *Harper's*, October 2006, 89–91.

## A Zelman

The time of Annette's arrest comes from Laurent Joly's *Denoncer Les Juifs Sous l'Occupation*. Details of her journey in the "salad basket" were compiled from multiple sources, including Raya Kagan, Claudette Bloch, descriptions of arrests found in France Hamelin's book, *Femmes Dans La Nuit: L'internement à La Petite Roquette et Au Camp Des Tourelles*, and field work. In August 2020, we got into our car at midnight and retraced what would almost certainly have been the *panier*'s route from Boulevard Strasbourg to the Palais de Justice. Paris never sleeps but the streets around the Palais were dark and eerily quiet as we walked beneath the imposing walls and peered through the iron gates into the prisoner's entrance. Additional material is based on a tour with attorney, Boris Khalvadjian, in August 2020. We constructed dialogue based on Annette's description of her arrest, thus quote marks were not used.

228 **"It has come to my attention"**: Theodor Dannecker, "Lettre Du 23/05/1942 de Theodor Dannecker, Chef de La Section Juive de La Sipo-SD à Louis Darquier de Pellepoix, Commissaire Général Aux Questions Juives, et Réponse de Ce Dernier En Date Du 03/06/1942, à Propos Des Mariages Mixtes, et Notamment Celui d'Annette Zelman Avec Monsieur Jean Jausion (Non-Juif)," *Memorial de La Shoah* CXVIII–2a. CGQ-J - CXVIII (May 23, 1942).

## The Depot

The primary source for this chapter is Annette's letter 49 to Jean Jausion. We also consulted a video showing the cells: *Plongée au coeur du dépôt de Paris*, and the combined testimonial memoirs of Alice Courouble, Claudette Bloch Kennedy, Jo Massey, and Raya Kagan. Descriptions of the oratory where the women slept come from Annette's letters, as well as the memoirs of Alice Courouble and Raya Kagan.

231 **"What is this Jew doing here?"**: Claudette Bloch Kennedy, Kennedy, Claudette, 1910– (2 of 6), The Living Memory of the Jewish Community—Jewish survivors of the Holocaust—Oral history, British Library—Sounds, interview by Natasha Burchardt, Sounds.bl.uk, December 7, 1988, Transcript p. 36.

232 **"In cell 13"**: Raya Kagan. ררעיה כגן and Lubich, S. נשים בלשכת הגיהנום] / [מכתב-היד ש. ליוביץ. Women in the Chamber of Hell. *Nashim Be-lishkat Ha-Gehinom | [mi-ketv-ha-yad Sh. Lyubits]*. Merchavyah: Ha-Kibuts Ha-artsi Ha-shomer Ha-tsa'ir, 1947, p. 36.

229 **"the most cruel people I ever met"**: Courouble, p. 25.

232 **the canteen:** Ibid.

238 **"royal road to the unconscious"**: Phrase used by Sigmund Freud.

238 REM sleep: Rubin Naiman, "Dreamless: The Silent Epidemic of REM Sleep Loss," *Annals of the New York Academy of Sciences*. 1406, no. 1 (August 15, 2017): 77–85.

239   **The young Jewish diarist:** *Journal of Hélène Berr*, p. 50.

239   **An onerous new law:** Theodore Dannecker, "Lettre de Theodor Dannecker à Louis Darquier de Pellepoix, 23 Mai 1942. Le Commissariat Général Aux Questions Juives Répond Qu'une Telle Mesure Est à L'étude," *Centre de Documentation Juive Contemporaine* (CDJC) CXVIII–2a. AJ38 9, June 3, 1942.

243   **"As for Choléra":** A novel written in 1932 by Joseph Delteil. "The story of a boy and his love affairs with three charming young girls. Delteil's first novel *Sur le fleuve Amour* attracted the attention of Louis Aragon and Andre Breton. In fact, Breton quotes him in the Surrealist Manifesto. Delteil participated in the first issue of *La Révolution surréaliste*, but after an interview in which he declared that he never dreamed, he received a letter of rupture from Breton." He did maintain a long friendship with Henry Miller and other notable poets, performers, and writers.

243   **Manhattan Transfer:** "Registers a fervent denunciation of a society that subsumes and crushes the individual," Jay McInerney wrote in the foreword to the Penguin Modern Classics New Edition. Written by John Dos Passos, *Manhattan Transfer* was published in the same year as F. Scott Fitzgerald's *The Great Gatsby*, but never reached the same heights of acclaim.

243   **99 percent:** Henry Bordeaux, *Images Du Maréchal Pétain* (Paris: Sequana, 1941).

244   **"Paul Uccello":** Andrea Paganini notes in his helpful analysis that Paul Uccello [Annette spelled his name incorrectly] "greatly impressed French writers, from the symbolist Marcel Schwob to the Dadaists and Surrealists (Tristan Tzara, Philippe Soupault, André Breton, Louis Aragon). And of course Antonin Artaud, who dedicated two prose poems to 'his friend, his chimera,' texts that are more than astonishing, especially the one in which Uccello is the main character: 'Paul les Oiseaux [= Paolo Uccello] ou la place de l'amour' (1925), later published in *L'ombilic des limbes*. And guess what: Rouch was very fond of Paolo Uccello (about whom he even spoke on television in the 1970s)."

249   **island of Levant:** The details about this plot of land come from Michele Kersz. She and her brother, Charles, visited Ile du Levant after the war to try and find out details, but could not locate any deeds.

## Yellow Stars

Material for this chapter comes primarily from Annette's letter 53 to Jean Jausion. Other sources include the archives of the Memorial de la Shoah, Yad Vashem, USC Shoah Foundation–Visual Archive, US Holocaust Memorial Museum, Service historique de la défense, and the memoirs of Alice Courouble, Claudette Bloch Kennedy, Raya Kagan, and prisoner recollections found in France Hamelin's book, *Femmes Dans La Nuit: L'internement à La Petite Roquette et Au Camp Des Tourelles: 1939–1944*.

252 **Among them she noted:** Alice Courouble, *Amie Des Juifs* (Paris: Bloud & Gay, 1946), p. 25.

253 **"Shit me":** Ibid., p. 24.

## Les Tourelles

The description of the route to Les Tourelles from the Depot was drawn from our own re-creation of the journey in the summer of 2020, when we also visited the prison. Today, it is the HQ of the French Secret Service, so, obviously we could not go inside! We used the transport list to identify countries of origin of the first Frenchwomen in Auschwitz, as well as their ages and arrest dates.

Alice Courouble and Raya Kagan's testimonies differ on what time the girls were removed from the prison population (Courouble says it was morning; Kagan reports it was evening). Since Kagan writes that Jean and Annette saw each other every two weeks and they were only in Tourelles for a week and a half, which would have been impossible. They would have seen each other only once or twice before she was deported. Kagan also remembered the date, and states they were being served cabbage soup, which seems more likely to have been served at supper. Therefore we suggest that Annette and the others were separated on Thursday, after visitation.

260 **"Silence stifled reunions":** Courouble, p. 25.

260 **Yellow Star protester Jo Massey:** France Hamelin, *Femmes Dans La Nuit: L'internement à La Petite Roquette et Au Camp Des Tourelles: 1939–1944* (Paris: Renaudot et Cie, 1988), pp. 251–53.

264 **"great event of our reclusive lives":** Courouble, p. 30.

265 **"an English magistrate":** Ibid.

267 **"All Jews between eighteen and forty-two go to one side!":** Bloch, Kagan and Courouble report different times of day that the separation occurred, but the orders are identical.

267 **"not a cry, not a word":** Courouble, p. 32.

268 **"My daughter, my little one":** Alice Courouble describes this entire scene and the dialogue in her testimony, p. 33.

272 **Barred from entry:** This is supposition, based on logic. Claude and Jean had to have been torn apart by the sudden turn of events. Bella would have been able to elucidate what had happened when she saw Claude at the next visitation (if that was allowed; we have no idea if it was).

267 **next to their beds:** This scene was witnessed and recorded by Alice Courouble, p. 33-34.

271 **aluminum drinking cups:** Bloch Kennedy, Transcript, p. 23.

273 **"One gendarme was weeping":** Bloch Kennedy. Transcript, p. 22.

275 **"Lempert! Zimmerman!":** USHMM. The transport list shows the two women's names crossed off. Since Kagan and Bloch report that two women were taken off the bus, we know the names of the women removed before the bus departed.

275 **Josette Delimal:** Claudette quoted in Kagan, p. 53.

## The Third Convoy

The images in the first paragraph are drawn from a poem Simon wrote on the day we toured Drancy and the train stations. We also cite the memo from the *Sicherheits-Dienst* (Security Service–Intelligence Agency of the SS) office, found in Annette's dossier at the United States Holocaust Memorial Museum (USHMM). For the journey to Auschwitz, the testimonial memoirs of Claudette Bloch and Raya Kagan, as well as Heather Dune's research into the 1942 women's camps in her books *999* and *Rena's Promise*, have informed much of the next three chapters. Weather records were also consulted and we used the map of the train journey available at Yad Vashem to track the stations the third convoy passed on its way through Germany to Poland.

277   **The doors to the wagons:** Bloch Kennedy. Transcript, p. 23.

277   **at 9:20 that morning:** Danuta Czech, *Auschwitz Chronicle 1939–1945* (New York: Henry Holt, 1997), p. 184.

277   **"The atmosphere in this train":** Bloch Kennedy. Transcript, p. 23.

278   **Claudette used a nail file:** Ibid.

280   **"Water! Water":** Ibid.

281   **"I think we are in Upper Silesia":** Ibid.

281   **a place called Auschwitz:** Ibid.

281   **Anya Litvac:** Quoted in Kagan, *Women in the Bureau of Hell*, p. 54

## Auschwitz

For the next three chapters, multiple sources have been drawn on to re-create these chapters, including the memoirs of Raya Kagan and Rena Kornreich Gelissen, the testimony/transcript of Claudette Bloch Kennedy, USC Shoah Visual History testimonies, and personal interviews conducted by Heather Dune in her research for her book and documentary film *999*, as well as *Auschwitz Chronicle 1939–1945* by Danuta Czech. We used the foreign languages that were spoken in Auschwitz at the time, so readers get a sense of reality and understand how difficult it was to survive in a world where your native tongue is not spoken; German and French translations are thanks to Simon Worrall; Slovak and Polish are thanks to DeepL.

284   **only 186 of those men:** Czech, *Auschwitz Chronicle*, p. 186.

286   **baritone laughter of braggarts:** Bloch Kennedy, transcript of interview Cassette 4, Side A. Reel 2, Side 1, p. 24. "Hoess... Like Rudolf Hoess... Wanted to enjoy the sight of the first French women arriving in his camp. He came with his retinue. And enjoyed especially those of us who had some red varnish on their toes." We refer back to that varnish to show the passage of time and the degradation of their lives and bodies.

287   **Roza Zimmerspitz:** The cousin of Eta Zimmerspitz, interviewed in 2019, was head of one of the Nissen huts and is confirmed by Claudette Bloch and Raya Kagan. Roza and her sisters had a terrible

reputation among prisoners. More about the sisters and their cousins story can be found in Heather Dune Macadam's book *999*.

287  **carry large sacks of laundry:** Bloch Kennedy, Cassette 4, Side A. Reel 2, Side 1. p. 25.

288  **"In our imagination:** Júlia Škodová. "Three Years without a Name" by Júlia Škodová: A Chapter to Read." Haartz.com. 27 Apr. 2022.

## Roll Call

290  **"It was impossible to squeeze":** Manca Schwalbová, *Vyhasnuté Oči* (Bratislava: Marenčin Pt, 2011).

290  **Laced with bromide:** This information comes from multiple sources, including Rena Kornreich Gelissen, coauthor of *Rena's Promise: A Story of Sisters in Auschwitz*, and is eloquently substantiated by Edith Valo in her USC Shoah testimony.

292  **"The 'green' female prisoners":** Rudolf Höss, *Commandant of Auschwitz: The Autobiography of Rudolf Höss* (London: Phoenix Press, 2001), p. 135.

293  **marching out barefoot:** Edith Grosman. *Personal interview for book and documentary film 999.* (Toronto, Canada. March - July 2017).

294  **The Mattock has a pick:** "Mattock," Wikipedia, Wikimedia Foundation, July 24, 2019.

296  **Budy Penal Colony:** Czech, *Auschwitz Chronicle*, p. 186, and Piotr Cywiński, Jacek Lachendro, and Piotr Setkiewicz, *Auschwitz from A to Z: An Illustrated History of the Camp* (Muzeum Auschwitz, 2021), "Budy."

297  **"The Budy blood-bath":** Höss, *Commandant of Auschwitz*, p. 135. Despite efforts to find who from the third convoy was murdered that day, we have not been able to find their names.

298  **"You had to sleep with your bread":** Judith Spielberger Mittelman, *Personal Interview for documentary film, 999.* (New York. November 29, 2021).

298  **"declared incapable of working":** Czech, *Auschwitz Chronicle*, p. 189.

298  **The first selection of Jews:** Czech, p. 191–2.

298  **"Every day some of us":** Bloch Kennedy, Cassette 4, Side A. Reel 2, Side 1. p. 26. Inaccurate death dates are recorded in both the Caen and Yad Vashem archives; they indicate death dates for six of the women from the third convoy as being June 25 and 27. Annette is one of those victims inaccurately listed among those dead. Thanks to Raya Kagan's memoir, we were able to confirm that Annette was alive in Birkenau in August 1942. It is important to note that neither testimony of Claudette Bloch nor Raya Kagan mention any of their group dying in those first few days. If one of them had died that early surely they would have recalled the incident for the historic record. Therefore, we conclude that those dates are erroneous. Women's death dates were not recorded until August 1942.

298 **Saturday, July 4:** Höss, *Commandant of Auschwitz*, p. 184, and Czech, *Auschwitz Chronicle*, pp. 191–92. "Of the Jews registered in camp the men were given numbers 44727–44990; and 108 women are tattooed at 8389–8496."

## Operation Spring Breeze—Paris

Multiple sources have been used in this section, including Serge and Beate Klarsfeld's penultimate history of *French Children of the Holocaust (Le Bulletin Des Les Fils et Filles Des Deportee Juifs de France)*, witness testimonies, and articles.

300 **Parti Populaire Français (PPF):** Claude Cattaert and Liliane Grunwald, *Le Vél' d'Hiv'*, 1903–1959.

300 **Sarah Lichtsztejn-Montard:** Stéphanie Trouillard, "The Vél d'Hiv Roundup: 75 Years On, a Survivor Remembers," *France 24*, July 15, 2017.

301 **"smoky light":** Ernest Hemingway, *A Moveable Feast* (New York: Vintage, 2012), pp. 64–65.

301 **"gave off a glaucous light":** Trouillard, "The Vél d'Hiv Roundup."

302 **thirteen thousand Jews arrested:** "Vel D'Hiv Roundup of Paris Jews Remembered, 78 Years Later," Algemeiner, July 16, 2020.

## Himmler Inspects Auschwitz

304 **Friday, July 17:** Czech, pp. 198–99.

306 **Langefeld was working:** Höss, *Commandant of Auschwitz*, 138, and Heather Dune Macadam, *999* (New York: Kensington Citadel, 2020), p. 191.

307 **Bella arrived:** Caen Archive, AC 21 P 262544 and AC 21 P 475969.

308 **Hélène Berger, Syma Berger:** Yad Vashem archive states that Hélène died on August 19, which is impossible, as that was the date that she was deported to Auschwitz. Hélène arrived on the twenty-first convoy on August 21. Of the 1,000 Jews on that transport, 817 were gassed upon arrival, 373 of whom were children under the age of thirteen; Hélène was thirteen and probably went straight to the gas chamber. There is no death date for her sister, Syma. In 1978, their surviving brother, Ferdinand, filed *Feuille Témoignage, à l'Institut Commémoratif des Martyrs et des Héros*, at Yad Vashem in Jerusalem, looking for any information about his sisters.

## Birkenau

312 **In 1961 Raya Kagan:** Session No. 70, 73, 75, 82, 87, YouTube video *EichmannTrialEN*, March 9, 2011.

312 **on August 15:** Czech, p. 186. In 2014 Macadam analyzed the records of the first Jewish transport, comparing the original transport list with the Arrival list typed in camp and all death records (at the time) available through the Auschwitz Museum and Yad Vashem. Due to an inordinate number of deaths on August 15 and the reports by survivors that the first selections began in August, her conclusion is that August 15, 1942, is the date of the first selection of women prisoners. In the future, other researchers may analyze deportation lists and discover additional information about this date, the first selection of women prisoners, and the number of women who were selected to die.

312 **"the first ruthless, terrible selection":** Manca Schwalbová is one of those survivors who wrote about that first selection in her memoir on p. 29.

314 **Monday, August 17:** This date was reached by comparing Kagan's testimony with the Czech arrival logs for Auschwitz-Birkenau. The last time Raya Kagan sees Annette and their friends is four days before she is moved to *Stabsgebäude*; she mentions a new transport of French-speaking Jews is standing at roll call. The only transport that arrived the week before she was relocated was the third convoy from Belgium, which arrived on Monday, August 17.

316 **Ruth and Nadine were standing:** Kagan, p. 86. Ruth may be Ruchla Plewa (nineteen years old and Polish/French) or Ryuak (Rachel) Szepsman (twenty-one, Polish). There was no Nadine on the third convoy but that may have been a nickname.

316 **third transport from Malines, Belgium:** Ibid., and Czech, *Auschwitz Chronicle*, p. 185. The third transport from Belgium arrived on August 17, 1942, with 1,000 Jews from Malines; of the 486 women on that transport, 205 were registered in camp. In a rare detail, the number of children were recorded: eighty-six boys and eighty-six girls were gassed, most likely with their mothers.

317 **"Merci":** Annette quoted in Kagan, p. 86.

## The Empty Seat

Information about the Sobibor Concentration Camp comes from the Memorial Museum of Sobibor and Arlson Archive in Germany.

321 **"gay and beautiful girls":** de Beauvoir, *Prime of Life*, p. 423.

322 **"victim of another woman's":** Ibid.

322 **designer and model Sonia Mossé:** Eugene Briffault, *Paris Dans l' Eau* (Gallica.bnf.fr Collection XIX, 2016).

322 *Le Rouge et le Bleu:* A weekly "journal of Socialist thought" started by the left-wing politician Charles Spinasse in 1941. Though it was regarded as a collaborationist publication, meaning it appeared with the assent of the Germans, it did not toe the Nazi line. It ceased publica-

tion in September 1942, which may have been one of the reasons Jean left for Limoges that fall.

324  **A photograph taken at the house:** This is the only surviving photograph we have managed to find of Jean Jausion. Most likely, Claude Crotelle had photos of his best friend, and possibly of Annette with Jean, but in a clear-out of his *chambres de bonne* apartment everything was tossed.

325  **Allied troops had landed in North Africa:** Gerhard Schreiber et al., *Germany and the Second World War*, vol. 3, *The Mediterranean, South-East Europe, and North Africa, 1939–1941: From Italy's Declaration of Non-Belligerence to the Entry of the United States into the War*, trans. by Dean S. McMurry, Ewald Osers, and Louise Willmot, trans. ed. P.S. Falla.

## Dispersal

We fleshed out Michele's memories with additional source material and survivors' testimonies.

328  **Balthazard, aka Saint-André:** Ville d'Annemasse, "Les Personnalités Importantes," Annemasse, and Dozol, "Annemasse, Ville Frontière 1940–1944."

328  **When the *passeur*, Mila Racine:** Mila Racine, "Mila Racine's Last Letter," www.yadvashem.org, July 1944.

328  **aka Marie Colin:** "Late June, Early July 1944: Annemasse, France; 'Love Her Like a Mother'—Last Letters from the Holocaust: 1944 YV."

329  **One hundred and fifty SS:** Dozol, "Annemasse, Ville Frontière 1940–1944."

331  **between February 1943 and April 1944:** Ibid.

331  **"Every morning, Marianne":** Julie Kangisser, "Ernst's Wife Renee's Story of Survival," Holocaust Matters, December 28, 2017.

## To the Barricades!

333  **informers and denouncers:** Alan Moorehead, *Eclipse* (New York: Andesite Press, 2015), p. 167.

333  **By 1944, the French resistance:** C. N. Trueman, "The French Resistance," History Learning Site, May 18, 2015.

334  **"We played records":** de Beauvoir, *Force of Circumstance*, p. 609.

334  **Are they finally leaving:** Mathew Cobb, *Eleven Days in August: The Liberation of Paris in 1944* (London: Simon & Schuster, 2019), p. 114.

334  **"Bread! Bread!":** Ibid.

335  **Free French resistance:** Ibid., pp. 145–49.

335  **Hundreds of resistants:** Cobb, *Eleven Days in August*, p. 147

335  **Fighting erupted all over:** de Beauvoir, *Prime of Life*, p. 467.

335  **"The sound of revolution":** Ibid., pp. 142–49.

335  **Dogs are barking:** Ibid., p. 163.

335　**Jean was captured:** Joly, *Dénoncer Les Juifs Sous l'Occupation.*

336　**"The whole neighborhood is here":** Quoted in Cobb, *Eleven Days in August,* p. 211.

336　**a pile of innards:** Ibid., p. 233.

336　**Notre Dame's bells:** Ibid., p. 277.

336　**under clear skies and hot sunshine:** Ibid., p. 291, and Moorehead, *Eclipse,* pp. 167–70.

337　**"The pandemonium of a free":** Cobb, *Eleven Days in August,* p. 325.

337　**Twelve days later:** Joly, *Dénoncer Les Juifs Sous l'Occupation,* p. 106.

## The Road to Lorraine

The description of Jean setting off to look for Annette comes from Georges Hugnet's memoir, *Pleins et Delies.* Key source material comes from *7th Armored Division Liberation of Western Europe, WWII Archival Film Footage* (distributed by Combat Reels) taken on the days in question on the exact route that Jean Jausion took to Lorraine, as well as our own retracing of the journey in the summer of 2020. To get firsthand knowledge of Jean's experience, we retraced his route along the Voie de la Liberté, visiting the village of Gravelotte and the Mogador Farm. We used archival photographs to describe this section, as well as reviewing newspaper headlines in France and England.

338　**"All fire, all flame":** Georges Hugnet, *Pleins et Delies: Souvenirs et Témoignages* (Paris, G. Authier, 1972), p. 237.

339　**In Provins:** Tyler Alberts, ed., *7th Armored Division—Raw and Uncensored WWII Archival Film Footage,* DVD, Combat Reels—Military History on Film, September 6, 1944.

339　**"fighting among themselves":** "Battle of Germany Opening: Only a Few Miles to Go Now," *The People,* September 3, 1944.

340　**"My men can eat their belts":** Chester Wilmot, *The Struggle for Europe* (Hertfordshire, UK: Wordsworth Editions, 2003), p. 473.

340　**The Citroën 11:** Citroën, "Citroën Traction Avant 11."

341　**Production had continued:** François Bonal, *Le Livre d'Or du Champagne* (Lausanne: Editions du Grand-Pont, Jean-Pierre Laubscher, 1984).

341　**Count Robert-Jean de Vogue:** Ibid. De Vogue later returned, frail and half-starved from his internment, and began the task of rebuilding the champagne industry.

341　**Patton's army had liberated Épernay:** Maire Machet, "Archives Municipales d'Épernay—Service Éducatif," August 28, 1944.

341　**"are topped by slender:** Hannah Nawalfleh, "Gothic Architecture Styles." *Issuu.com.*

342　**It had almost been destroyed:** Thomas W. Gaehtgens, "Bombing the Cathedral of Reims," *Getty Iris,* January 23, 2015.

342　**Echoes of the Great War:** Sueddeutsche Zeitung Photo, German Commemoration Celebration in Verdun, 1940, Alamy Stock Photo,

1940; Sueddeutsche Zeitung Photo, Ossuary of Douaumont during the Occupation of France, 1940, Alamy Stock Photo, 1940; Sueddeutsche Zeitung Photo, World War II from German Propaganda News. Parade of Wehrmacht Soldiers in Occupied Verdun, France, 1940, Alamy Stock Photo, 1940. In WWI, the battle went from February 1916 to December 1916; approximately 230,000 men died.

342    **The recent German retreat:** Photographic and newspaper resources include, *Evening Standard*, Alamy image 2BEPG21; Kathy deWitt, *Evening Standard* WWII British Newspaper Headline 1 September 1944 "Patton Takes Verdun" across the Meuse and Germany Is 49 Miles Away, Spring 2, 2020, Alamy Stock Photo, Spring 2, 2020; and F. P., "Commémoration—Mercredi Prochain Se Dérouleront Les Cérémonies Du 72e Anniversaire de La Libération de La Ville Au Monument Legay, Hénon, Schluck et Evins Ainsi Qu'au Monument Des Fusillés de Tavannes. En Souvenir Du 31 Août 1944, Jour de La Libération de Verdun," *L'Est Républicain*, August 25, 2016.

343    **"to the last man:** Cole, Hugh M. "Chapter IX the November Battle for Metz (Concluded)." *U.S. Army World War II - European Theater of Operations - the Lorraine Campaign*, 1997.

343    **"German high command":** *Daily Herald*, Front page. September 6, 1944, BNF-G.

343    **Les Wirkkala:** Gary Bedingfield, "Les Wirkkala—Baseball's Greatest Sacrifice," Baseball's Greatest Sacrifice, May 29, 2012.

344    **battle-hardened units:** The *kampfgruppe* of 1,800 mostly officer cadets was led by the veteran commander Major General Joachim von Siegroth, who would receive one of the highest honors of the German military, the *Ritterkreuz des Eisernen Kreuzes*, or Knight's Cross, for his leadership at Gravelotte. "Siegroth, Von, Joachim," STIWOT—Traces of War—Foundation for Information World War Two (STIWOT, 1999).

344    **The editors of *Franc-Tireur*:** "Le Franc-Tireur: Organe des Mouvements Unis de Résistance: Mensuel Malgré la Gestapo et la Police de Vichy: Édition de Paris." *Gallica*, November 9, 1944.

## *Return to the City of Light*

Details of the Zelmans' return to Paris and the effect of the disappearance of Annette come from our interviews with Michele Kersz. For details about the Hôtel Lutetia as a reception center for concentration camp survivors, we used survivor testimonies, Michele's own memories, and archival photographs.

346    **"The liberation of Limoges":** *Combat*, Gallica-BNF, September 20, 1944.

347    **the Sentier was a warren:** Eric Hazan, *The Invention of Paris* (London: Verso, 2011), pp. 50–51.

348    **on January 27:** Czech, p. 785–805.

350    **Buchenwald, the camp:** *Combat*, April 20, 1945.

351 **Hôtel Lutetia:** Mark Seal, "Paris' Hotel Lutetia Is Haunted by History," *Smithsonian Magazine*, April 2019.

353 **between eighteen and twenty thousand:** Ibid.

354 **Many found themselves alone:** Quoted in Rosie Whitehouse, "A Paris Luxury Hotel Filled with Concentration Camp Survivors," *Tablet Magazine*, May 8, 2020.

354 **Maurice Cling was sixteen:** Ibid.

354 **"Did you know so and so":** Ibid.

354 **"empty faces":** Ibid.

355 **Marceline Loridan:** After the war, Marceline Loridan and her family became a close friend of the Zelmans. Indeed, her father wanted their son, Guy, to marry her. Camille later fell in love with her but nothing came of it. She went on to marry Dutch documentary filmmaker Joris Ivens. She also became a close collaborator and friend of Jean Rouch, who had played such an important role in Annette's Café de Flore days. It truly is a small world.

## *Poland*

360 **Josette Delimal was gone:** Raya Kagan tells Claudette about Josette on p. 108. There is no death date recorded for Josette Delimal.

361 **Tamara Isserlis, of whom:** Claudette Bloch quoted in Kagan, p. 108. According to the Caen Archive, Tamara Isserlis died on September 1, 1942, of typhus. She was working as a nurse, so may have died in the prisoner hospital. Generally, ill prisoners were sent to Block 25, also known as the Block of Death, where they were removed for gassing. Since Tamara's death date concurs with Ida Levine's, they may have been taken together from Block 25 to the gas. *The Auschwitz Chronicle* does not report a mass selection on that day, but it is still possible that Ida, Tamara, Sonia, Bella, and Annette all died together on the same day, in all likelihood they died within days or weeks of each other. "In comparison to this, Dante's Inferno seems almost like a comedy. Not for nothing is Auschwitz called the camp of extermination," SS Dr. Johann Paul Kremer wrote in his diary on September 2, 1942. Czech, p. 232.

361 **the historic "Big" selection:** Personal interviews with Edith Grosman #1970, 999; Rena Gelissen #1716, *Rena's Promise*; the testimony of Linda Reich Breder #1173, from the USC Shoah testimony; and the memoirs *I Escaped Auschwitz*, by Rudolph Vrba, and *Extended Eyes*, by Dr. Manca Schwalbová.

## *Epilogue*

The quote that begins this chapter is a tribute to the young Spanish Jew, Bourla, whose incarceration in Drancy and subsequent murder, de Beauvoir and Sartre grieved. She wrote about him in her memoir and he was the character, Diégo, in *Les Mandarins*. It is interesting to also note that her character "Lambert" which is how Jean Rouch spelled Bella's last name, may be a nod to Bella; that character is also a journalist whose fiancée is denounced to the Gestapo by his father, just like Jean Jausion.

Material about the postwar lives of the Zelman family comes from our interviews with Michele Kersz in the summer of 2020. We also made an emotional return with her to the Café de Flore and her childhood haunts on Boulevard de Strasbourg. Because the layout of the building at No. 58 has been altered, we were not able to see the actual apartment Annette and her family lived in.

Our research into Jean's death comes from a journey we took from Paris to Gravelotte, in Lorraine, that same summer. We visited the Mogador Farm, where General Patton had holed up for a fortnight and where Jean's bullet-riddled body was believed to have been laid out. But we could not find a grave, nor any further information.

The letter from Dr. Hubert Jausion to Annette's brother, Guy, about the Jausions' own investigation, is quoted in *Dénoncer les Juifs Sous l'Occupation*, by Laurent Joly. The reference to the erroneous rumor that Jean committed vehicular suicide, first mentioned by Simone de Beauvoir, comes from her postwar memoir, *Force of Circumstance*.

The correspondence between Dannecker and Darquier de Pellepoix about legislation banning mixed marriages between Aryans and Jews comes from the *Centre de Documentation Juive Contemporaine, Memorial de la Shoah*, Paris.

# Bibliography

We gratefully acknowledge the USC Shoah Foundation and the Institute for Visual History and Education for the following testimonies: Edita Valo, 1996; Linda Breder, 1990; Margaret Rosenberg, 1996. For more information, visit sfi.usc.edu.

*Adolf Hitler's Visit to Paris: June 1940.* https://war-documentary.info/eng/, April 4, 2021; https://war-documentary-info-hitler-in-Paris-june-1940.

Alberts, Tyler, ed. *7th Armored Division—Raw and Uncensored WWII Archival Film Footage.* DVD. *Combat Reels—Military History on Film,* September 6, 1944.

Alvarez, Andrea. "La Caserne Des Tourelles/La Piscine." Mapping Modiano's *Dora Bruder.* Projet numérique des étudiants de RLFR 305 (Williams College), 2018. https://sites.williams.edu/rlfr305-f18/uncat egorized/la-caserne-des-tourelles-la-piscine/.

"Arno Breker." www.artnet.com. Accessed July 29, 2021. http://www.artnet .com/artists/arno-breker/.

Audry, Colette. "Sisters in the Resistance: Transcript of Interview with Colette Audry (English)." Margaret Collins Weitz Papers, 1945–2006 (MS109). Moakley Archive & Institute; Suffolk University Boston, April 26, 1982. https://moakleyarchive.omeka.net/items/show/9211.

Auschwitz-Birkenau Memorial and Museum. "Budy." n.d. http://ausch-witz.org/en/history/auschwitz-sub-camps/budy/.

"Battle of Germany Opening: Only a Few Miles to Go Now." *The People,* September 3, 1944. https://gallica.bnf.fr.

Bedingfield, Gary. "Les Wirkkala—Baseball's Greatest Sacrifice." www.base-ballsgreatestsacrifice.com, May 29, 2012. https://www.baseballsgreat-estsacrifice.com/biographies/wirkkala_les.html.

Berr, Hélène. *The Journal of Hélène Berr.* Translated by David Bellos. London: Maclehose, 2009.

———. *The Journal of Hélène Berr.* New York: Weinstein Books, 2008.

Berson, Roger. "Captain Vézille Giving a Present to the 100,001th Visitor. World War II. Le Juif et La France, Anti-Jewish Exhibition at the Berlitz Palace, Paris." Roger-Viollet. *LAPI Granger*, September 1941.

———. *Walck, Young Man. Exhibition Le Juif et La France. World War II. 0764195.* Roger-Viollet. *LAPI Granger*, September 1941. https://www.granger.com/results.asp?image=0764195&itemw=0&itemf=0001&itemstep=1&itemx=1.

Birman, Renée. *Mémoire de Mon Bonheur.* Paris: L'Harmattan, 2004.

Blakemore, Erin. "The French Resistance's Secret Weapon? The Mime Marcel Marceau." History, January 2, 2019. https://www.history.com/news/marcel-marceau-wwii-french-resistance-georges-loinger.

Bloch, Claudette. *Témoignages sur Auschwitz: Récits par le Dr B. Krewer, Claudette Bloch, J. Furmansk, Les Drs Désiré Haffner et Golse, Mme Kleinowa, etc. Avant-Propos de Claudette Bloch.*

Bloch Kennedy, Claudette. "Claudette Kennedy—Living Memory of the Jewish Community." (3–6 of 6) Interview by Natasha Burchardt. Oral History—British Library Sound Archive, July 10, 1988. http://www.europeana.eu/en/item/2059209/data_sounds_C0410X0027XX_0300. This transcript is copyright of the British Library. Please refer to the oral history section at the British Library prior to any publication or broadcast from this document.

Bloch Kennedy, Claudette, Simone Franck-Floersheim, Lore Shelley, and Aude Hoyrup. *Claudette: Auschwitz-Birkenau, 1942–1945: Recherche en Laboratoire.* Chambéry: Ed. De La Librairie J.-J. Rousseau, 2002.

Bonal, François. *Le Livre d'Or du Champagne.* Lausanne: Editions du Grand-Pont, Jean-Pierre Laubscher, 1984.

Bordeaux, Henry. *Images du Maréchal Pétain.* Paris: Sequana, 1941.

Boubal, Christophe. *Café de Flore, l'Esprit d'un Siècle.* Paris: Lanore, 2004.

Boyd, Julia. *Travellers in the Third Reich: The Rise of Fascism through the Eyes of Everyday People.* London: Elliott & Thompson, 2018.

Brendel, Jürgen. "Édith Piaf: The Dark Life of the Singer of Love." www.dw.com. Deutsche Welle, December 2015. https://www.dw.com/en/%C3%A9dith-piaf-the-dark-life-of-the-singer-of-love/a-18925386.

Breton, André. *Le Surrealisme au Service de la Revolution: Numbers 1 to 6, July 1930 to May 1933. Complete Collection.* Paris: Jean-Michel Place, 2002.

———. *Manifeste du Surréalisme—Poisson Soluble.* Paris: Éditions du Sagittaire, 1924.

Briffault, Eugène. *Paris dans l'Eau (1799–1854). Gallica.bnf.fr.* Collection XIX, 2016. J. Hetzel, 1844. https://gallica.bnf.fr/ark:/12148/bpt6k1030068/f3.item.

Brookner, Anita. *Incidents in the Rue Laugier.* New York: Vintage Books, 1997.

Bucher Jaeger, Jeanne. "Jeanne Bucher Gallery 1925–2008." Jeanne Bucher Jaeger, 2008. https://jeannebucherjaeger.com/about/jeanne-bucher/.

Buck, Stephanie. "Zazous: What Punk Culture Meant in World War II France." Timeline, October 4, 2016. https://timeline.com/zazou -france-world-war-ii-9f26b36e0ee3.

Cain, Abigail. "What Were 1960s 'Happenings,' and Why Do They Matter?" Artsy, March 2016. https://www.artsy.net/article/artsy-editorial-what- were-1960s-happenings-and-why-do-they-matter.

Callil, Carmen. *Bad Faith: A Forgotten History of Family and Fatherland*. London: Jonathan Cape, 2006.

Camus, Albert. *Notebooks 1942–1951*. Translated by Justin O'Brien. 1964. Reprint. New York: Alfred A. Knopf, 1965.

Camus, Albert, and Alexandre De Gramont. *Between Hell and Reason: Essays from the Resistance Newspaper Combat, 1944–1947*. Middletown, CT: Wesleyan University Press, 1991.

Cardon-Hamet, Claudine. "L'aide d's '45 000' Aux Femmes de Birkenau." https://politique-auschwitz.blogspot.com, 2005. https://politique -auschwitz.blogspot.com/2011/04/laide-des-45-000-aux-femmes-de- birkenau.html.

Cassou, Jean. "La Liberation de la Zone Sud." Gallica. Combat: Organe du Mouvement de libération française, September 11, 1944. https:// gallica.bnf.fr/ark:/12148/bpt6k47485795/.

Cattaert, Claude, and Liliane Grunwald. *Le Vél' d'Hiv', 1903–1959*. Paris: Éditions Ramsay, 1979.

The Central Database of Shoah Victims' Names. List of persecuted persons. Yad Vashem. Item ID, 6986086. https://yvng.yadvashem.org/name Details.html?language=en&itemId=6986086&ind=4

Century, Rachel. Phone Interview. London, 29 April 2021.

Chevalier, Maurice. "Ma Pomme." 1936.

Chornyi, Maksym. "Adolf Hitler's Visit to Paris: June 1940." https://war-doc umentary.info/eng/, April 4, 2021. https://war-documentary.info/ hitler-in-paris-june-1940/.

"Citroën Traction Avant 11CV." CITROËNËT. www.citroenet.org.uk. Accessed July 30, 2021. http://www.citroenet.org.uk/passenger-cars/ michelin/traction/11CV/traction-avant-11cv-1.html.

Cobb, Matthew. *Eleven Days in August: The Liberation of Paris in 1944*. London: Simon & Schuster, 2019.

"Cohn, Marianne (1921–1944)." Encyclopedia.com. www.encyclopedia.com, n.d. https://www.encyclopedia.com/women/encyclopedias-almanacs -transcripts-and-maps/cohn-marianne-1921-1944.

Cole, Hugh M. "Chapter IX the November Battle for Metz (Concluded)." U.S. Army World War II—European Theater of Operations—the

Lorraine Campaign, 1997. Ibiblio, www.ibiblio.org/hyperwar/USA/ USA-E-Lorraine/index.html. Accessed 4 Apr. 2021.

"Colette Audry." Wikipedia, July 2021. https://en.wikipedia.org/wiki/Colette _Audry.

"Combat: Organe du Mouvement de Libération Française." Gallica, September 20, 1944. https://gallica.bnf.fr/ark:/12148/bpt6k4748587q. Map of the front line.

"Commémoration—Mercredi Prochain se Dérouleront les Cérémonies du 72e Anniversaire de la Libération de la Ville au Monument Legay, Hénon, Schluck et Evins Ainsi Qu'au Monument des Fusillés de Tavannes. En Souvenir du 31 Août 1944, Jour de la Libération de Verdun." *L'Est Republicain,* August 25, 2016. https://www.estrepublicain .fr/edition-de-verdun/2016/08/24/en-souvenir-du-31-aout-1944-jour -de-la-liberation-de-verdun.

Cone, Michèle C. "Remembering Arno Breker—Artnet Magazine." www .artnet.com. Accessed July 2021. http://www.artnet.com/magazineus/ features/cone/cone7-31-06.asp.

Cornil, Mme. (Ed.) *Cent Ans de Mode Francaises 1800–1900.* Paris & Liege: R. Ducher, 1932.

Courouble, Alice. *Amie des Juifs.* Paris: Bloud & Gay, 1946. Memorial de la Shoah Cote: 1.368.

"Couverture." Wikipedia, June 2021. https://en.wikipedia.org/wiki/Couverture.

Coward, David. "Monocled Baron Charged." *London Review of Books,* June 8, 2006. https://www.lrb.co.uk/the-paper/v28/n11/david-coward/ monocled-baron-charged.

Cywiński, Piotr, Jacek Lachendro, and Piotr Setkiewicz. *Auschwitz from A to Z: An Illustrated History of the Camp.* Muzeum Auschwitz, 2021. https:// www.amazon.com/Auschwitz-Z-Illustrated-History-Camp-ebook/dp/ B09FM5BP41/ref=sr_1_1?dchild=1&keywords=Auschwitz+from+A +to+Z&qid=1631872282&sr=8-1.

Czech, Danuta. *Auschwitz Chronicle 1939–1945: From the Archives of the Auschwitz Memorial and the German Federal Archives.* New York: Henry Holt, 1997.

D'Adamo, Cristiano. "Bombardments of Bordeaux." www.regiamarina.net. Direzione Generale del Personale Militare-Regia Marina Italiana, 1996. http://www.regiamarina.net/detail_text.asp?nid=91&lid=1.

Dannecker, Theodor. "Lettre du 23/05/1942 de Theodor Dannecker, Chef de la Section Juive de la Sipo-SD à Louis Darquier de Pellepoix, Commissaire Général aux Questions Juives, et Réponse de Ce Dernier en Date du 03/06/1942, à Propos des Mariages Mixtes, et Notamment Celui d'Annette Zelman avec Monsieur Jean Jausion (Non-Juif)." *Memorial de La Shoah* CXVIII–2a, no. CGQJ—CXVIII, May

23, 1942. https://ressources.memorialdelashoah.org/notice.php?q
=id%3A%28591215%20OR%20id%3A591211%29&from=panier&start
=-&sort_define=tri_titre&sort_order=0.

"Dannecker, Theodor—Instruction by regarding the Campaign of Detentions
against the Jews of Paris." Yad Vashem Documents Archive. Yad Vashem,
April 7, 1942. Item ID: 386038; Record Group: M.9—Jewish Historical
Documentation Center, Linz (Simon Wiesenthal Collection) File
Number: 289. https://documents.yadvashem.org/index.html?language=
en&search=global&strSearch=3686038&GridItemId=386038.

Dave, Kim. "How To: Draft Box Pleated Circle Skirt Pattern." March 2018.
https://www.youtube.com/watch?v=3I-TLlkM4QM&t=0s.

———. "How To: Make Full Circle Skirt Pattern." February 2018. https://
www.youtube.com/watch?v=b1K2BKo3aHg.

de Balzac, Honoré. *Un Episode sous la Terreur.* Bielefeld: Velhagen & Klasing, 1939.

de Beauvoir, Simone. *After the War: Force of Circumstance, 1944–1952.* Boston:
Da Capo Press, 1994.

———. *La Force de l'Âge.* Paris: Gallimard, 1960.

———. *Prime of Life: The Autobiography of Simone de Beauvoir.* Translated by
Peter Green. 1960. Reprint. London: Andrea Deutsch and Weidenfeld and Nicolson, 1963.

Delbo, Charlotte, and Rosette C. Lamont. *Auschwitz and After.* New Haven,
CT: Yale University Press, 2014.

Delteil, Joseph. *Choléra.* Paris: Grasset, 2013.

"Demarcation Line Ministry of Defence General Secretariat for Administration Directorate of Memory, Heritage and Archives." Ministry of Defence. Accessed September 2020. http://www.civs.gouv.fr/images/pdf/
documents_utiles/documents_dhistoire/the_demarcation_line.pdf.

de Ronsard, Pierre. "Mignonne Allons Voir si la Rose—Pierre de Ronsard—
French Moments." French Moments, March 4, 2014. https://french-
moments.eu/mignonne-allons-voir-si-la-rose/.

Dorléac, Laurence Bertrand. *Art of the Defeat: France 1940–1944.* Los An-
geles: Getty Research Institute, 2009.

Dos Passos, John. *Manhattan Transfer.* Boston: Vintage Books, 2021.

"Dossier Individuel de Personnel de Isserlis, Tamara, Denise | Service His-
torique de la Défense." Caen. www.servicehistorique.sga.defense
.gouv.fr. Accessed June 11, 2020. https://www.servicehistorique.sga
.defense.gouv.fr/en/node/123989.

"Dossier Individuel de Personnel de Lempert, Bella," March 12, 2020. Service Historique de la Défense." Caen. Accessed June 11, 2020.. www
.servicehistorique.sga.defense.gouv.fr.

Dozol, Vincent. "Annemasse, Ville Frontière 1940–1944." Institut d'Etudes
Politques de Lyon. Lyon: Université de Lyon, 2010.

Drake, David. *Paris at War: 1939–1944*. Cambridge, MA: Belknap Press, 2015.

Dregny, Michael. *Django: The Life and Music of a Gypsy Legend*. New York: Oxford University Press, 2006.

Dumas, Alexandre. *The Three Musketeers*. Adapted by Saviour Pirotta. Illustrated by John Manders. New York: Starry Forest Books, 2021.

Durand-Boubal, Christophe. *Café de Flore: L'esprit d'un Siècle*. Paris: Éd. Lanore, 2004.

"Eichmann Trial—Session No. 70, 73, 75, 82, 87." YouTube video. *Eichmann-TrialEN,* March 9, 2011. https://www.youtube.com/watch?v=TtXJNcwTɪcE. Continuation of the cross-examination.

"Eichmann Trial—Testimony of Raya Kagan, Born in 1910, Regarding Her Experiences in Paris, in the Tourelles Camp and in Auschwitz, 29 May 1961." Yad Vashem Documents Archive. Yad Vashem, May 29, 1961. ID: 3664457; Record: TR–3—Eichmann Trial; File: 1645. https://documents.yadvashem.org/index.html?language=en&search=global&strSearch=3664457&GridItemId=3664457.

Eismann, G. "The Militärbefehlshaber in Frankreich and the Genesis of the 'Final Solution' in France (1941–1942)." *Vingtième Siècle. Revue d'histoire* 132, no. 4 (2016). https://doi.org/.

"84 Avenue Foch." Wikipedia, December 20, 2019. https://en.wikipedia.org/wiki/84_avenue_foch.

Elphick, James. "This Is What the Army's 'Iron Men of Metz' and Attila the Hun Have in Common." We Are the Mighty, April 16, 2021. https://www.wearethemighty.com/mighty-history/iron-men-of-metz-and-attila-the-hun/.

Evezard, Juliette. *Un Art Autre: Le Rêve de Michel Tapié*. Paris: Les Presses des Réel, 2023.

"Fable Jean de La Fontaine: La Fille, Le Héron." www.la-fontaine-ch-thierry.net. Accessed April 16, 2021. http://www.la-fontaine-ch-thierry.net/heron.htm.

Fauré, Michel. *Histoire du Surréalisme sous l'Occupation: Les Réverbères, la Main à Plume*. Paris: La Table Ronde, 2003.

Finley-Croswhite, Annette, and Gayle K. Brunelle. "Creating a Holocaust Landscape on the Streets of Paris: French Agency and the Synagogue Bombings of October 3, 1941." Oxford: *Holocaust and Genocide Studies* 33 (2019): 60–89. https://doi.org/10.1093/hgs/dcz009.

Flambard-Weisbart, Veronique. "Analysis of Annette Zelman Letters." July 2, 2021.

Fogg, Shannon Lee. "Denunciations, Community Outsiders, and Material Shortages in Vichy France." *Proceedings of the Western Society for French History* 31 (2003), https://quod.lib.umich.edu/w/wsfh/0642292.0031.017/.

———. "Refugees and Indifference: The Effects of Shortages on Attitudes towards Jews in France's Limousin Region during World War II." *Holocaust and Genocide Studies* 21, no. 1 (2007): 31–54. https:// muse.jhu.edu/article/215310.

Foot, Michael R. D. *Resistance: An Analysis of European Resistance to Nazism.* London: Methuen, 1976.

Fox Maura, Soledad. *Exile, Writer, Soldier, Spy: Jorge Semprún.* New York: Arcade, 2018.

"France Pays Tribute to Six-Year-Old Resistance Hero Marcel Pinte." *Guardian.* Staff and agencies in Aixe-sur-Vienne, November 11, 2020. https://www.theguardian.com/world/2020/nov/11/france-pays-tribute-to-six-year-old-resistance-hero-marcel-pinte.

Fraser, Nicholas. "[Reviews] Toujours Vichy, by Nicholas Fraser." *Harper's Magazine,* October 1, 2006. https://harpers.org/archive/2006/10/toujours-vichy/.

French Ministry of Defence. "Remembrance and Citizenship," *The Demarcation Line.* Series 7. Directorate of Memory, Heritage and Archives, n.d. Accessed Sept. 2020. http://www.civs.gouv.fr/images/pdf/documents_utiles/documents_dhistoire/the_demarcation_line.pdf.

"French Poet Pierre de Ronsard and Cassandre Salviati, Engraving For…" Getty Images, November 22, 1547. https://www.gettyimages.com/detail/news-photo/french-poet-pierre-de-ronsard-and-cassandre-salviati-news-photo/89865923.

"Fresnes Prison—Fresnes—TracesOfWar.com." www.tracesofwar.com. Accessed July 28, 2021. https://www.tracesofwar.com/sights/108777/Fresnes-Prison.htm.

Gaehtgens, Thomas W. "Bombing the Cathedral of Reims." *Getty Iris,* January 23, 2015. https://blogs.getty.edu/iris/bombing-the-cathedral-of-rheims/.

Gandoulou, Justin-Daniel. *Entre Paris et Bacongo.* Paris: Centre Georges Pompidou, Centre De Création Industrielle, 1984.

Gay, Valentine. "La Défaite Récupérée École Nationale Supérieure des Beaux-Arts." PhD thesis, 2011.

"Gedenkstätte und Museum Sachsenhausen." Gedenkstätte und Museum Sachsenhausen, n.d. https://www.sachsenhausen-sbg.de/en/history/1933-1934-oranienburg-concentration-camp/.

Gilbert, Martin. *The Second World War.* Revised. 1989. Reprint, London: Fontana/Collins, 1990.

"Great Synagogue of Paris—La Victoire." Grande Synagogue de Paris. Accessed July 23, 2021. http://www.lavictoire.org/English/index.html.

Grosman, Edith. Multiple Personal Interviews, Toronto, CN, and Poprad, Slovakia, 2017–2020.

Hamelin, France. *Femmes dans la Nuit: L'internement à la Petite Roquette et au Camp des Tourelles: 1939–1944.* Paris: Renaudot et Cie, 1988.

Hazan, Éric, and David Fernbach. *The Invention of Paris: A History in Footsteps.* London: Verso, 2011.

Headquarters Third US Army and Eastern Military District: Apprehension of Dannecker, Theo. December 10, 1945. Declassified April 20, 2001. CIA. https://www.jewishvirtuallibrary.org/jsource/Holocaust/OSS/dannecker.pdf.

Heath, Nick. "The Zazous—1940–1945." *Organise! The Theoretical Journal of the Anarchist Federation* 59. libcom.org, n.d. https://libcom.org/history/1940-45-the-zazous.

Heeckeren, Axel de. "Jean Auguste Marembert—Monographie et Biographie." Jean Marembert, 2019. https://www.jeanmarembert.com/english-bio.

Heim, Susanne, Carola Sachse, and Mark Walker. *The Kaiser Wilhelm Society under National Socialism.* New York: Cambridge University Press, 2009.

Hemingway, Ernest. *A Moveable Feast.* New York: Vintage, 2012.

"Henry Bordeaux." April 20, 2021. https://en.wikipedia.org/wiki/Henry_Bordeaux.

"Heron and the Fish, The." Wikipedia, November 5, 2019. Accessed March 1, 2021. https://en.wikipedia.org/wiki/The_Heron_and_the_Fish.

Hidalgo, Louise. "Witness History—The Paris Hotel That Hosted Holocaust Survivors—BBC Sounds." www.bbc.co.uk, October 29, 2019. https://www.bbc.co.uk/sounds/play/w3csyx2s.

"Hitler: Fight on to End, Ignore Allied Pledges." *Daily Herald,* January 31, 1945. www.britishnewspaperarchive.co.uk. 001.

Höss, Rudolf. *Commandant of Auschwitz: The Autobiography of Rudolf Höss.* London: Phoenix Press, 2000.

Hugnet, Georges. *Pleins et Delies: Souvenirs et Temoignages, 1926–1972.* Paris: G. Authier, 1972.

Hugnet, Georges, and Pablo Picasso. *Non Vouloir.* Paris: Jeanne Bucher, 1940.

Hulton Archive and Gettty Images. "French Poet Pierre de Ronsard (1524–1585) and Cassandre Salviati, Engraving for 1552 Edition of 'Amours.'" Apic, 1552. https://www.gettyimages.com/detail/news-photo/french-poet-pierre-de-ronsard-and-cassandre-salviati-news-photo/89865923.

Hutton, Margaret Anne. *Testimony from the Nazi Camps: French Women's Voices.* London: Routledge, 2004. https://play.google.com/books/reader?id=pG1_AgAAQBAJ&hl=en&pg=GBS.PT56.

Jackson, Julian. *France: The Dark Years, 1940–1944.* New York: Oxford University Press, 2003.

Jahan, Pierre. "Pierre JAHAN (1909–2003)—Site Officiel du Photograhe." pierrejahan.free.fr, 2006. http://pierrejahan.free.fr/pjahan/galerie/displayimage.php?album=15&pos=12.

Jausion, Jean. *Un homme Marche dans la ville (A ManWalks in the City)*. Paris: Gallimard, 1945.

Jausion, Jean & Michel Tapié. *Polyphème, ou, L'escadron Bleu*. Paris: Éditions des Réverbères, 1939.

Jausion, Raymond. "J'ai Chasse le Poisson a l'Arbalete—au Large du Bandolier." *Paris-soir*, November 21, 1941. https://gallica.bnf.fr/ark:/12148/bpt6k7642998d/f2.item.r=Jausion.

Jézégou, Frédérick. "Les plus Accomodants Sont les plus Habiles—Dictionnaire des Citations." https://dicocitations.lemonade.fr/blog/les-plus-accommodants-sont-les-plus-habiles/.

Joly, Laurent. *Dénoncer les Juifs Sous l'Occupation, 1940–1944*. Paris: Cnrs, 2017.

———. *Les Collabos. Treize Portraits d'Après les Archives des Services Secrets de Vichy, des RG et de l'Épuration Édition Revue et Augmentée—Laurent Joly*. www.decitre.fr. 2011. Reprint, Paris: Tallandier, 2019.

Jortner, Claire. Personal interview about Claude Croutelle. Interview by Heather Dune Macadam and Simon Worrall, July 12, 2021.

Kagan, Raya. *Women in the Bureau of Hell* (Auschwitz Chapters). Merhavyah: ha-Kibuts ha-artsi ha-shomer ha-tsa'ir, 1947. Electronic reproduction. HathiTrust Digital Library, 2010. MiAaHDL.

———. *Des Femmes dans le Bureau de l'Enfer*. Edited by Serge Klarsfeld. Translated by Fabienne Bergmann. 1947. Reprint, Paris: F.F.D.J.F. Serge et Beate Klarsfeld Foundation, 2020.

Kangisser, Julie. "Ernst's Wife Renee's Story of Survival." *Holocaust Matters*, December 28, 2017. https://www.holocaustmatters.org/ernsts-wife-renees-story-of-survival/.

Kennedy, Claudette. "Personal Recollections of Durkheim, Mauss, the Family and Others." *Durkheimian Studies/Études Durkheimiennes* 16, no. 1. (2010): 36–56. https://doi.org/10.3167/ds.2010.160104.

"Kennedy, Claudette, 1910– (2 of 6)." The Living Memory of the Jewish Community—Jewish Survivors of the Holocaust—Oral History. British Library—Sounds. Interview by Natasha Burchardt. Sounds.bl.uk, December 7, 1988. https://sounds.bl.uk/Oral-history/Jewish-Holocaust-survivors/021M-C0410X0027XX-0200V0.

Kershaw, Alex. *Blood and Champagne: The Life and Times of Robert Capa*. New York: Da Capo Press, 2004.

Kersz, Laurence. *La Cuisine de Nos Grands-Mères Juives-Polonaises*. Monaco: Éditions Du Rocher, 2005.

Kersz, Michele. Multiple interviews, July 2–3, 2019, and July–August 2020.

Kladstrup, Don, and Petie Kladstrup. *Wine and War: The French, the Nazis, and the Battle for France's Greatest Treasure*. New York: Broadway Books, 2002.

Klarsfeld, Serge. *French Children of the Holocaust: A Memorial*. Edited by Susan Cohen, Howard M. Epstein, and Serge Klarsfeld. Translated by Glorianne Depondt and Howard M. Epstein. New York: New York University Press, 1996.

Klarsfeld, Serge and Beate, eds. *Le Bulletin des les Fils et Filles des Deportee Juifs de France,* March 2020.

Klein, Julia M. "Review: 'Avenue of Spies' by Alex Kershaw." *Chicago Tribune,* August 6, 2015. https://www.chicagotribune.com/entertainment/books/ct-prj-avenue-of-spies-alex-kershaw-20150806-story.html.

"L'Action Française—Organe Du Nationalisme Intégral/Directeur Politique: Henri Vaugeois; Rédacteur En Chef: Léon Daudet." *Gallica,* April 1914. https://gallica.bnf.fr/ark:/12148/bpt6k7583137/f3.item.zoom.

"La Première Aventure Céléste de Mr. Antipyrine | La Première Aventure Céléste de Mr. Antipyrine · Dada & Surrealism." dada.lib.uiowa.edu, n.d. https://dada.lib.uiowa.edu/items/show/223.

"La Première Aventure Céléste de Mr Antipyrine." www.goodreads.com. Accessed March 19, 2021. https://www.goodreads.com/book/show/6871022-la-premi-re-aventure-c-l-ste-de-mr-antipyrine.

"La Voie de la Liberté Markers." Atlas Obscura. Accessed July 30, 2021. https://www.atlasobscura.com/places/la-voi-de-la-liberte-markers.

Le Boterf, Hervé. *La Vie Parisienne Sous l'Occupation.* Paris: Éditions France-Empire, 1997.

"Le Dernier Tournant." Lux Compagnie Cinématographique de France, 1939.

Lefrançois, Michèle, and Elisabeth Caillet. "Journal de Paul Landowski." Journal.paul-landowski.com. Musée des Années Trente-Musée à Boulogne-Billancourt, 2009. http://journal.paul-landowski.com.

"Le Franc-Tireur: Organe des Mouvements Unis de Résistance: Mensuel Malgré la Gestapo et la Police de Vichy: Édition de Paris." *Gallica,* November 9, 1944. https://gallica.bnf.fr/ark:/12148/bpt6k4105349v/f2.item.r=Jausion.zoom. Blue jacket with fur collar, yellow shoes.

Lehrer, Steven. *Wartime Sites in Paris: 1939–1945.* New York: Sf Taffel, 2013.

"Le Projet | Mémoires des Déportations 1939–1945." memoiresdesdeportations.org, 2017. http://memoiresdesdeportations.org/fr/page/le-projet.

Le Roy, Eric. *Yannick Bellon: La Mirada de Frente.* San Sebastian, Spain: Euskadiko Filmategia/Filmoteca Vasca, D.L, 2019.

"L'Information Universitaire: Journal Hebdomadaire." BNF-Gallica, October 18, 1941. https://gallica.bnf.fr/ark:/12148/bpt6k4585954d/fl.image.r=Univeritarie%20Octobre%20Sciences%20Academie%20Beaux%20Arts%20Prix?rk=21459. Page 6.

"'Love Her Like a Mother'—Last Letters from the Holocaust: Late June, Early July 1944: Annemasse, France." Yad Vashem. www.yadvashem.org. Accessed July 29, 2021. https://www.yadvashem.org/yv/en/exhibitions/last-letters/1944/cohn_marianne.asp.

"Lyon—Statue de la République." statues.vanderkrogt.net, August 2018. https://statues.vanderkrogt.net/object.php?webpage=ST&record= frra046.

Macadam, Heather Dune. Letter to Eva Langer. "Jewish Sisters Disappeared in the Holocaust." Email, 13 March, 2017.

———. *999: The Extraordinary Young Women of the First Official Jewish Transport to Auschwitz*. New York: Citadel Press Books, 2020.

———. *Rena's Promise: A Story of Sisters in Auschwitz*. Boston: Beacon Press, 1994 and 2015.

Machet, Maire. "Archives Municipales d'Epernay—Service Éducatif." August 28, 1944. http://archivesmunicipales.epernay.fr/La_Liberation_d _Epernay_dossier_dicactique.pdf.

Macintyre, Ben. *Double Cross: The True Story of the D-Day Spies*. New York: Random House, 2012.

"Marianne." Wikipedia, July 2021. https://en.wikipedia.org/wiki/Marianne.

Mar, Alexandre. *Un Univers Surréaliste: Succession Myrtille et Georges Hugnet*. Paris: Christie's, December 15, 2015. https://www.christies.com/ PDF/catalog/2015/PAR12467_SaleCat.pdf.

Marrus, Michael R., and Robert O. Paxton. *Vichy France and the Jews*. Stanford, CA: Stanford University Press, 1996.

Marrus, Michael Robert. *The Nazi Holocaust. Part 6: The Victims of the Holocaust*. Vol. 2. De Gruyter Saur, 1989.

Martinique, Elena. "The Avantgarde Nature of Surrealist Manifesto." *Widewalls*, December 18, 2016. https://www.widewalls.ch/magazine/ Surrealist-manifesto.

Maslin, Janet. "On the Unsavory Trail of a Vichy-Era Monster." *New York Times*, October 12, 2006, sec. Books. https://www.nytimes.com/ 2006/10/12/books/12masl.html.

Matthews, Nicholas. "Collaboration, Resistance, and State-Sanctioned Journalism in Vichy France." Aleph Humanities Dept. UCLA, July 26, 2015. http://aleph.humanities.ucla.edu/2015/07/26/collaboration-resistance -and-state-sanctioned-journalism-in-vichy-france/.

"Mattock." Wikipedia. Wikimedia Foundation, July 24, 2019. https://en .wikipedia.org/wiki/Mattock.

Maurois, André. *Les Trois Dumas*. Paris: Hachette, 1976.

McCarthy, Meagan. "Remembering Vélodrome D'Hiver." *Kaleidoscope Journal* 5, no. 2 (2014): 16–23. The Boston College International Relations and Global Studies. https://doi.org/.

McQueen, Paul. "Remembering the Legacy of France's World War 2 Punk Culture." Culture Trip, August 6, 2017. https://theculturetrip.com/ europe/france/paris/articles/remembering-the-legacy-of-frances-world -war-2-punk-culture/.

Mees, Bernard Thomas. *The Science of the Swastika*. Central European University Press, 2008. https://books.google.com/books/about/The_Science_of_the_Swastika.html?id=hLNUx6YK9RIC.

Megargee, Geoffrey P., Joseph White, Mel Hecker, and United States. *The United States Holocaust Memorial Museum Encyclopedia of Camps and Ghettos, 1933–1945*. Vol. 3: *Camps and Ghettos under European Regimes Aligned with Nazi Germany*. Bloomington: Indiana University Press, 2018.

Mellby, Julie. "Les Réverbères." *Graphic Arts,* March 2019. https://graphicarts.princeton.edu/2019/03/13/les-reverberes/.

Miller, Roderick. "Bordeaux Fort du Hâ Prison." Frank Falla Archive, n.d. https://www.frankfallaarchive.org/prisons/bordeaux-fort-du-ha-prison/.

Mindel, Lee F., and FAIA. "Tour Paris's École des Beaux-Arts, the Venerable Art School That Trained Some of History's Top Artists and Designers." *Architectural Digest,* December 2014. https://www.architecturaldigest.com/gallery/tae-ecole-des-beaux-art-slideshow.

Ministry of Information - photography division. 1945. "Parisian Traffic, Spring 1945: Everyday Life In Paris, France, 1945." Imperial War Museums. 1945. https://www.iwm.org.uk/collections/item/object/205201712.

Mittelman, Judith Spielberger. Personal Interview. Rena's Promise Foundation, New York. November 29, 2021.

Modiano, Patrick. *Dora Bruder*. Paris: Gallimard, 1999.

"MoMA | Tapping the Subconscious: Automatism and Dreams." Moma.org, 2019. https://www.moma.org/learn/moma_learning/themes/Surrealism/tapping-the-subconscious-automatism-and-dreams/.

Moorehead, Alan. *Eclipse*. New York: Andesite Press, 2015.

Mossé, Sonia. "Artland—Discover and Buy Art Online." www.artland.com. Accessed May 5, 2021. https://www.artland.com/artists/sonia-mosse.

———. "Sonia Mossé (1897–1943)—Find a Grave Memorial." www.findagrave.com. Accessed May 5, 2022. https://www.findagrave.com/memorial/32084134/sonia-mosse.

Mouvement de libération nationale (France) Auteur du texte. "Recherche." *Le Franc-Tireur : Organe Des Mouvements Unis de Résistance : Mensuel Malgré La Gestapo et La Police de Vichy : Édition de Paris,* 9 Nov. 1944, p. 2, gallica.bnf.fr/ark:/12148/bpt6k4105349v/f2.item.r=raymondjausion+jausion. Accessed 9 Aug. 2020.

Nahum, Henri. "2013/1 the Annette Zelman Affair or the Dramatic Consequences of Ordinary Anti-Semitism." *Cairn* 46 (May 2013). https://doi.org/https://doi.org/10.3917/aj.461.0045.

Nawalfleh, Hannah. "Gothic Architecture Styles." *Issuu.com,* issuu.com/hala nawafleh7739/docs/_____/s/12292987. Accessed 10 Aug. 2021.

Naiman, Rubin. "Dreamless: The Silent Epidemic of REM Sleep Loss." *Annals of the New York Academy of Sciences* 1406, no. 1 (August 15, 2017): 77–85. https://doi.org/10.1111/nyas.13447.

Nicole, Courtney. "DIY: How to a Sew a Pleated Skirt!" www.youtube.com, June 2015. https://www.youtube.com/watch?v=N-9wc1KfYOo.

"1939–1940: Evacuation—Phony War and Collapse, May–June 1940." Mémorial Alsace Moselle, 2017. https://www.memorial-alsace-moselle .com/en/le-memorial/un-peu-d-histoire/1939-1940-evacuation-phony-war-and-collapse-may-june-1940.

"Nisko Plan." Jewishgen.org, 2013. https://kehilalinks.jewishgen.org/lublin/ Nisko_Plan.html.

Nordmann-Cohen, Marie-Elisa. "Te Rappelles Tu Ma Chere Claudette." *Memoires des Deportations, France—Temoignages,* 1955. http://memoires desdeportations.org/fr/texte/te-rappelles-tu-ma-chere-claudette.

"Origins of Neo-Nazi and White Supremacist Terms and Symbols: A Glossary." Ushmm.org, 2017. https://www.ushmm.org/antisemitism/what -is-antisemitism/origins-of-neo-nazi-and-white-supremacist-terms-and-symbols.

Ousby, Ian. *Occupation: The Ordeal of France, 1940–1944.* New York: Cooper Square Press, 2000.

P., F. "Commémoration—Mercredi Prochain se Dérouleront les Cérémonies du 72e Anniversaire de la Libération de la Ville au Monument Legay, Hénon, Schluck et Evins Ainsi Qu'au Monument des Fusillés de Tavannes. en Souvenir du 31 Août 1944, Jour de la Libération de Verdun." *L'est Républican,* August 25, 2016. https://www.estrepublicain .fr/edition-de-verdun/2016/08/24/en-souvenir-du-31-aout-1944-jour -de-la-liberation-de-verdun.

Paganini, Andrea. "Analysis of Annette Zelman's Letters," July 5, 2021, and August 7, 2021.

Paganini, Andrea. Email with text from his biography on Jean Rouch, 24 August 2021. Translated by Simon Worrall.

*Par 18 Mètres de Fond [18 Meters Deep]—1942.* CG-45. YouTube, September 2015. https://www.youtube.com/watch?v=OlTyUagouCM.

"Place de la Nation." Wikipedia, February 2021. https://en.wikipedia.org/ wiki/Place_de_la_Nation.

Portis, Larry. *French Frenzies: A Social History of Popular Music in France.* College Station, TX: Virtualbookworm.com, 2004.

Poulhès, Louis. *Un Camp d'Internement en Plein Paris: La Caserne des Tourelles: 1940–1945.* Neuilly-Sur-Seine (Hauts-De-Seine): Atlande, Dl, 2019.

Poznanski, Renée. *Jews in France during World War II.* Waltham, MA, and Hanover, NH: Brandeis University Press in Association with the United States Holocaust Memorial Museum, 2001.

Pressfield, Steven. *The War of Art: Break through the Blocks and Win Your Inner Creative Battles*. 16th ed. New York: Black Irish Entertainment, 2012.

Prevert, Jacques. *Les Enfants Qui S'Aiment*. In *Spectacle*. Paris: Gallimard, 1949.

Reich Breder, Linda. Interview 22979. Segment 3 of 9. Visual History Archive, USC Shoah Foundation. Retrieved February 12, 2018.

Ribemont-Dessaignes, Georges. *Déja Jadis: Ou du Mouvement Dada à l'Espace Abstrait*. Paris: Rene Juilliard, 1958.

Richter, Hans. *Dada: Art and Anti-Art*. 1985. Reprint. New York: Thames Hudson, 2004.

Riding, Alan. *And the Show Went On: Cultural Life in Nazi-Occupied Paris*. New York: Alfred A. Knopf, 2010.

Rimbaud, Arthur, Paul Schmidt, and Robert Mapplethorpe. *A Season in Hell*. New York: Little, Brown, 1997.

"Robert Hossein—Biographie, Spectacles, Films, Théâtre et Photos." Théâtres et Producteurs Associés. Accessed July 2021. https://tpa.fr/acteurs-theatre/hossein-robert-111.html.

Roberts, Adam. "The Swimming Pool That Sank and Other Watery Tales." *Invisible Paris*, January 27, 2013. http://parisisinvisible.blogspot.com/2013/01/ the-swimming-pool-that-sank-and-other.html.

Rosbottom, Ronald C. *When Paris Went Dark: The City of Light under German Occupation, 1940–1944*. New York: Back Bay Books, 2015.

Rouch, Jean, and Andrea Paganini. *"Saluts d'Irrémédiable!" & Autres Saluts, Hommages et Portraits*. Montreuil: Editions De L'oeil, 2021.

Rouch, Jocelyn. Interview with the authors, August 8, 2020.

Rubenfeld, Sheldon, and Susan Benedict, eds. *Human Subjects Research after the Holocaust*. Foreword by Arthur L. Caplan. Cham, Switzerland: Springer, 2014.

"Rules of the Game, The." Wikipedia. Wikimedia Foundation, March 2019. https://en.wikipedia.org/wiki/The_Rules_of_the_Game.

Sandomir, Richard. "Georges Loinger, Wartime Rescuer of Jewish Children, Dies at 108." *New York Times*, January 4, 2019, sec. Obituaries. https://www.nytimes.com/2019/01/04/obituaries/georges-loinger-dead.html.

Sartre, Jean-Paul. *Paris under the Occupation*. Translated by Lisa Lieberman. New York: Now and Then Reader, 2011.

Sartre, Jean-Paul, and Simone de Beauvoir. *Quiet Moments in a War: The Letters of Jean-Paul Sartre to Simone de Beauvoir, 1940–1963*. London: Penguin, 1995.

Sauvy, Jean. *Jean Rouch tel que je l'ai connu*. Paris: L'Harmattan, 2006.

Schöpe, Björn. "A Relic from Germany's Post-War Era: A Hoard of Cigarette Boxes | CoinsWeekly." https://coinsweekly.com/. Coins Weekly, Oc-

tober 14, 2009. https://coinsweekly.com/a-relic-from-germanys-post
-war-era-a-hoard-of-cigarette-boxes/.

Schreiber, Gerhard, and Bernd Stegemann, Detlef Vogel, and Militärges-chichtliches Forschungsamt. *Germany and the Second World War.* Vol. 3, *The Mediterranean, South-East Europe, and North Africa, 1939–1941: From Italy's Declaration of Non-Belligerence to the Entry of the United States into the War.* Translated by Dean S. McMurry, Ewald Osers, and Louise Willmot; translation editor P. S. Falla. New York: Clarendon Press, 1995.

Schwalbová, Manca. *Vyhasnuté Oči.* Bratislava, Marenčin Pt, 2011.

Seal, Mark. "Paris' Hotel Lutetia Is Haunted by History." *Smithsonian,* April 2019. https://www.smithsonianmag.com/travel/paris-hotel-lutetia-haunted-history-180971629/.

Sebba, Anne. *Les Parisiennes: How the Women of Paris Lived, Loved, and Died under Nazi Occupation.* New York: St. Martin's Press, 2017.

Seymour-Jones, Carole. *A Dangerous Liaison: A Revelatory New Biography of Simone de Beauvoir and Jean-Paul Sartre.* New York: Overlook Press, 2009. Jean-Pierre Bourla, whom de Beauvoir referred to as her kid, was arrested for not wearing the yellow star and deported to Drancy.

Shakespeare, William. *Romeo and Juliet.* London: The New Arden Shakespeare, 2012.

"Siegroth, Von, Joachim." Traces of War—Foundation for Information World War Two. STIWOT (Stichting Informatie Wereldoorlog Twee), 1999. https://www.tracesofwar.com/persons/18695/Siegroth-von-Joachim .htm.

Signoret, Simone. *Nostalgia Isn't What It Used to Be.* New York: Penguin Books, 1979.

Škodová, Júlia. יוליה, שקודובה, et al. *Three Years without a Name.* שלוש שנים 1942–1945 אושוויץ שם ללא/*Shalosh Shanim Le-Lo Shem : A'ushvits 1942-1945.* משו די, ידיעות אחרונות Jerusalem, Yerushalayim. Yad Va-Shem, Rashut Ha-Zikaron La-Sho'ah Vela-Gevurah, Mar. 2022.

Škodová, Júlia. "Three Years without a Name" by Júlia Škodová: A Chapter to Read." 27 Apr. 2022, www-haaretz-co-il.translate.goog/blogs/ somethingtoread/2022-04-27/ty-article/00000180-7ee4-d9ba-a3f7 -ffef06c20000?_x_tr_sl=iw&_x_tr_tl=en&_x_tr_hl=en&_x_tr_pto=sc. Accessed 1 Aug. 2022.

Slocomb, Romain. *L'étoile Jaune de l'Inspecteur Sadorski: Roman.* Paris: Robert Laffont, 2018.

Speer, Albert. *Inside the Third Reich: Memoirs.* Translated by Richard and Clara Winston. 1969. Reprint. New York: Macmillan, 1970.

Spotts, Frederic. *The Shameful Peace: How French Artists and Intellectuals Survived the Nazi Occupation.* New Haven, CT: Yale University Press, 2008.

Steur, Claudia. *Theodor Dannecker: Ein Funktionär der "Endlösung."* Cologne: Klartext-Verl, 1997.

Suleiman, Susan Rubin. "Memory Troubles: Remembering the Occupation in Simone de Beauvoir's Les Mandarins." *French Politics, Culture & Society*, vol. 28, no. 2, 1 Jan. 2010, 10.3167/fpcs.2010.280202. Accessed 30 Nov. 2021.

Swaffer, Hannan. "As Hannan Swaffer Sees It." www.britishnewspaperarchive.co.uk.April 22, 1942.https://www.britishnewspaperarchive.co.uk/viewer/bl/0000729/19450422/045/0004.

Toulgoat, Bernard J. "Life in Paris under Nazi Occupation (May 1940–August 1944), Part 2; 1941." HubPages, December 2012. https://discover.hubpages.com/education/Life-in-Paris-under-Nazi-occupation-May-1940-August-1944-Part-2-1941.

Travers, James. "Review of the Film *L'Assassinat du Père Noël* (1941)." frenchfilms.org, 2002. http://www.frenchfilms.org/review/l-assassinat-du-pere-noel-1941.html.

Tronel, Jacky. "Au Sujet des Atrocités Commises par les Allemands à la Prison Militaire de Bordeaux…" Histoire Pénitentiaire et Justice Militaire, July 2010. https://prisons-cherche-midi-mauzac.com/des-prisons/au-sujet-des-atrocites-commises-par-les-allemands-a-la-prison-militaire-de-bordeaux%E2%80%A6-3187.

Trouillard, Stéphanie. "The Vél d'Hiv Roundup: 75 Years On, a Survivor Remembers." France 24, July 15, 2017. www.france24.com/En/20170712-Vel-Dhiv-Roundup-Holocaust-France-Survivor-Remembers-World-War.

Trueman, C. N. "French Resistance, The." History Learning Site. May 18, 2015. Accessed November 15, 2020. www.Historylearningsite.Co.Uk/World-War-Two/Resistance-Movements/The-French-Resistance/.

———. "Milice, The." History Learning Site, April 21, 2015. Accessed November 15, 2020. https://www.historylearningsite.co.uk/world-war-two/world-war-two-in-western-europe/france-during-world-war-two/the-milice/.

Tzara, Tristan. "ArtSalve." http://artsalve-productions.eu/art/Tristan_Tzara.html. Accessed March 19, 2021.

———. "La Première Aventure Céléste de Mr. Antipyrine | La Première Aventure Céléste de Mr. Antipyrine · Dada & Surrealism." dada.lib.uiowa.edu, n.d. https://dada.lib.uiowa.edu/items/show/223. Collection Dada. Weinbrgstr, Switzerland, 1916.

Union des femmes françaises. Section (Rhône)., and Tatiana Oks. "La Voix des Femmes. Edité par l'Union des Comités des Femmes de France de la Région Lyonnaise 'Puis' par l'Union des Femmes Françaises.

Région Lyonnaise!" Gallica, April 8, 1945. https://doi.org/oai:bnf.fr: gallica/ark:/12148/bpt6k954461t.

Van der Krogt, René and Peter. "Lyon—Statue de la République. *Emile Peynot.*" statues.vanderkrogt.net, August 10, 2018. Accessed March 10, 2021. https://statues.vanderkrogt.net/object.php?webpage=ST&record =frrao46.

"Vel d'Hiv Roundup of Paris Jews Remembered, 78 Years Later." The Algemeiner, July 16, 2020. https://www.algemeiner.com/2020/07/16/veldhiv-roundup-of-paris-jews-remembered-78-years-later/.

Vergnon, Gilles, and Bruno Benoit. *Annemasse,Ville Frontière 1940–1944.* Lyon, Université de Lyon. June 21, 2010. http://doc.sciencespo-lyon.fr/ Ressources/Documents/Etudiants/Memoires/Cyberdocs/MFE2010/ dozol_v/pdf/dozol_v.pdf.

Vian, Boris. *Manuel de Saint-Germain-des-Prés.* Paris: Editions Du Chene, 1974.

Ville d'Annemasse. "Les Personnalités Importantes." Annemasse: Site Internet, 2021. https://www.annemasse.fr/que-faire-a-annemasse/decouvrir/ memoire-et-patrimoine/annemasse-dhier-a-aujourdhui/les-personnalites -importantes.

Vrba, Rudolf. *I Escaped from Auschwitz.* New York, Barricade ; Hadleigh, 2003.

Weindling, Paul. *Epidemics and Genocide in Eastern Europe, 1890–1945.* Oxford, New York: Oxford University Press, 2000.

"What Is Cross of Lorraine—History and Meaning." Symbol Sage, August 2020. https://symbolsage.com/cross-of-lorraine-symbol/.

Whitehouse, Rosie. "A Paris Luxury Hotel Filled with Concentration Camp Survivors." *Tablet Magazine,* May 8, 2020. https://www.tabletmag .com/sections/arts-letters/articles/convoy-61-ve-day.

Wilmot, Chester. *The Struggle for Europe.* Hertfordshire, UK: Wordsworth Editions, 2003.

"Witness History, the Paris Hotel That Hosted Holocaust Survivors." *BBC,* BBC World Service, 29 Oct. 2019, www.bbc.co.uk/programmes/ w3csyx2s. Accessed 8 May 2021.

Yad Vashem: The World Holocaust Remembrance Center. "Mila Racine's Last Letter." www.yadvashem.org. Accessed July 29, 2021. https://www .yadvashem.org/yv/en/exhibitions/last-letters/1944/racine.asp.

Yad Vashem map. "Transport 3 from Drancy, Camp, France, to Auschwitz Birkenau, Extermination Camp, Poland, on 22/06/1942." Yad Vashem. Accessed August 10, 2020. https://deportation.yadvashem.org/index .html?language=en&itemId=5092602.

Zelman, Camille, and Claude Levy-Lambert. "Lettre du 15/05/1992 de Camille Zelman à Madame Maslhiah, du Centre de Documentation Juive Contemporaine, Rappelant l'Histoire de la Déportation de Sa

Soeur Annette Zelman et Documents la Concernant." *Memorial de La Shoah* CXVIII–2a(bis), no. CGQJ-CXVIII (May 15, 1992): 6. https://ressources.memorialdelashoah.org/notice.php?q=fulltext%3A %28CXVIII-2a%29%20AND%20id_not%3A%28%2A%29&spec_ex pand=1&start=0.

Zweite, Armin. *Fritz Hofmann und die Städtische Galerie 1937—Eine national-sozialistische Museumskarriere, ihre Vorgeschichte und Konsequenzen.* In Ausst. Cat.: *The "City of Art": Munich, National Socialism, and "Degenerate Art."* Staatsgalerie moderner Kunst, Munich 1987, pp. 262–78.

# Index

Pages numbers followed by f indicate illustrations

437